# An Introduction to Language
## The Essentials

Victoria Fromkin
Robert Rodman
Nina Hyams

Cengage

Australia • Brazil • Mexico • Singapore • United Kingdom • United States

*Introduction to Language Essential Version*

**Victoria Fromkin**
**Robert Rodman**
**Nina Hyams**



ISBN-13: 978-89-6218-446-4

**Cengage Learning Korea Ltd.**
14F YTN Newsquare 76 Sangamsan-ro
Mapo-gu Seoul 03926 Korea

Cengage is a leading provider of customized learning solutions with employees residing in nearly 40 different countries and sales in more than 125 countries around the world. Find your local representative at: **www.cengage.com.**

Visit our website at **www.cengageasia.com.**

Printed in Korea
Print Number: 03 Print Year: 2024

## Classification of American English Vowels

**Part of the Tongue Involved**

| Tongue Height | FRONT ⟵ | CENTRAL | ⟶ BACK |
|---|---|---|---|
| HIGH | i beet | | u boot |
| ↑ | ɪ bit | ROUNDED → | ʊ put |
| MID | e bait | | o boat |
| | ɛ bet | ə about | |
| ↓ | | ʌ butt | |
| LOW | æ bat | a balm | ɔ bawd |

## A Phonetic Alphabet for English Pronunciation

| Consonants | | | | | | Vowels | | | |
|---|---|---|---|---|---|---|---|---|---|
| p | **p**ill | t | **t**ill | k | **k**ill | i | b**ee**t | ɪ | b**i**t |
| b | **b**ill | d | **d**ill | g | **g**ill | e | b**ai**t | ɛ | b**e**t |
| m | **m**ill | n | **n**il | ŋ | ri**ng** | u | b**oo**t | ʊ | f**oo**t |
| f | **f**eel | s | **s**eal | h | **h**eal | o | b**oa**t | ɔ | b**o**re |
| v | **v**eal | z | **z**eal | l | **l**eaf | æ | b**a**t | a | p**o**t/b**a**r |
| θ | **th**igh | ʧ | **ch**ill | r | **r**eef | ʌ | b**u**tt | ə | sof**a** |
| ð | **th**y | ʤ | **g**in | j | **y**ou | aɪ | b**i**te | aʊ | b**ou**t |
| ʃ | **sh**ill | ʍ | **wh**ich | w | **w**itch | ɔɪ | b**oy** | | |
| ʒ | mea**s**ure | | | | | | | | |

**The Vocal Tract.** Places of articulation: 1. bilabial; 2. labiodental; 3. interdental; 4. alveolar; 5. (alveo)palatal; 6. velar; 7. uvular; 8. glottal.

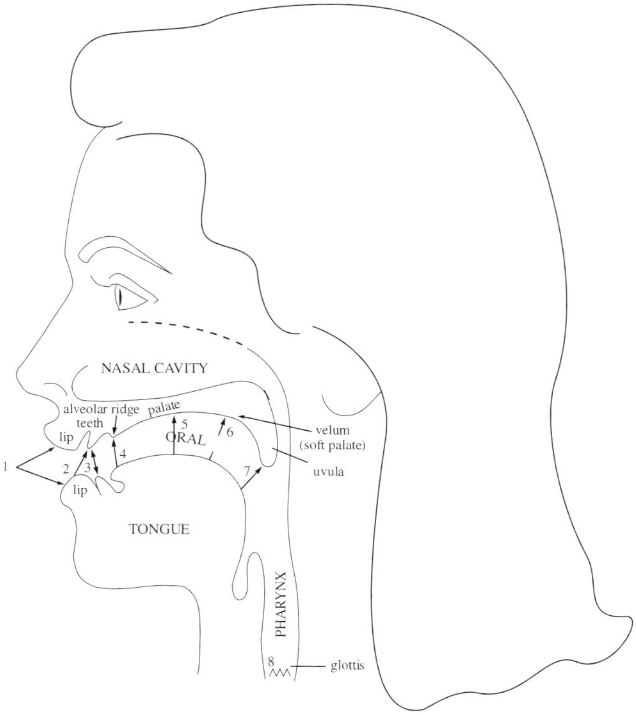


## Some Phonetic Symbols for American English Consonants

| | Bilabial | Labiodental | Interdental | Alveolar | Palatal | Velar | Glottal |
|---|---|---|---|---|---|---|---|
| **Stop** (oral) | | | | | | | |
| voiceless | p | | | t | | k | ʔ |
| voiced | b | | | d | | g | |
| **Nasal** (voiced) | m | | | n | | ŋ | |
| **Fricative** | | | | | | | |
| voiceless | | f | θ | s | ʃ | | h |
| voiced | | v | ð | z | ʒ | | |
| **Affricate** | | | | | | | |
| voiceless | | | | | ʧ | | |
| voiced | | | | | ʤ | | |
| **Glide** | | | | | | | |
| voiceless | ʍ | | | | | ʍ | |
| voiced | w | | | | j | w | |
| **Liquid** (voiced) | | | | | | | |
| (central) | | | | r | | | |
| (lateral) | | | | l | | | |

*In memory of Robert David Rodman and Joseph Hyams*

# Contents

CHAPTER 6

## Phonology: The Sound Patterns of Language 168



CHAPTER 7

## Language in Society 207

# Preface

> Well, this bit which I am writing, called Introduction, is really the er-h'r'm of the book, and I have put it in, partly so as not to take you by surprise, and partly because I can't do without it now. There are some very clever writers who say that it is quite easy not to have an er-h'r'm, but I don't agree with them. I think it is much easier not to have all the rest of the book.
>
> **A. A. MILNE,** *Now We Are Six,* 1927

> The last thing we find in making a book is to know what we must put first.
>
> **BLAISE PASCAL** (1623–1662)

Robert Rodman passed away on January 15, 2017, shortly after the completion of the eleventh edition of *An Introduction to Language*. His breadth of knowledge, charm, and wit touch every page of this new edition, and will be sorely missed in future editions. Robert and Vicki Fromkin published the first edition of *An Introduction to Language* in 1974. Their goal was to share with students their love of language and linguistics by presenting complex material in a lighthearted and personal way that included witty quotations (A. A. Milne was one of Vicki's favorites) and cartoons (Robert kept a huge file of them, which he regularly updated). This edition continues in the style and spirit of my friends, colleagues, and co-authors, Robert Rodman and Victoria Fromkin.

The first ten editions of *An Introduction to Language* succeeded, with the help of dedicated teachers, in introducing the nature of human language to hundreds of thousands of students. This is a book that students enjoy and understand and that professors find effective and thorough. Not only have majors in linguistics benefited from the book's easy-to-read yet comprehensive presentation, but also majors in fields as diverse as teaching English as a second language, foreign language studies, general education, the cognitive and neurosciences, psychology, sociology, and anthropology have enjoyed learning about language from this book.

## Highlights of This Edition

This edition has been rewritten for improved clarity, conciseness, and currency. It includes **new developments in linguistics and related fields** that will strengthen its appeal to a wider audience. Much of this information will enable students to gain insight and understanding about linguistic issues and debates appearing in the national media and will help professors and students stay current with important linguistic research. We hope that it may also dispel certain common misconceptions that people have about language and language use.

The eleventh edition has been reduced to nine chapters from the original twelve of earlier editions. The chapters on Computer Processing of Human Language and Writing have been eliminated, with some of the material on the history of writing incorporated into Chapter 8 (Language Change). This more streamlined edition will enable teachers and students on a quarter system to more fully utilize the material, and for those on the semester system, it allows extra time for the more challenging chapters such as phonology and syntax.

**Exercises** (more than 200) continue to be abundant in this edition, and additional research-oriented exercises have been added for those instructors who wish their students to pursue certain topics more deeply. Some exercises continue to be marked as "challenge" questions: they go beyond the scope of what is ordinarily expected in a first course in language study. An **answer key** is available to instructors to assist them in areas outside of their expertise.

**Chapter 1, "What Is Language?"** continues as a concise introduction to the general study of language. It contains many "hooks" for engaging students, including "Language and Thought," which takes up the Sapir–Whorf hypothesis; the universal properties of languages; a consideration of animal "languages"; and the occasional silliness of self-appointed mavens of "good" grammar who beg us not to carelessly split infinitives and who find sentence-ending prepositions an abomination not to be put up with.

**Chapter 2, "Morphology: The Words of Language,"** launches the book into the study of grammar with morphology, the study of word formation, as that is the most familiar and intuitive aspect of grammar to most students. The subject is treated with clarity and an abundance of simple illustrations from English emphasize the word structure, including the essentials of derivational versus inflectional morphology, free and bound morphemes, and the hierarchical structure of words. The section on compounds words has been expanded to include a detailed discussion of their internal structure.

**Chapter 3, "Syntax: The Sentence Patterns of Language,"** is the most heavily revised chapter from the previous edition. The first half of the chapter introduces the universal and easily understood notions of constituency, syntactic categories (parts of speech), phrase structure trees and rules, structural ambiguity, and the infinite scope of language. Phrase structure trees are painstakingly built up, level by level, using traditional (pre-X-Bar) notation. The second half of the chapter delves into the internal structure of phrases, including the concepts of heads, complements, and selection. Current X-bar notation is introduced at this point, in a very restricted and clear way, to describe some of the deeper and more subtle syntactic structures of English and other languages. The chapter ends with a basic introduction to grammatical dependencies, including agreement rules and the transformational analysis of questions, carefully explained and illustrated. Formalisms are held to the bare minimum required to enhance clarity.

**Chapter 4, "The Meaning of Language,"** on semantics, is finely structured so that the challenging topics of this complex subject can be digested in smaller pieces. The chapter first introduces students to truth-conditional semantics. Following are discussions of what happens when compositionality fails, as with idioms, metaphors, and semantically anomalous sentences. Lexical semantics take up various approaches to word meaning, including the concepts of reference and sense, semantic features, argument structure, and thematic roles. The most heavily revised parts of this chapter are the sections on argument structure, thematic roles, and semantic features, the latter now containing a discussion of how these features affect the syntax. In the final section on pragmatics, we discuss and illustrate in depth the influence of situational versus linguistic context on the communicative content of utterances, the significance of implicature in comprehension, Grice's Maxims of Conversation, presuppositions, and J. L. Austin's speech acts.

**Chapter 5, "Phonetics: The Sounds of Language,"** retains its former organization and continues to embrace IPA (International Phonetics Association) notation for English in keeping with current practices, with the sole exception of using /r/ in place of the technically correct /ɹ/ when illustrating English. We continue to mention alternative notations that students may encounter in other publications.

**Chapter 6, "Phonology: The Sound Patterns of Language,"** continues to be presented with a greater emphasis on insights through linguistic data accompanied by small amounts of well-explicated formalisms, so that the student can appreciate the need for formal theories without experiencing the burdensome details. In this spirit, we have eliminated the section on Optimality Theory, which we now feel is beyond the scope of an introductory text. The chapter covers central concepts in segmental and prosodic phonology, and contains numerous exercises structured to guide students through the basics of phonological analysis.

**Chapter 7, "Language in Society,"** retains its forward position in the book from earlier editions reflecting its growing importance as a major sub-field of linguistics. The chapter presents the established facts and principles of sociolinguistics while bringing up to date subjects such as banned languages (it's still happening); dead and dying languages (also still happening); gender differences; minority dialects such as African American English. In addition, included are sections on contact languages such as pidgins, creoles, and lingua francas that may be found in linguistically heterogeneous areas.

**Chapter 8, "Language Change: The Syllables of Time,"** has been updated with the latest research on language families and language relatedness. The thematically related section on the history of writing is also included, moved from its previous location in a separate chapter.

**Chapter 9, "Language Acquisition,"** has been heavily revised for clarity and conciseness. It covers the basic stages and data from childhood language development including sections on bilingual language acquisition and child second language acquisition, all couched in the more general theoretical question of how children accomplish the complex task of learning a language.

The **order of presentation of Chapters 2 through 6** was once thought to be nontraditional. Our experience, backed by previous editions of the book and the recommendations of colleagues throughout the world, has convinced us that it is easier for the novice to approach the structural aspects of language by first looking at morphology (the structure of the most familiar linguistic unit, the word). This is followed by syntax (the structure of sentences), which is also familiar to many students, as are numerous semantic concepts. We then proceed to the more novel (to students) phonetics and phonology, which students often find daunting. However, the book is written so that individual instructors can present material in the traditional order of phonetics, phonology, morphology, syntax, and semantics (Chapters 5, 6, 2, 3, and 4) without confusion, if they wish.

As in previous editions, the primary concern has been basic ideas rather than detailed expositions. This book assumes no previous knowledge on the part of the reader. An updated list of references at the end of each chapter is included to accommodate any reader who wishes to pursue a subject in more depth. Each chapter concludes with a summary and exercises to enhance the students' interest in and comprehension of the textual material.

## Additional Resources

### MindTap: Empower Your Students

MindTap is a platform that propels students from memorization to mastery. It gives you complete control of your course, so you can provide engaging content, challenge every learner, and build student confidence. Customize interactive syllabi to emphasize priority topics, then add your own material or notes to the eBook as desired. This outcomes-driven application gives you the tools needed to empower students and boost both understanding and performance.

#### Access Everything You Need in One Place

Cut down on prep with the preloaded and organized MindTap course materials. Teach more efficiently with interactive multimedia, assignments, quizzes, and more. Give your students the power to read, listen, and study on their phones, so they can learn on their terms.

#### Empower Students to Reach Their Potential

Twelve distinct metrics give you actionable insights into student engagement. Identify topics troubling your entire class and instantly communicate with those struggling. Students can track their scores to stay motivated toward their goals. Together, you can be unstoppable.

### Control Your Course—and Your Content

Get the flexibility to reorder textbook chapters, add your own notes, and embed a variety of content including Open Educational Resources (OER). Personalize course content to your students' needs. They can even read your notes, add their own, and highlight key text to aid their learning.

### Get a Dedicated Team, Whenever You Need Them

MindTap isn't just a tool, it's backed by a personalized team eager to support you. We can help set up your course and tailor it to your specific objectives, so you'll be ready to make an impact from day one. Know we'll be standing by to help you and your students until the final day of the term.

## Answer Key

The Answer Key for *An Introduction to Language* contains answers to all of the exercises in the core text, and is available to instructors through the publisher.

## Instructor Companion Web Site

This password-protected companion site contains useful resources for instructors—including chapter-level PowerPoint lecture slides, and a downloadable version of the Answer Key. Go to www.cengagebrain.com to access the site.

# Acknowledgments

We would like to express our deep appreciation to UCLA Professors Susan Curtiss and Jesse Harris for helping us revise the previous edition.

Brook Danielle Lillehaugen undertook the daunting task of writing the Answer Key to the ninth, tenth, and eleventh editions. Her thoroughness, accuracy, and insightfulness in construing solutions to problems and discussions of issues are appreciated by all who avail themselves of this useful document, including us, the authors.

We also express deep appreciation for the incisive comments of the reviewers of the tenth edition, whose frank assessment of the work, both critical and laudatory, heavily influenced this new edition:

Ellyn Arwood, University of Portland; Craig Barrette, Brescia University; Althea Bradford, Winston-Salem State University; Ulrike Christofori, San Joaquin Delta College; Liliana Cobas, Carlos Albizu University; Anthony DeFazio, New York University; Michael Duffett, San Joaquin Delta College; Laurie Durzo, Penn State University; Carmen Fought, Pitzer College; Brent Green, Salt Lake Community College; Alicia Holland, Capella University; Susan Inouye, Kapiolani Community College; John Jeep, Miami University; McLoddy Kadyamusuma, State University of New York at Fredonia; Patti Kurtz, Minot State University; Nancy Lee-Jones, Endicott College; Sally LeVan, Gannon University; Keming Liu, The City University of New York; Deanna Nisbet, Regent University; Silvia Peart, United States Naval Academy; Edward Rielly, Saint Joseph's College; Kelly Schroeder, Fresno Pacific University; Jefferey Taylor, Metropolitan State University of Denver; and Elizabeth Winkler, Western Kentucky University.

We continue to be deeply grateful to the individuals who have sent us suggestions, corrections, criticisms, cartoons, language data, and exercises over the course of many editions. Their influence is still strongly felt in this eleventh edition. The list is long and reflects the global, communal collaboration that a book about language—the most global of topics—merits. To each of you, our heartfelt thanks and appreciation. Know that in this eleventh edition lives your contribution:[1]

Natasha Abner, Montclair State University; Byron Ahn, Princeton University; Adam Albright, Massachusetts Institute of Technology; Otto Santa Ana, University of California, Los Angeles; Rebecca Barghorn, University of Oldenburg; Seyed Reza Basiroo, Islamic Azad University; Karol Boguszewski, Poland; Melanie Borchers, Universität Duisburg-Essen; Donna Brinton, Emeritus, University of California, Los Angeles; Daniel Bruhn, University of California, Berkeley; Lynn A. Burley, University of Central Arkansas; Ivano Caponigro, University of California, San Diego; Ralph S. Carlson, Azusa Pacific University; Robert Channon, Purdue University; Judy Cheatham, Greensboro College; Leonie Cornips, Meertens Institute; Antonio Damásio, University of Southern California; Hanna Damásio, University of Southern California; Julie Damron, Brigham Young University; Rosalia Dutra, University of North Texas; Christina Esposito, Macalester College; Fred Field, California State University, Northridge; Susan Fiksdal, Evergreen State College; Beverly Olson Flanigan and her teaching assistants, Ohio University; Jackson Gandour, Purdue University, West Lafayette; Jule Gomez de Garcia, California State University, San Marcos; Deborah Grant, Independent consultant; Loretta Gray, Central Washington University; Xiangdong Gu, Chongqing University; Helena Halmari, University of London; Karin Hedberg, Sam Houston State University; Sharon Hargus, University of Washington; Benjamin H. Hary, Emory University; Tometro Hopkins, Florida International University; Eric Hyman, University of North Carolina, Fayetteville; Dawn Ellen Jacobs, California Baptist University; Seyed Yasser Jebraily, University of Tehran; Kyle Johnson, University of Massachusetts, Amherst; Paul Justice, San Diego State University; Simin Karimi, University of Arizona; Edward Keenan, University of California, Los Angeles; Robert D. King, University of Texas; Sharon M. Klein, California State University, Northridge; Nathan Klinedinst, Institut Jean Nicod/CNRS, Paris; Otto Krauss Jr., late, unaffiliated; Elisabeth Kuhn, Virginia Commonwealth University; Peter Ladefoged, late, University of California, Los Angeles; Mary Ann Larsen-Pusey, Fresno Pacific University; Rabbi Robert Layman, Philadelphia; Byungmin Lee, Korea; Virginia "Ginny" Lewis, Northern State University; David Lightfoot, Georgetown University; Ingvar Lofstedt, University of California, Los Angeles; Giuseppe Longobardi, Università di Venezia; Harriet Luria, Hunter College, City University of New York; Jeff MacSwan, Arizona State University; Tracey McHenry, Eastern Washington University; Craig Melchert, University of California, Los Angeles; Pamela Munro, University of California, Los Angeles; Tom Nash, Southern Oregon University; Carol Neidle, Boston University; Don Nilsen, Arizona State University; Reiko Okabe, Nihon University, Tokyo; John Olsson, Forensic

[1]Some affiliations may have changed or are unknown to us at this time.

Linguistic Institute, Wales, UK; Robyn Orfitelli, Sheffield University; Anjali Pandey, Salisbury University; Barbara Hall Partee, University of Massachusetts, Amherst; Maria "Masha" Polinsky, University of Maryland; Fernanda Pratas, Universidade Nova de Lisboa; Vincent D. Puma, Flagler College; Mousa Qasem, Kuwait University; Ian Roberts, Cambridge University; Tugba Rona, Istanbul International Community School; Natalie Schilling-Estes, Georgetown University; Philippe Schlenker, Institut Jean-Nicod, Paris and New York University; Carson Schütze, University of California, Los Angeles; Bruce Sherwood, North Carolina State University; Koh Shimizu, Beijing; Dwan L. Shipley, Washington University; Muffy Siegel, Temple University; Andrew Simpson, University of Southern California; Neil Smith, University College London; Nancy Stenson, University of Minnesota, Twin Cities; Donca Steriade, Massachusetts Institute of Technology; Mel Storm, Emporia State University; Nawaf Sulami, University of Northern Iowa; Megha Sundara, University of California, Los Angeles; Erik Thomas, North Carolina State University; Robert (Bob) Trammell, Florida Atlantic University, Boca Raton; Dalys Vargas, College of Notre Dame; Willis Warren, Saint Edwards University; Donald K. Watkins, University of Kansas; Walt Wolfram, North Carolina State University; Maria Luisa Zubizarreta, University of Southern California; and Kie Zuraw, University of California, Los Angeles.

Please forgive us if we have inadvertently omitted any names, and if we have spelled every name correctly, then we shall believe in miracles.

Finally, we wish to thank our editorial and production teams. They have been superb and supportive in every way: Vanessa Coloura, product manager; Julia Giannotti, project manager; Melissa Sacco, content development project manager, Michael Lepera, content project manager. Our thanks also to Eleanor Glewwe, University of California, Los Angeles, for her editorial assistance and to Nicoletta Loccioni, for her meticulous work on the tree diagrams in Chapter 3.

Last but certainly not least, we acknowledge our debt to those we love and who love us and who inspire our work when nothing else will: Nina's son, Michael; Robert's children Zack and Emily together with a quartet of grandchildren: Cedar, Luke, Juniper, and Henry; our parents and siblings; and our dearly beloved and still deeply missed colleagues, Vicki Fromkin and Peter Ladefoged.

The responsibility for errors in fact or judgment is, of course, ours alone. We continue to be indebted to the instructors who have used the earlier editions and to their students, without whom there would be no eleventh edition.

Robert Rodman<br>
Nina Hyams

# About the Authors

**VICTORIA FROMKIN** received her bachelor's degree in economics from the University of California, Berkeley, in 1944 and her M.A. and Ph.D. in linguistics from the University of California, Los Angeles, in 1963 and 1965, respectively. She was a member of the faculty of the UCLA Department of Linguistics from 1966 until her death in 2000, and served as its chair from 1972 to 1976. From 1979 to 1989 she served as the UCLA Graduate Dean and Vice Chancellor of Graduate Programs. She was a visiting professor at the Universities of Stockholm, Cambridge, and Oxford. Vicki served as president of the Linguistics Society of America in 1985, president of the Association of Graduate Schools in 1988, and chair of the Board of Governors of the Academy of Aphasia. She received the UCLA Distinguished Teaching Award and the Professional Achievement Award, and served as the U.S. Delegate and a member of the Executive Committee of the International Permanent Committee of Linguistics (CIPL). She was an elected Fellow of the American Academy of Arts and Sciences, the American Association for the Advancement of Science, the New York Academy of Science, the American Psychological Society, and the Acoustical Society of America, and in 1996 was elected to membership in the National Academy of Sciences. She published more than one hundred books, monographs, and papers on topics concerned with phonetics, phonology, tone languages, African languages, speech errors, processing models, aphasia, and the brain/mind/language interface—all research areas in which she worked. Vicki Fromkin passed away on January 19, 2000, at the age of 76.

**ROBERT RODMAN** received his bachelor's degree in mathematics from the University of California, Los Angeles, in 1961, a master's degree in mathematics in 1965, a master's degree in linguistics in 1971, and his Ph.D. in linguistics in 1973. He was on the faculties of the University of California at Santa Cruz, the University of North Carolina at Chapel Hill, Kyoto Industrial College in Japan, and North Carolina State University. His research areas included forensic linguistics and computer speech processing. In 2009, he was elected into the American Academy of Social Sciences as an Associate Fellow for his achievements in computational forensic linguistics. Robert Rodman passed away on January 15, 2017, at the age of 76.

**NINA HYAMS** received her bachelor's degree in journalism from Boston University in 1973 and her M.A. and Ph.D. degrees in linguistics from the Graduate Center of the City University of New York in 1981 and 1983, respectively. She joined the faculty of the University of California, Los Angeles, in 1983, where she is currently a professor of linguistics. Her main areas of research are childhood language development and syntax. She is author of the book *Language Acquisition and the Theory of Parameters* (D. Reidel Publishers, 1986), a milestone in language acquisition research. She has also published numerous articles on the development of syntax, morphology, and semantics in children. She has been a visiting scholar at the University of Utrecht and the University of Leiden in the Netherlands and has given lectures throughout Europe and Japan. Nina lives in Los Angeles with her pal Spot, a rescued border collie mutt, and his olde English bulldogge companion, the ever soulful Nellie.

1

# What Is Language?

Whatever else people do when they come together—whether they play, fight, make love, or make automobiles—they talk. We live in a world of language. We talk to friends, associates, wives and husbands, lovers, teachers, parents, rivals, and even enemies. We talk face-to-face and over all manner of electronic media, and everyone responds with more talk. Hardly a moment of our waking lives is free from words, and even our dreams are filled with talk. We also talk when there is no one to answer. Some of us talk aloud in our sleep. We talk to our pets and sometimes to ourselves.

The capacity for language, perhaps more than any other attribute, distinguishes humans from other animals. According to the philosophy expressed in many myths and religions, language is the source of human life and power. To some people of Africa, a newborn child is a *kintu*, a "thing," not yet a *muntu*, a "person." It is only by the act of learning language that the child becomes a human being. To understand our humanity, we must understand the nature of language that makes us human. That is the goal of this book. We begin with a simple question: What does it mean to "know" a language?

## Linguistic Knowledge

When you know a language, you can speak and be understood by others who also know that language. This means you are able to produce strings of sounds that signify certain meanings and to understand or interpret the sounds produced by others. But language is much more than speech. Deaf people produce and understand sign languages just as hearing persons produce and understand spoken languages. The languages of the deaf communities throughout the world are equivalent to spoken languages, differing only in their modality of expression.

Most everyone knows at least one language. Five-year-old children are nearly as proficient at speaking and understanding as their parents. Yet, the ability to carry out the simplest conversation requires profound knowledge that most speakers are unaware of. This is true for speakers of all languages, from Albanian to Zulu. A speaker of English can produce a sentence having two relative clauses without knowing what a relative clause is. For example:

> My goddaughter who was born in Sweden and who now lives in Iowa is named Disa, after a Viking queen.

In a parallel fashion, a child can walk without understanding or being able to explain the principles of balance and support or the neurophysiological control mechanisms that permit one to do so. The fact that we may know something unconsciously is not unique to language.

## Knowledge of the Sound System

Part of knowing a language means knowing what sounds (or signs) are in that language and what sounds are not. One way this unconscious knowledge is revealed is by the way speakers of one language pronounce words from another language. If you speak only English, for example, you may substitute an English sound for a non-English sound when pronouncing "foreign" words such as French *ménage à trois*. If you pronounce it as the French do, you are using sounds outside the English sound system.

French people speaking English often pronounce words such as *this* and *that* as if they were spelled *zis* and *zat*. The English sound represented by the initial letters *th* in these words is not part of the French sound system, and the mispronunciation reveals the French speaker's unconscious knowledge of this fact.

Knowing the sound system of a language includes more than knowing the inventory of sounds. It means also knowing which sounds may start a word, end a word, and follow each other. The name of a former president of Ghana was *Nkrumah*, pronounced with an initial sound like the sound ending the English word *sink*. While this is an English sound, no word in English begins with the *nk* sound. Speakers of English who have occasion to pronounce this name often mispronounce it (by Ghanaian standards) by inserting a short vowel sound, like *Nekrumah* or *Enkrumah*, making the word correspond to the English system. Children develop the sound patterns of their language very rapidly. A one-year-old learning English already knows that *nk* cannot begin a word, just as a Ghanaian child of the same age knows that it can in his language. We will learn more about sounds and sound systems in Chapters 5 and 6.

## Knowledge of Words

Sounds and sound patterns of our language constitute only one part of our linguistic knowledge. Beyond that we know that certain sequences of sounds signify certain concepts or **meanings**. Speakers of English understand what *boy* means, and that it means something different from *toy* or *girl* or *pterodactyl*.

We also know that *toy* and *boy* are words, but *moy* is not. When you know a language, you know words in that language; that is, you know which sequences of sounds have specific meanings and which do not.

## Arbitrary Relation of Form and Meaning

If you do not know a language, the words (and sentences) of that language will be mainly incomprehensible, because the relationship between speech sounds and the meanings they represent is, for the most part, an **arbitrary** one. When you are acquiring a language, you have to learn that the sounds represented by the letters *house* signify the concept 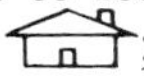; if you know French, this same meaning is represented by *maison*; if you know Russian, by *dom*; if you know Spanish, by *casa*. Similarly,  is represented by *hand* in English, *main* in French, *nsa* in Twi, and *ruka* in Russian. The same sequence of sounds can represent different meanings in different languages. The word *bolna* means "speak" in Hindi–Urdu and "aching" in Russian; *bis* means "devil" in Ukrainian and "twice" in Latin; a *pet* is a domestic animal in English and a fart in Catalan; and the sequence of sounds *taka* means "hawk" in Japanese, "fist" in Quechua, "a small bird" in Zulu, and "money" in Bengali.

These examples show that the words of a particular language have the meanings they do only by convention. Despite a penchant that biologists have for Greek roots, a pterodactyl could have been called *ron, blick*, or *kerplunkity*.

This **conventional** and arbitrary relationship between the **form** (sounds) and **meaning** (concept) of a word is also true in sign languages. If you see someone using a sign language you do not know, it is doubtful that you will understand the message from the signs alone. A person who knows Chinese Sign Language (CSL) would find it difficult to understand American Sign Language (ASL), and vice versa.

Many signs were originally like miming, where the relationship between form and meaning is not arbitrary. Bringing the hand to the mouth to mean "eating," as in miming, would be nonarbitrary as a sign. Over time these signs may change, just as the pronunciation of words changes, and the miming effect is lost. These signs become conventional, so that the shape or movement of the hands alone does not reveal the meaning of the signs.

There is some **sound symbolism** in language—that is, words whose pronunciation suggests their meanings. Most languages contain **onomatopoeic** words like *buzz* or *murmur* that imitate the sounds associated with the objects or actions they refer to. But even here, the sounds differ from language to language and reflect the particular sound system of the language. In English *cock-a-doodle-doo* is an onomatopoeic word whose meaning is the crow of a rooster, whereas in Finnish the rooster's crow is *kukkokiekuu*. Forget *gobble gobble* when you're in Istanbul; a turkey in Turkey goes *glu-glu*.

Sometimes particular sound combinations seem to relate to a particular concept. Many English words beginning with *gl* relate to sight, such as *glare, glint, gleam, glitter, glossy, glaze, glance, glimmer, glimpse,* and *glisten*. However, *gl* words and their like are a very small part of any language, and *gl* may have nothing to

HERMAN®/LaughingStock Licensing Inc., Ottawa, Canada

do with "sight" in another language, or even in other words in English, such as *gladiator, glucose, glory, glutton,* and *globe.*

To know a language, we must know words of that language. But no speaker knows all the entries in an unabridged dictionary—and even if someone did, he would still not know that language. Imagine trying to learn a foreign language from an online dictionary. However, many words you learned, you would not be able to form nor understand very many phrases. And even if you could manage to get your message across using a few words from a traveler's dictionary, such as "car—gas—where?" the best you could hope for is to be pointed in the direction of a gas station. If you were answered with a sentence, it is doubtful that you would understand what was said or be able to look it up, because you would not know where one word ended and another began. Chapter 3 will discuss how words are put together to form phrases and sentences, and Chapter 4 will explore word and sentence meanings.

## The Creativity of Linguistic Knowledge

Knowledge of a language enables you to combine sounds to form words, words to form phrases, and phrases to form sentences. No matter how smart your smartphone is, it cannot contain all the sentences of a language because the number is infinite. Knowing a language means being able to produce and understand new sentences never spoken before. This is the **creative aspect** of language. Not every speaker can create great literature, but everybody who knows a language can create and understand novel sentences.

That language is creative and sentences potentially infinite in length and number is shown by the fact that any sentence can be made indefinitely longer. In English, you can say:

> This is the house.

or

> This is the house that Jack built.

or

> This is the malt that lay in the house that Jack built.

or

> This is the dog that worried the cat that killed the rat that ate the malt that lay in the house that Jack built.

The longer these sentences become the less likely we are to hear or say them. A sentence such as "The old, old, old, old, old, old man fell" with half-dozen occurrences of *old* would be highly unusual in either speech or writing, even to describe Methuselah. But such a sentence is theoretically possible. If you know English, you have the knowledge to add any number of adjectives to a noun, and any number of clauses to a sentence, as in "the house that Jack built."

All human languages permit their speakers to increase the length and complexity of sentences in these ways; creativity is a universal property of human language.

Our creative ability is reflected not only in what we say, but also in our understanding of new or novel sentences. Consider the following sentence: "Daniel Boone decided to become a pioneer because he dreamed of pigeon-toed giraffes and cross-eyed elephants dancing in pink skirts and green berets on the wind-swept plains of the Midwest." You may not believe the sentence; you may question its logic; but you can understand it, although you probably never heard or read it before now.

In pointing out the creative aspect of language, Noam Chomsky, who many regard as the father of modern linguistics, argued persuasively against the view that language is a set of learned responses to stimuli. It's true that if someone steps on your toes, you may automatically respond with a scream or a grunt, but these sounds are not part of language. They are involuntary reactions to stimuli. After we reflexively cry out, we can then go on to say: "Thank you very much for stepping on my toe, because I was afraid I had elephantiasis and now that I can feel the pain I know I don't," or any one of an infinite number of sentences, because the particular sentences we produce are not controlled by any stimulus.

Even some involuntary cries such as "ouch" change according to the language we speak. Step on an Italian's toes and he will cry "ahi." French speakers often fill their pauses with the vowel sound that starts their word for "egg"—*oeu(f)*—a sound that does not occur in English. Even conversational fillers such as *er, uh,* and *you know* in English are constrained by the language in which they occur.

The fact of human linguistic creativity was well expressed more than 400 years ago by Huarte de San Juan (1530–1592): “Normal human minds are such that . . . without the help of anybody, they will produce 1,000 (sentences) they never heard spoke of . . . inventing and saying such things as they never heard from their masters, nor any mouth.”

## Knowledge of Sentences and Nonsentences

Our knowledge of language not only allows us to produce and understand an infinite number of well-formed (even if silly and illogical) sentences. It also permits us to distinguish well-formed (grammatical) from ill-formed (ungrammatical) sentences. This is further evidence of our linguistic creativity because ungrammatical sentences are typically novel, not sentences we have previously heard or produced, precisely because they are ungrammatical!

Consider the following sentences:

**a.** John kissed the little old lady who owned the shaggy dog.
**b.** Who owned the shaggy dog John kissed the little old lady.
**c.** John is difficult to love.
**d.** It is difficult to love John.
**e.** John is anxious to go.
**f.** It is anxious to go John.
**g.** John, who was a student, flunked his exams.
**h.** Exams his flunked student a was who John.

If you were asked to put an asterisk or star before the examples that seemed ill formed or ungrammatical or “not good” to you, which ones would you mark? Our intuitive knowledge about what is or is not an allowable sentence in English convinces us to star *b, f,* and h. Which ones did you star?

Would you agree with the following judgments?

**a.** What he did was climb a tree.
**b.** *What he thought was want a sports car.[1]
**c.** Drink your beer and go home!
**d.** *What are drinking and go home?
**e.** I expect them to arrive a week from next Thursday.
**f.** *I expect a week from next Thursday to arrive them.
**g.** Linus lost his security blanket.
**h.** *Lost Linus security blanket his.

If you find the starred sentences unacceptable, as we do, you see your linguistic creativity at work.

These sentences also illustrate that not every string of words constitutes a well-formed sentence in a language. Sentences are not formed simply by placing one word after another in any order, but by organizing the words according to

[1]The asterisk is used before examples that speakers find ungrammatical. This notation will be used throughout the book.

the rules of sentence formation of the language. These rules are finite in length and finite in number so that they can be stored in our finite brains. Yet, they permit us to form and understand an infinite set of new sentences. They also enable us to judge whether a sequence of words is a well-formed sentence of our language or not. These rules are not determined by a judge or a legislature, or even taught in a grammar class. They are unconscious rules that we acquire as young children as we develop language and they are responsible for our linguistic creativity. Linguists refer to this set of rules as the **grammar** of the language.

Returning to the question we posed at the beginning of this chapter—what does it mean to know a language? It means knowing the sounds and meanings of many, if not all, of the words of the language, and the rules for their combination—the grammar, which accounts for infinitely many possible sentences. We will have more to say about these rules of grammar in later chapters.

## Linguistic Knowledge and Performance

Speakers of all languages have the knowledge to understand or produce sentences of any length. Here is an example from the ruling of a federal judge:

> We invalidate the challenged lifetime ban because we hold as a matter of federal constitutional law that a state initiative measure cannot impose a severe limitation on the people's fundamental rights when the issue of whether to impose such a limitation on these rights is put to the voters in a measure that is ambiguous on its face and that fails to mention in its text, the proponent's ballot argument, or the state's official description, the severe limitation to be imposed.

Theoretically, there is no limit to the length of a sentence, but in practice very long sentences are unlikely, the verbose federal judge's ruling notwithstanding. Evidently, there is a difference between having the knowledge required to produce or understand sentences of a language and applying this knowledge. It is a difference between our knowledge of words and grammar, which is our **linguistic competence**, and how we use this knowledge in actual speech production and comprehension, which is our **linguistic performance**.

Our linguistic knowledge permits us to form longer and longer sentences by joining sentences and phrases together or adding modifiers to a noun. However, there are physiological and psychological reasons that limit the number of adjectives, adverbs, clauses, and so on that we actually produce and understand. Speakers may run out of breath, lose track of what they have said, or die of old age before they are finished. Listeners may become tired, bored, disgusted, or confused, like poor Alice when being interrogated by the Red Queen.

When we speak we usually wish to convey some message. At some stage in the act of producing speech, we must organize our thoughts into strings of words. Sometimes the message is garbled. We may stammer, or pause, or produce **slips of the tongue** such as saying *preach seduction* when *speech production* is meant.

# What Is Grammar?

## Descriptive Grammars

The way we are using the word *grammar* differs from most common usages. In our sense, the grammar is the knowledge speakers have about the units and rules of their language—rules for combining sounds into words (called *phonology*), rules of word formation (called *morphology*), rules for combining words into phrases and phrases into sentences (called *syntax*), as well as rules for assigning meaning (called *semantics*). The grammar, together with a mental dictionary (called a *lexicon*) that lists the words of the language, represents our linguistic competence. To understand the nature of language, we must understand the nature of grammar.

Every human being who speaks a language knows its grammar. When linguists wish to describe a language, they make explicit the rules of the grammar that exist in the minds of the speakers of the language. There will be some differences among speakers, but there must be shared knowledge too. The shared knowledge—the common parts of the grammar—makes it possible to communicate through language. To the extent that the linguist's description is a true model of a speaker's linguistic capacity, it is a successful description of the grammar and of the language itself. Such a model is called a **descriptive grammar**. It does not tell you how you *should* speak; it tells you how you *do* speak. It explains how it is possible for you to speak and understand and make judgments about well-formedness, and it describes what you know about the sounds, words, phrases, and sentences of your language.

When we say that a sentence is **grammatical**, we mean that it conforms to the rules of the mental grammar (as described by the linguist); when we say that it is **ungrammatical**, we mean it deviates from the rules in some way. If, however, we posit a rule for English that does not agree with your intuitions as a speaker, then the grammar we are describing differs in some way from the mental grammar that represents your linguistic competence; that is, your language is not the one described. That's okay. No language or variety of a language (called a *dialect*) is superior or inferior to any other in a linguistic sense. Every grammar is equally complex, logical, and capable of producing an infinite set of sentences to express any thought. (We will have more to say about dialects in Chapter 7.)

## Prescriptive Grammars

Not all grammarians, past or present, share the view that all grammars are equal. Language "purists" of all ages believe that some versions of a language are better than others, that there are certain "correct" forms that all educated people should use in speaking and writing, and that language change is corruption.

The Greek Alexandrians in the first century, the Arabic scholars at Basra in the eighth century, and numerous English grammarians of the eighteenth and nineteenth centuries held this view. They wished to *prescribe* rather than *describe* the rules of grammar, which gave rise to the writing of **prescriptive grammars**.

In the Renaissance, a new middle class emerged who wanted their children to speak the dialect of the "upper" classes. This desire led to the publication of many prescriptive grammars. In 1762, Bishop Robert Lowth wrote *A Short Introduction to English Grammar with Critical Notes*. Lowth prescribed a number of new rules for English, many of them influenced by his personal taste. Before the publication of his grammar, practically everyone—upper-class, middle-class, and lower-class—said *I don't have none* and *You was wrong about that*. Lowth, however, decided that "two negatives make a positive" and therefore one should say *I don't have any*; and that even when *you* is singular it should be followed by the plural *were*. Many of these prescriptive rules were based on Latin grammar and made little sense for English. Because Lowth was influential and because the rising new class wanted to speak "properly," many of these new rules were legislated into English grammar, at least for the **prestige dialect**—that variety of the language spoken by people in positions of power.

Prescriptive grammars such as Lowth's are different from the descriptive grammars that linguists develop. Their goal is not to describe the rules people know, but to tell them what rules they should follow. The great British Prime Minister Winston Churchill is credited with this response to the "rule" against ending a sentence with a preposition: "This is the sort of nonsense up with which I will not put."

rhymeswithorange.com Distributed by King Features Syndicate

Even today language purists write books and blogs attempting to "save the English language." For example, they criticize the use of *enormity* to mean "enormous" instead of "monstrously evil", its original meaning. But languages change in the course of time and words change meaning. Language change is a natural process, as we discuss in Chapter 8. Over time *enormity* has been used increasingly used to mean "enormous," and now that former U.S. President Barack Obama has used it that way (in his victory speech of November 4, 2008), and that British author J. K. Rowling uses it similarly in the immensely popular *Harry Potter and the Deathly Hallows*, that usage will gain acceptance.

Still, the "saviors" of the English language will never disappear. They will continue to blame TV, the Internet, and especially texting for corrupting the English language, and are likely to continue to dis (oops, we mean disparage) anyone who suggests that African American English (AAE)[2] and other dialects are viable, complete languages.

## Universal Grammar

There are rules of particular languages such as English or Arabic or Zulu that form part of the individual grammars of these languages, and then there are rules that hold in all languages. The universal rules are of particular interest because they give us a window into the human "faculty of language," which enables us to learn and use any particular language.

Interest in language universals has a long history. Early scholars encouraged research into the nature of language in general and promoted the idea of *general grammar* as distinct from *special grammar*. General grammar was to reveal those features common to all languages.

Students trying to learn Latin, Greek, French, or Swahili as a second language are generally so focused on learning aspects of the new language that differ from their native language that they may overlook the universal laws of language. Yet, there is much that all language learners know unconsciously even before they begin to learn a new language. They know that a language has its own set of sounds, perhaps thought of as its alphabet, that combine according to certain patterns to form words, and that the words themselves recombine to form phrases and sentences. Learners will expect to find verbs and nouns—as these are universal grammatical categories; they will know that the language—like all languages—has a way of negating, forming questions, issuing commands, referring to past or future time, and more generally, has a system of rules that will allow them to produce and understand an infinite number of sentences.

The more linguists explore the intricacies of human language, the more evidence we find to support Chomsky's view that there is a **Universal Grammar (UG)** that is part of the biologically endowed human language faculty. We can think of UG as the blueprint that all languages follow that forms part of the child's innate capacity for language learning. It specifies the different components of the grammar and their relations, how the different rules of these components are constructed, how they interact, and so on. A major aim of **linguistic theory** is to discover the nature of UG.

The linguist's goal is to reveal the "laws of human language," as the physicist's goal is to reveal the "laws of the physical universe." The complexity of language undoubtedly means this goal will never be fully achieved. All scientific theories are incomplete, and new hypotheses must be proposed to account for new data. Theories are continually changing as new discoveries are made. Just as physics

[2]AAE is also called African American Vernacular English (AAVE), Ebonics, and Black English (BE). It is spoken by some (but by no means all) African Americans. It is discussed in Chapter 7.

was enlarged by Einstein's theories of relativity, so grows the linguistic theory of UG as new discoveries shed new light on the nature of human language. The comparative study of many different languages is of central importance to this enterprise.

## What Is Not (Human) Language

Patrick McDonnell/King Features Syndicate

All languages share certain fundamental properties, and children naturally acquire these languages because human beings are designed for human language. But what of the "languages" of other species: Are they like human languages? Can other species be taught a human language?

## The Birds and the Bees

Most animal species possess some kind of communication system. Humans also communicate through systems other than language such as head nodding or facial expressions. The question is whether the communication systems used by other species are at all like human language with its very specific properties, most notably its creative aspect.

Many species have a non vocal system of communication. Among certain species of spiders there is a complex system for courtship. Before approaching his ladylove, the male spider goes through an elaborate series of gestures to tell her that he is indeed a spider and a suitable mate, and not a crumb or a fly to be eaten. These gestures are invariant. One never finds a creative spider changing or adding to the courtship ritual of his species.

A similar kind of gestural language is found among the fiddler crabs. There are forty species, and each uses its own claw-waving movement to signal to another member of its "clan." The timing, movement, and posture of the body never change from one time to another or from one crab to another within the particular variety. Whatever the signal means, it is fixed. Only one meaning can be conveyed.

An essential property of human language not shared by the communication systems of spiders, crabs, and other animals is its **discreteness**. Human languages are not simply made up of a fixed set of invariant signs. They are composed of discrete units—sounds, words, phrases—that are combined according to the rules of the grammar of the language. The word *top* in English has a particular meaning, but it also has individual parts that can be rearranged to produce other meaningful sequences—*pot* or *opt*. Similarly, the phrase *the cat on the mat* means something different from *the mat on the cat*. We can arrange and rearrange the units of our language to form an infinite number of expressions. The creativity of human language depends on discreteness.

In contrast to crabs and spiders, birds communicate vocally and bird-songs have always captured the human imagination. Musicians and composers have been moved by these melodies, sometimes imitating them in their compositions, other times incorporating birdsongs directly into the music. Birdsongs have also inspired poets as in Percy Bysshe Shelley's *To a Skylark*:

> Teach me half the gladness
> That thy brain must know;
> Such harmonious madness
> From my lips would flow,
> The world should listen then, as I am listening now.

Birds do not sing for our pleasure, however. Their songs and calls communicate important information to other members of the species and sometimes to other animals. **Birdcalls** (consisting of one or more short notes) convey danger, feeding, nesting, flocking, and so on. **Bird songs** (more complex patterns of notes) are used to stake out territory and to attract mates. Like the messages of crabs and spiders, however, there is no evidence of any internal structure to these songs; they cannot be segmented into discrete meaningful parts and rearranged to encode different messages as can the words, phrases, and sentences of human language.

In his territorial song, the European robin alternates between high-pitched and low-pitched notes to indicate how strongly he feels about defending his territory. The different alternations indicate intensity and nothing more. The robin is creative in his ability to sing the same song in different ways, but not creative in his ability to use the same units of the system to express different messages with different meanings. Recently, scientists have observed that finches will react when the units of a familiar song are rearranged. It is unclear, however, whether the birds recognize a violation of the rules of the song or are just responding to a pattern change.

Though crucial to the birds' survival, the messages conveyed by these songs and calls are limited, relating only to a bird's immediate environment and needs. Human language is different of course. Our words and sentences are not simply responses to internal and external stimuli. If you're tired you may yawn, but you may also say "I'm tired," or "I'm going to bed," or "I'm going to Starbucks for a double espresso." Notably, you also have the right to remain silent, or talk about things completely unrelated to your physical state—the weather, Facebook, your plans for the weekend, or most interesting of all, your linguistics class.

Linguists call this property of human language **displacement**: the capacity to talk (or sign) messages that are unrelated to here and now. Displacement and discreteness are two fundamental properties that distinguish human language from the communication systems of birds and other animals.

One respect in which birdsongs do resemble human languages is in their development. In many bird species, the full adult version of the birdsong is acquired in several stages, as it is for children acquiring language. The young bird sings a simplified version of the song shortly after hatching and then learns the more detailed, complex version by hearing adults sing. However, he must hear the adult song during a specific fixed period after birth—the period differs from species to species; otherwise song acquisition does not occur. For example, the chaffinch is unable to learn the more detailed song elements after ten months of age. A baby nightingale in captivity may be trained to sing melodiously by another nightingale, a "teaching bird," but only before its tail feathers are grown. These birds show a **critical period** for acquiring their "language" similar to the critical period for human language acquisition. As with human language acquisition, the development of the birdsongs of these species involves an interaction of both learned and innate structure.

An interesting consequence of the fact that some birdsongs are partially learned means that variation can develop. There can be "regional dialects" within the same species, and as with humans, these dialects are transmitted from parents to offspring. Researchers have noted, in fact, that dialect differences may be better preserved in songbirds than in humans because there is no homogenization of regional accents due to radio or TV. We will discuss human language dialects in Chapter 7.

Honeybees have a particularly interesting signaling system. When a forager bee returns to the hive she communicates to other bees where a source of food is located by performing a dance on a wall of the hive that reveals the location and quality of the food source. For one species of Italian honeybee, the dancing may assume one of three possible patterns: *round* (which indicates locations near the hive, within 20 feet or so); *sickle* (which indicates locations at 20 to 60 feet from the hive); and *tail-wagging* (for distances that exceed 60 feet). The number of repetitions per minute of the basic pattern in the tail-wagging dance indicates the precise distance: the slower the repetition rate, the longer the distance. The number of repetitions and the intensity with which the bee dances the round dance indicates the richness of the food source: the more repetitions and the livelier the bee dance the more food to be gotten.

Bee dances are discrete in some sense, consisting of separate parts, and in principle they can communicate infinitely many different messages, like human language; but unlike human language the topic is always the same, namely food. They lack the displacement property. As experiments have shown, when a bee is forced to walk to a food source rather than fly, she will communicate a distance many times farther away than the food source actually is. The bee has no way of communicating the special circumstances of its trip. This absence of creativity makes the bee's dance qualitatively different from human language.

## Language and Thought

Many people are fascinated by the question of how language relates to thought. It is natural to imagine that something as powerful and fundamental to human nature as language would influence how we think about or perceive the world around us. This is clearly reflected in the appendix of George Orwell's masterpiece *1984*, quoted above. Over the years, there have been many claims made regarding the relationship between language and thought. The claim that the structure of a language influences how its speakers perceive the world around them is most closely associated with the linguist Edward Sapir and his student Benjamin Whorf, and is therefore referred to as the **Sapir–Whorf hypothesis**. In 1929 Sapir wrote:

> Human beings do not live in the objective world alone, nor in the world of social activity as ordinarily understood, but are very much at the mercy of the particular language which has become the medium of expression for their society . . . we see and hear and otherwise experience very largely as we do because the language habits of our community predispose certain choices of interpretation.[3]

Whorf made even stronger claims:

> The background linguistic system (in other words, the grammar) of each language is not merely the reproducing instrument for voicing ideas but rather is itself the shaper of ideas, the program and guide for the individual's mental activity, for his analysis of impressions, for his synthesis of his mental stock in trade . . . We dissect nature along lines laid down by our native languages.[4]

The strongest form of the Sapir–Whorf hypothesis is called **linguistic determinism** because it holds that the language we speak *determines* how we perceive and think about the world. According to this view, language acts like a filter on reality. One of Whorf's best-known claims in support of linguistic determinism was that the Hopi Indians do not perceive time in the same way as speakers of European languages because the Hopi language does not make the grammatical distinctions of tense that, for example, English does with words and word endings such as *did, will, shall, -s, -ed,* and *-ing*.

A weaker form of the hypothesis is **linguistic relativism**, which says that languages differ in the categories they encode and therefore speakers of different languages think about the world in different ways. For example, languages break up the color spectrum at different points. In Navaho, blue and green are one word. Russian has different words for dark blue *(siniy)* and light blue *(goluboy)*, while in English we need to use the additional words *dark* and *light* to

[3]Sapir, E. 1929. *Language*. New York: Harcourt, Brace & World, p. 207.

[4]Whorf, B. L., and J. B. Carroll. 1956. *Language, thought, and reality: Selected writings*. Cambridge, MA: MIT Press.

express the difference. The American Indian language Zuni does not distinguish between the colors yellow and orange.

Languages also differ in how they express locations. For example, in Italian, you ride "in" a bicycle and you go "in" a country while in English you ride "on" a bicycle and you go "to" a country. In English, we say that a ring is placed "on" a finger and a finger is placed "in" the ring. Korean, on the other hand, has one word for both situations, *kitta*, which expresses the idea of a tight-fitting relation between the two objects. Spanish has two different words for the inside of a corner *(rincón)* and the outside of a corner *(esquina)*.

That languages show linguistic distinctions in their lexicons and grammar is certain, and we will see many examples of this in later chapters. The question is to what extent—if at all—such distinctions determine or influence the thoughts and perceptions of speakers. The Sapir–Whorf hypothesis is controversial, but it is clear that the strong form of this hypothesis is false. Peoples' thoughts and perceptions are not determined by the words and structures of their language. We are not prisoners of our linguistic systems. If speakers were unable to think about something for which their language had no specific word, translations would be impossible, as would learning a second language. English may not have separate words for the inside of a corner and the outside of a corner, but we are perfectly able to express these concepts using more than one word. In fact, we just did. If humans could not think about something for which we don't have a word, how would infants ever learn their first words, much less languages?

Many of the specific claims of linguistic determinism have been shown to be wrong. For example, the Hopi language may not have words and word endings for specific tenses, but the language has other expressions for time, including words for the days of the week, parts of the day, yesterday and tomorrow, lunar phases, seasons, and so on. The Hopi people use various kinds of calendars and various devices for time-keeping based on the sundial. Clearly, they have a sophisticated concept of time despite the lack of a tense system in the language.

The Munduruku, an indigenous people of the Brazilian Amazon, have no words in their language for triangle, square, rectangle, or other geometric concepts, except circle. The only terms to indicate direction are words for upstream, downstream, sunrise, and sunset. Yet, Munduruku children understand many

SHERMAN'S LAGOON © 2011 JIM TOOMEY

principles of geometry as well as American children, whose language is rich in geometric and spatial words.

Though languages differ in their color words, speakers can readily perceive colors that are not named in their language. Grand Valley Dani is a language spoken in New Guinea with only two color words, black and white (dark and light). In experimental studies, however, speakers of the language showed recognition of the color red, and they did better with fire-engine red than off-red. This would not be possible if their color perceptions were fixed by their language. Our perception of color is determined by the structure of the human eye, not by the structure of language. However, some experiments have shown that speakers are better at discriminating two colors when their language has different words for each, supporting a weaker version of the Whorfian hypothesis.

One Whorfian claim that has taken on the cast of an urban legend is that the Inuit language, spoken in the Canadian Arctic, has many more words for snow than English, and that this affects the worldview of the Inuit people. However, anthropologists have shown that Inuit has no more words for snow than English does: around a dozen, including *sleet, blizzard, slush,* and *flurry*. But even if it did, this would not show that language conditions the Inuits' experience of the world. Rather, it suggests that experience with a particular world creates the need for certain words. In this respect, the Inuit speaker is no different from the computer programmer, who has a technical vocabulary for Internet protocols, or the linguist, who has many specialized words regarding language. In this book, we will introduce you to many new words and linguistic concepts, and surely you will learn them! This would be impossible if your thoughts about language were determined by the linguistic vocabulary you now have.

Politicians and marketers certainly believe that language can influence our thoughts and values. One political party may refer to "assisted suicide" while another "compassion and choices." In the abortion debate, some refer to the "right to choose" and others to the "right to life." The terminology reflects different ideologies, but the choice of expression is primarily intended to sway public opinion. Politically correct (PC) language also reflects the idea that language can influence thought. Many people believe that by changing the way we talk, we can change the way we think; that if we eliminate racist and sexist terms from our language, we will become a less racist and sexist society. As we will discuss in Chapter 7, language itself is not sexist or racist, but people can be, and because of this, particular words take on negative meanings.

In his book *The Language Instinct*, the psychologist Steven Pinker uses the expression *euphemism treadmill* to describe how the euphemistic terms that are created to replace negative words often take on the negative associations of the words they were coined to replace. For example, *handicapped* was once a euphemism for the offensive term *crippled*, and when *handicapped* became politically incorrect it was replaced by the euphemism *disabled*, which was then replaced by yet another euphemism, *challenged*, and most recently, *person with a disability*. Nonetheless, in all such cases, changing language has not resulted in a new worldview for the speakers. Rather, it is changing sensibilities that drive the changes in language.

Some language changes inspired by political correctness can be quite extreme. For example, a local council in Britain banned the term *brainstorming* and replaced it with *thought showers* because local lawmakers worried that the original term might offend people with epilepsy. Or the instruction to newly recruited holiday Santa Clauses in Sidney, Australia, to not say *Ho Ho Ho* deemed too close to the American slang for prostitute and therefore degrading to women.

Prescient as Orwell was with respect to how language could be used for social control, he was more circumspect with regard to the relation between language and thought. He was careful to qualify his notions with the phrase "at least so far as thought is dependent on words." Current research shows that language does not determine how we think about and perceive the world. Future research should show the extent to which language influences other aspects of cognition such as memory and categorization.

## Summary

We are all intimately familiar with at least one language, our own. Yet, few of us ever stop to consider what we know when we know a language. No book contains, or could possibly contain, the English or Russian or Zulu language. The words of a language can be listed in a dictionary, but not all the sentences can be. Speakers use a finite set of rules to produce and understand an infinite set of possible sentences.

These rules are part of the **grammar** of a language, which develops when you acquire the language and includes the sound system (the **phonology**), the structure and properties of words (the **morphology** and **lexicon**), how words may be combined into phrases and sentences (the **syntax**), and the ways in which sounds and meanings are related (the **semantics**). The sounds and meanings of individual words are related in an **arbitrary** fashion. If you had never heard the word *syntax*, you would not know what it meant by its sounds. The gestures used by signers are also arbitrarily related to their meanings. Language, then, is a system that relates sounds (or hand and body gestures) with meanings. When you know a language, you know this system.

This knowledge **(linguistic competence)** is different from behavior **(linguistic performance)**. You have the competence to produce a million-word sentence but performance limitations such as memory and endurance keep this from occurring.

There are different kinds of "grammars." The **descriptive grammar** of a language represents the (often unconscious) linguistic knowledge of its speakers. Such a grammar is a model of the **mental grammar** every speaker of the language possesses. It does not teach the rules of the language; it describes the rules that are already there. A grammar that attempts to legislate what your grammar should be is called a **prescriptive grammar**. It specifies a standard of usage. It does not describe, except incidentally.

The more linguists investigate the nearly 7,000 languages of the world and describe the ways in which they differ from one another, the more they discover that these differences are limited. There are linguistic universals that pertain to the components of the grammar, the ways in which these components are related, and the forms of rules that govern them. These principles compose

**Universal Grammar (UG)**, which provides a blueprint for the grammars of all possible human languages. Universal Grammar constitutes the innate component of the human language faculty that makes language development in children possible.

Strong evidence for Universal Grammar is found in the way children acquire language. Children learn language by exposure. They need not be deliberately taught, though parents may enjoy "teaching" their children to speak or sign. Children will learn any human language to which they are exposed, and they learn it in definable stages, beginning at a very early age.

If language is defined merely as a system of communication, or the ability to produce speech sounds, then language is not unique to humans. There are, however, certain characteristics of human language not found in the communication systems of any other species. A basic property of human language is its **creativity**—a speaker's ability to combine the basic linguistic units to form an infinite set of "well-formed" grammatical sentences, most of which are novel, never before produced or heard.

Human languages consist of discrete units that combine according to the rules of the grammar of the language. Human languages also allow us to talk about things that are removed in time and space from our immediate environment or mental or physical state. These are the properties of **discreteness** and **displacement** and they distinguish human language from the "languages" of other species.

The **Sapir–Whorf hypothesis** holds that the particular language we speak determines or influences our thoughts and perceptions of the world. Much of the early evidence in support of this hypothesis has not stood the test of time. More recent experimental studies suggest that the words and grammar of a language may affect certain aspects of cognition such as memory.

## References for Further Reading

Bickerton, D. 1990. *Language and species*. Chicago: Chicago University Press.

Chomsky, N. 1986. *Knowledge of language: Its nature, origin, and use*. New York and London: Praeger.

Emmorey, K. 2002. *Language, cognition and the brain: Insights from sign language research*. London, UK: Routledge

Gentner, D., and S. Goldin-Meadow. 2003. *Language in mind*. Cambridge, MA: MIT Press.

Klima, E. S., and U. Bellugi. 1979. *The signs of language*. Cambridge, MA: Harvard University Press.

Pilley, J. W. 2013. Chaser: *Unlocking the genius of the dog who knows a thousand words*. Boston: Houghton Mifflin Harcourt.

Pinker, S. 1999. *Words and rules: The ingredients of language*. New York: HarperCollins.

____. 1994. *The language instinct*. New York: William Morrow.

Premack, A. J., and D. Premack. 1972. Teaching language to an ape. *Scientific American* (October): 92–99.

Terrace, H. S. 1979. *Nim: A chimpanzee who learned sign language*. New York: Knopf.

## Exercises

1. Consider the following sentences. Put a star (*) after those that do not seem to conform to the rules of your grammar, that are ungrammatical for you. State, if you can, why you think the sentence is ungrammatical.
   - **a.** Robin forced the sheriff go.
   - **b.** Napoleon forced Josephine to go.
   - **c.** The devil made Faust go.
   - **d.** He passed by a large pile of money.
   - **e.** He drove by my house.
   - **f.** He drove my house by.
   - **g.** Did in a corner little Jack Horner sit?
   - **h.** Elizabeth is resembled by Charles.
   - **i.** Nancy is eager to please.
   - **j.** It is easy to frighten Emily.
   - **k.** It is eager to love a kitten.
   - **l.** That birds can fly flabbergasts.
   - **m.** The fact that you are late to class is surprising.
   - **n.** Has the nurse slept the baby yet?
   - **o.** I was surprised for you to get married.
   - **p.** I wonder who and Mary went swimming.
   - **q.** Myself bit John.
   - **r.** What did Alice eat the toadstool with?
   - **s.** What did Alice eat the toadstool and?

2. Although sounds and meanings of most words in all languages are arbitrarily related, there are some communication systems in which the "signs" unambiguously reveal their "meanings."
   - **a.** Describe (or draw) five different signs that directly show what they mean. *Example*: a road sign indicating an S curve.
   - **b.** Describe any other communication system that, like language, consists of arbitrary symbols. *Example*: traffic signals, in which red means stop and green means go.

3. Consider these two statements: I learned a new word today. I learned a new sentence today. Do you think the two statements are equally probable, and if not, why not?

4. Suppose you taught a dog to *heel, sit up, roll over, play dead, stay, jump,* and *bark* on command, using the italicized words as cues. Would you be teaching it language? Why or why not?

5. State some rule of grammar that you have learned is the correct way to say something, but that you do not generally use in speaking. For example, you may have heard that *It's me* is incorrect and that the correct form is *It's I*. Nevertheless, you always use *me* in such sentences; your friends do also, and in fact *It's I* sounds odd to you.

Write a short essay presenting arguments against someone who tells you that you are wrong. Discuss how this disagreement demonstrates the difference between descriptive and prescriptive grammars.

**6.** English (especially British English) has many words for woods and woodlands. Here are some:

woodlot, carr, fen, firth, grove, heath, holt, lea, moor, shaw, weald, wold, coppice, scrub, spinney, copse, brush, bush, bosquet, bosky, stand, forest, timberland, thicket

**a.** How many of these words do you recognize?
**b.** Look up several of these words in the dictionary and discuss the differences in meaning. Many of these words are obsolete, so if your dictionary doesn't have them, try the Internet.
**c.** Do you think that English speakers have a richer concept of woodlands than speakers whose language has fewer words? Why or why not?

**7.** English words containing *dge* in their spelling *(trudge, edgy)* are said mostly to have unfavorable or negative connotations. Research this notion by accumulating as many *dge* words as you can and classifying them as unfavorable *(sludge)* or neutral *(bridge)*. What do you do about *budget?* Unfavorable or not? Are there other questionable words?

**8.** **Research project**: Read the Cratylus Dialogue—it's online. In it is a discussion (or "dialogue") of whether names are "conventional" (i.e., what we have called *arbitrary*) or "natural." Do you find Socrates' point of view sufficiently well-argued to support the thesis in this chapter that the relationship between form and meaning is indeed arbitrary? Argue your case in either direction in a short (or long, if you wish) essay.

**9.** In the sci-fi movie *Arrival* (based on Ted Chiang's novella *Story of Your Life*), linguist Louise Banks learns the language (Heptapod B) of aliens visiting the Earth and then realizes she can see the future. Watch the movie and explain how the Sapir–Whorf hypothesis shapes the story.

2

# Morphology: The Words of Language

Every speaker of every language knows tens of thousands of words. Unabridged dictionaries of English contain nearly 500,000 entries, but most speakers don't know all of these words. It has been estimated that a child of six knows as many as 13,000 words and the average high school graduate about 60,000. A college graduate presumably knows many more than that, but whatever our level of education, we learn new words throughout our lives, such as the many words in this book that you will learn for the first time.

Words are an important part of linguistic knowledge and constitute a component of our mental grammars, but one can learn thousands of words in a language and still not know the language. Anyone who has tried to communicate in a foreign country by merely using a dictionary knows this is true. On the other hand, without words we would be unable to convey our thoughts through language or understand the thoughts of others.

Someone who doesn't know English would not know where one word begins or ends in an utterance like *Thecatsatonthemat.* We separate written words by spaces, but in the spoken language there are no pauses between most words. Without knowledge of the language, one can't tell how many words are in an utterance. Knowing a word means knowing that a particular sequence of sounds is associated with a particular meaning. A speaker of English has no difficulty in segmenting the stream of sounds into six individual words—*the, cat, sat, on, the,* and *mat*—because each of these words is listed in his or her mental dictionary, or lexicon (the Greek word for *dictionary*), that is part of a speaker's linguistic knowledge. Similarly, a speaker knows that *uncharacteristically,* which has more letters than *Thecatsatonthemat,* is nevertheless a single word.

When you know a word, you know its sound (pronunciation) and its meaning. Because the sound-meaning relation is arbitrary, it is possible to have words with the same sound and different meanings (*bear* and *bare*) and words with the same meaning and different sounds (*sofa* and *couch*).

Because each word is a sound-meaning unit, its pronunciation is stored in our mental lexicon alongside the corresponding meaning. For literate speakers, the spelling of most of the words is also included.

Each word in your mental lexicon includes other information as well, such as whether it is a noun, a pronoun, a verb, an adjective, an adverb, a preposition, or a conjunction. That is, the mental lexicon also specifies the **grammatical category** or **syntactic class** of the word. You may not consciously know that a form such as *love* is listed as both a verb and a noun, but as a speaker you have such knowledge, as shown by the phrases *I love you* and *You are the love of my life*. If such information were not in the mental lexicon, we would not know how to form grammatical sentences, nor would we be able to distinguish grammatical from ungrammatical sentences.

## Content Words and Function Words

Languages make an important distinction between two kinds of words—content words and function words. Nouns, verbs, adjectives, and adverbs are the **content words**. These words denote concepts such as objects, actions, attributes, and ideas that we can think about like *children*, *build*, *beautiful*, and *seldom*. Content words are sometimes called the **open class** words because we can and regularly do add new words to these classes, such as *Facebook* (noun), *blog* (noun, verb), *frack* (verb), and *online* (adjective, adverb).

Other classes of words do not have clear lexical meanings or obvious concepts associated with them, including conjunctions such as *and*, *or*, and *but*; prepositions such as *in* and *of*; the articles *the* and *a/an*, and pronouns such as *it*. These kinds of words are called **function words** because they specify grammatical relations and have little or no semantic content. For example, the articles indicate whether a noun is definite or indefinite—*the* boy or *a* boy. The preposition *of* indicates possession, as in "the book of yours," but this word indicates many other kinds of relations too. The *it* in *it's raining* and *the archbishop of Canterbury found it advisable* are further examples of words whose function is purely grammatical—they are required by the rules of syntax and are indispensable to the grammar.

Function words are sometimes called **closed class** words. This is because it is difficult to think of any articles, conjunctions, prepositions, or pronouns that have recently entered the language. The small set of personal pronouns such as *I, me, mine, he,* and *she,* are part of this class. So are the complementizers *if, that,* and *whether* which we will discuss the next chapter.

The difference between content and function words is illustrated by the following test that has circulated over the Internet:

> Count the number of Fs in the following text without reading further, then check the footnote:[1]

[1]Most people come up with three. If you came up with fewer than six, count again, and this time, pay attention to the function word *of*.

FINISHED FILES ARE THE
RESULT OF YEARS OF SCIENTIFIC
STUDY COMBINED WITH THE
EXPERIENCE OF YEARS.

This little test illustrates that the brain treats content and function words (such as *of*) differently. A great deal of psychological and neurological evidence supports this claim. In reading tasks people tend to skip over the function words. And some brain-damaged patients with language impairments are unable to read function words such as *in* or *which*, but can read the lexical content words *inn* and *witch*.

The two classes of words also seem to function differently in **slips of the tongue** produced by normal individuals. For example, a speaker may inadvertently switch words producing "the journal of the editor" instead of "the editor of the journal," but the switching or exchanging of function words has not been observed. There is also evidence for this distinction from language acquisition. In the early stages of development, children often omit function words from their speech as in "doggie barking."

The linguistic evidence suggests that content words and function words play different roles in language. Content words bear the brunt of the meaning, whereas function words connect the content words to the larger grammatical context.

## Morphemes: The Minimal Units of Meaning

"They gave it me," Humpty Dumpty continued, "for an un-birthday present."

"I beg your pardon?" Alice said with a puzzled air.

"I'm not offended," said Humpty Dumpty.

"I mean, what is an un-birthday present?"

"A present given when it isn't your birthday, of course."

LEWIS CARROLL, *Through the Looking-Glass*, 1871

Humpty Dumpty is well aware that the form *un-* means "not," as further shown in the following pairs of words:

| **A** | **B** |
|---|---|
| desirable | undesirable |
| likely | unlikely |
| inspired | uninspired |
| happy | unhappy |
| developed | undeveloped |
| sophisticated | unsophisticated |

Thousands of English adjectives begin with *un-*. If we assume that the most basic unit of meaning is the word, what do we say about parts of words, such as *un-*, which has a fixed meaning? In all the words in the B column, *un-* means the same thing—"not." *Undesirable* means "not desirable," *unlikely* means "not likely," and so on. All the words in column B consist of at least two meaningful units: *un* + *desirable*, *un* + *likely*, *un* + *inspired*, and so on.

Just as *un-* occurs with the same meaning in the previous list of words, so does *phon-* in the following words. (You may not know the meaning of some of them, but you will when you finish this book.)

| | | |
|---|---|---|
| phone | phonology | phoneme |
| phonetic | phonologist | phonemic |
| phonetics | phonological | allophone |
| phonetician | telephone | euphonious |
| phonic | telephonic | symphony |

*Phon-* is a minimal form in that it can't be decomposed. *Ph* doesn't mean anything; *pho*, though it may be pronounced like *foe*, has no relation in meaning to it; and *on* is not the preposition spelled *o-n*. In all the words on the list, *phon* has the identical meaning "pertaining to sound."

These examples illustrate that many words are composed by rules and have internal structure. *Uneaten, undisputed,* and *ungrammatical* are words in English, but **eatenun*, **disputedun*, and **grammaticalun* (to mean "not eaten," "not disputed," "not grammatical") are not words because we form a negative meaning of a word by adding *un-* to the beginning of a word not the end.

When Samuel Goldwyn, the pioneer moviemaker, announced, "In two words: impossible," he was reflecting the common view that words are the basic meaningful elements of a language. We have seen that this cannot be so, because some words contain several distinct units of meaning. The linguistic term for the most elemental unit of grammatical form is **morpheme**. The word is derived from the Greek word *morphe*, meaning "form." If Goldwyn had taken a linguistics course, he would have said, more correctly, "In two morphemes: im-possible."

The study of the internal structure of words, and of the rules by which words are formed, is **morphology**. This word itself consists of two morphemes, *morph* + *ology*. The morpheme *-ology* means "branch of knowledge," so the meaning of *morphology* is "the branch of knowledge concerning (word) forms." Morphology also refers to our internal grammatical knowledge concerning the words of our language, and like most linguistic knowledge we are not consciously aware of it.

A single word may be composed of one or more morphemes:

| | |
|---|---|
| One morpheme | boy |
| | desire |
| | meditate |
| two morphemes | boy + ish |
| | desire + able |
| | meditate + tion |
| three morphemes | boy + ish + ness |
| | desire + able + ity |
| four morphemes | gentle + man + li + ness |
| | un + desire + able + ity |

more than four    un + gentle + man + li + ness
                  anti + dis + establish + ment + ari + an + ism

A morpheme may be represented by a single letter such as the morpheme *a-* meaning "without" as in *amoral* and *asexual,* or by a single syllable, such as *child* and *ish* in *child* + *ish.* A morpheme may also consist of more than one syllable: of two syllables, as in *camel, lady,* and *water;* of three syllables, as in *Hackensack* and *crocodile;* or of four or more syllables, as in *hallucinate, apothecary, helicopter,* and *accelerate.*

A morpheme—the minimal linguistic unit—is thus an arbitrary union of a sound and a meaning (or grammatical function) that cannot be further analyzed. So, solidly welded is this union in the mind that it is impossible for you to hear or read a word you know and not be aware of its meaning, even if you try! These two sides of the same coin are often called a **linguistic sign**, not to be confused with the *sign* of sign languages. Every word in every language is composed of one or more morphemes.

## The Discreteness of Morphemes

9 CHICKWEED LANE © 2011 Brooke McEldowney. Reprinted by permission of Universal Uclick for UFS. 

Internet bloggers love to point out "inconsistencies" in the English language. They observe that while singers sing and flingers fling, it is not the case that fingers "fing." However, English speakers know that *finger* is a single morpheme, or a **monomorphemic word**. The final *-er* syllable in *finger* is not a separate morpheme because a finger is not "something that fings." Similarly, *butter* when not referring to goat-like behavior is monomorphemic food stuff, and *buttress,* to be sure, is neither a feminine form of *butt* nor has anything to do with locks of hair.

The meaning of a morpheme must be constant. The agentive morpheme *-er* means "one who does" in words such as *singer, painter, lover,* and *worker,* but the same sounds represent the comparative morpheme, meaning "more," in *nicer, prettier,* and *taller.* Thus, two different morphemes may be pronounced identically. The identical form represents two morphemes because of the different meanings. The same sounds may occur in another word and not represent a separate morpheme at all, as in *finger.*

Conversely, the two morphemes *-er* and *-ster* have the same meaning, but different forms. Both *singer* and *songster* mean "one who sings." And like *-er*, *-ster* is not a morpheme in *monster* because a monster is not something that "mons" or someone that "is mon" the way *youngster* is someone who is young. All of this follows from the concept of the morpheme as a *sound* plus a *meaning* unit.

The decomposition of words into morphemes illustrates one of the fundamental properties of human language—discreteness—a property that sets it apart from the animal communication systems, as discussed in Chapter 1. In all languages, sound units combine to form morphemes, morphemes combine to form words, and words combine to form larger units—phrases and sentences.

Discreteness is an important part of linguistic creativity. We can combine morphemes in novel ways to create new words whose meaning will be apparent to other speakers of the language. If you know that "to tweet" means to post an update to the social media site Twitter, you automatically understand that a *tweetable* message is one that is suitable for posting on Twitter; that a *tweeter* is someone who tweets, and that when a *tweet* is *retweeted* thousands of times, it has gone viral! You know the meanings of all these words by virtue of your knowledge of the discrete morphemes *tweet, re-, -able,* and *-er*, and the rules for their combination.

## Bound and Free Morphemes

Our morphological knowledge has two components: knowledge of the individual morphemes and knowledge of the rules that combine them. We will see a similar situation in the next chapter where our syntactic knowledge consists of knowledge of words and the rules for combining them, and we will see yet another example of the discreteness of human language in succeeding chapters where speakers have knowledge of the individual sounds of their language and the rules for combining them into morphemes and words.

One of the things we know about particular morphemes is whether they can stand alone or whether they must be attached to a base morpheme. Some morphemes such as *boy, desire, gentle,* and *man* may constitute words by themselves. These are **free morphemes**. Other morphemes such as *-ish, -ness, -ly, pre-, trans-,* and *un-* are never words by themselves but are always parts of words. These **affixes** are **bound morphemes** and they may attach at the beginning, the end, in the middle, or both at the beginning and end of a word. The humor in the cartoon is Brad's stumbling over the bound morpheme *un-* in a questionable attempt to free it.

### Prefixes and Suffixes

We know whether an affix precedes or follows other morphemes, for example, *un-, pre- (premeditate, prejudge),* and *bi- (bipolar, bisexual)* are **prefixes**. They occur before other morphemes. Some morphemes occur only as **suffixes**, following other morphemes. English examples of suffix morphemes are *-ing (sleeping, eating, running, climbing), -er (singer, performer, reader), -ist (typist, pianist, novelist, linguist),* and *-ly (manly, sickly, friendly),* to mention only a few.

Many languages have prefixes and suffixes, but languages may differ in how they deploy these morphemes. A morpheme that is a prefix in one language may be a suffix in another and vice versa. In English, the plural morphemes *-s* and *-es* are suffixes (*boys, lasses*). In Isthmus Zapotec, spoken in Mexico, the plural morpheme *ka-* is a prefix:

| | | | |
|---|---|---|---|
| zigi | "chin" | kazigi | "chins" |
| zike | "shoulder" | kazike | "shoulders" |
| diaga | "ear" | kadiaga | "ears" |

Languages may also differ in what meanings they express through affixation. In English, we do not add an affix to derive a noun from a verb. We have the verb *dance* as in "I like to dance," and we have the noun *dance* as in "There's a dance or two in the old dame yet." The form is the same in both cases. In Turkish, you derive a noun from a verb with the suffix *-ak*, as in the following examples:

| | | | |
|---|---|---|---|
| dur | "to stop" | durak | "stopping place" |
| bat | "to sink" | batak | "sinking place" or "marsh/swamp" |

To express reciprocal action in English we use the phrase *each other*, as in *understand each other, love each other*. In Turkish, a morpheme is added to the verb:

| | | | |
|---|---|---|---|
| anla | "understand" | anla*sh* | "understand each other" |
| sev | "love" | sev*ish* | "love each other" |

The reciprocal suffix in these examples is pronounced *sh* after a vowel and *ish* after a consonant. This is similar to the process in English in which we use *a* as the indefinite article morpheme before a noun beginning with a consonant, as in *a dog*, and *an* before a noun beginning with a vowel, as in *an apple*. The same morpheme may have more than one slightly different form (see Exercise 6, for example). We will discuss the various pronunciations of morphemes in more detail in Chapter 6.

## Roots and Stems

Morphologically complex words consist of a morpheme **root** and one or more affixes. Some examples of English roots are *paint* in *painter, read* in *reread, ceive* in *conceive,* and *ling* in *linguist.* A root may or may not stand alone as a word (*paint* and *read* do; *ceive* and *ling* don't).

When a root morpheme is combined with an affix, it forms a **stem**. Other affixes can be added to a stem to form a more complex stem, as shown in the following:

| | | |
|---|---|---|
| **root** | Chomsky | (proper) noun |
| **stem** | Chomsky + ite | noun + suffix |
| **word** | Chomsky + ite + s | noun + suffix + suffix |
| **root** | believe | verb |
| **stem** | believe + able | verb + suffix |
| **word** | un + believe + able | prefix + verb + suffix |
| **root** | system | noun |
| **stem** | system + atic | noun + suffix |
| **stem** | un + system + atic | prefix + noun + suffix |
| **stem** | un + system + atic + al | prefix + noun + suffix + suffix |
| **word** | un + system + atic + al + ly | prefix + noun + suffix + suffix + suffix |

With the addition of each new affix, a new stem and a new word are formed. Linguists sometimes use the word **base** to mean any root or stem to which an affix is attached. In the preceding example, *system, systematic, unsystematic,* and *unsystematical* are bases.

## Bound Roots

Bound roots do not occur in isolation and they acquire meaning only in combination with other morphemes. For example, words of Latin origin such as *receive, conceive, perceive,* and *deceive* share a common root, *-ceive*; and the words *remit, permit, commit, submit, transmit,* and *admit* share the root *-mit*. For the original Latin speakers, the morphemes corresponding to *ceive* and *mit* had clear meanings, but for modern English speakers, Latinate morphemes such as *ceive* and *mit* have no independent meaning. Their meaning depends on the entire word in which they occur.

A similar class of words is composed of a prefix affixed to a bound root morpheme. Examples are *ungainly*, but no **gainly*; *discern*, but no **cern*; *nonplussed*, but no **plussed; downhearted* but no **hearted*, and others to be seen in this section's epigraph.

The morpheme *huckle*, when joined with *berry*, has the meaning of a berry that is small, round, and purplish blue; *luke* when combined with *warm* has the meaning "somewhat." Both these morphemes and others like them (*cran, boysen*) are bound morphemes that convey meaning only in combination.

# Rules of Word Formation

> "I never heard of 'Uglification,'" Alice ventured to say. "What is it?" The Gryphon lifted up both its paws in surprise. "Never heard of uglifying!" it exclaimed. "You know what to beautify is, I suppose?" "Yes," said Alice doubtfully: "it means—to make—prettier." "Well, then," the Gryphon went on, "if you don't know what to uglify is, you are a simpleton."
>
> LEWIS CARROLL, *Alice's Adventures in Wonderland*, 1865

When the Mock Turtle listed the branches of Arithmetic for Alice as "Ambition, Distraction, Uglification, and Derision," Alice was very confused. She wasn't really a simpleton, since *uglification* was not a common word in English until Lewis Carroll used it. Still, most English speakers would immediately know the meaning of *uglification* even if they had never heard or used the word before because they would know the meaning of its individual parts—the root *ugly* and the affixes *-ify* and *-cation*.

We said earlier that knowledge of morphology includes knowledge of individual morphemes, their pronunciation, their meaning, and knowledge of the rules for combining them into complex words. The Mock Turtle added *-ify* to the adjective *ugly* and formed a verb. Many verbs in English have been formed from adjectives in this way: *purify, amplify, simplify, falsify*; and from nouns, too: *objectify, glorify, personify*. Notice that the Mock Turtle went even further: he added the suffix *-cation* to *uglify* and formed a noun, *uglification*, as in *glorification, simplification, falsification,* and *purification*. By using the **morphological rules** of English, he created a new word. The rules that he used are as follows:

| | | | |
|---|---|---|---|
| Adjective + ify | → | Verb | "to make Adjective" |
| Verb + cation | → | Noun | "the process of making Adjective" |

## Derivational Morphology

Bound morphemes such as *-ify, - cation,* and *- arian* are called **derivational morphemes**. When they are added to a base, a new word with a new meaning is derived. The addition of *-ify* to *pure—purify*—means "to make pure," and the addition of *-cation—purification*—means "the process of making pure." If we invent an adjective, *pouzy*, to describe the effect of static electricity on hair, you will immediately understand the sentences "Walking on that carpet really pouzified my hair" and "The best method of pouzification is to rub a balloon on your head." This means that we must have a list of the derivational morphemes in our mental dictionaries as well as the rules that determine how they are added to a root or stem. The form that results from the addition of a derivational morpheme is called a **derived word**.

Derivational morphemes have clear semantic content. In this sense, they are like content words, except that they are not words. As we have seen, when a derivational morpheme is added to a base, it adds meaning. The derived word may also be of a different grammatical class than the original word, as shown

Macnelly/King Features Syndicate

by suffixes such as *-able* and *-en*. When a verb is suffixed with *-able*, the result is an adjective, as in *desire* + *able*. When the suffix *-en* is added to an adjective, a verb is derived, as in *dark* + *en*. One may form a noun from an adjective, as in *sweet* + *ie*. Other examples are:

**Noun to Adjective**

boy + -ish
virtu + -ous
Elizabeth + -an
pictur + -esque
affection + -ate
health + -ful
alcohol + -ic

**Verb to Noun**

acquitt + -al
clear + -ance
accus + -ation
sing + -er
conform + -ist
predict + -ion

**Adjective to Adverb**

exact + -ly

**Noun to Adverb**

home + -ward
side + -ways
length + -wise

**Noun to Verb**

moral + -ize
vaccin + -ate
hast + -en
im- + prison
be- + friend
en- + joy
in- + habit

**Adjective to Noun**

tall + -ness
specific + -ity
feudal + -ism
free + -dom

**Verb to Adjective**

read + -able
creat + -ive
migrat + -ory
run(n) + -y

**Adjective to Verb**

en- + large
en- + dear
en- + rich

Some derivational affixes do not cause a change in grammatical class.

**Noun to Noun**

friend + -ship
human + -ity
king + -dom
New Jersey + -ite
vicar + -age
Paul + -ine

**Verb to Verb**

un- + do
re- + cover
dis- + believe
auto- + destruct

**Adjective to Adjective**

pink + -ish
red + -like
a- + moral
il- + legal
in- + accurate
un- + happy

America + -n
libr(ary) + -arian
mono- + theism
dis- + advantage
ex- + wife
auto- + biography
un- + employment
semi- + annual
dis- + agreeable
sub- + minimal

When a new word enters the lexicon by the application of morphological rules, other complex derivations may be **blocked**. For example, when *Commun + ist* entered the language, words such as *Commun + ite* (as in *Trotsky + ite*) or *Commun + ian* (as in *grammar + ian*) were not needed; their formation was blocked. Sometimes, however, alternative forms do coexist: for example, *Chomskyan* and *Chomskyist* and perhaps even *Chomskyite* (all meaning "follower of Chomsky's views of linguistics"). *Semanticist* and *semantician* are both used for linguists who study meaning in language, but the possible word *semantite* is not.

Finally, derivational affixes appear to come in two classes. In one class, the addition of a suffix triggers subtle changes in pronunciation. For example, when we affix *-ity* to *specific* (pronounced "specifik" with a *k* sound), we get specificity (pronounced "specifisity" with an *s* sound). When deriving *Elizabeth + -an* from *Elizabeth*, the fourth vowel sound changes from the vowel in *Beth* to the vowel in *Pete*. Other suffixes such as *-y, -ive,* and *-ize* may induce similar changes: *sane/sanity, deduce/deductive, critic/criticize.*

On the other hand, suffixes such as *-er, -ful, -ish, -less, -ly,* and *-ness* may be tacked onto a base word without affecting the pronunciation, as in *baker, wishful, boyish, needless, sanely,* and *fullness*. Moreover, affixes from the first class cannot be attached to a base containing an affix from the second class: **need + less + ity, *moral + ize +* ive; but affixes from the second class may attach to bases with either kind of affix: *moral + iz(e) + er, need + less + ness.*

## Inflectional Morphology

Function words such as *to, it,* and *be* are free morphemes. Many languages, including English, also have bound morphemes that have a strictly grammatical function. They mark properties such as tense, number, person, and so forth. Such bound morphemes are called **inflectional morphemes**. Unlike derivational morphemes, they never change the grammatical category of the stems to which they are attached. Consider the forms of the verb in the following sentences:

1. I sail the ocean blue.
2. He sails the ocean blue.
3. John sailed the ocean blue.
4. John has sailed the ocean blue.
5. John is sailing the ocean blue.

In sentence (2) the *-s* at the end of the verb is an agreement marker; it signifies that the subject of the verb is third-person and is singular, and that the verb

Zits Partnership/King Features Syndicate

is in the present tense. It doesn't add lexical meaning. The suffix *-ed* indicates past tense, and is also required by the syntactic rules of the language when verbs are used with auxiliary *have*, just as *-ing* is required when verbs are used with auxiliary *be*. (This will be discussed in Chapter 3.)

Inflectional morphemes represent relationships between different parts of a sentence. For example, *-s* expresses the relationship between the verb and the third-person singular subject; *-ed* expresses the relationship between the time the utterance is spoken (e.g., now) and the time of the event (past). If you say "John danced," the *-ed* affix places the activity before the utterance time. Inflectional morphology is closely connected to the syntax and semantics of the sentence.

English also has other inflectional endings, such as the plural suffix, which is attached to certain singular nouns, as in *boy/boys* and *cat/cats*. In contrast to Old and Middle English, which were more richly inflected languages, Modern English has only eight bound inflectional affixes:

| English | Inflectional Morphemes | Examples |
|---|---|---|
| **-s** | third-person singular present | She wait-s at home. |
| **-ed** | past tense | She wait-ed at home. |
| **-ing** | progressive | She is eat-ing the donut. |
| **-en** | past participle | Mary has eat-en the donuts. |
| **-s** | plural | She ate the donut-s. |
| **-'s** | possessive | Disa's hair is short. |
| **-er** | comparative | Disa has short-er hair than Karin. |
| **-est** | superlative | Disa has the short-est hair. |

Inflectional morphemes in English follow the derivational morphemes in a word. Thus, to the derivationally complex word *commit* + *ment* one can add a plural ending to form *commit* + *ment* + *s*, but the order of affixes may not be reversed to derive the impossible *commit* + *s* + *ment* = **commitsment*.

Yet another distinction between inflectional and derivational morphemes is that all inflectional morphemes are **productive**: They apply freely to nearly every appropriate base (except "irregular" forms such as *feet*, not **foots*). Most nouns take an *-s* inflectional suffix to form a plural and most verbs take *-ed* to form a past tense, and any new verb added to the language will immediately take these inflections, witness *tweets, tweeting, tweeted.* Derivational morphemes vary a lot in their productivity; only some nouns take the derivational suffix *-ize* to form a verb: *idolize,* but not **picturize,* while *-er* can attach to almost any verb (even very new ones) to make an agent, *sing/singer, dance/dancer, blog/blogger, tweet/tweeter.*

The differences between inflectional and derivational morphemes in Modern English are summarized in the table below and in Figure 2.1 that follows it:

| Inflectional | Derivational |
|---|---|
| Grammatical function | Lexical function |
| No word class change | May cause word class change |
| Small or no meaning change | Some meaning change |
| Often required by rules of grammar | Never required by rules of grammar |
| Follow derivational morphemes in a word | Precede inflectional morphemes in a word |
| Productive | Some productive, many nonproductive |

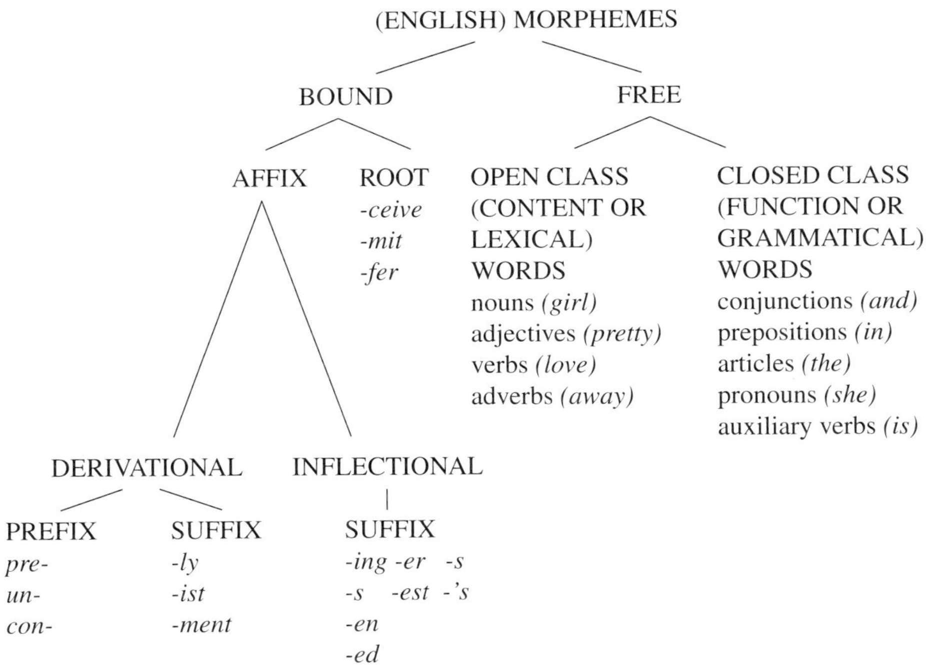


**FIGURE 2.1** | Classification of English morphemes.

## The Hierarchical Structure of Words

We saw earlier that morphemes are added in a fixed order. This order reflects the *hierarchical structure* of the word, entirely analogous to the hierarchical structure of sentences that we observed in the previous chapter. A word is not a simple sequence of morphemes just as a sentence is not a simple sequence of words. It has an internal structure. For example, the word *unsystematic* is composed of three morphemes: *un-, system,* and *-atic*. The root is *system,* a noun, to which we add the suffix *-atic,* resulting in an adjective, *systematic*. To this adjective, we add the prefix *un-,* forming a new adjective, *unsystematic*.

The hierarchical organization of words can be represented using tree diagrams, as illustrated for *unsystematic*:

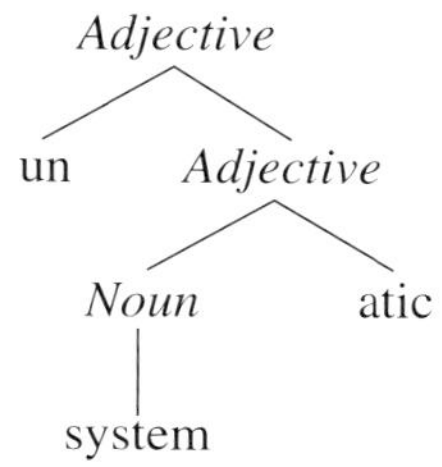


This tree represents the application of two morphological rules:

1. Noun + atic → Adjective
2. un + Adjective → Adjective

Rule 1 attaches the derivational suffix *-atic* to the root noun, forming an adjective. Rule 2 takes the adjective formed by rule 1 and attaches the derivational prefix *un-*. The diagram shows that the entire word—*unsystematic*—is an adjective that is composed of an adjective—*systematic*—plus *un*. The adjective is itself composed of a noun—*system*—plus the suffix *-atic*.

Hierarchical structure is an essential property of human language. Words (and sentences) have component parts which relate to each other in specific, rule-governed ways. Despite appearances, it is not the case that the morphemes *un-* and *-atic* each relate to the root *system* in the same way. The root *system* is "closer" to *-atic* than it is to *un-,* which is actually connected to the adjective *systematic,* and not directly to the noun *system*. Indeed, **unsystem* is not a word, as may be inferred from the *un-* rule in (2).

Further morphological rules can be applied to the given structure. For example, English has a derivational suffix *-al,* as in *egotistical, fantastical,* and *astronomical*. In these cases, *-al* is added to an adjective—*egotistic, fantastic, astronomic*—to form a new adjective. The rule for *-al* is as follows:

3. Adjective + al → Adjective

Another affix is -ly, which is added to adjectives—*happy, lazy, hopeful*—to form adverbs *happily, lazily, hopefully*. Following is the rule for -ly:

**4.** Adjective + ly → Adverb

Applying these two rules to the derived form *unsystematic,* we get the following tree for *unsystematically:*

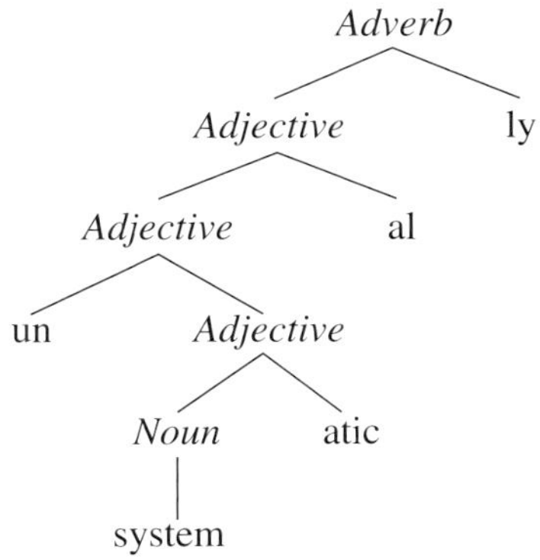


This is a rather complex word. Despite its complexity, it is well-formed because it follows the morphological rules of the language. On the other hand, a very simple word can be ungrammatical. Suppose in the above example we first added *un-* to the root *system.* That would have resulted in the nonword **unsystem.*

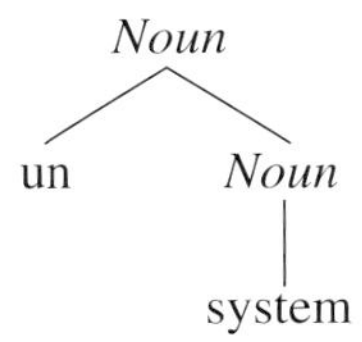


**Unsystem* is not a possible word because the rule of English that allows *un-* to be added to nouns is restricted to very few cases, and those are always nouns that already have a suffix such as *un + employment, un +cceptance* or *un + feasability*. The large soft-drink company whose ad campaign promoted the *Uncola* successfully flouted this linguistic rule to capture people's attention. Part of our linguistic competence includes the ability to recognize possible versus impossible words, such as **unsystem* and **Uncola.* Possible words are those that conform to the rules; impossible words are those that do not.

Tree diagrams make explicit the way speakers represent the internal structure of sentences as well as morphologically complex words. In speaking and writing, we appear to string morphemes together sequentially as in *un + system + atic.* However, our mental representation of words is hierarchical as well as linear, and this is shown by tree diagrams.

Inflectional morphemes are equally well represented. The following tree shows that the inflectional agreement morpheme *-s* follows the derivational morphemes *-ize* and *re-* in *refinalizes:*

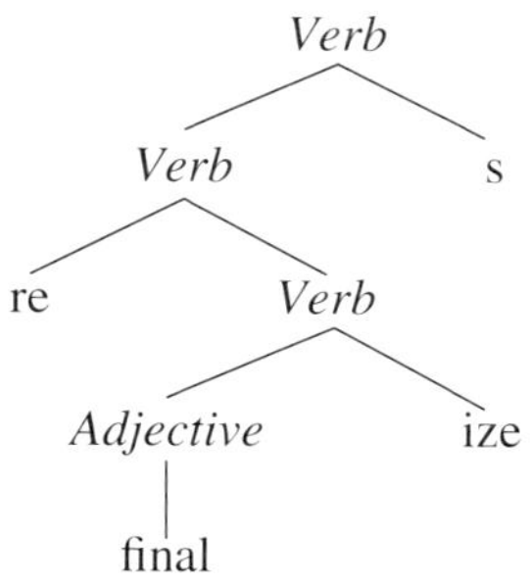


The tree also shows that *re-* applies to *finalize,* which is correct as **refinal* is not a word, and that the inflectional morpheme follows the derivational morpheme.

The hierarchical organization of words is even more clearly shown by structurally ambiguous words, words that have more than one meaning by virtue of having more than one structure. Consider the word *unlockable.* Imagine you are inside a room and you want some privacy. You would be unhappy to find the door is *unlockable*—"not able to be locked." Now imagine you are inside a locked room trying to get out. You would be very relieved to find that the door is *unlockable*—"able to be unlocked." These two meanings correspond to two different structures, as follows:

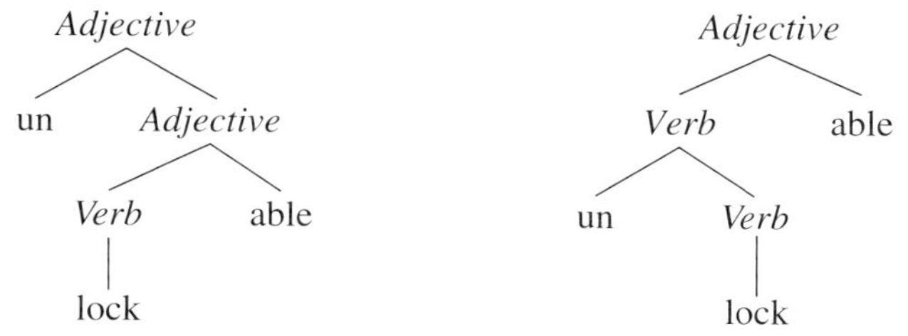


In the first structure, the verb *lock* combines with the suffix *-able* to form an adjective *lockable* ("able to be locked"). Then, the prefix *un-,* meaning "not," combines with the derived adjective to form a new adjective *unlockable* ("not able to be locked"). In the second case, the prefix *un-* combines with the verb *lock* to form a derived verb *unlock.* Then, the derived verb combines with the suffix *-able* to form *unlockable,* "able to be unlocked."

An entire class of words in English follows this pattern: *unbuttonable, unzippable,* and *unlatchable,* among others. The ambiguity arises because the prefix *un-* can combine with an adjective, as illustrated in rule 2, or it can combine with a verb, as in *undo, unstaple, unearth,* and *unloosen.*

If words were only strings of morphemes without any internal organization, we could not explain the ambiguity of words such as *unlockable.* These words also illustrate another key point, which is that structure is important to determining meaning. The same three morphemes occur in both versions of *unlockable,* yet there are two distinct meanings. The different meanings arise because of the different structures.

## Rule Productivity

We have noted that some morphological processes, inflection in particular, are productive, meaning that they can be used freely to form new words from the list of free and bound morphemes. Among derivational morphemes, the suffix *-able* can be conjoined with any verb to derive an adjective with the meaning of the verb and the meaning of *-able,* which is something like "able to be" as in *accept + able, laugh + able, pass + able, change + able, breathe + able, adapt + able,* and so on. The productivity of this rule is illustrated by the fact that we find *-able* affixed to new verbs such as *tweetable,* meaning a message suitable for posting on Twitter (140 characters or fewer).

The prefix *un-* derives same-class words with an opposite meaning: *unafraid, unfit, un-American,* and so on. Additionally, *un-* can be added to derived adjectives that have been formed by morphological rules, resulting in perfectly acceptable words such as *un + believe + able* or *un + pick + up + able.*

Yet, *un-* is not fully productive. We find *happy* and *unhappy, cowardly* and *uncowardly,* but not *sad* and **unsad, brave* and **unbrave,* or *obvious* and **unobvious.* It appears that the "un-Rule" is most productive for adjectives that are derived from verbs, such as *unenlightened, unsimplified, uncharacterized, unauthorized,* and *undistinguished.* It also appears that most acceptable *un*-words have polysyllabic bases, and while we have *unfit, uncool, unread,* and *unclean,* many of the unacceptable *un-* forms have monosyllabic stems such as **unbig, *ungreat, *unred, *unsad, *unsmall,* and **untall.*

The rule that adds *-er* to verbs in English to produce a noun meaning "one who does" is a nearly productive morphological rule, giving us *examiner, examtaker, sleepwalker, stir-fryer* for your favorite chef and even *force-feeder* for *thwarters* of *hunger-strikers,* but fails full productivity owing to "unwords" such as **chairer,* which is not "one who chairs."

The "other" *-er* suffix, the one that means "more" as in *greedier,* also fails to be entirely productive as Alice's **curiouser* points out. The more syllables a word has, the less likely *-er* will work and we will need the word *more,* as in *more beautiful* (but not **beautifuler*) compared with the well-formed *prettier* and *lovelier.*

Other derivational morphemes fall farther short of productivity. Consider:

| | | |
|---|---|---|
| *sincerity* | from | *sincere* |
| *warmth* | from | *warm* |
| *moisten* | from | *moist* |

The suffix *-ity* is found in many other words in English, such as *chastity, scarcity,* and *curiosity;* and *-th* occurs in *health, wealth, depth, width,* and *growth.* We find *-en* in *sadden, ripen, redden, weaken,* and *deepen.* Still, the phrase "*The tragicity of Hamlet" sounds somewhat strange, as does "*I'm going to *heaten* the sauce." Someone may say *coolth,* but when "words" such as *tragicity, heaten,* and *coolth are* used, it is usually either a slip of the tongue or an attempt at humor. Most adjectives will not accept any of these derivational suffixes.

Even less productive to the point of rareness are such derivational morphemes as the diminutive suffixes in the words *pig + let* and *sap + ling.*

In the morphologically complex words that we have seen so far, we can generally predict the meaning based on the meanings of the morphemes that make up the word. *Unhappy* means "not happy" and *acceptable* means "fit to be accepted." However, one cannot always know the meaning of the words derived from free and derivational morphemes by knowing the morphemes themselves. The following *un-* forms have unpredictable meanings:

| | |
|---|---|
| unloosen | "loosen, let loose" |
| unrip | "rip, undo by ripping" |
| undo | "reverse doing" |
| untread | "go back through in the same steps" |
| unearth | "dig up" |
| unfrock | "deprive (a cleric) of ecclesiastic rank" |
| unnerve | "fluster" |

Morphologically complex words whose meanings are not predictable must be listed individually in our mental lexicons. However, the morphological rules must also be in the grammar, revealing the relation between words and providing the means for forming new words.

### Exceptions and Suppletions

The morphological rule that forms plural nouns from singular nouns does not apply to words like *child, man, foot,* and *mouse*. These words are exceptions to the rule. Similarly, verbs such as *go, sing, bring, run,* and *know* are exceptions to the inflectional rule for producing past-tense verbs in English. These exceptional forms must be stored in the lexicon. There are therefore two mechanisms for forming complex words; regular forms such as *danced* and *books* are formed by applying morphological rules to the base morpheme, which is stored in the lexicon. Irregular, also called **suppletive**, forms must be retrieved directly from the lexicon.

When children are learning English (or any other language), they first learn the regular rules, which they apply to all forms. Thus, we often hear them say *mans* and *goed*. Later in the acquisition process, they specifically learn irregular plurals such as *men* and *mice,* and irregular past tense forms such as *came* and *went*. These children's errors are actually evidence that the regular rules exist. It also suggests that the "rule route" for forming complex words is more accessible to the child than accessing irregular forms in the lexicon. Children's morphological learning is discussed more fully in Chapter 9.

When a new word enters the language, the regular inflectional rules generally apply. The plural of *geek,* when it was a new word in English, was *geeks,* not **geeken,* although we are advised that some geeks wanted the plural of *fax* to be **faxen,* like *oxen,* when *fax* entered the language as a shortened form of *facsimile*. Never fear: its plural is *faxes*. The exception to this may be a word "borrowed" from a foreign language. For example, the plural of Latin *datum* has always been *data,* never *datums,* though nowadays *data,* the one-time plural, is treated by many as a singular word like *information*.

The past tense of the verb *hit,* as in the sentence *Yesterday you hit the ball,* and the plural of the noun *sheep* as in *The sheep are in the meadow,* show that some morphemes have no phonological shape at all. We know that *hit* in the above sentence is *hit* + *past* because of the time adverb *yesterday,* and we know that *sheep* is the phonetic form of *sheep* + *plural* because of the plural verb form *are.*

When a verb is derived from a noun, even if it is pronounced the same as an irregular verb, the regular rules apply to it. Thus, *ring,* when used in the sense of encircle, is derived from the noun *ring,* and as a verb it is regular. We say *the police ringed the bank with armed men,* not **rang the bank with armed men.* In the jargon of baseball one says that *the hitter flied out* (hit a lofty ball that was caught), rather than **flew out,* because the verb came from the compound noun *fly ball.*

## Lexical Gaps

The vast majority of letter (sound) sequences that could be words of English—*crint, spleek, feg*—are not. Similar comments apply to morphological derivations like *disobvious* or *inobvious.* "Words" that conform to the rules of word formation but are not truly part of the vocabulary are called **accidental gaps** or **lexical gaps**. Accidental gaps are well-formed but non-existing words.

The actual words in a language constitute a mere subset of the possible words. There are always gaps in the lexicon—words not present but that could be added. Some of the gaps are due to the fact that a permissible sound sequence has no meaning attached to it (such as *blick,* or *slarm,* or *krobe*). The sequence of sounds must be in keeping with the constraints of the language, however; **bnick* is not a "gap" because no word in English can begin with *bn.* We will discuss such constraints in chapter 6.

Other gaps result when possible combinations of morphemes never come into use. Speakers can distinguish between impossible words such as **unsystem* and **needlessity* and possible but nonexisting words such as *magnificenter* or *disobvious* (cf. *distrustful*). The latter are blocked, as noted earlier, owing to the presence of *more magnificent* and *nonobvious*. Psycholinguistic experiments show that listeners respond more slowly to "possible" nonwords such as *floop* and *plim* than to "impossible" nonwords such as *tlat* and *mrock*. The ability to make this distinction is further evidence that the morphological component of our mental grammar consists of not just a lexicon—a list of existing words—but also of rules that enable us to create and understand new words, and to recognize possible and impossible words.

## Other Morphological Processes

The various kinds of affixation that we have discussed are by far the most common morphological processes among the world's languages. But, as we continue to emphasize in this book, the human language capacity is enormously creative, and that creativity extends to ways other than affixation in which words may be altered and created.

### Back-Formations

Misconception can sometimes be creative, and nothing in this world both misconceives and creates like a child, as we shall see in Chapter 9. A new word may enter the language because of an incorrect morphological analysis. *Peddle* was derived from *peddler* on the mistaken assumption that the *-er* was the agentive suffix. Such words are called **back-formations**. The verbs *hawk, stoke, swindle, burgle*, and *edit* all came into the language as back-formations—of *hawker, stoker, swindler, burglar,* and *editor*. *Pea* was derived from a singular word, *pease,* by speakers who thought *pease* was a plural.

Some word creation comes from deliberately miscast back-formations. The word *bikini* comes from the Bikini atoll of the Marshall Islands. Because the first syllable *bi-* is a morpheme meaning "two" in words like *bicycle,* some clever person called a topless bathing suit a *monokini* and a tank top with a bikini bottom a *tankini*. Historically, a number of new words have entered the English lexicon in a similar way, some of the most recent being the *appletini, chocotini, mintini,* and *God-knows-what-else-tini* to be found as flavor additives to the traditional martini libation. Based on analogy with such pairs as *act/action, exempt/exemption,* and *revise/revision,* new words *resurrect, preempt,* and *televise* were formed from the existing words *resurrection, preemption,* and *television*.

Language purists sometimes rail against back-formations and cite *enthuse* and *liaise* (from *enthusiasm* and *liaison*) as examples of language corruption. However, language is not corrupt; it is adaptable and changeable. Don't be surprised to discover in your lifetime that *shevelled* and *chalant* have infiltrated the English language (from *disheveled* and *nonchalant*) to mean "tidy" and "concerned," and if it happens do not cry "havoc" and let slip the dogs of prescriptivism; all will be well.

## Compounds

Two or more words may be joined to form new, compound words. English is very flexible in the kinds of combinations permitted, as the following table of compounds shows.

| | **Adjective** | **Noun** | **Verb** |
|---|---|---|---|
| **Adjective** | bittersweet | smartwatch | whitewash |
| **Noun** | headstrong | homework | spoonfeed |
| **Verb** | feel-good | pickpocket | sleepwalk |
| **Preposition** | overeager | outpatient | undergo |

Some compounds that have been recently introduced into English are *Facebook, LinkedIn, android apps, e-commerce, crowdfunding, cyber café, flash mob,* and *robocall.*

In English, the rightmost word in a compound is the **head** of the compound. The head is the part of a word or phrase that determines its broad meaning and grammatical category. The head of the compound *smartwatch* is *watch,* which determines the core meaning (*smartwatch* is a kind of watch), and syntactic category (*watch* is a noun so *smartwatch* is also a noun). The head of *sleepwalk* (a kind of walking) is *walk,* a verb, so *sleepwalk* is also a verb. If you go through the examples given above, you will see that they mostly conform to this "right-hand head rule." But there are exceptions. Compounds whose rightmost member is a preposition are not themselves prepositions. A *meet-up* is a kind of meeting, not a direction, *meltdown* and *knockout* are nouns, not prepositions. This is further evidence that prepositions form a closed-class category that does not readily admit new members, in contrast to nouns, verbs, and adjectives.

Some compounds are said to be "unheaded" because the rightmost member does not determine their core meaning. An example is *flatfoot,* which is not a kind of *foot,* but a slang term meaning policeman. *Policeman* is also a compound, but unlike *flatfoot,* it is headed by *man.* A policeman is a kind of man. The head of a compound transmits not only its meaning and syntactic category to the compound, but also whatever irregular morphological form it takes. The plural of *man* is the irregular form *men* and the plural of *policeman* is *policemen* (same for *policewomen*). But in the case of unheaded compounds such as *flatfoot,* irregular morphology is not inherited by the compound—just as the meaning is not inherited. A *flatfoot* is not a kind of foot, and its plural is not *flatfeet,* but rather *flatfoots.* It undergoes the regular rule. Absent a head the compound transmits neither its meaning nor its irregular morphology. Similar examples are given below:

| | | | |
|---|---|---|---|
| walkman | *walkmen | walkmans | (device for playing music) |
| sabertooth | *saberteeth | sabertooths | (extinct species of tiger) |
| lowlife | *lowlives | lowlifes | (a disreputable person) |

There are a few English compounds that appear to be left-headed. An *attorney-general* is not a general but an attorney, a *mother-in-law* is a kind of mother. A *passer-by* is a person who passes. In these and similar cases the, plural inflection occurs "inside" the compound, on the head, *attorneys-general, passers-by, sons-in-law, courts-martial, sergeants-major.* Many of these left-headed compounds are legal or military terms. They were borrowed into English from

French—a language in which adjectives follow nouns—during the Norman occupation of England when French was used for legal, military, and other affairs of state (see Chapter 8). It is fair to say, however, that for many people outside the military and legal professions these compounds behave like regular plurals, *attorney generals*, *court-martials*, and so on.

Although two-word compounds are the most common in English, it would be difficult to state an upper limit: Consider *three-time loser, four-dimensional space-time, sergeant-at-arms, mother-of-pearl, master of ceremonies, daughter-in-law,* and the military slang *fire-in-the-hole* meaning "watch out!"

Spelling does not tell us what sequence of words constitutes a compound; whether a compound is spelled with a space between the two words, with a hyphen, or with no separation at all depends on the idiosyncrasies of the particular compound, as shown in *blackbird, six-pack,* and *smoke screen.*

Like derived words, compounds have internal structure. This is clear from the ambiguity of a compound such as *top + hat + rack,* which can mean "a rack for top hats" corresponding to the structure in tree diagram (1), or "the highest hat rack," corresponding to the structure in (2).

(1)

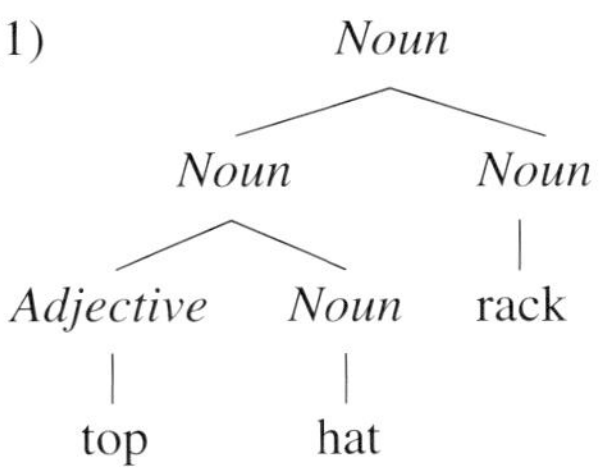


(2)

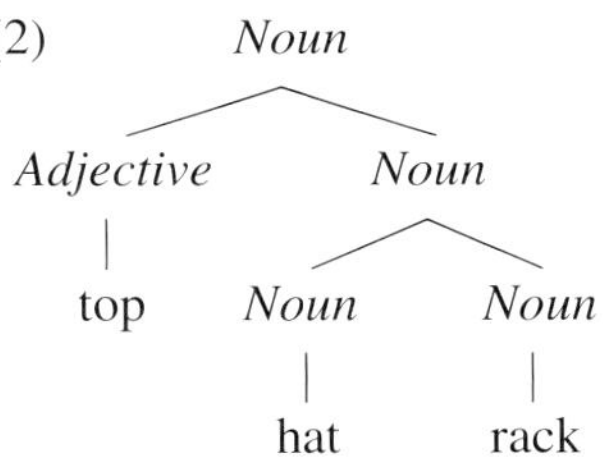


## Meaning of Compounds

The head of compound carries its core or basic meaning. *Homework* is a kind of work done at home. But the meaning of a compound is not always simply the sum of the meanings of its parts; a *blackboard* may be green or white, an online newspaper is still a *newspaper* though no paper is involved, an albino *goldfish* would still be a goldfish, and a rattlesnake, though more stealthy, remains a *rattlesnake* even without its rattle.

Other compounds reveal other meaning relations between the parts, which are not entirely consistent because many compounds are idiomatic (idioms are discussed in Chapter 4). A *boathouse* is a house for boats, but a *cathouse* is not a house for cats. (It is slang for a house of prostitution or whorehouse.) A *jumping bean* is a bean that jumps, a *falling star* is a star that (appears to) fall, and a *magnifying glass* is a glass that magnifies; but a *looking glass* is not a glass that looks, nor is an *eating apple* an apple that eats, and *laughing gas* does not laugh. *Peanut oil* and *olive oil* are oils made from something, but what about *baby oil*? And is this a contradiction: "horse meat is dog meat"? Not at all, since the first is meat *from* horses and the other is meat *for* dogs.

In the examples so far, the meaning of each compound includes at least to some extent the meanings of the individual parts. However, many compounds nowadays do not seem to relate to the meanings of the individual parts at all. A *jack-in-a-box* is a tropical tree, and a *turncoat* is a traitor. A *highbrow* does not necessarily have a high brow, nor does a *bigwig* have a big wig, nor does an *egghead* have an egg-shaped head.

Like certain words with the prefix *un-*, the meaning of many compounds must be learned as if they were individual whole words. Some of the meanings may be figured out, but not all. If you had never heard the word *hunchback*, it might be possible to infer the meaning; but if you had never heard the word *flatfoot*, it is doubtful you would know it means "detective" or "policeman," even though the origin of the word, once you know the meaning, can be figured out.

The pronunciation of English compounds differs from the way we pronounce the sequence of two words that are not compounded. In an actual compound, the first word is usually stressed (pronounced somewhat louder and higher in pitch), and in a noncompound phrase the second word is stressed. Thus, we stress *hot* in *hotdog* the food, but *dog* in *hot dog* the canine. (Stress, pitch, and other similar features are discussed in Chapters 5 and 6.)

## Morphological Analysis: Identifying Morphemes

As we have seen in this chapter, speakers of a language know the internal structure of words because they know the morphemes of their language and the rules for their combination. This is unconscious knowledge of course and it takes a trained linguist to make this knowledge explicit as part of a descriptive grammar of the language. The task is challenging enough when the language you are analyzing is your own, but linguists who speak one language may nevertheless analyze languages for which they are not native speakers.

Suppose you were a linguist from the planet Zorx who wanted to analyze English. How would you discover the morphemes of the language? How would you determine whether a word had one, two, or more morphemes, and what they were?

The first thing to do would be to ask native speakers how they say various words. (It would help to have a Zorxese–English interpreter along; otherwise, copious gesturing is in order.) Assume you are talented in miming and manage to collect the following forms:

| Adjective | Meaning |
|---|---|
| ugly | "very unattractive" |
| uglier | "more ugly" |
| ugliest | "most ugly" |
| pretty | "nice looking" |
| prettier | "more nice looking" |
| prettiest | "most nice looking" |
| tall | "large in height" |
| taller | "more tall" |
| tallest | "most tall" |

To determine what the morphemes are in such a list, the first thing a field linguist would do is to see whether some forms mean the same thing in different words, that is, to look for *recurring* forms. We find them: *ugly* occurs in *ugly, uglier,* and *ugliest,* all of which include the meaning "very unattractive." We also find that *-er* occurs in *prettier* and *taller,* adding the meaning "more" to the adjectives to which it is attached. Similarly, *-est* adds the meaning "most." Furthermore, by having our Zorxese–English interpreter pose additional questions to our native English-speaking consultant we find that *-er* and *-est* do not occur in isolation with the meanings of "more" and "most." We can therefore conclude that the following morphemes occur in English:

| | |
|---|---|
| ugly | root morpheme |
| pretty | root morpheme |
| tall | root morpheme |
| -er | bound morpheme "comparative" |
| -est | bound morpheme "superlative" |

As we proceed, we find other words that end with *-er* (e.g., *singer, lover, bomber, writer, teacher*) in which the *-er* ending does not mean "comparative" but, when attached to a verb, changes it to "a noun who 'verbs,'" (e.g., *sings, loves, bombs, writes, teaches*). So, we conclude that this is a different morpheme, even though it is pronounced the same as the comparative. We go on and find words such as *number, somber, butter,* and *member* in which the *-er* has no separate meaning at all—a *somber* is not "one who sombs" and a *member* does not *memb*—and therefore these words must be monomorphemic.

## Summary

Knowing a language means knowing the **morphemes** of that language, which are the elemental units that constitute words. *Moralizers* is an English word composed of four morphemes: *moral* + *ize* + *er* + s. When you know a word or morpheme, you know both its **form** (sound or gesture) and its **meaning**; these are inseparable parts of the **linguistic sign**. The relationship between form and meaning is **arbitrary**. There is no inherent connection between them (i.e., the words and morphemes of any language must be learned).

Morphemes may be free or bound. **Free morphemes** stand alone such as *girl* or *the,* and they come in two types: **open class**, containing the content words of the language, and **closed class,** containing function words such as *the* or *of.* **Bound morphemes** may be **affixes** or bound roots such as *-ceive*. Affixes may be **prefixes** or **suffixes**. Affixes may be derivational or inflectional. **Derivational affixes** derive new words; **inflectional affixes**, such as the plural affix *-s,* make grammatical changes to words. Complex words contain a **root** around which **stems** are built by affixation. Rules of morphology determine what kind of affixation produces actual words such as *un* + *system* + *atic,* and what kind produces nonwords such as **un* + *system*.

Words have hierarchical structure evidenced by ambiguous words such as *unlockable,* which may be *un* + *lockable* "unable to be locked" or *unlock* + *able* "able to be unlocked."

Some morphological rules are **productive**, meaning they apply freely to the appropriate stem; for example, *re-* applies freely to verbal stems to give words like *redo, rewash,* and *repaint.* Other rules are more constrained, forming words such as *young* + *ster* but not **smart* + *ster.* Inflectional morphology is extremely productive: the plural *-s* applies freely even to nonsense words. **Suppletive forms** escape inflectional morphology, so instead of **mans* we have *men;* instead of **bringed* we have *brought.*

There are many ways for new words to be created other than affixation. **Compounds** are formed by uniting two or more root words in a single word, such as *homework*. The **head** of the compound (the rightmost word) bears the basic meaning, so *homework* means a kind of work done at home, but often the meaning of compounds is not easily predictable and must be learned as individual lexical items, such as *laughing gas.* **Back-formations** are words created by misinterpreting an affix look-alike such as *-er* as an actual affix, so, for example, the verb *peddle* was formed under the mistaken assumption that peddler was *peddle* + *-er.*

Morphological analysis is the process of identifying form-meaning units in a language, taking into account small differences in pronunciation, so that prefixes *in-* and *im-* are seen to be variants of the "same" prefix in English (cf. *intolerable, impeccable*) just as *democrat* and *democrac* are stem variants of the same morpheme, which shows up in *democratic* with its "t" and in *democracy* with its "c."

## References for Further Reading

Aronoff, M. and Fudeman, K. 2011. *What is morphology? 2nd ed.* Malden, MA: Wiley-Blackwell Publishing.

Bauer, L. 2003. *Introducing linguistic morphology, 2nd ed.* Washington, DC: Georgetown University Press.

Haspelmath, M. and Sims, A. 2010. *Understanding morphology, 2nd ed.* New York, NY: Routledge.

Katamba, F. and Stonham, J. 2006. *Morphology, 2nd ed.* New York, NY: Palgrave MacMillan.

Pinker, S. 1999. *Words and rules: the ingredients of language.* New York: Harper Collins.

Stockwell, R., and D. Minkova. 2009. *English words: History and structure, 2nd ed.* New York: Cambridge University Press.

## Exercises

1. Divide the following words by placing a + between their morphemes. (Some of the words may be monomorphemic and therefore indivisible.) *Example*: replaces = re + place + s

   a. retroactive
   b. befriended
   c. televise
   d. margin
   e. endearment
   f. psychology
   g. unpalatable
   h. holiday
   i. grandmother
   j. morphemic
   k. mistreatment
   l. deactivation
   m. saltpeter
   n. airsickness
   o. bureaucrat
   p. democrat
   q. aristocrat
   r. plutocrat
   s. democracy
   t. democratic
   u. democratically
   v. democratization
   w. democratize
   x. democratizer
   y. democratizing
   z. democratized

2. Match each expression under A with the one statement under B that characterizes it.

| A | B |
|---|---|
| a. noisy crow | (1) compound noun |
| b. scarecrow | (2) root morpheme plus derivational prefix |
| c. the crow | (3) phrase consisting of adjective plus noun |
| d. crowlike | (4) root morpheme plus inflectional affix |
| e. crows | (5) root morpheme plus derivational suffix |
| | (6) grammatical morpheme followed by lexical morpheme |

3. Write the one proper description from the list under B for the italicized part of each word in A.

| A | B |
|---|---|
| a. terrorized | (1) free root |
| b. *uncivilized* | (2) bound root |
| c. terrorize | (3) inflectional suffix |
| d. *lukewarm* | (4) derivational suffix |
| e. impossible | (5) inflectional prefix |
| | (6) derivational prefix |
| | (7) inflectional infix |
| | (8) derivational infix |

4. a. Draw tree diagrams for the following words: *construal, disappearances, irreplaceability, misconceive, indecipherable, redarken.*
   b. Draw two tree diagrams for *undarkenable* to reveal its two meanings: "able to be less dark" and "unable to be made dark."

5. There are many asymmetries in English in which a root morpheme combined with a prefix constitutes a word, but without the prefix is a non-word. A number of these are given in this chapter.

   a. Following is a list of such nonword roots. Add a prefix to each root to form an existing English word.

| Word | Nonwords |
|---|---|
| ______________ | descript |
| ______________ | cognito |
| ______________ | beknownst |
| ______________ | peccable |
| ______________ | promptu |
| ______________ | plussed |
| ______________ | domitable |
| ______________ | nomer |
| ______________ | crat |

   b. There are many more such multimorphemic words for which the root morphemes do not constitute words by themselves. Can you list five more?

6. We have seen that the meaning of compounds is often not revealed by the meanings of their composite words. Crossword puzzles and riddles often make use of this by providing the meaning of two parts of a compound and asking for the resulting word. For example, infielder = diminutive/cease. Read this as asking for a word that means "infielder" by combining a word that means "diminutive" with a word that means "cease." The answer is *shortstop*. See if you can figure out the following:

   a. sci-fi TV series = headliner/journey
   b. campaign = farm building/tempest
   c. at-home wear = tub of water/court attire
   d. kind of pen = formal dance/sharp end
   e. conservative = correct/part of an airplane

7. Consider the following dialogue between parent and schoolchild:

   PARENT: When will you be done with your eight-page book report, dear?
   CHILD: I haven't started it yet.
   PARENT: But it's due tomorrow, you should have begun weeks ago. Why do you always wait until the last minute?
   CHILD: I have more confidence in myself than you do.
   PARENT: Say what?
   CHILD: I mean, how long could it possibly take to read an eight-page book?

   The humor is based on the ambiguity of the compound *eight-page book report*. Draw two trees similar to those in the text for *top hat rack* to reveal the ambiguity.

8. **Research project:** Consider what are called "interfixes" such as *-o-* in English *jack-o-lantern*. They are said to be meaningless morphemes attached to two morphemes at once. What can you learn about that notion? Where do you think the *-o-* comes from? Are there languages other than English that have interfixes?

3

# Syntax: Infinite Use of Finite Means

It is a remarkable fact that any speaker of a human language can learn and store in his or her mental lexicon thousands of words, each of which is an arbitrary pairing of sound and meaning. Even more astonishing is our ability to combine these words to produce and understand an infinite number of novel sentences, as we showed with the following sentence:

> This is the dog that worried the cat that killed the rat that ate the malt that lay in the house that Jack built . . .

To further illustrate, consider the following:

> Snorlax is asleep.
> The monster is asleep.
> The friend of the monster is asleep.
> The rightmost person in the first row is asleep.
> The person immediately to the left of the rightmost person in the front row is asleep.
> The person behind the person immediately to the left of the rightmost person in the first row is asleep.
> Snorlax is asleep.
> Pikachu noticed that Snorlax is asleep.
> Nobody cares that Pikachu noticed that Snorlax is asleep.
> Squirtle knows that nobody cares that Pikachu noticed that Snorlax is asleep.

We can do this because we know (a finite number of) rules, which can be applied repeatedly. All spoken language is governed by rules—the set of rules is called a **grammar**. Every speaker has a mental grammar of the rules of his or her language that he or she follows in producing, understanding, and making judgments of well-formedness (grammaticality) about his or her language.

If we modify the order of words or omit some of the words, the sentences sound "weird" or "odd." (Recall that the asterisk or star preceding a sentence is the linguistic conventio or indicating that the sentence is ungrammatical or ill-formed according to the rules of the grammar.)

*Asleep is Homer.
*Professor the is asleep.
*Rightmost person the in the first row is asleep.
*Homer asleep.
*Right most person front row is asleep.

The oddness of these sentences indicates that some rule of the language has been violated. The sentences are ungrammatical.

To further illustrate this idea let's look at a simple made-up rule of English that we'll call the "everybody knows" rule:

Rule: If S is a sentence of English then *Everybody knows that S* is a sentence of English.

This rule can be iterated (repeated) any number of times to produce an arbitrary number of new sentences.

Snorlax is asleep.
Everybody knows that Snorlax is asleep.
Everybody knows that everybody knows that Snorlax is asleep.
Everybody knows that everybody knows that everybody knows that Snorlax is asleep.

This simple rule in the mind of a speaker enables him or her to produce and understand a potentially infinite number of sentences. The "everybody knows" rule describes (generates) an infinite set of sentences. Any sentence that conforms to the rule is judged well-formed and any sentence that does not conform to the rule is judged ungrammatical, such as the following:

*Knows everybody that Snorlax is asleep.

Given any sentence a speaker could create another sentence by adding a (nother) prepositional phrase, relative clause, or by embedding one sentence inside another as in the "everybody knows" examples. Or simply by adding another adjective:

The kindhearted boy had many girlfriends.
The kindhearted, intelligent boy had many girlfriends.
The kindhearted, intelligent, handsome boy had many girlfriends.

All languages have mechanisms of this sort that make the number of sentences limitless. Like words, discussed in the previous chapter, sentences are composed of finitely many discrete units that are combined by rules. Thus languages make infinite use of finite means. In this respect knowledge of language is like knowledge of integers. There is no limit to the number of even integers you could enumerate: 2, 4, 6, 8, 10, . . . . Clearly, you didn't memorize all of them. Rather, you know a rule that allows you to produce new integers from old ones.

Rule: If E is an integer, E+2 is an integer.

This ability to make infinite use of finite means shows the creative nature of human linguistic knowledge—not creative in the sense that we are all accomplished poets, but creative in that none of us is limited to a fixed repertoire of expressions. Rather, we can exploit the resources of our language and grammar to produce, understand and make judgments about a limitless number of sentences embodying a limitless range of ideas and emotions.

The part of grammar that represents a speaker's knowledge of sentences and their structures is called **syntax**. The aim of this chapter is to first show you what syntactic structures look like and then to familiarize you with some of the rules that determine them. Most of the examples will be from the syntax of English, but the principles that account for syntactic structures are universal.

## What the Syntax Rules Do

The rules of syntax combine words into phrases and phrases into sentences. Among other things, the rules define the correct word order for a language. For example, English is a Subject–Verb–Object (SVO) language. The English sentence in (1) is grammatical because the words occur in the right order; the sentence in (2) is ungrammatical because the word order is incorrect for English.

1. The President nominated a new Supreme Court justice.
2. *President the Supreme new justice Court a nominated.

The rules of the syntax also specify the **grammatical relations** of a sentence, such as **subject** and **direct object**. In other words, they provide information about who is doing what to whom. This information is crucial to understanding the meaning of a sentence. For example, the grammatical relations in (3) and (4) are reversed, so the otherwise identical sentences have very different meanings.

3. Your dog chased my cat.
4. My cat chased your dog.

The word order of a sentence is crucial to its meaning. The sentences in (5) and (6) contain the same words, but the meanings are quite different, as the Mad Hatter points out.

5. I mean what I say.
6. I say what I mean.

Although the structure of a sentence contributes to its meaning, as illustrated in the examples 3–6, grammaticality and meaningfulness are not the same thing. Consider the following sentences:

Colorless green ideas sleep furiously.
A verb crumpled the milk.

Although these sentences do not make much sense, they are syntactically well–formed. They sound funny, but their funniness is different from what we find in the following strings of words, which are not syntactically well-formed:

*Furiously sleep ideas green colorless.
*Milk the crumpled verb a.

There are also sentences that we understand even though they are not well-formed according to the rules of the syntax. We can easily interpret Yoda's words to Luke Skywalker although the word order is incorrect for English.

". . . when gone I am . . . the last of the Jedi will you be"

To be a sentence, words must conform to specific patterns determined by the specific syntactic rules of the language.

Some sentences are grammatical even though they are difficult to interpret because they include nonsense words, that is, words with no agreed-on meaning. This is illustrated by the following lines from the poem "Jabberwocky" by Lewis Carroll:

'Twas brillig, and the slithy toves
Did gyre and gimble in the wabe

These lines are grammatical in the linguistic sense that they obey the word order and other constraints of English. Such nonsense poetry is amusing precisely because the sentences comply with syntactic rules and sound like English. Ungrammatical strings of nonsense words are not entertaining:

*Toves slithy the and brillig 'twas
wabe the in gimble and gyre did

Grammaticality does not depend on the truth of sentences. If it did, lying would be easy to detect. Nor does it depend on whether real objects are being discussed or whether something is possible in the real world. Untrue sentences can be grammatical, sentences discussing unicorns can be grammatical, and sentences referring to pregnant fathers can be grammatical.

The ability to produce, understand, and judge the grammaticality of a sentence depends on whether it conforms to the unconscious rules of our mental grammar. This grammar is different from the prescriptive grammar rules that we are taught in school. We develop the mental rules of grammar long before we attend school, as we shall see in Chapter 9.

# Sentence Structure

The job of the linguist is to describe the structure of the sentences in a language in a way that matches the linguistic knowledge of its speakers. We can compare two competing hypotheses. The first says that a sentence consists simply of a string of words organized in a flat structure as in (1).

**1.**

We have already seen that word order is an important aspect of syntactic knowledge and this simple diagram correctly captures the SVO word order of English:

The subject (S) *the child*, comes before the verb (V) *found*, which comes before the object (O) *a puppy*.

Let us contrast this kind of description with another, one that says that sentences have a tree-like structure in which words are grouped together into natural units nested within other natural units in a hierarchical arrangement, as in (2).

**2.**

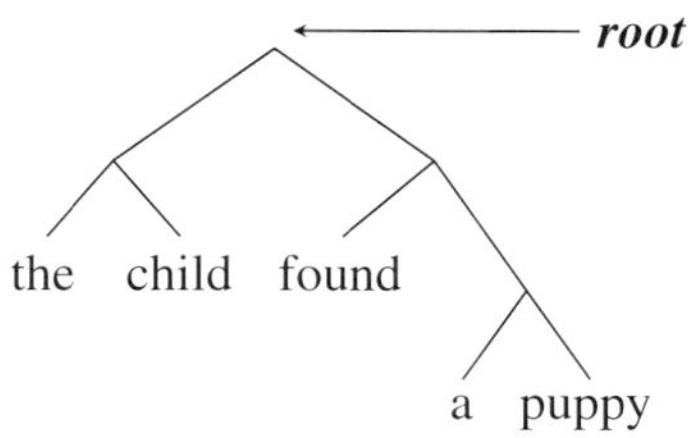


The "tree" in (2) is upside down with its "root" encompassing the entire sentence, "The child found a puppy," and its "leaves" being the individual words *the, child, found, a,* and *puppy*. The **tree diagram** in (2), embodies the hypothesis that these words are organized into subunits (or subtrees) and that speakers mentally represent sentences not as flat strings of words, but as complex structures with an internal organization. The subunits (or subtrees) of the sentence are called **constituents**.

In the tree diagram in (2), the words *a* and *puppy* form a constituent, as indicated below:

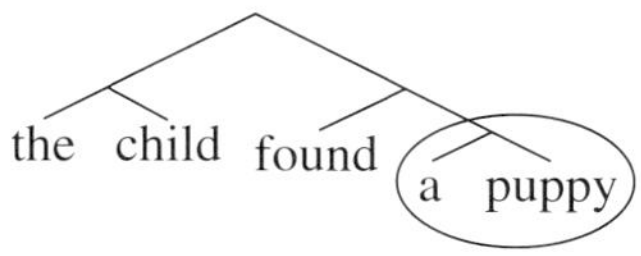


We can also represent constituents by using square brackets around the words [a puppy]. Constituents can be nested inside one another. So, [a puppy] occurs inside the constituent [found a puppy], as illustrated in the following tree.

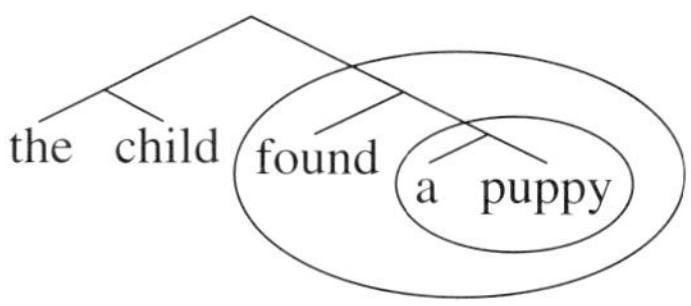


Using bracket notation, we would write this as [found [a puppy]].

There is one more constituent in the tree in (2). Do you know what it is? If you guessed [the child] you would be correct.

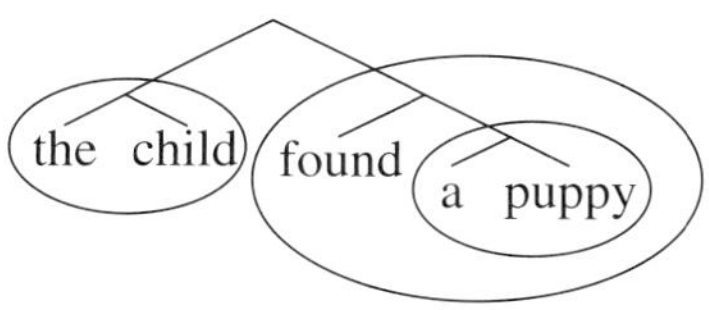

A constituent consists not just of the words, but of the subtree that branches into the words, and it ends at the **node** where the branches meet. A constituent corresponds to a node on the tree. And to be a constituent all the words under the node must be included. The words that form a constituent are contiguous (next to one another), but not all contiguous words form a constituent. In the following tree, the words *found a* are contiguous but they do not form a constituent. They are not contained exclusively under the same node.

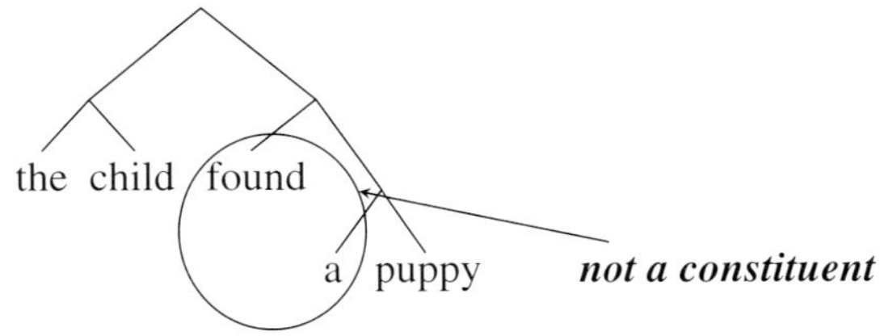


We began our discussion with a simple sentence "The child found a puppy," but this simple sentence belies a complex internal structure. The tree diagram in (2) groups the words of the sentence into the constituents *the child* and *found a puppy*, corresponding to the subject and predicate of the sentence. A further division of the phrase *found a puppy* divides naturally into two branches, one for the verb *found* and the other for the direct object *a puppy*. This division conforms to our intuitions about the natural units of the sentence in a way that a different division, say, *found a* and *puppy*, would not.

## Constituents and Constituency Tests

In addition to our intuitions of naturalness, various linguistic tests reveal the constituents of a sentence. The first test is the "stand alone" test. If a group of words can stand alone, for example, as an answer to a question, they form a constituent. So, in response to the question "What did the child find?" a speaker might answer *a puppy*, but not *found a*. *A puppy* can stand alone while *found a* cannot. We have a clear intuition that one of these is a meaningful unit and the other is just a list of words.

The second test is "replacement by a pronoun." Pronouns can substitute for natural groups. In answer to the question, "Where did the child find *a puppy*?" a speaker can say, "I found *him* in the park." Words such as *do* (which is not a pronoun per se) can also take the place of the entire predicate *found a puppy*, as in "The boy found a puppy and the girl *did* too." If a group of words can be replaced by a pronoun or a word like *do*, it forms a constituent.

A third test of constituency is the "move-as-a-unit" test. If a group of words can be moved together and remain grammatical, they form a constituent. For example, if we compare the following sentences to the sentence "The child found a puppy," we see that certain elements have moved:

It was *a puppy* that the child found.
*A puppy* was found by *the child*.

In the first example, the constituent *a puppy* has moved from its position following *found*; in the second example, the positions of *a puppy* and *the child* have been changed. In all such rearrangements, the constituents *a puppy* and *the child* remain intact. *Found a* does not remain intact, because it is not a constituent. Nor does *child found* for the same reason. Even though both these pairs of words occur next to each other in the original sentence *The child found a puppy*; they do not pass constituency tests, illustrating again that sentences are not simply string of words.

Some sentences have prepositional phrases in the predicate, for example:

The puppy played in the garden.

We can use our tests to show that *in the garden* is also a constituent, as follows:

Where did the puppy play? *In the garden* (stand alone)
The puppy played *there*. (replacement by a pronoun-like word)
*In the garden* the puppy played. (move as a unit)
It was *in the garden* that the puppy played. (move as a unit)

The prepositional phrase in this example passes all three constituent tests. But in general a constituent need not pass all three tests. It is sufficient to pass one.

As before, our knowledge of the **constituent structure** of a sentence may be graphically represented by a tree diagram. The tree diagram for the sentence "The puppy played in the garden" is as follows:

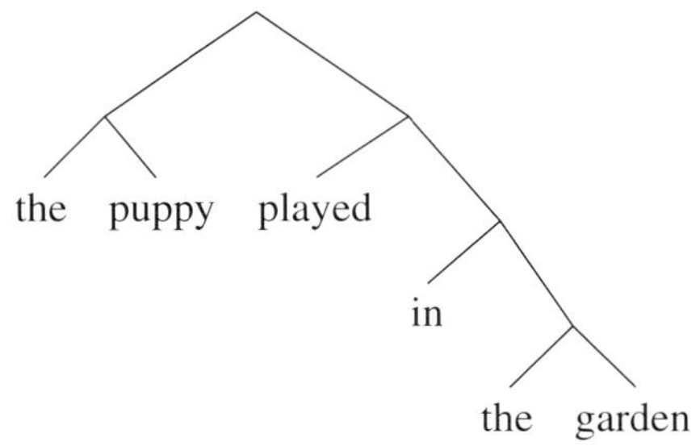


The move-as-a-unit test can also tell us when what appears to be a constituent, such as a prepositional phrase, is in fact something different. The two phrases *ran up the hill* and *ran up the bill* are superficially quite similar, but we see in (3) and (4) that they behave quite differently. Consider first the expression *ran up the hill*, as in (3a). The rules of the syntax allow the word orders in (3b, c) as variants, revealing that *up the hill* is a constituent. By contrast, the expression *run up the bill* in (4a) does not have these same options, as shown in (4b, c), which means that *up the bill* is neither a prepositional phrase nor a constituent.

**3.** **(a)** Jack ran up the hill.
**(b)** Up the hill Jack ran.
**(c)** Up the hill ran Jack.

**4.** **(a)** Jack ran up the bill.
**(b)** *Up the bill Jack ran.
**(c)** *Up the bill ran Jack.

## Structural Ambiguity

Hilary B. Price/King Features Syndicate

Syntactic trees reflect our judgments about the internal organization of sentences; flat structures do not. They can also account for other linguistic judgments, such as when a sentence is **ambiguous**. A sentence is ambiguous if it has two or more meanings. Sometimes an ambiguity arises because a word has more than one meaning, as in the following sentence:

This will make you smart.

The two interpretations of this sentence are due to the two meanings of *smart*—"clever" and "burning sensation." This is referred to as a **lexical ambiguity** and will be discussed further in Chapter 4. Other times multiple meanings arise because a sentence has more than one tree structure associated with it, resulting in a **structural ambiguity**. Each tree will correspond to one of the possible meanings of the sentence. For example, the sentence:

Sue saw the man with the telescope.

has two different meanings:

Meaning 1: The seeing is done with the telescope.
Meaning 2: The man is holding the telescope.

Notice that none of the individual words is ambiguous. The ambiguity is structural: The sentence has two different trees. Meaning 1 corresponds to the tree in (1), what we might call the instrumental meaning in which Sue is using the telescope to see the man. In this tree, the *the man* and the prepositional phrase *with the telescope* do not form a constituent.

**1.**

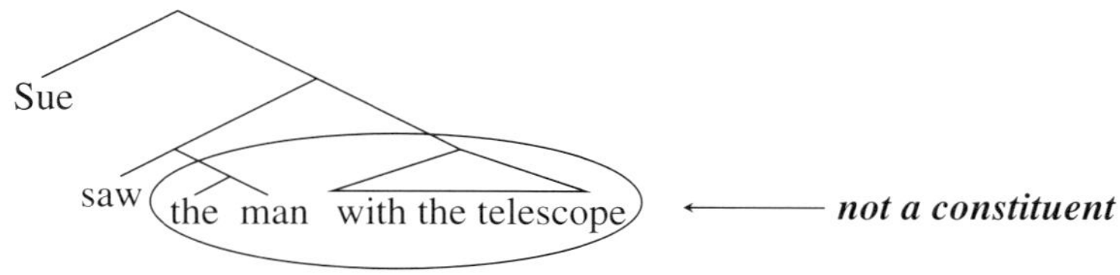

Meaning 2 corresponds to the tree in (2). In this case, the phrases *the man* and *with a telescope* do form a constituent, reflecting the meaning in which the man is holding the telescope.

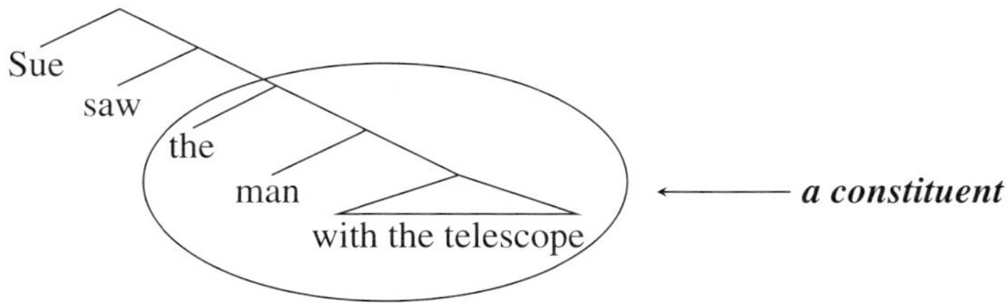


The availability of these two structures leads to a prediction: If we do a constituency test that forces *the man with the telescope* to be a constituent (e.g. move it as a unit), then meaning 1 (instrumental) should disappear and we should only have the meaning corresponding to the tree in (2). The following sentences confirm this prediction:

It was the man with the telescope that Mary saw.

The man with the telescope was seen by Mary.

What Mary saw was the man with the telescope.

None of these sentences has the interpretation in which the seeing is done with the telescope. In each, the only possible meaning is that the man is holding the telescope. This shows us that the structure of a sentence contributes importantly to its meaning, a point we will come back to in Chapter 4.

Structural ambiguities of the sort just discussed provide striking evidence in support of our hypothesis that sentences have a tree-like (hierarchical) structure, and against the idea that they are simply strings of words. The flat structure hypothesis could not explain how there can be two different meanings associated with *the same string of words*.

The cartoon at the head of this section illustrates both lexical and structural ambiguity. The lexical ambiguity is on the two meanings of *ring*; the structural ambiguity is whether *nose ring* is understood as a compound noun or a noun followed by a verb.

## Syntactic Categories

In the previous section, we illustrated how tree structures reflect our knowledge of the hierarchical organization of sentences. Speakers also have implicit knowledge of the categories of each of the subgroupings in a sentence.

Each grouping in the tree diagrams of "The child found a puppy" is a member of a large family of similar expressions. For example, *the child* belongs to a family that includes *the police officer, your neighbor, this yellow cat, he, John,* and countless others. We can substitute any member of this family for *the child* without affecting the grammaticality of the sentence, although the meaning of course would change.

A police officer found a puppy.
Your neighbor found a puppy.
This yellow cat found a puppy.

A family of expressions that can substitute for one another without loss of grammaticality is called a **syntactic category**, or more informally, a "part of speech." *The child, a police officer, John*, and so on belong to the syntactic category **noun phrase (NP)**. NPs may function as subjects or as objects in sentences. An NP often contains a *determiner* (such as *a* or *the*) and a noun, but it may also consist of a proper name (*Ann*), a pronoun (*I*), a noun without a determiner (*fish*), or even a clause or a sentence (*that dogs bark*). Even though a proper noun such as *John* and pronouns such as *he* and *him* are single words, they are technically NPs, because they pattern like NPs in being able to fill a subject, object or other NP slot.

John found the puppy.
He found the puppy.
Boys love puppies.
The puppy loved him.
The puppy loved John.

NPs can be quite complex, as illustrated by the sentence:

The girl that Professor Snape loved married the man of her dreams.

The NP subject of this sentence is *the girl that Professor Snape loved*, and the NP object is *the man of her dreams*. We know this because each of these lengthy expressions fills a slot otherwise occupied by a simpler NP as in *Mary loved John*.

Syntactic categories are part of a speaker's knowledge of syntax. That is, speakers of English know that only items (a), (b), (e), (f), and (g) in the following list are NPs even if they have never heard the term *noun phrase* before.

1. **(a)** a bird
   **(b)** the red banjo
   **(c)** have a nice day
   **(d)** with a balloon
   **(e)** the woman who was laughing
   **(f)** it
   **(g)** John
   **(h)** went

You can test this claim by inserting each expression into three contexts: *What/who I heard was* __________, *Who found* __________*?* and __________ *was seen by everyone*. For example, **Who found with a balloon?* is ungrammatical, as is **Went was seen by everyone*, as opposed to *Who found it?* or *John was seen by everyone*. Only NPs fit into these contexts because only NPs can function as subjects and objects.

There are other syntactic categories. The expression *found a puppy* is a **verb phrase (VP)**. A verb phrase always contains a **verb (V)**, and it may contain other categories, such as a noun phrase or **prepositional phrase (PP)**, which is a preposition followed by an NP, such as *in the park, on the roof,* and *with a balloon.* In (2) the VPs are those phrases that can complete the sentence "The child __________."

**2.** **(a)** saw a clown
**(b)** a bird
**(c)** slept
**(d)** smart
**(e)** ate the cake
**(f)** found the cake in the cupboard
**(g)** realized that the Earth was round

Inserting (a), (c), (e), (f), and (g) will produce grammatical sentences, whereas the insertion of (b) or (d) would result in an ungrammatical sentence. Thus, (a), (c), (e), (f), and (g) are verb phrases.

## Lexical and Functional Categories

*"Very traditional. He's the noun. She's the adjective."*



Syntactic categories include both phrasal categories such as NP, VP, AP (adjective phrase), PP (prepositional phrase), and AdvP (adverbial phrase), as well as lexical categories such as noun (N), verb (V), preposition (P), adjective (A), and adverb (Adv). Each lexical category has a corresponding phrasal category. Following is a list of phrasal categories and lexical categories with some examples of each type:

**Phrasal categories**

| | |
|---|---|
| Noun Phrase (NP) | *men, the man, the man with a telescope sees, always* |
| Verb Phrase (VP) | *sees, rarely sees the man, often sees the man with a telescope* |
| Adjective Phrase (AP) | *happy, very happy, very happy about winning* |

| | |
|---|---|
| Prepositional Phrase (PP) | *over, nearly over, nearly over the hill* |
| Adverbial Phrase (AdvP) | *brightly, more brightly, more brightly than the Sun* |
| **Lexical categories** | |
| Noun (N) | *puppy, boy, man, soup, happiness, fork, kiss, pillow* |
| Verb (V) | *find, run, sleep, throw, realize, see, try, want, believe* |
| Preposition (P) | *up, down, across, into, from, by, with, over* |
| Adjective (A) | *red, big, happy, candid, hopeless, fair, idiotic, lucky* |
| Adverb (Adv) | *again, always, brightly, often, never, very, fairly* |

Many of these categories may already be familiar to you. Other categories may be less familiar such as the category **determiner (Det)**, which includes the articles *a* and *the*, as well as **demonstratives** such as *this, that, these,* and *those*, and "quantifiers" such as *each* and *every*. Another less familiar category is **T**(ense), which includes the **modal** auxiliaries *may, might, can, could, must, shall, should, will,* and *would,* and abstract tense elements that we discuss below. Lastly, there are **complementizers (Comp)** words such as *that, for,* and *if, whether* that occur in complex (multi-clause), sentences such as the following:

John thinks that Mary is pretty.
John wonders whether/if Mary will date him.

T, Det, and Comp are **functional categories**, so called because their members have grammatical functions rather than descriptive meanings. For example, determiners specify whether a noun is indefinite or definite (*a boy* versus *the boy*), or the proximity of the person or object to the context (*this boy* versus *that boy*). Tense provides the verb with a time frame, whether present *(John knows Mary)*, or past *(John danced)*. And complementizers introduce embedded clauses. In English, T is expressed as a (sometimes silent) morpheme on the verb, except in the future tense, which is expressed with the modal *will*. Modals also express notions such as possibility *(John may dance);* necessity *(John must dance);* and ability *(John can dance)*. The modals belong to a larger class of verbal elements traditionally referred to as **auxiliaries** or helping verbs, which also include *have* and *be* in sentences such as *John is dancing* or *John has danced*.

Each lexical category typically has a particular kind of meaning associated with it. For example, verbs usually refer to actions, events, and states *(kick, marry, love);* adjectives to qualities or properties *(lucky, old);* common nouns to general entities *(dog, elephant, house);* and proper nouns to particular individuals *(Noam Chomsky)* or places *(Dodger Stadium)* or other things that people give names to, such as commercial products *(Coca-Cola, Viagra)*.

But the relationship between grammatical categories and meaning is more complex than these few examples suggest. For example, some nouns refer to events *(marriage* and *destruction)* and others to states *(happiness, loneliness)*. We can use abstract nouns such as *honor* and *beauty*, rather than adjectives, to refer to properties and qualities. In the sentence "Seeing is believing," *seeing* and *believing* are nouns, but they are not entities. Prepositions are generally used to express relationships between two entities involving a location (e.g., *the boy is in the room, the cat is under the bed*), but this is not always the case; the prepositions *of, by, about,* and *with* often have nonlocational meanings.

Because of the difficulties involved in specifying the precise meaning of lexical categories, we do not define grammatical categories in terms of their meanings, but rather on the basis of where they occur in a sentence, what categories co-occur with them, and what kind of inflections they can take. For example, we define a noun as a word that can occur with a determiner *(the boy)* and that can (ordinarily) take a plural marker *(boys);* a verb as a word that can occur with an adverb *(run fast)* or modal *(may go, will dance);* an adjective as a word that can occur with a degree word *(very hungry)* or a comparative or superlative marker *(hungrier, hungriest)*, among other properties.

All languages have syntactic categories such as N, V, and NP. Speakers know the syntactic categories of their language even if they do not know the technical terms. Our knowledge of syntactic classes is revealed when we substitute equivalent phrases, as we just did in examples (1) and (2) above, and when we use the various syntactic tests that we have discussed.

Our knowledge of syntactic categories is also revealed through our intuitions about nonsensical sentences. Recall the sentences in (1) and (2) below. Although neither of these sentences makes sense, we have a clear intuition that (1) is grammatical in a way that (2) is not.

**1.** Colorless green ideas sleep furiously.
**2.** *Sleep colorless green furiously ideas.

This is because sentence (1) obeys the word order constraints of English while sentence (2) does not. In other words, we recognize the category of each of the words: *Colorless* is an adjective, *ideas* is a noun, *colorless green ideas* is a noun phrase, and *sleep furiously* is a verb phrase, and know that they fit properly together in (1) but not in (2). We are not taught these categories nor their word order. We know this implicitly before we go to school. They are part of our grammar that we develop as a child growing up (see Chapter 9).

In these sentences, we can identify when the order is correct and when it is not, even though the meanings of the different words and constituents do not jibe. An idea cannot be green or colorless, (except in a metaphorical sense), but even if ideas had color we would say *colorless green ideas* and not *ideas green colorless* or *green ideas colorless.*

Similarly, we may not be able to make sense of Lewis Carroll's Jabberwocky, but we can identify the words *brillig, slithy*, and *mimsy* as adjectives, *toves, wabe, borogoves, and momeraths* as nouns, and *outgrabe, gyre, and gimble* as verbs, all based on their position in the sentences.

'Twas brillig, and the slithy toves
Did gyre and gimble in the wabe:
All mimsy were the borogoves,
And the momeraths outgrabe.

Speakers know the syntactic category of the various constituents and how they are ordered with respect to one another. They also know how to group words into units—*constituents*. This knowledge is graphically represented in tree structures that reveal the grammatical organization of the words of a sentence.

Tree structures also explain how the grouping of words in a sentence relates to its meaning, such as when a sentence or phrase is ambiguous. And even when the meaning is nonsensical the structure must obey the syntactic rules of the language. The rules of syntax also permit speakers to produce and understand a limitless number of sentences never produced or heard before—*the creative aspect of linguistic knowledge*, illustrated at the beginning of this chapter. A major goal of linguistics is to show clearly and explicitly how syntactic rules account for what speakers implicitly know about their language.

## Phrase Structure Trees

Now that you know something about constituent structure and grammatical categories, you are ready to learn how the phrases and sentences of a language are constructed. We will begin by illustrating trees for simple phrases and then proceed to more complex structures. The trees that we will build here are more detailed than those we saw in the previous sections, because the branches of the tree will have category labels identifying each constituent. In this section, we will also introduce the kind of syntactic rules that **generate** (a technical term for describe or specify) the different structures.

The tree diagram in (1) provides labels for each of the constituents of the sentence "The child found a puppy." These labels show that the entire sentence belongs to the syntactic category of S (because the S-node encompasses all the words). It also reveals that *the child* and *a puppy* belong to the category NP, that is, they are noun phrases, and that *found a puppy* belongs to the category VP or is a verb phrase, consisting of a verb and an NP. It also shows the syntactic category of each of the words in the sentence.

1.

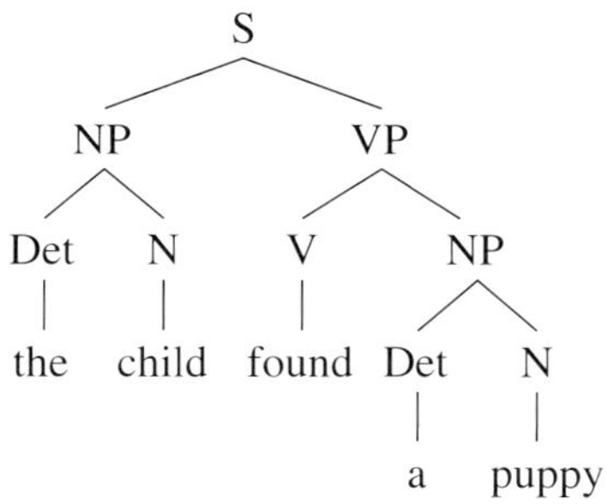


A tree diagram with syntactic category information is called a **phrase structure tree** or a **constituent structure tree**. Phrase Structure trees (PS trees) represent three aspects of a speaker's syntactic knowledge:

1. The linear order of the words in the sentence
2. The identification of the syntactic categories of words and groups of words
3. The hierarchical structure of the syntactic categories (e.g., an S is composed of an NP followed by a VP, a VP is composed of a V that may be followed by an NP, and so on).

The syntactic category of each word is listed in our mental dictionaries, as we will discuss in more detail in Chapter 4. This lexical information guides the syntax of the language. Words appear in trees under labels that correspond to their syntactic category. Nouns are under *N*, determiners under *Det*, verbs under *V*, and so on.

The larger syntactic categories such as *VP* consist of all the syntactic categories and words below that node in the tree. The *VP* in the PS tree above consists of syntactic category nodes *V* and *NP* and the words *found*, *a*, and *puppy*. Because *a puppy* can be traced up the tree to the node *NP*, this constituent is a noun phrase. Because *found* and *a puppy* can be traced up to the node *VP*, this constituent is a verb phrase. In discussing trees, every higher node is said to **dominate** all the categories beneath it. S dominates every node. A node is said to **immediately dominate** the categories one level below it. VP immediately dominates V and NP, the categories of which it is composed. Categories that are immediately dominated by the same node are **sisters**. V and NP are sisters in the phrase structure tree of "the child found a puppy."

PS trees are also useful for defining various grammatical relations in a precise way. For example, the subject of a sentence is the NP immediately dominated by S (*the child* in the tree in (1) and the direct object is the NP immediately dominated by VP (*the puppy* in the tree in (1).

## Phrase Structure Rules

The information shown in a PS tree can also be represented by another formal device: phrase structure (PS) rules. PS rules capture the knowledge that speakers have about the possible structures of a language. Just as a speaker cannot have an infinite list of sentences in his or her head, so he or she cannot have an infinite set of PS trees in his or her head. Rather, a speaker's knowledge of the permissible and impermissible structures must exist as a finite set of rules that characterize a tree for any sentence in the language. To express the structure given above, we need the following PS rules:

1. S → NP VP
2. NP → Det N
3. VP → V NP

You can think of PS rules as templates that a tree must match to be grammatical. They express the regularities of the language and make explicit a speaker's knowledge of the order of words and the grouping of words into syntactic categories. For example in English an NP may contain a determiner followed by a noun. This is represented by rule 2. This rule conveys two facts:

> A noun phrase may contain a determiner followed by a noun in that order.
> A determiner followed by a noun is a noun phrase.

Phrase structure rules specify the well-formed structures of a language precisely and concisely. To the left of the arrow is the dominating category NP. The categories that it immediately dominates appear on the right side, in this case Det and N. The right side of the arrow also shows the linear order of these components. Thus, the subtree for the English NP looks like this:

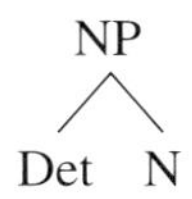


Rule 1 says that a sentence (S) contains (immediately dominates) an NP and a VP in that order. Rule 3 says that a verb phrase consists of a verb (V) followed by an NP. These rules are general statements and do not refer to any specific VP, V, or NP. The subtrees represented by rules 1 and 3 are as follows:

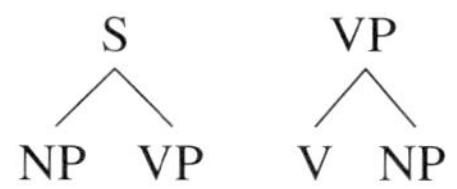


A VP need not contain an NP object, however. It may include a verb alone, as in the following sentences:

The woman laughed.
The man danced.
The horse galloped.

These sentences have the structure:

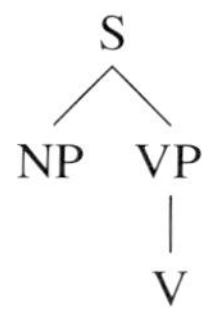


Thus, a tree may have a VP that immediately dominates only V, as specified by rule 4, which we include in our grammar:

**4.** VP → V

The following sentences contain prepositional phrases following the Verb:

The puppy played in the garden.
The boat sailed up the river.
A girl laughed at the monkey.
The sheepdog rolled in the mud.

The PS tree for such sentences is

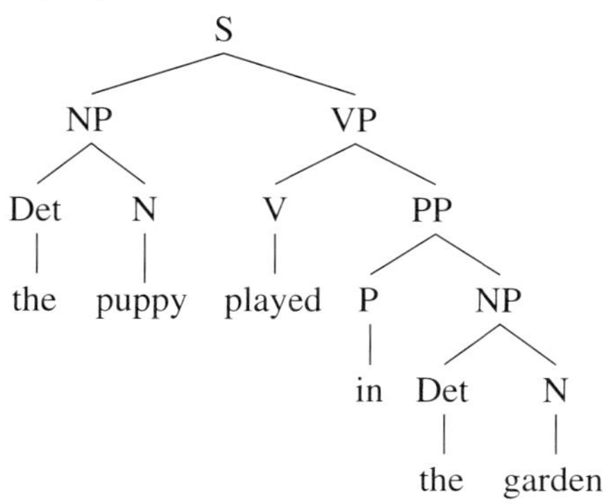

To generate structures of this type we need two additional PS rules as in 5 and 6.

**5.** VP → V PP
**6.** PP → P NP

Another option open to the VP is to contain or *embed* a sentence. For example, the sentence "The professor hoped that the students read the chapter" contains the sentence "the students read the chapter." Preceding the **embedded sentence** is the word *that*, which belongs to the category of complementizers C(omp), a functional category like T(ense) and Det. Here is the structure of such sentence types:

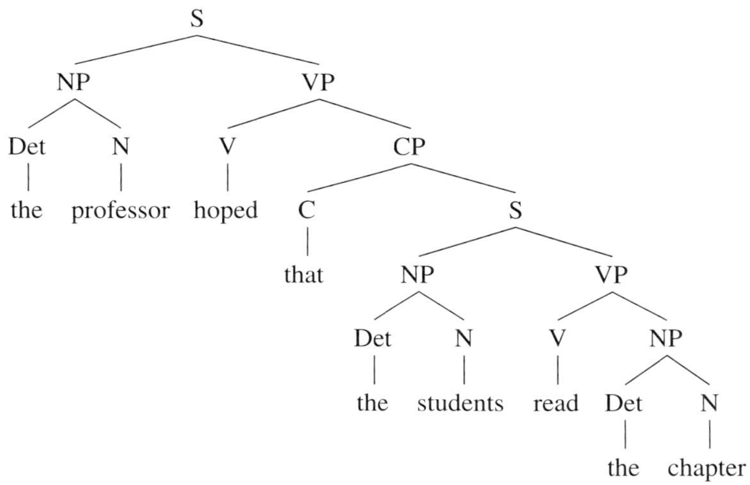


To allow such embedded sentences, we need to add these two new rules to our set of phrase structure rules.

**7.** VP → V CP
**8.** CP → C S

CP stands for complementizer phrase. Rule 8 says that CP contains a complementizer such as *that* followed by the embedded sentence. Other complementizers are *if* and *whether* in sentences such as

I don't know whether I should talk about this.
The teacher asked if the students understood the syntax lesson.

which have structures similar to the one above.

Here are the PS rules we have discussed so far. The rules have been slightly renumbered to keep all the VP rules together. We will introduce some other rules later.

**1.** S → NP VP
**2.** NP → Det N
**3.** VP → V NP
**4.** VP → V
**5.** VP → V PP
**6.** VP → V CP

7. PP → P NP
8. CP → C S

## Building Phrase Structure Trees

The phrase structure rules can be used as a guide for building trees that follow the structural constraints of the language. In so doing, certain conventions are followed. The S occurs at the top or "root" of the tree (remember the tree is upside down). So, first find the rule with S on the left side of the arrow (rule 1) and put the categories on the right side below the S, as shown here.

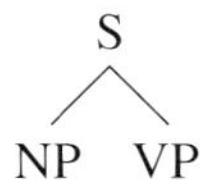


Continue by matching any syntactic category at the bottom of the partially constructed tree to a category on the left side of a rule, then expand the tree with the categories on the right side. For example, we may expand the tree by applying the NP rule to produce:

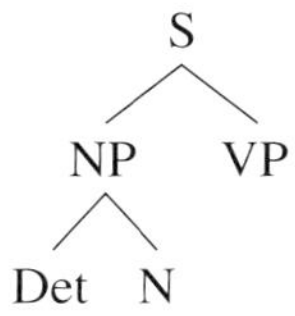


The categories at the bottom are Det, N, and VP, but only VP occurs to the left of an arrow in the set of rules and so needs to be expanded using one of the VP rules. Any one of the rules will work. The order in which the rules appear in the list of rules is irrelevant. (We could have begun by expanding the VP rather than the NP.) Suppose we use rule 4 next. Then, the tree has grown to look like this:

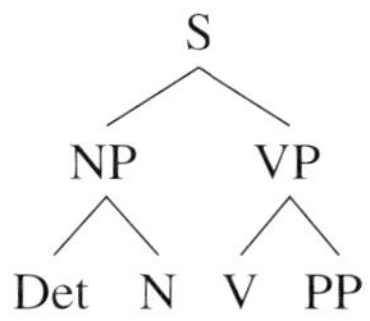


We continue in this way until all phrasal categories are expanded, that is, none of the categories at the bottom of the tree appears on the left side of any rule. The PP must expand into a P and an NP (rule 7), and the NP into a Det and an N. (Proper names and pronouns which are NPs and not nouns are an exception to the "full expansion convention.") We can use a rule as many times as it can apply. In this tree, we used the NP rule twice. After we have applied all the rules that can apply, the tree looks like this:

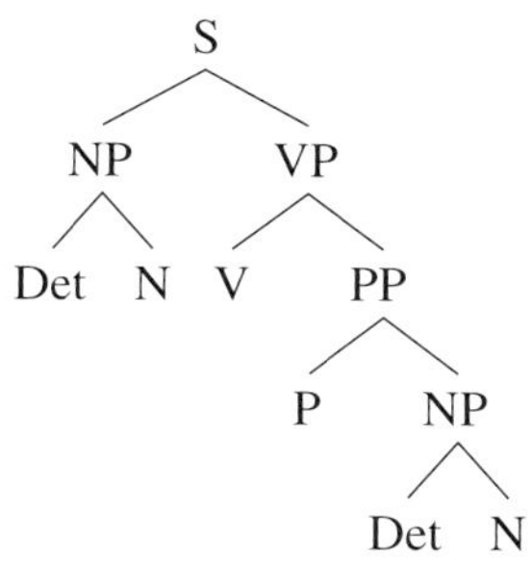


By following these conventions, we generate only trees specified by the PS rules, and hence only trees that conform to the syntax of the language. By implication, any tree not so specified will be ungrammatical, that is, not permitted by the syntax. At any point during the construction of a tree, any rule may be used as long as its left-side category occurs somewhere at the bottom of the tree. By choosing different VP rules, we could specify different structures corresponding to sentences such as:

The boys left. (VP → V)
The wind blew the kite. (VP → V NP)
The senator hopes that the bill passes. (VP → V CP)

Because the number of possible sentences in a language is infinite, there are also an infinite number of trees. However, all trees are built out of a finite set of phrase structure rules.

## The Infinity of Language: Recursive Rules

Though incomplete, the set of PS rules we have introduced thus far is sufficient to illustrate the mechanisms by which languages generate a limitless number of sentences. Consider the following set of sentences, similar to those discussed at the beginning of this chapter.

1. Homer caught a pokémon.
2. Marge noticed that Homer caught a pokémon.
3. Bart wonders whether Marge noticed that Homer caught a pokémon.
4. Lisa knows that Bart wonders whether Marge noticed that Homer caught a pokémon.

We see that sentence 1 is embedded inside sentence 2, sentence 2 inside sentence 3, sentence 3 inside sentence 4. We could continue this process indefinitely. This is made possible by the fact that rule phrase structure rule 6 (VP → V CP) in combination with rules 8 (CP → C S) and 1 (S → NP VP) form a **recursive** set, in which the symbols S and VP occur on both the left and right side of the rules. Therefore, the rules allow S to contain VP, which in turn contains CP, which in turn contains S, which in turn again contains VP and so on, potentially without end. Recursive rules are of critical importance because they allow the grammar to generate an infinite set of sentences. The PS tree for sentence 4 illustrates the application of these rules (here we use triangles under the NPs to indicate that proper names are full NPs, not nouns):

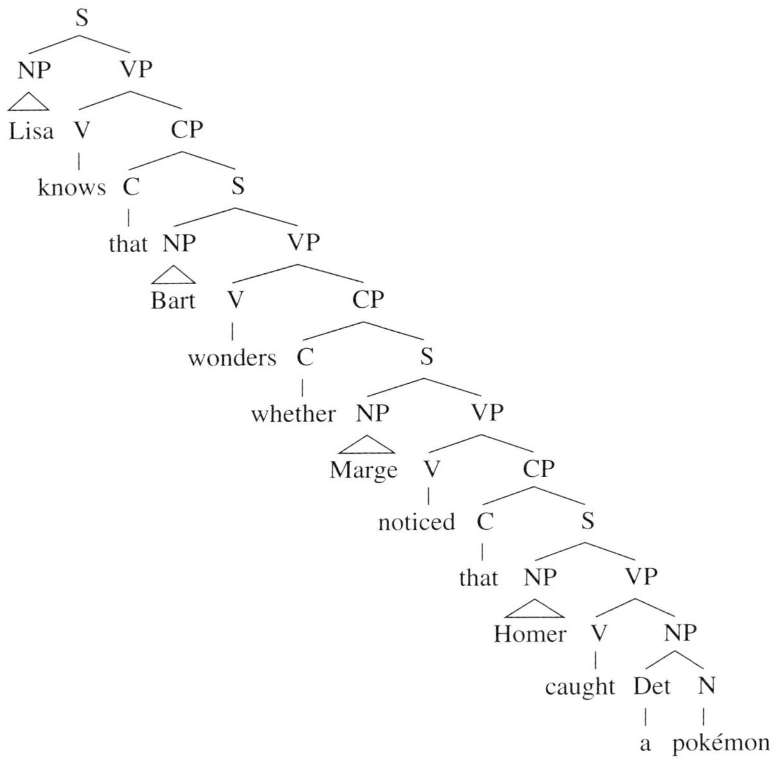


The property of recursion also illustrates the difference between competence and performance, discussed in Chapter 1. All speakers of English (and all other languages) have as part of their linguistic competence—their mental grammars—the ability to embed phrases within each other ad infinitum. However, as the structures grow longer, they become increasingly more difficult to produce and understand. This can be due to short-term memory limitations, muscular fatigue, breathlessness, boredom, or any number of performance factors. Nevertheless, these very long sentences would be well-formed according to the rules of the grammar.

Below, we will see other examples of recursive rule sets such as the one responsible for the potentially infinite number of prepositional phrases in sentences like:

> The person behind the person immediately to the left of the rightmost person in the first row is asleep.

# The Internal Structure of Phrases

In the previous sections, we focused on the hierarchical organization of sentences into phrasal categories such as NP, VP, and PP. In this section, we will look at the internal structure of phrases themselves.

## Heads, Complements, and Selection

One of the striking things we observe when we consider the various phrase structure rules given above (and the subtrees they generate) is that they have a similar organization. Consider the following examples of each of the phrasal categories we have discussed:

NP: the *mother* of James Whistler
VP: *sing* an aria
PP: *over* the hill

For completeness, we add the category AP (adjective phrase), illustrated by the example

AP: *wary* of snakes
generated by the following rule:

**9.** AP → A PP

As we noted in our discussion of grammatical categories, the core of every phrase is a lexical category of its same syntactic type (italicized), which is its **head**; for example, the NP *the mother of James Whistler* is headed by the noun *mother;* the VP *sing an aria* is headed by the verb *sing;* the AP *wary of snakes* is headed by the adjective *wary;* the PP *over the hill* is headed by the preposition *over*. Loosely speaking, the entire phrase refers to whatever the head refers to. For example, the VP *sing an aria* refers to a "singing" event; the NP *the mother of James Whistler* to someone's mother.

In addition to the head, the phrasal categories may contain other categories such as NP, PP or CP. These sister categories are called **complements**. A complement is a phrasal category that occurs next to a head, and only there, and which elaborates on the meaning of the head. The complements are underlined: For example, the head N *mother* takes the PP complement of James Whistler; the head V *sing* takes the NP complement an aria; the head A(djective) *wary* takes the PP of snakes, and the P(reposition) *over* takes the NP the hill as complement.

## Selection

Complements are not always present in the phrase structure. They are optional; only the head is obligatory. The choice of complement type for any particular phrase depends on the specific properties of the head of that phrase. For example, verbs select different kinds of complements: *find* is a transitive verb and requires an NP complement (direct object), as in *The boy found the ball*, but not **The boy found*, or **The boy found in the house*. Some verbs such as *eat* are optionally transitive. *John ate* and *John ate a sandwich* are both grammatical. *Sleep* is an **intransitive verb**; it cannot take an NP complement:

Michael slept.
*Michael slept the baby.

Some verbs, such as *think*, may select both a PP and a sentence complement (underlined):

Let's think about it.
I think a girl won the race.

Other verbs, such as *tell*, select an NP and a sentence:

I told the boy a girl won the race.

Yet other verbs such as *feel* select either an AP or a sentence complement:

Paul felt strong as an ox.
He feels he can win.

Categories besides verbs also select their complements. For example, the noun *belief* selects either a PP or a sentence, while the noun *sympathy* selects a PP, but not a sentence, as shown by the following examples:

the belief in freedom of speech
the belief that freedom of speech is a basic right
their sympathy for the victims
*their sympathy that the victims are so poor

Adjectives can also have complements. For example, the adjectives *tired* and *proud* select PPs:

tired of stale sandwiches
proud of her children

The information about the complement types selected by particular verbs and other lexical items is called **C-selection** or **subcategorization**, and is included in the lexical entries of the items in our mental lexicons. (C stands for "category.")

A verb also includes in its lexical entry a specification that imposes certain semantic requirements its subjects and complements, just as it selects for syntactic categories. This kind of selection is called **S-selection**. (S stands for "semantic.") For example, the verb *murder* requires its subject and object to be animate, while the verb *quaff* requires its subject to be animate and its object liquid. Verbs such as *like,* and *hate* select animate subjects. The following sentences violate S-selection and can only be used in a metaphorical sense. (We will use the symbol "!" to indicate a semantic anomaly.)

!Golf plays John.
!The beer drank the student.
!The tree liked the boy.

The famous sentence *Colorless green ideas sleep furiously* cited above is anomalous because (among other things) S-selection is violated (e.g., the verb *sleep* requires an animate subject). In Chapter 4, we will discuss the semantic relationships between a verb and its subject and objects in far more detail.

The well-formedness of a phrase depends, then, on at least two factors: whether the phrase conforms to the structural constraints of the language as expressed in the PS rules, and whether it obeys the selectional requirements of the head—both syntactic (C-selection) and semantic (S-selection).

## The Three Levels of Phrases

In addition to the head and its complements, a phrase may have an element preceding the head. These elements are called **specifiers**. For example, in the NP *the mother of James Whistler,* the determiner *the* is the specifier of the NP. In English, possessives may also be specifiers of NP, as in *Nellie's ball.* The specifier position may also be empty, as in the NP *dogs with bones*. PPs, APs, and VPs also have specifiers, but for various reasons they are harder to see. They usually show up when the phrase is embedded in another sentence, as in

**a.** Betty made [Jane wary of snakes].
**b.** I heard [Pavarotti sing an aria].
**c.** I saw [everyone at the stadium].

In (a) *Jane* is the specifier of the AP *wary of snakes,* in (b) *Pavarotti* is the specifier of the VP *sing an aria*, and in (c) *everyone* is the specifier of the PP *at the stadium. Specifier* is a purely structural notion. In English, it is the first position in the phrase, if it is present at all, and a phrase may contain at most one specifier.

Unlike complements, specifiers are not sisters of the head, but rather sisters of the phrase formed by the head and the complement. These observations tell us that all of the phrasal categories, NP, VP, AP, and PP, have a similar three-tiered structure, as follows:

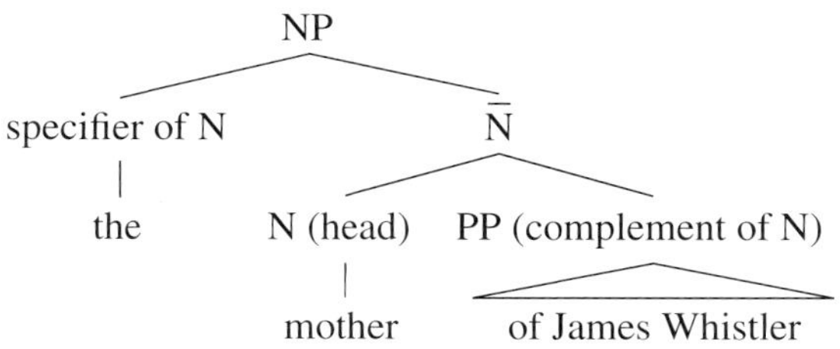


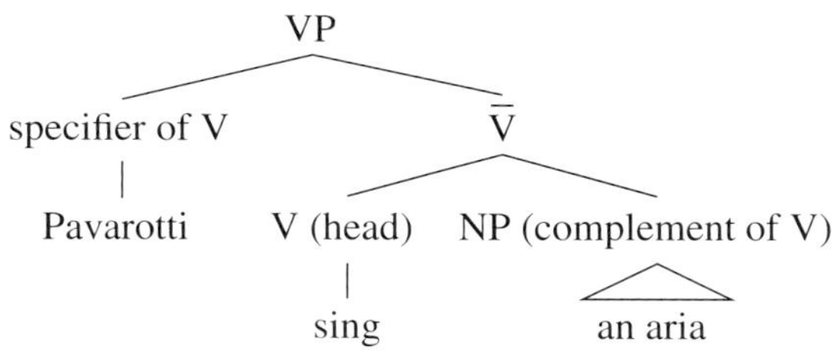

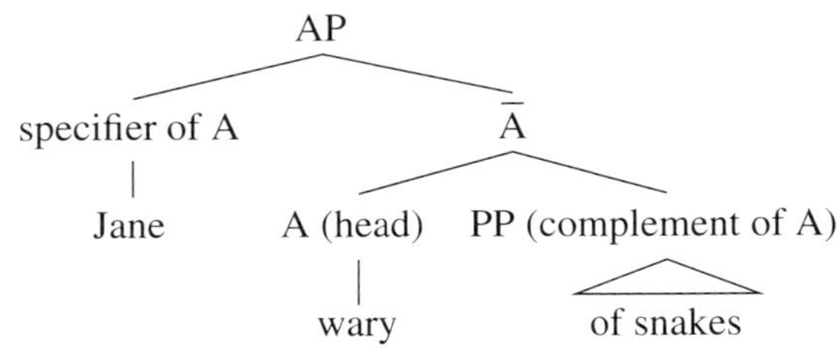


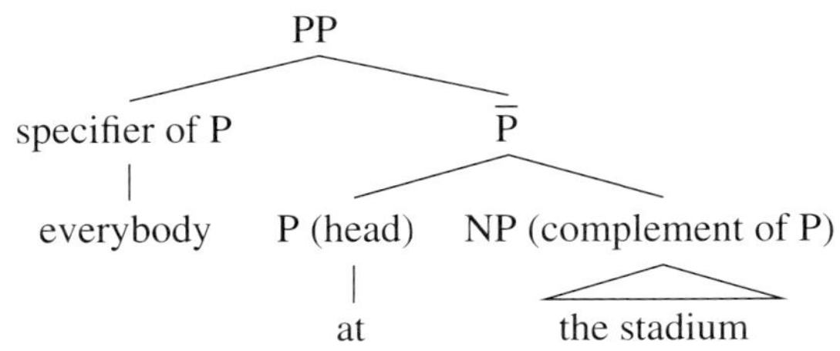


To capture the generalization that each phrasal category has the same internal structure, we substitute X in place of N, V, P, A and we get the following tree:

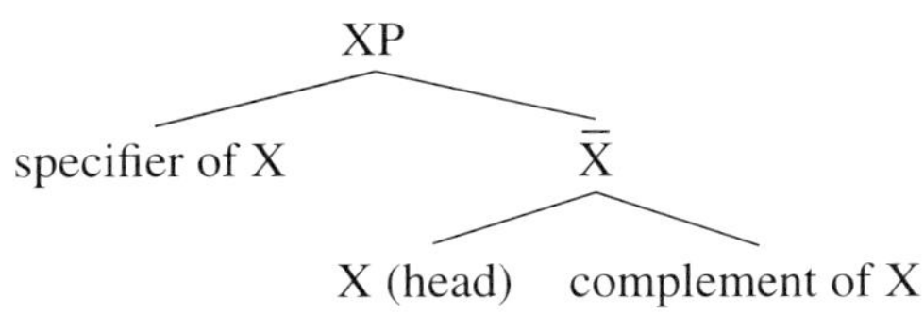


This three-tiered structure, referred to as **X-bar ($\overline{X}$) schema**, is a template or blueprint that specifies how the phrases of a language are organized, or alternatively, how PS rules are formed. The X-bar schema "stands for" the various phrasal categories given above (and others we will see later) and applies to all syntactic phrases. The parentheses around the specifier and complement indicate that these expansions are optional and depend on the selectional properties of the head. The head is the only obligatory category of a phrase. The "bar" category is an intermediate level category necessary to account for certain syntactic phenomena that we'll see shortly.

Assuming X-bar schema we must modify our PS rules to incorporate the three tiers. Here are the revised rules for NP:

2a: NP $\rightarrow$ (Det) $\overline{N}$
2b: $\overline{N}$ $\rightarrow$ N (XP)

Under the new rules, NP expands as an optional Det and $\overline{N}$ and $\overline{N}$ expands as N and an optional complement of any category (XP). These rules will generate the PS tree for phrase *the mother of Whistler*, illustrated on the previous page, where XP stands for the PP *of Whistler* as complement to the head N *mother*.

We have several VP rules in our list showing the different complements to V (rules 3–6). X-bar allows us to collapse these VP rules as follows:

3a: VP → (Spec) $\overline{\text{V}}$
3b: $\overline{\text{V}}$ → V (XP)

Under the new rules, VP expands to include an optional specifier (*Pavarotti* in sentence b above), and $\overline{\text{V}}$, which in turn contains V and an optional complement of any category such as NP as direct object in *found* <u>*a puppy*</u>. Here is the revised set of rules. Notice that the rules have been renumbered and are more compact:

1. S → NP VP
2. NP → (Det) $\overline{\text{N}}$
3. $\overline{\text{N}}$ → N (XP)
4. VP → (Spec) $\overline{\text{V}}$
5. $\overline{\text{V}}$→V (XP)
6. PP → P NP
7. CP → C S
8. AP → A PP

Our PS rules for PP, and AP (rules 6 and 8) also adhere to X-bar (e.g., PP → (Spec) $\overline{\text{P}}$ etc.) but we omit the details. We will revisit the rules for S (rule 1) and CP (rule 7) below.

The X-bar schema is hypothesized to be part of Universal Grammar. As such, all languages have phrases that consist of heads, specifiers, and complements that relate to each other as just described. However, the order of the head and complement may differ in different languages. In English, for example, we see that the head comes first, followed by the complement. In Japanese, complements precede the head, as shown in the following examples:

| Taro-ga | inu-o | mitsuketa | |
|---|---|---|---|
| Taro-subject marker | dog-object marker | found | "Taro found a dog" |

| Inu-ga | niwa-de | asonde | iru | |
|---|---|---|---|---|
| Dog-subject marker | garden-in | playing | is | "The dog is playing in the garden" |

In the first sentence, the direct object complement *inu-o*, "dog," precedes the head verb *mitsuketa*, "found." In the second, the NP complement *niwa*, "garden," precedes the head preposition *de*, "in." English is a VO language, meaning that the verb ordinarily precedes its object. Japanese is an OV language, and this difference is reflected in the head/complement word order. For Japanese, the X-bar schema looks like this:

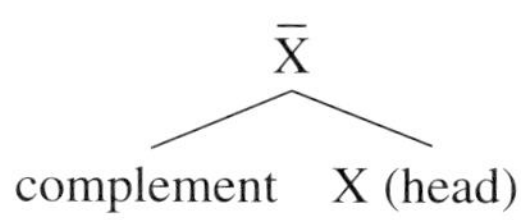


Compare this to the English schema:

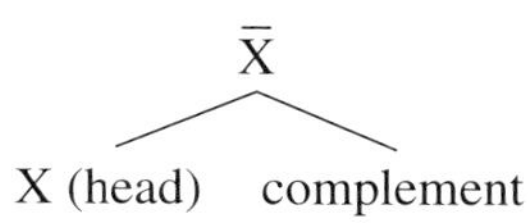

X-bar schema specifies a vast amount of syntactic knowledge in a concise way. If, as many linguistics believe, X-bar is universal (order aside) and hence part of children's innate endowment for language, it also helps explain how they so quickly learn the abstract hierarchical structures of phrases in their language (see Chapter 9). Upon hearing *Taro-ga inu-o mitsuketa* (Taro dog finds), the Japanese child automatically knows not only that NP complements precede the verb in his or her language, but also that all other complements do so as well. For example, NPs precede their prepositional heads, as in *niwa-de* (garden in). The English-speaking child will just as easily come to the opposite order based on sentences such as *John found the dog.*

## What Heads the Sentence

We have suggested that the structure of all phrasal categories follows the X-bar schema. One category that we have not yet discussed in this regard is sentence (S). To preserve the powerful syntactic generalization that the X-bar schema offers, we want all the phrasal categories to have a three-tiered structure with specifiers, heads, and complements, but what would these be in the case of S? To answer this question, we first observe that sentences are always "tensed." Tense provides a time-frame for the event or state described by the verb. In English, present and past tenses are marked on the verb:

John dance**s**. (present)
John danc**ed**. (past)

Future tense is expressed with the modal *will* (*John* will *dance*). Modals also express notions such as possibility (*John* may *dance*); necessity (*John* must *dance*); and ability (*John can dance*). A modal such as *may* says it is possible that the event will occur at some future time, *must* that it is necessary that the event occur at some future time, and so on. The English modals are inherently "tensed," as shown by their compatibility with various time expressions:

John may/must/can win the race today/tomorrow.
*John may/must/can win the race yesterday.
John could/would have tantrums when he was a child.
John could leave the country tomorrow.

Just as the VP is about the situation described by the verb—*eat ice cream* is about "eating"—so a sentence is about a situation or state of affairs that occurs at some point in time. Thus, the category Tense is a natural category to head S.

Using this insight, linguists refer to sentences as TPs (Tense Phrases) with the following structure conforming to the X-bar schema:

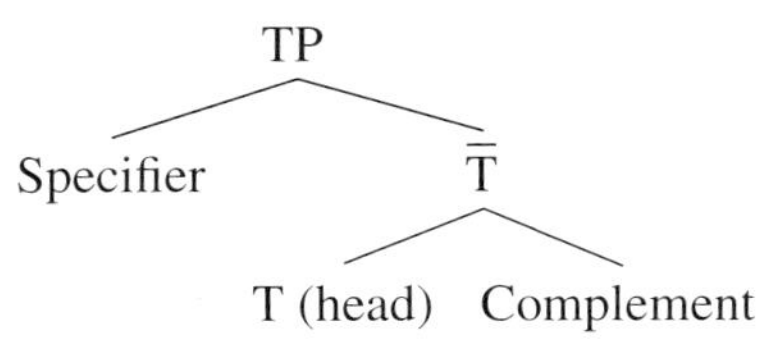

For sentences, or TPs, the specifier is the subject of the sentence and the complement of the T is a verb phrase. The head T contains the tense (±pst) and modal verbs such as *can* or *would* and takes VP as its complement. The introduction of $\overline{\text{T}}$ gives the sentence its traditional subject–predicate form.

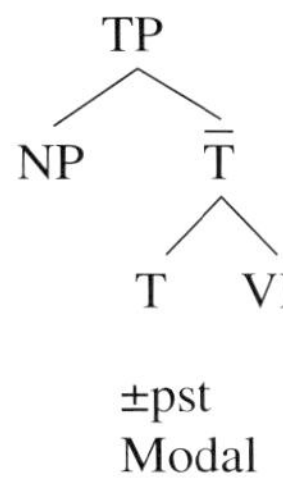


The NP left daughter of the TP functions as the subject of the sentence; the $\overline{\text{T}}$ right daughter is what is traditionally called the predicate. We are now able to represent the structures of such sentences as *The girl may cry* and *The child ate*:

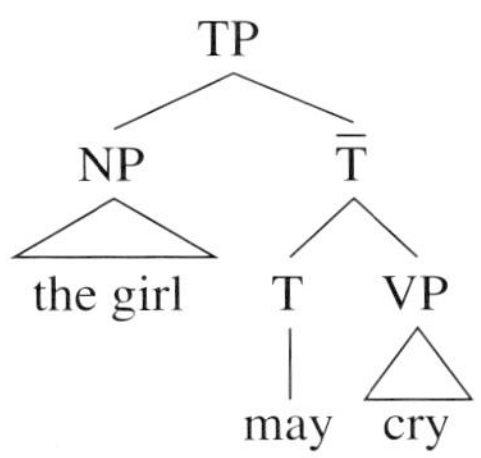


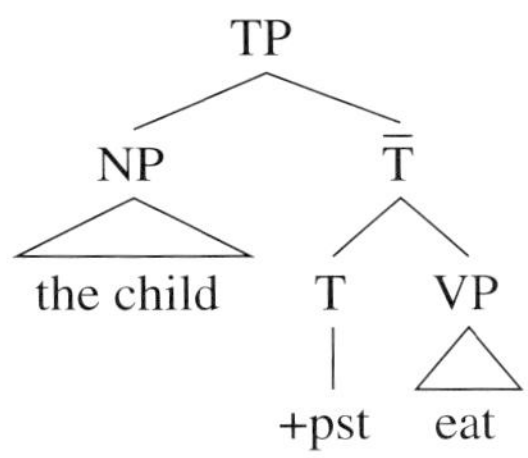


In these structures, the T containing +pst and *eat* is ultimately pronounced *ate*. When there is no modal under T, the present or past tense is realized on the verbal head of the VP.

Another way tense is expressed in English is by the tense-bearing word *do* that is inserted into negative sentences such as *John did not go* and questions such as *Where did John go?* In these sentences, *did* means "past tense." Later in this chapter, we will see how *do*-insertion works.

While many of the details of X-bar syntax are beyond the scope of an introductory text, we will briefly show how the inclusion of an intermediate $\overline{\text{X}}$ tier allows the grammar to generate a wide range of sentences that could not be otherwise produced, and also further explains the recursive property of human languages.

## The Infinity of Language Revisited

We noted at the beginning of the chapter that languages have various means of creating longer and longer sentences. For example, an NP may contain any number of adjectives as in the *kind-hearted, intelligent, handsome boy*. One benefit of positing the abstract category $\overline{\text{N}}$ is that it allows us to account for the potentially limitless number of adjectives. Here we need a recursive rule—one that repeats itself—on $\overline{N}$:

**9.** $\overline{N} \rightarrow A\ \overline{N}$

This rule generates the NP structure in question:

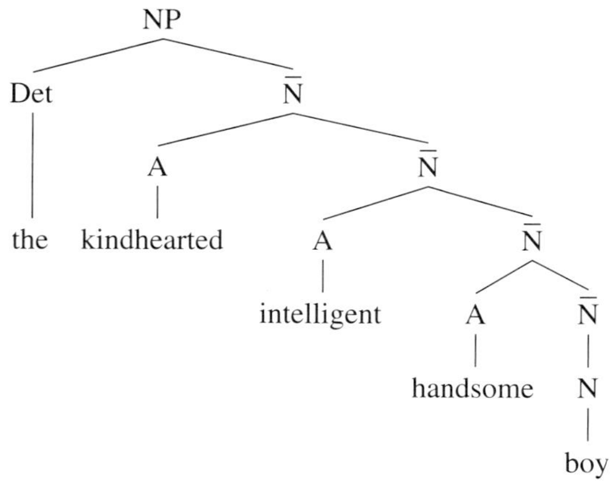


Without $\overline{N}$ we would be forced to have a recursive rule on NP such as NP → A NP. Such a rule would capture the recursion of the adjective, but it would also allow the Det to show up in an impossible place as in *kind-hearted, intelligent, the boy:*

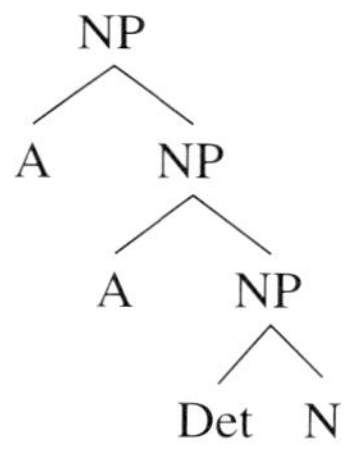


A similar kind of recursion occurs in this cartoon:

Another way speakers of English can build structures of theoretically limitless size is by repeating the category of Intensifier (Int) within an AP. The recursive rule looks like this and would not only handle Hattie's 100-word essay but also takes care of the more modest expression *really very pretty:*

**10.** $\overline{A} \rightarrow \text{Int}\ \overline{A}$

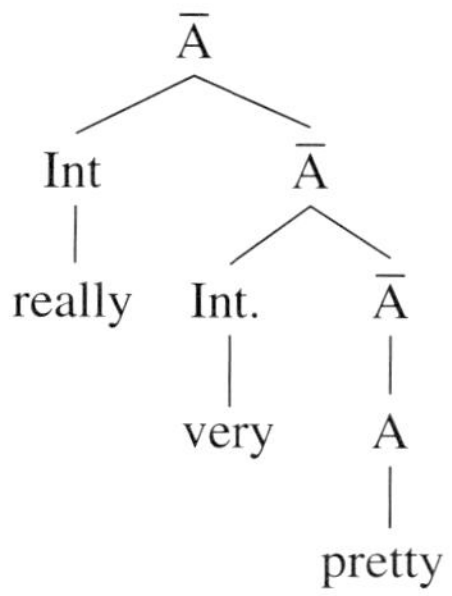

A slightly different form of recursion involves PP recursion, as illustrated by *she went over the hills through the woods to grandmother's house. . . .* Sentences of this sort requires recursion on $\overline{\text{V}}$.

**11.** $\overline{\text{V}} \rightarrow \overline{\text{V}}$ PP

giving rise to the following subtree

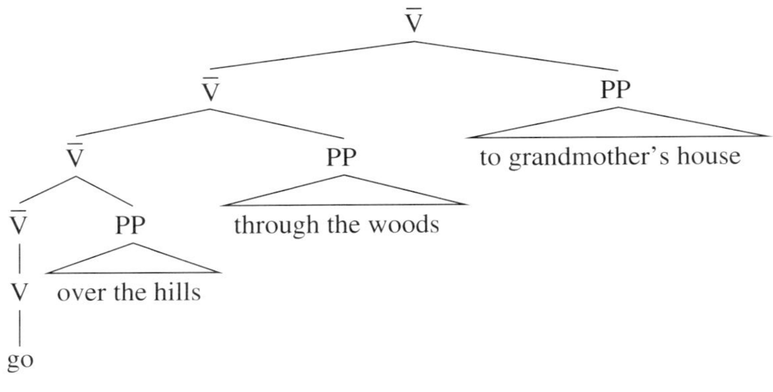


Note that the PP in (11), like the adjective in (9) and the intensifier in (10), are not complements, they are not sisters to the head of the phrase. Rather, they are sisters to $\overline{\text{V}}$, $\overline{\text{N}}$, and $\overline{\text{A}}$ respectively. A phrasal category that is sister to an $\overline{\text{X}}$

and daughter of a higher $\overline{X}$, as in the above structures, is called an **adjunct**. Like complements, adjuncts may be of any grammatical category.

Distinguishing between complements and adjuncts is not always straightforward. Structurally, the distinctions are unambiguous: complements are sisters to X; adjuncts are sisters to $\overline{X}$. But in analyzing sentences it is not always clear whether an addendum to a head is a complement or an adjunct. Here's one example illustrating the difference between a complement and an adjunct, an example that will bring us back to our discussion of the structural ambiguity of the sentence:

Sue saw the man with the telescope.

As discussed earlier, this sentence has more than one PS tree, each corresponding to a different meaning. Under the "instrumental" meaning (Sue used the telescope to see the man) the complement of *saw* is the simple NP *the man* and the PP is an *adjunct* introduced by rule 11. The sentence has the following constituent structure: (From now on we'll adopt the convention of using a triangle when we are not concerned with the internal structure of the category.)

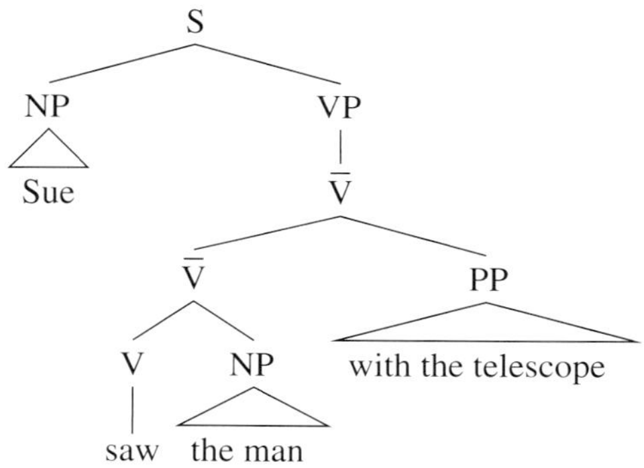


Under the second meaning of the sentence (the man is holding the telescope), *the man* and *with the telescope* form an NP constituent and the PP is a *complement* to the head noun, as illustrated in the following structure:

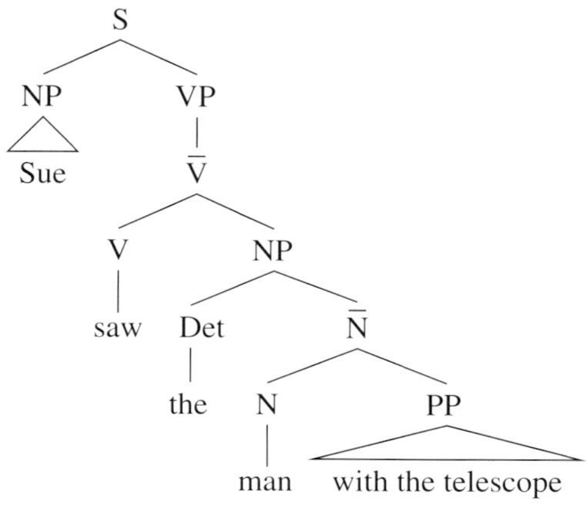

Thus, the different meanings arise from the fact that in the first case the PP *with the telescope* is sister to (hence modifies) the $\overline{\text{V}}$ *see the man*; but in the second case it is sister to (hence modifies) *man*. The two interpretations of this sentence are possible because the rules of syntax permit different structures for the same linear order of words.

Let us sum up our discussion thus far. We have seen that sentences have a tree-like organization. They are not simply "flat" strings of words, as shown by various constituency tests, as well as structural ambiguities. Phrase structure trees specify (i) the grammatical categories of words and groups of words in a sentence, for example, N, V, VP, and so on, (ii) the position of categories with respect to each other, that is, word order, and (iii) the internal organization of words into hierarchically arranged phrases. The PS rules for a language thus define the (infinite set) of well-formed (grammatical) structures in that language.

# Grammatical Dependencies

In addition to the properties discussed above, the syntactic component of the grammar must describe various relationships and dependencies that hold across and within sentences. It is clear that certain sentence types are related, for example, the declarative-question pair below:

Homer will sleep.
Will Homer sleep?

Our grammar must reflect the speaker's knowledge of relationships of this sort.

Similarly, within a sentence two elements can be related even when they are separated by an arbitrary number of words. These "dependencies at a distance" provide further evidence for the hierarchical organization of sentences provided by the PS rules. Two such rules are subject–verb agreement, and question formation.

## Subject–Verb Agreement

In many languages, including English, the verb must agree with the subject. The verb (in English) is marked with an *-s* when the subject is third-person singular and otherwise unmarked.

1. This **guy seems** kind of cute.
2. These **guys seem** kind of cute.

A simple rule that expresses the agreement relationship in terms of the linear adjacency of the noun (*guy/guys*) and verb (*seem/seems*) would work for the sentences in 1 and 2:

## Linear Agreement Rule

The verb agrees in person and number with the word to its left.

But what about the sentences in 3 and 4?

3. The **guy** we met at the party next door **seems** kind of cute.
4. The **guys** we met at the party next door **seem** kind of cute.

The verb *seem* must agree with the head of the subject NP, *guy* or *guys*, regardless of the number of words between the head noun and the verb. Moreover, there is no limit to how many words may intervene, or whether they are singular or plural, as the following sentence illustrates:

> The **guy (guys)** we met at the party next door that lasted until 3 a.m. and was finally broken up by the cops who were called by the neighbors **seems (seem)** kind of cute.

The (much abbreviated) phrase structure tree below explains why this is so.

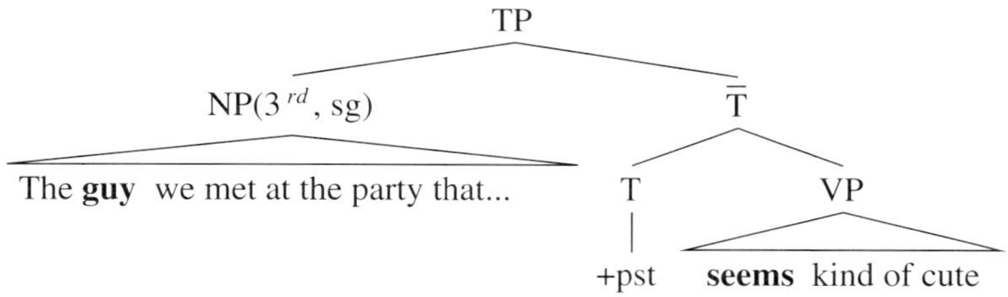


In the tree, the NP may in principle be indefinitely long and complex. However, speakers of English (and all other languages) know that agreement depends on sentence structure and not on the linear order of words: agreement is between the head of the subject NP and the main verb. As far as the rule of agreement is concerned, all other material can be ignored. (Although in actual performance, if the distance is too great, the speaker may forget what the subject was.) Thus, the rules of grammar that relate different elements in the sentence are **structure dependent** and therefore a more accurate agreement rule must be stated in terms of hierarchical structure:

> ***Structure dependent agreement rule***: The verb agrees in person and number with the *subject* of the sentence, where *subject* is defined as the NP immediately dominated by S (TP).

The fact that rules are structure dependent supports the tree-like arrangement of constituents in a sentence. If sentences were just flat strings of words, it would be impossible to state an agreement rule.

## Question Formation Rules

## Yes–no questions

Within any language certain sentence types relate systematically to other sentence types, such as the following pairs:

| | |
|---|---|
| The boy will sleep. | Will the boy sleep? |
| The dog is barking. | Is the dog barking? |
| The man has eaten a fish. | Has the man eaten a fish? |

Each pair of sentences is about the same situation. For example, the first sentence asserts that a "boy-sleeping" situation will happen. Such sentences are called **declarative** sentences. The corresponding question asks whether such a "boy-sleeping" situation will occur. Sentences of the second sort are called **yes–no questions**. The only actual difference in meaning between these sentences is that one asserts information while the other asks for confirmation of information. This meaning difference is indicated by the different word orders, illustrating that two sentences may have a structural difference that corresponds *in a systematic way* to a meaning difference. The grammar of the language must account for this fact.

The standard way of describing these relationships is to say that the related sentences come from a common underlying structure. Yes–no questions are a case in point. A yes–no question begins life as a declarative sentence, a TP in the X-bar schema, for example:

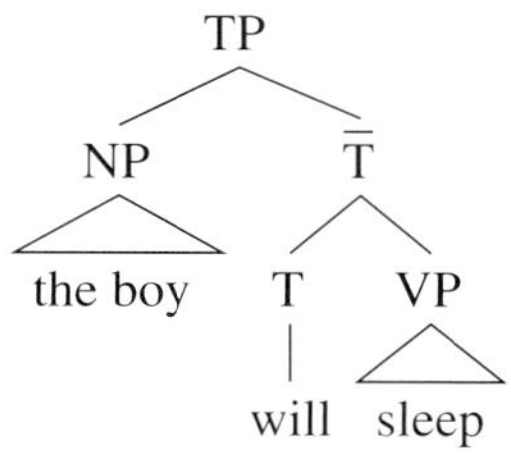


The head of the TP, namely T (the modal *will* in this example), is central to the formation of yes–no questions as well as certain other types of sentences in English. In yes–no questions, the modal or auxiliary verb *have* or *be* appears in a different position; it precedes the subject.

The relationship between a declarative sentence and a yes–no question can be described by a rule that moves the material in T before the subject NP. This rule applies to the tree structure.

For the sentence *The boy will sleep* shown on the previous page to derive the structure below:

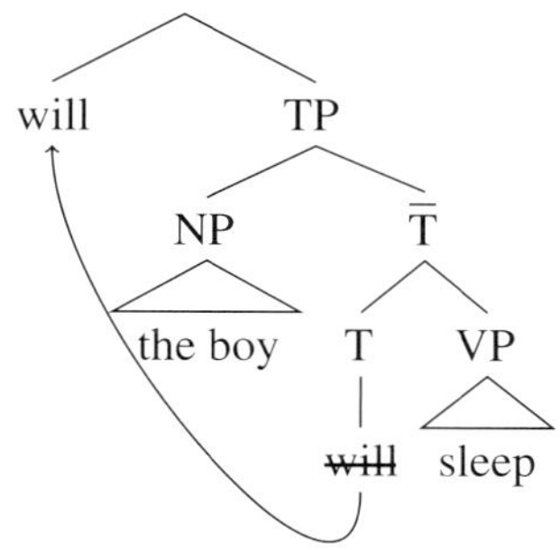


For descriptive purposes, we'll call this rule **Aux inversion**. Aux inversion is an example of what is traditionally referred to as a **transformational rule**. For now, we will leave unspecified the structural position that the auxiliary moves to in the tree above. We return to that below.

Thus, yes–no questions are thus generated in two steps:

1. PS-rules generate a basic structure.
2. Aux inversion applies to the basic structure to produce the derived structure.

By generating questions in two steps, we are claiming that a principled structural relationship exists between a question and its corresponding statement. Intuitively, we know that such sentences are related. The transformational rule is a formal way of representing this knowledge.

More generally, the basic structures of sentences are called **deep structures** or **d-structures**. Variants on the basic sentence structures are derived via transformational rules. The derived structures—the ones that follow the application of transformational rules—are called **surface structures** or **s-structures**. Loosely said, we *speak* and *hear* s-structures but mentally connect s-structures to d-structures. If no transformations apply, then d-structure and s-structure are the same. If transformations apply, then s-structure is the result after all transformations have taken effect.

In our discussion of the constituency test "move as a unit," we saw other rules that dislocate elements of a sentence, for example, the active-passive pair in 1 and PP-preposing in 2:

1. The child found a puppy → A puppy was found by the child.
2. The puppy played in the garden → In the garden the puppy played.

We saw earlier that the rule of subject–verb agreement is sensitive to structure and not to the linear position of elements in a sentence. We can now go further and state that all grammatical rules are structure dependent. For example, the PP-preposing rule in 2 cannot move just any string of words that begins with a preposition: It looks at the specific structure of the sentence containing the PP. This is made evident by the fact that *with a telescope, Sue saw the man* is not ambiguous. It has only the meaning "Sue used a telescope to see the man," corresponding to the first phrase structure on page 78 where the PP is immediately dominated by the $\overline{V}$. In the structure corresponding to the other meaning, "the boy saw a man who had a telescope," the PP is in the NP, as in the second tree on page 78. The PP-preposing transformation applies to the first structure but not the second.

Aux inversion provides yet another illustration of structure dependency.

1. The boy who **can** run fastest **will** win.
2. **Will** the boy who **can** run fastest win?
3. ***Can** the boy who run fastest **will** win?

The contrast in grammaticality of the sentences in 2 and 3 shows that to form a question Aux inversion applies to the modal within the $\overline{T}$ that is dominated by the root (highest) TP, and not simply to the *first* modal in the sentence, as illustrated in this highly abbreviated structure.

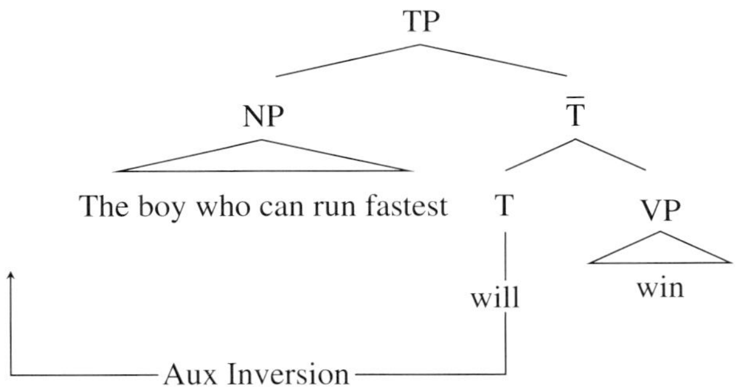

Let's now look at the structure of "Will the boy sleep?" in more detail. Thus far we have been assuming S (TP) is the root of the sentence. Strictly speaking, this is not correct. Remember our PS rule 7, repeated below.

**7.** CP → C S

From this rule, we see that CP (Complementizer Phrase) dominates S (TP). Though this rule was previously used only for embedded sentences such as *Marge noticed that Homer caught a pokémon*, yes–no questions (and many other structures) tell us that all sentences have CP as their root. Like all other categories, CP conforms to X-bar schema and hence we modify rule 7 accordingly:

**7(a).:** CP → (Spec) $\overline{\text{C}}$
**7(b).:** $\overline{\text{C}}$ → C TP

The sentence root is CP and TP is the complement to the head C. C contains the abstract element +Q for questions or −Q for declaratives. Putting aside the specifier of CP for the moment, the X-bar analysis of CP has the advantage that C provides a home for T when Aux inversion relocates it. The d-structure for questions is:

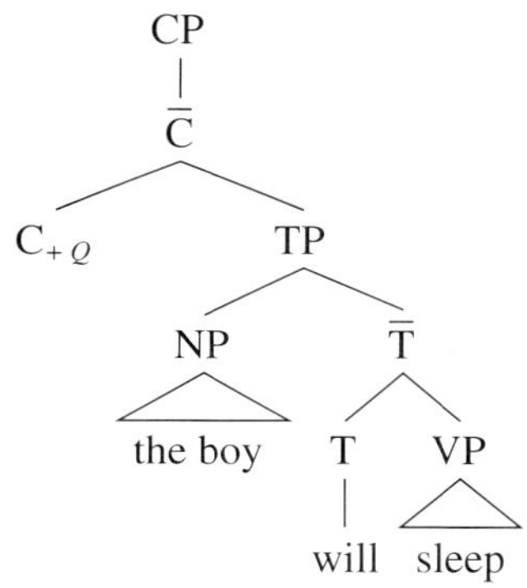


and the modal is moved to C:

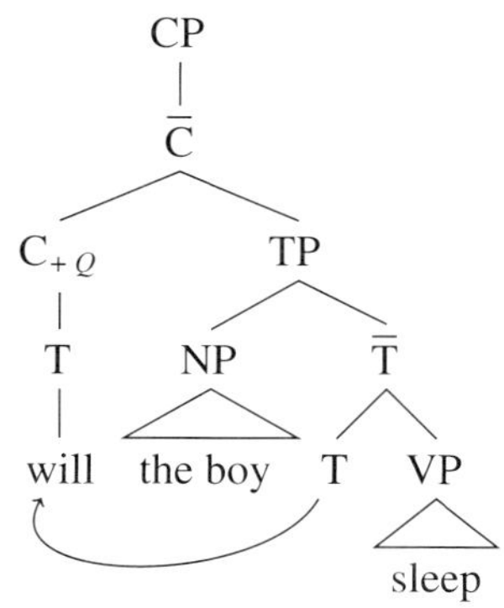

The auxiliaries *have* and *be* also undergo Aux inversion in yes–no question:

| | |
|---|---|
| Spot has chased a squirrel. | Has Spot chased a squirrel? |
| Nellie is snoring. | Is Nellie snoring? |

But the d-structure position of these auxiliaries is not under T. We know this because they can also occur with modals (which occupy the T position) as in:

Nellie may be snoring.
Spot must have found a squirrel.

Moreover, like other verbs in English (and unlike modals) *have* and *be* inflect for tense (and agreement): *am, is, are,* was, were, *have, has, had.* These observations lead us to conclude that *have/be* originate under V. When there is no modal in the sentence, *have* or *be* can undergo a movement that is not available to other verbs: they can "raise" from the position under V to T, and then undergo a second movement to C to form a question, as follows:

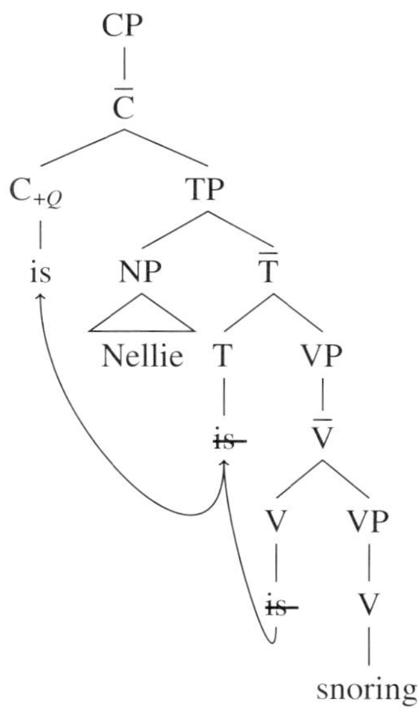


Additional PS rules would be needed to account for sentences with both *have* and *be* such as *Spot has been chasing squirrels* and even such unusual sentences as *The squirrels have been being chased by Spot.*

In addition to questions, the need for the complementizer phrase (CP) is provided by phrasal categories that take sentences (TPs) in their complements (underlined):

belief that iron floats (CP complement to head N)
wonders if iron floats (CP complement to head V)
happy that iron floats (CP complement to head A)
about whether iron will sink (CP complement to head P)

The words *that, if,* and *whether* are complementizers and the CP has a place for them under its head C, for example:

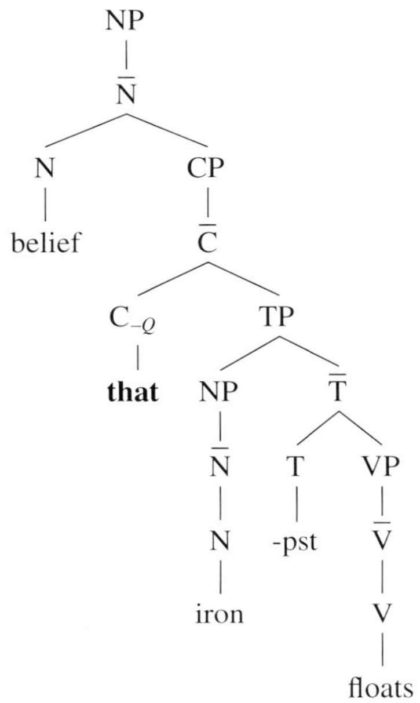


## *Wh* Questions

We have shown that syntactic rules are structure dependent and do not pay attention to the length or content of the words in a sentence. Nowhere is this better illustrated than in ***wh* questions** such as the following.

1. **(a)** What will Max chase __________?
   **(b)** Where should Pete put his dog bone __________?
   **(c)** Which toys does Pete like __________?

*Wh* questions contain *wh* phrases of various syntactic categories, for example, *what* is an NP, *which* is a determiner, and *where* is a PP. They are inserted into a PS tree under the appropriate category node, like all other words. In English and many other languages, *wh* phrase generally have to move from their d-structure position, indicated by the __________ in the sentences in (1), to the beginning of the sentence ("echo questions" like *you ate what!*? behave differently and we'll ignore them here).

Several clues tell us that the *wh* phrases in (1) have undergone movement. For example, the verb *chase* in sentence (a) is transitive, yet there is no direct object following it. There is a "gap" where the direct object should be. The verb *put* in sentence (b) is subcategorized for a direct object and a prepositional phrase, yet there is no PP following *his bone*. Finally, in sentence (c) *like* is followed by a gap and also has the third-person singular *-s* morpheme though it is preceded by a plural noun.

We can explain the grammaticality of the sentences in (1) despite these "abnormalities" by assuming that in each case the *wh* phrase originates in the position of the gap, as in (2), and is then moved to the beginning of the sentence by transformational rule.

**2.** **(a)** Max will chase *what?*
**(b)** Pete should put his dog bone *where?*
**(c)** Pete likes *which toys?*

The sentences in (1) are grammatical because the requirement that *chase* and *like* have a direct object is satisfied by the *what* and *which toys*, while the PP requirement of *put* is satisfied by *where*. The subcategorization requirements of the verbs are met prior to movement of the *wh* phrase. In any *wh* question, there is a dependency between the *wh* phrase at the beginning of the sentence and a gap somewhere else in the sentence.

*Wh* questions such as those in (1) are generated in several steps: phrase structure principles provide the basic declarative word orders in (2) (or more precisely the d-structure) with the *wh* expression in complement position, as required by the X-bar schema and the selectional properties of the verbs *chase*, *put* and *like*. Transformational operations then apply. Taking (2a) as illustrative, the rule *wh* movement relocates the *wh* expression from its d-structure position to a structural position at the beginning of the sentence, which we now identify as the Specifier of CP. Aux inversion moves the modal to the C, as in the derivation of yes–no questions. Following are the d-structure and s-structure trees for the sentence "What will Max chase?" is:

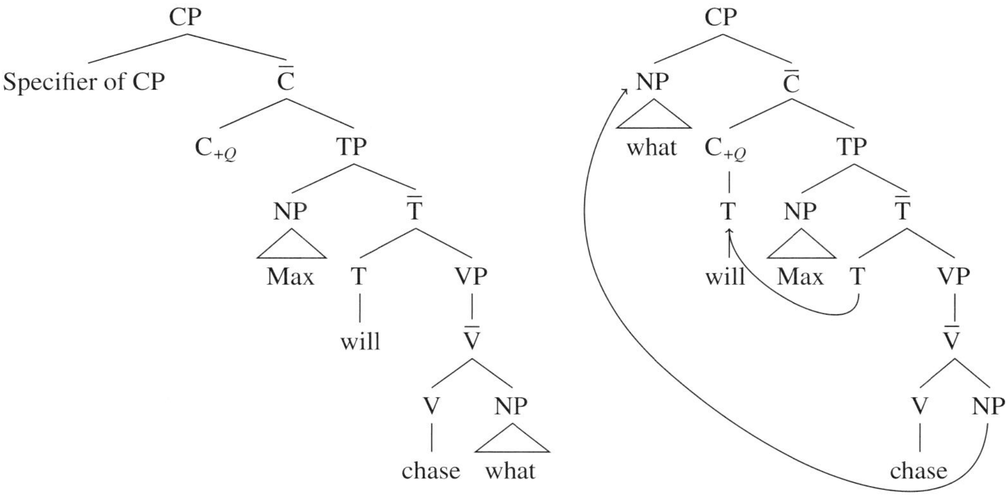


At this point, it is worth observing that like proper names and pronouns, *wh* expressions such as *what* and *who* are full NPs, not Ns. Unlike nouns, *who* and *what* cannot appear with a determiner, an adjective, or any other NP element.

*The what did you see?
*The fast who won the race?

However, *what* can be a determiner, like *which*. This is reflected in the structure for the sentence *Which toys does Pete like?* Following is the d-structure of this sentence:

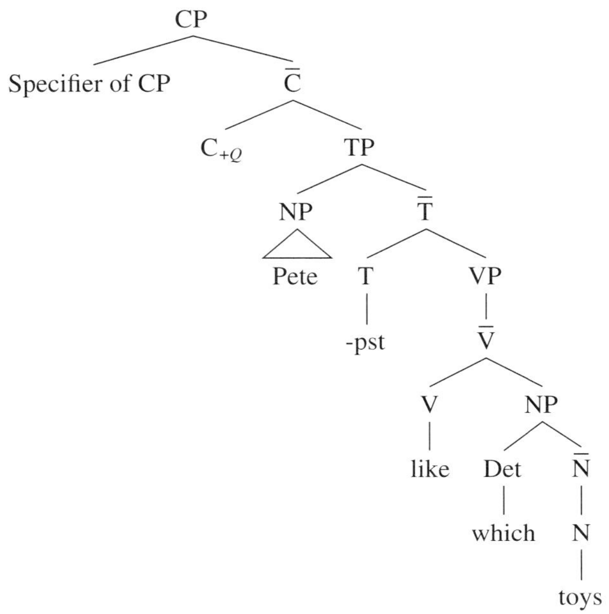


After *wh* movement and Aux Inversion have done their work we have this near s-structure:

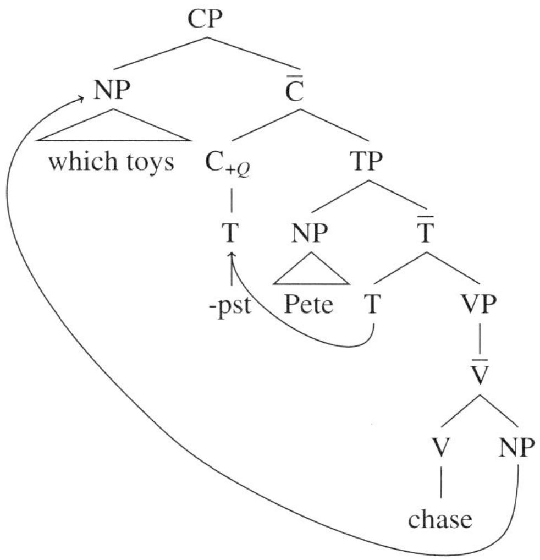


Additionally, when T lacks an actual word and carries only the present tense, as in this sentence, it still undergoes movement because Aux Inversion is *structure dependent* and doesn't pay attention to the particular words (or lack thereof) under a category. With T separated from the main verb by an NP, something is needed to carry the tense. That something is the "dummy" word *do*, and it is put in place by a transformational rule of *do-insertion*, yielding the final s-structure:

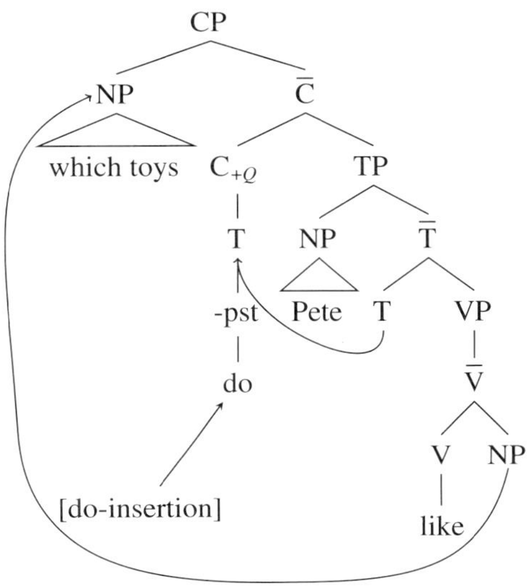


*Do* combines with [-pst] to yield the present tense *does*. Rules that convert inflectional features such as *past tense* or *third-person present tense* into their proper phonological forms are called **spell-out rules**. They apply to the syntactic output of s-structures.

A notable property of *wh* questions is that the *wh* phrase is relocated to a position outside its original d-structure clause. Indeed, there is no limit to the distance that a *wh* phrase can move, as illustrated by the following sentences. The dashes indicate the d-structure position from which the *wh* phrases has been moved.

Who did Helen say the senator wanted to hire _______?
Who did Helen say the senator wanted the congressional representative to try to hire _______?
Who did Helen say the senator wanted the congressional representative to try to convince the Speaker of the House to get the Vice President to hire _______?

"Long-distance" dependencies such as those created by *wh* movement are a fundamental part of human language. They provide still further evidence that sentences are not simply strings of words but are supported by a rich scaffolding of phrase structure trees. These trees express the underlying structure of a sentence as well as its relation to other sentences in the language, and as always reflect a person's knowledge of syntax.

## Summary

Speakers of a language recognize the grammatical sentences of their language and know how the words in a sentence must be ordered and grouped to convey a certain meaning. All speakers are capable of producing and understanding an unlimited number of new sentences that have never before been spoken or heard. They also recognize ambiguities, know when different sentences mean the same thing, and correctly interpret the grammatical relations in a sentence, such as **subject** and **direct object**. This kind of knowledge comes from their knowledge of the rules of syntax.

Sentences have structure that can be represented by **phrase structure trees** containing **syntactic categories**. Phrase structure trees reflect the speaker's mental representation of sentences. Ambiguous sentences may have more than one phrase structure tree.

Phrase structure trees reveal the linear order of words and the constituency of each syntactic category. There are different kinds of syntactic categories: **Phrasal categories**, such as NP and VP, are composed of other syntactic categories; **lexical categories**, such as Noun and Verb, and **functional categories**, such as Det and T, often correspond to individual words. The hierarchical structure of the phrasal categories is universal and is specified by ***X-bar schema***. NPs, VPs, and so on are headed by nouns, verbs, and the like. The sentence (S or TP) is headed by T, which carries such information as tense and modality.

The particular order of elements within the phrase is subject to language-particular variation and can be expressed through the **phrase structure rules** of each language, which conform to the X-bar schema. Here is a composite of all the phrase structure rules given in this chapter renumbered to keep phrasal types together.

1. S (=TP) → NP $\overline{\text{T}}$
2. $\overline{\text{T}}$ → T VP
3. NP → (Det) $\overline{\text{N}}$
4. $\overline{\text{N}}$ → N (XP)
5. $\overline{\text{N}}$ → A $\overline{\text{N}}$
6. VP → (Spec) $\overline{\text{V}}$
7. $\overline{\text{V}}$→V (XP)
8. $\overline{\text{V}}$ → $\overline{\text{V}}$ PP
9. PP → P NP
10. CP → (Spec) $\overline{\text{C}}$
11. $\overline{\text{C}}$ → C TP (=S)
12. AP → A PP
13. $\overline{\text{A}}$ → Int $\overline{\text{A}}$

A grammar is a formally stated, explicit description of the mental grammar or the speaker's linguistic competence. The **lexicon** represents the knowledge that a speaker has about the vocabulary of his or her language. This knowledge includes the syntactic categories of words as well as the **subcategorization** or **C-selection** properties of particular lexical items that specify the complements they can take, for example, whether a verb is **transitive** or **intransitive**. The lexicon also contains semantic information, including the kinds of NPs that can function as semantically coherent subjects and objects: **S-selection**. Selectional restrictions must be satisfied in the **d-structure** representation of the sentence.

**Transformational rules** such as Aux Inversion, Wh Movement, and do-insertion account for relationships between sentences such as declarative and interrogative pairs, including *wh* questions. The output of the transformational rules is the **s-structure** of a sentence, the structure that most closely determines how the sentence is to be pronounced (or signed). Inflectional information, such as tense, may be represented as abstract features in the phrase structure tree. After the rules of the syntax have applied, these features are sometimes spelled out as affixes such as *-ed* or as function words such as *do*.

## References for Further Reading

Baker, M. C. 2001. *The atoms of language: The mind's hidden rules of grammar.* New York: Basic Books.

Carney, A. 2012. *Syntax: A generative introduction, 3rd ed.* Cambridge, MA: Blackwell.

Chomsky, N. 1995. *The minimalist program.* Cambridge, MA: MIT Press.

____. 1972. *Language and mind, rev. ed.* New York: Harcourt Brace Jovanovich.

____. 1965. *Aspects of the theory of syntax.* Cambridge, MA: MIT Press.

Jackendoff, R. S. 1994. *Patterns in the mind: Language and human nature.* New York: Basic Books.

Pinker, S. 1999. *Words and rules: The ingredients of language.* New York: HarperCollins.

Radford, A. 2009. *Analysing English sentences: A minimalist approach.* Cambridge, UK: Cambridge University Press.

____. 2004. *English syntax: An introduction.* Cambridge, UK: Cambridge University Press.

## Exercises

1. Consider the following sentences:
   **a.** I hate war.
   **b.** You know that I hate war.
   **c.** He knows that you know that I hate war.
      **i.** Write another sentence that includes sentence (c).
      **ii.** What does this set of sentences reveal about the nature of language?
      **iii.** How is this characteristic of human language related to the difference between linguistic competence and performance? (Hint: Review these concepts in Chapter 1.)

2. Paraphrase each of the following sentences in two ways to show that you understand the ambiguity involved:

   *Example*: Smoking grass can be nauseating.
      **i.** Putting grass in a pipe and smoking it can make you sick.
      **ii.** Fumes from smoldering grass can make you sick.

   **a.** Dick finally decided on the boat.
   **b.** The professors appointment was shocking.

c. The design has big squares and circles.
d. That sheepdog is too hairy to eat.
e. Could this be the invisible mans hair tonic?
f. The governor is a dirty street fighter.
g. I cannot recommend him too highly.
h. Terry loves his wife and so do I.
i. They said she would go yesterday.
j. No smoking section available.
k. We will dry clean your clothes in 24 hours.
l. I bought cologne for my boyfriend containing 25% alcohol.
m. The new magazine has between one and two billion readers.

3. Here are two examples where structural ambiguities lead to humorous results.

   *For sale: an antique desk suitable for lady with thick legs and large drawers.*

   *We will oil your sewing machine and adjust tension in your home for $10.00.*

   Using square brackets to delineate constituents, explained the ambiguity and the resulting humor of these two sentences by doing a constituent analysis.

4. Following the X-bar schema, draw two phrase structure trees to represent the two meanings of the sentence *The magician touched the child with the wand.* Be sure you indicate which meaning goes with which tree. (Hint: this is similar to an example in the text)

5. Indicate the grammatical category of each of the words in the following sentences.

   a. The girls love sushi.
   b. That boy has won many races.
   c. Mary will finish her homework in the library.
   d. A strong wind uprooted the tall trees.
   e. My dog is exceptionally smart.

6. Consider the phrase structure rule NP $\rightarrow$ (Det) $\overline{\text{N}}$ as given in this chapter to account for NPs such as *dogs* in *dogs bark*. Why would this rule not work for expressions such as *who, he, Mary.*

7. Draw the NP subtrees for the italicized NPs in the following sentences:

   a. *Every mother* hopes for good health.
   b. *A big black dog is* barking.
   c. *Angry men in dark glasses* roamed the streets.
   d. Challenge exercise: *Melissa's garden* is beautiful.

8. In all languages, sentences can occur within sentences. For example, in Exercise 2, sentence (b) contains sentence (a), and sentence (c) contains sentence (b). Put another way, sentence (a) is embedded in sentence (b), and sentence (b) is embedded in sentence (c). Sometimes embedded

sentences appear slightly changed from their normal forms, but you should be able to recognize and underline the embedded sentences in the following examples. Underline in the non-English sentences, when given, not in the translations (the first one is done as an example):

a. Yesterday I noticed <u>my accountant repairing the toilet</u>.
b. Becky said that Jake would play the piano.
c. I deplore the fact that bats have wings.
d. That Guinevere loves Lorian is known to all my friends.
e. Who promised the teacher that Maxine wouldn't be absent?
f. It's ridiculous that he washes his own Rolls-Royce.
g. The woman likes for the waiter to bring water when she sits down.
h. The person who answers this question will win $100.
i. The idea of Romeo marrying a 13-year-old is upsetting.
j. I gave my hat to the nurse who helped me cut my hair.
k. For your children to spend all your royalty payments on recreational drugs is a shame.
l. Give this fork to the person I'm getting the pie for.

9. Adhering to the X-bar schema, draw phrase structure trees for the following sentences.

a. The puppy found the child.
b. A surly passenger insulted the attendant.
c. The house on the hill collapsed in the earthquake.
d. The ice melted.
e. The hot sun melted the ice.
f. The old tree swayed in the wind.
g. The wondrous, beautiful, blue guitar sold for a song.

10. Create three phrase structure trees of 6, 7, 8, 9, and 10 words. Use your mental lexicon to fill in the bottoms of the trees.

11. Using one or more of the constituency tests (i.e., stand alone, move as a unit, replacement by a pronoun) discussed in the chapter, determine which of the boldfaced portions in the sentences are constituents (and which are not). Provide the grammatical category of the constituents.

a. Martha found **a lovely pillow** for the couch.
b. The **light in this room** is terrible.
c. I wonder **whether Bonnie has finished packing her books.**
d. Melissa slept **in her class**.
e. **Pete and Max** are fighting over the bone.
f. I gave a bone to Pete **and to Max** yesterday.
g. I gave a bone to **Pete and** to Max yesterday.

12. The two sentences below contain a **verbal particle** *up*:

He *ran* <u>up</u> the bill.
He *ran* the bill <u>*up*</u>.

**a.** The verbal particle *up* and the verb *run* depend on each other for the unique idiosyncratic meaning of the phrasal verb *run up*. (*Running up a bill* involves neither running nor the location up.) Does *up the bill* form a constituent? Give at least one argument that favors your answer.
**b.** List five other verb+ particle combinations in English.

**13.** In terms of C-selection restrictions, explain why the following are ungrammatical:

**a.** *The man located.
**b.** *Jesus wept the apostles.
**c.** *Robert is hopeful of his children.
**d.** *Robert is fond that his children love animals.
**e.** *The children laughed the man.

**14.** The complement of V may be a single NP direct object as for *find*. English also has **ditransitive verbs**, ones whose complement may be two NPs, such as *give*:

The emperor gave the vassal a castle.
Think of three other ditransitive verbs in English and give example sentences.

**15.** Tamil is a language spoken in India by upward of 70 million people. Following are word-for-word translations of PPs from Tamil to English:

| Tamil to English | Meaning |
|---|---|
| the bed on | "on the bed" |
| the village from | "from the village" |

**a.** Based on these data, is Tamil a head initial or a head final language?
**b.** What would the PS tree for a Tamil PP look like?

**16.** Here are three more word-for-word glosses in Tamil:

| | |
|---|---|
| a story tell | "tell a story" |
| the boy a cow saw | "the boy saw a cow" |
| woman this slept | "this woman slept" |

Do these additional data support or argue against your analysis in Exercise 16? What would the pertinent VP and NP trees look like in Tamil, based on these data?

**17.** Provide the d-structure for each of the following *wh* questions. Then state the grammatical function of the *wh* phrase (e.g., subject, object, etc.)

Example: Who did Mary see?
d-structure: Mary saw who
*Who* is the direct object

**a.** Who left the party early?
**b.** Where did Mary leave her wallet?
**c.** What did you eat for dinner last night?

**d.** Who did Mary write to?
**e.** Which book did Sue read?
**f.** Whose jacket are you wearing?
**g.** Who did Al forget that Betty invited to the party?
**h.** Which bear did Goldilocks say that Mama Bear gave porridge to?
**i.** What did Goldilocks say that Mama Bear gave to Baby Bear?

**18.** As illustrated in the last two examples of the previous question, a *wh* phrase can move a very long distance. But as we saw in the chapter, there are certain instances in which it cannot apply and these constraints are universal and structure dependent. Consider the following sentences and state (in your own words) the constraint that blocks *wh* movement in the ungrammatical examples.

**a.** Paul and John play beautiful music.
**b.** Who plays beautiful music?
**c.** Paul and who (else) play beautiful music?
**d.** *Who do Paul and play beautiful music.
**e.** The children love macaroni and cheese?
**f.** What do the children love?
**g.** What do the children love macaroni with?
**h.** *What do the children love macaroni and?

**19.** There are many systematic, structure-dependent relationships among sentences similar to the one discussed in the chapter between declarative and interrogative sentences. Here are some example sentences based on existential *there* sentences:

**a.** **(i)** A boy is on the roof
**(ii)** There is a boy on the roof.
**b.** **(i)** A boy danced on the roof.
**(ii)** *There danced a boy on the roof.
**c.** **(i)** A boy was dancing on the roof.
**(ii)** There was a boy dancing on the roof.
**d.** **(i)** A wallet was left in the restaurant.
**(ii)** There was a wallet left in the restaurant.
**e.** **(i)** The boy is on the roof.
**(ii)** *There is the boy on the roof.
**f.** **(i)** A man seems to be in the garden.
**(ii)** There seems to be a man in the garden.

Formulate in your own words a transformational rule relating the pairs in (i) and (ii). Be careful that your rule generates the grammatical pairs but not the ungrammatical ones.

**Challenge exercise:**
Now consider the following pair of sentences:

**g.** **(i)** Students must be in the dorm by midnight.
**(ii)** There must be students in the dorm by midnight.

Can you describe the difference in meaning between sentence (i) and (ii)?

Does this meaning difference undermine the transformational analysis of *there* sentences?

**20.** **Challenge exercise**: We noted that it is often not straightforward to distinguish adjuncts from complements. "One-replacement" provides a test: only nouns with adjuncts can be substituted for by *one,* as in *a patient with a broken arm and* one *with a broken leg* (adjunct), but nouns with true complements do not allow one-replacement, so that **a patient of the doctor and one of the chiropractor* is not well-formed. Here are four examples of complements and four of adjuncts. Apply the *one*-replacement test to determine which is which:

**a.** the man with the golden arm
**b.** a voter for proposition eighteen
**c.** my cousin's arrival at his home
**d.** the construction of a retaining wall
**e.** the boat in the river
**f.** the ocean white with foam
**g.** the desecration of the temple
**h.** the betrayal of Julius Caesar

**21.** **Challenge research exercise:** X-bar theory demands binary branching and that a head may have one and only one complement. Ditransitive verbs such as *write* and *give.* (they are numerous) pose problems insofar as fitting into the strict (dare we say "Procrustean") requirements of X-bar. This research project asks you to examine the work that has been done to accommodate the facts of ditransitive verbs with X-bar theory.

4

# The Meaning of Language

For thousands of years, philosophers have pondered the **meaning** of *meaning*, yet speakers of a language can easily understand what is said to them and can produce strings of words that are meaningful to other speakers. We use language to convey information to others *(My new bike is pink)*, ask questions *(Who left the party early?)*, give commands *(Stop lying!)*, and express wishes *(May there be peace on Earth)*.

What do you know about meaning when you know a language? You know when a "word" is meaningful *(flick)* or meaningless *(blick)*, and you know when a "sentence" is meaningful *(Jack swims)* or meaningless *(Colorless green ideas sleep furiously)*. You also know when a word has two meanings *(bear)* and when a sentence has two meanings *(Jack saw a man with a telescope)*. You know when two words have the same meaning *(sofa and couch)*, and when two sentences have the same meaning *(Jack put off the meeting, Jack put the meeting off)*. And you know when words or sentences have opposite meanings *(alive/dead; Jack swims/Jack doesn't swim)*.

You are generally familiar with the real-world objects that words refer to such as *the chair in the corner*; and even if the words do not refer to actual objects, such as *the unicorn behind the bush*, you still have a sense of what they mean.

Importantly, if you know the meaning of a (declarative) sentence, you know its **truth conditions**, or in other words, you know the circumstances under which the sentence is true or false. In some cases, it's obvious, or redundant *(all kings are male* [true], *all bachelors are married* [false]); in other cases, you need some further, nonlinguistic knowledge (*Molybdenum conducts electricity)*, but by knowing the meaning, you know the kind of world knowledge that is needed. Often, if you know that a sentence is true (*Nina bathed her dogs)*, you can infer that another sentence must also be true *(Nina's dogs got wet)*: that is, the first sentence **entails** the second sentence.

Like our syntactic knowledge, knowledge about meaning extends to an unlimited set of sentences, and is part of the grammar of the language. The study of the linguistic meaning of morphemes, words, phrases, and sentences is called **semantics**. Subfields of semantics are **lexical semantics**, which is concerned with the meanings of words and the meaning relationships among words. The study of how context affects meaning—for example, how the sentence *It's cold in here* comes to be interpreted as "close the windows" in certain situations—is called **pragmatics**.

## What Speakers Know about Sentence Meaning

For speakers to understand the meaning of (an infinite number of) sentences requires a system of semantic rules. These rules build the meaning of a sentence from the meanings of its words and its syntactic structure. They allow speakers to determine which conditions need to hold for a sentence to be true or false, when one sentence implies the truth or falseness of another, and whether a sentence has multiple meanings. This is called compositional semantics or **truth-conditional semantics** because it calculates the **truth conditions** of a sentence by composing, or putting together, the meanings of smaller units according to semantic rules. When you know the general truth conditions of a sentence, you can then apply them to any specific situation in which the sentence is used and determine the **truth value** of the sentence, that is, whether it is true or false in that situation.

We will limit our discussion to declarative sentences such as *Jack swims* and *Jack kissed Laura*, because we can specify precisely what the truth conditions are. For example, the sentence *Jack swims* is true if it's uttered in a situation in which the person named Jack can swim or is a habitual swimmer.

### Truth

Suppose you are at the poolside and Jack is swimming in the pool. If you hear the sentence *Jack swims*, and you know the meaning of that sentence, then you will judge the sentence to be true. On the other hand, if you are indoors and you happen to believe that Jack never learned to swim, then when you hear the very same sentence *Jack swims*, you will judge the sentence to be false and you will think the speaker is misinformed or lying. More generally, if you know the meaning of a sentence, then you can determine under what conditions it is true or false. Knowing the meaning tells you how to determine the truth value.

The converse is not true; you don't need to actually know whether a sentence is true or false to know its meaning. Rather, you just need to know (or be able to figure out) the conditions under which it is true or false. The sentence *copper conducts electricity* has meaning and is understood because we know how to determine whether it's true or false: for example, by use of a voltmeter. We could also comment sensibly on the sentence by noting the use of copper wire in lamps. On the other hand, we find the sentence *Crumple-horned snork-acks incarnadine nargles* is meaningless because we don't have the foggiest idea how to determine whether it is true or false.

For most sentences, it does not make sense to say that they are always true or always false. Rather, they are true or false in a given situation, as we previously saw with *Jack swims*. But a restricted number of sentences are indeed always true regardless of the circumstances. They are called **tautologies**. (The term **analytic** is also used for such sentences.) Examples of tautologies are sentences such as *Circles are round* and *A person who is single is not married*. Their truth is guaranteed solely by the meaning of their parts and the way they are put together. Similarly, some sentences are always false. These are called **contradictions**. Examples of contradictions are sentences such as *Circles are square* or *A bachelor is married*.

## Entailment and Related Notions

Much of what we know is deduced from what people say alongside our observations of the world. Sherlock Holmes took deduction to the ultimate degree, as illustrated in the quotation. Often, deductions can be made based on language alone.

If you know that the sentence *Jack swims beautifully* is true, then you also know that the sentence *Jack swims* is true. This meaning relation is called **entailment**. We say that *Jack swims beautifully* entails *Jack swims*. More generally, one sentence entails another if whenever the first sentence is true the second one is also true in all conceivable circumstances.

Generally, entailment goes only in one direction. So, while the sentence *Jack swims beautifully* entails *Jack swims*, the reverse is not true. Knowing merely that *Jack swims* is true does not necessitate the truth of *Jack swims beautifully*. Jack could be a poor swimmer. On the other hand, negating both sentences reverses the entailment. *Jack doesn't swim* entails *Jack doesn't swim beautifully*.

The notion of entailment can be used to reveal knowledge that we have about other meaning relations. For example, omitting tautologies and contradictions, two sentences are **synonymous** (or **paraphrases**) if they are both true or both false with respect to the same situation. Sentences such as *Jack put off the meeting* and *Jack postponed the meeting* are synonymous, because when one is true the other must be true; and when one is false the other must also be false. We can describe this pattern in a more concise way by using the notion of entailment:

Two sentences are synonymous if they entail each other.

Thus, if sentence A entails sentence B and vice versa, then whenever A is true B is true, and vice versa. Although entailment says nothing specifically about false sentences, it's clear that if sentence A entails sentence B, then whenever B is false, A must be false. (If A were true, B would have to be true.) And if B also entails A, then whenever A is false, B would have to be false. Thus, mutual entailment guarantees identical truth values in all situations; the sentences are synonymous. Two sentences are **contradictory** if, whenever one is true, the other is false or, equivalently, there is no situation in which they are both true or both false. For example, the sentences *Jack is alive* and *Jack is dead* are contradictory because if the sentence *Jack is alive* is true, then the sentence *Jack is* *dead* is false, and vice versa. In other words, *Jack is alive and Jack is dead* always have opposite truth values. Like synonymy, contradiction can be defined in terms of entailment.

Two sentences are *contradictory* if one entails the negation of the other. For instance, *Jack is alive* entails the negation of *Jack is dead*, namely *Jack is not dead*. Similarly, *Jack is dead* entails the negation of *Jack is alive*, namely *Jack is not alive*.

The notions of *contradiction* (always false) *and contradictory* (opposite in truth value) are related in that if two sentences are contradictory, their conjunction with *and* is a contradiction. Thus, *Jack is alive and Jack is dead* is a contradiction; it cannot be true under any circumstances.

Describing meaning in terms of truth conditions has proved to be very fruitful in understanding semantic properties of language such as entailment and synonymous or contradictory sentences.

## When Compositionality Goes Awry

The meaning of an expression is not always obvious, even to a native speaker of the language. Meanings may be obscured in many ways, or at least may require some imagination or special knowledge to be apprehended. Poets, pundits, and yes, even professors can be difficult to understand.

It is said that semantic rules compute sentence meaning compositionally based on the meanings of words and the syntactic structure that contains them. There are, however, interesting cases in which compositionality breaks down, either because there is a problem with words or with the semantic rules. If one or more words in a sentence do not have a meaning, then obviously we will not be able to compute a meaning for the entire sentence. Even when the individual words have meaning, if they cannot be combined together as required by the syntax and related semantic rules we will also not get to a meaning. Situations of this sort are referred to as semantic **anomaly**. Sometimes a lot of creativity and imagination are required to derive a meaning. This is what happens in **metaphors**. Finally, some expressions—called **idioms**—have a fixed meaning. Because the meaning of idioms is not given by the meaning of its parts applying compositional rules to them gives rise to funny or inappropriate meanings.

### Anomaly

The semantic properties of words determine what other words they can be combined with. A sentence widely used by linguists that we encountered in Chapter 2 illustrates this fact:

Colorless green ideas sleep furiously.

The sentence obeys all the syntactic rules of English. The subject is *colorless green ideas* and the predicate is *sleep furiously*. It has the same syntactic structure as the sentence

Dark green leaves rustle furiously.

but there is obviously something semantically wrong with the sentence. The meaning of *colorless* includes the semantic feature "without color," but it is combined with the adjective *green*, which has the feature "green in color." How can something be both "without color" and "green in color"? Other semantic violations occur in the sentence. Such sentences are semantically **anomalous**.

Other "sentences" make no sense at all because they include "words" that have no meaning; they are **uninterpretable**. They can be interpreted only if some meaning for each nonsense word can be dreamt up. Lewis Carroll's "Jabberwocky" is probably the most famous poem in which most of the content words have no meaning—they do not exist in the lexicon of the language. Still, all the sentences sound as if they should be or could be English sentences:

'Twas brillig, and the slithy toves
Did gyre and gimble in the wabe;
All mimsy were the borogoves,
And the mome raths outgrabe.

. . .

He took his vorpal sword in hand:
Long time the manxome foe he sought—
So rested he by the Tumtum tree,
And stood awhile in thought.

Without knowing what *vorpal* means, you nevertheless know that

He took his vorpal sword in hand means

the same thing as

He took his sword, which was vorpal, in hand

and

It was in his hand that he took his vorpal sword.

Knowing the language, and assuming that *vorpal* means the same thing in the three sentences (because the same sounds are used), you can decide that the sense—the truth conditions—of the three sentences are identical. In other words, you are able to decide that two sentences mean the same thing even though you do not know what either one means. You decide by assuming that the semantic properties of *vorpal* are the same whenever it is used.

We now see why Alice commented, when she had read "Jabberwocky": "It seems very pretty, but it's *rather* hard to understand!" (You see she didn't like to confess, even to herself, that she couldn't make it out at all.) "Somehow it seems to fill my head with ideas—only I don't exactly know what they are! However, *somebody* killed *something*: that's clear, at any rate—"

Semantic violations in poetry may form strange but interesting esthetic images, as in Dylan Thomas's phrase *a grief ago*. *Ago* is ordinarily used with words specified by some temporal semantic feature:

| | | |
|---|---|---|
| a week ago | | *a table ago |
| an hour ago | but not | *a dream ago |
| a month ago | | *a mother ago |
| a century ago | | |

When Thomas used the word *grief* with *ago*, he added a durational feature to grief for poetic effect, so while the noun phrase is anomalous, it evokes certain emotions.

In the poetry of E. E. Cummings, there are phrases such as

the six subjunctive crumbs twitch
a man . . . wearing a round jeer for a hat
children building this rainman out of snow[1]

Though all of these phrases violate semantic rules, we can understand them; breaking the rules creates the desired imagery. That we are able to assign some meaning to such expressions, and at the same time recognize that they are anomalous, demonstrates our knowledge of the semantic system, just as the recognition of ungrammatical sentences shows our knowledge of the rules of syntax.

## Metaphor

When what appears to be an anomaly is nevertheless understood in terms of a meaningful concept, the expression becomes a metaphor. There is no strict line between anomalous and metaphorical expressions. Technically, metaphors are anomalous, but the nature of the anomaly creates the salient meanings that metaphors usually have. The anomalous *A grief ago* might come to be interpreted by speakers of English as "the unhappy time following a sad event" and therefore become a metaphor.

Metaphors may have a literal meaning as well as their metaphorical meaning, so in some sense they are ambiguous. However, when the semantic rules are applied to an expression such as *Walls have ears*, the literal meaning is so unlikely that listeners use their imagination for another interpretation. The principle of compositionality is very "elastic" and when it fails to produce an acceptable literal meaning, listeners try to accommodate and stretch the meaning. This accommodation is based on semantic properties that are inferred or that provide some kind of resemblance or comparison that can end up as a meaningful concept.

To interpret a metaphor, we need to understand the individual words, the literal meaning of the whole expression, and facts about the world. To understand the metaphor

Time is money

it is necessary to know that in our society we are often paid according to the number of hours or days worked. In fact, "time," which is an abstract concept, is the subject of multiple metaphors. We "save time," "waste time," "manage time," push things "back in time," live on "borrowed time," and suffer the "ravages of time" as the "sands of time" drift away. In effect, the metaphors take the abstract concept of time and treat it as a concrete object of value.

Metaphor has a strong cultural component. Shakespeare used metaphors that are lost on many of today's playgoers. "I am a man whom Fortune hath cruelly scratched," is most effective as a metaphor in a society like Shakespeare's that commonly depicts "Fortune" as a woman. On the other hand, *There's a bug in my program* would make little sense in a culture without computers, even if the idea of having bugs in something indicates a problem.

Many expressions now taken literally may have originated as metaphors, such as "the fall of the dollar," meaning its decline in value on the world market. Many people wouldn't bat an eyelash (another metaphor) at the literal interpretation of saving or wasting time. Metaphorical use of language is language creativity at its highest. Nevertheless, the basis of metaphorical use is very much the ordinary linguistic knowledge that all speakers possess about words, their semantic properties, and their combinatorial possibilities.

## Idioms

Because the words (or morphemes) of a language are arbitrary (not predictable by rule), they must be listed in a mental lexicon. The lexicon is a repository of the words (or morphemes) of a language with their grammatical properties and their meanings. On the other hand, the meanings of morphologically complex words, phrases, and sentences are compositional and are derived by rules. We noted in Chapter 2 that the meaning of some words (e.g., compounds) is not entirely predictable, so these must also be given in the lexicon. It turns out that languages also contain many phrases whose meanings are not predictable on the basis of the meanings of the individual words. These phrases typically start out as metaphors that "catch on" and are repeated so often that they become fixtures in the language. Such expressions are called *idioms*, or **idiomatic phrases**, as in these English examples:

sell down the river
rake over the coals
drop the ball
let their hair down
put his foot in his mouth
throw her weight around
snap out of it
give a piece of your mind
bring a knife to a gunfight

The usual semantic rules for combining meanings do not apply in these cases. Idioms act very much like individual morphemes in that they are not decomposable, but have a fixed meaning that must be learned. Idioms are similar in structure to ordinary phrases except that they tend to be frozen in form and hence do not readily undergo rules that change word order or substitution of their parts.

The sentence in (1) has the same structure as the sentence in (2).

1. She put her foot in her mouth.
2. She put her bracelet in her drawer.

But while (2) is clearly related to the sentences in (3) and (4),

3. The drawer in which she put her bracelet was her own.
4. Her bracelet was put in her drawer.

the idiomatic sense of sentence (1) is lost in sentence (5) and (6), except, perhaps, humorously.

5. The mouth in which she put her foot was her own.
6. Her foot was put in her mouth.

In addition, if we know the meaning of (2) and the meaning of the word *necklace* we will immediately understand (7).

7. She put her necklace in the drawer.

But if we try substituting *hand* for *foot* in sentence (1), we lose the idiomatic meaning, and derive a literal compositional meaning.

There are exceptions: some idioms allow their parts to be moved without losing their idiomatic sense:

The FBI kept tabs on radicals.
Tabs were kept on radicals by the FBI.
Radicals were kept tabs on by the FBI.

Like metaphors, idioms can break the rules on combining semantic properties. The object of *eat* must usually be something with the semantic feature "edible," but in

He ate his hat.

and

Eat your heart out.

this restriction is violated.

Idioms often lead to humor:

What did the doctor tell the vegetarian about his surgically implanted heart valve from a pig?
That it was okay as long as he didn't "eat his heart out."

Idioms may even show disrespect for syntax, for example, the expression *deep six*, while containing parts that are never used as verbs, is itself a verb meaning "to put the kibosh on," yet another idiom.

With some imagination, idioms may also be used to create what appears to be a **paradox**, a situation to which it is impossible to ascribe a truth value. Consider the idiom "drop the ball" meaning to blunder. In many places such as Times Square in New York, a ball is dropped at midnight on New Year's Eve. Now, if the person in charge doesn't drop the ball, then he or she has "dropped the ball." And if that person does indeed drop the ball, then he or she has not "dropped the ball." Neither can be true nor false, right?

Because of their special semantic and syntactic properties idioms must be listed in the mental lexicon as single items with their meanings specified, and speakers must learn the special restrictions on their use.

Although all languages have idioms, they rarely if ever translate word for word from one language to another. Most speakers of American English understand the idiom *to kick the bucket* as meaning "to die." The same combination of words in Spanish (*patear el cubo*) has only the literal meaning of striking a specific bucket with a foot. On the other hand, *estirar la pata*, literally "to stretch the (animal) leg," has the idiomatic sense of "to die" in Spanish.

## Lexical Semantics (Word Meanings)

As just discussed, the meaning of a phrase or sentence is partially a function of the meanings of the words it contains. Similarly, the meaning of a morphologically complex word is a function of its component morphemes, as we saw in Chapter 2. However, there is a fundamental difference between word meaning—or *lexical semantics*—and sentence meaning. The meaning of most sentences is constructed by the application of semantic rules. The meaning of words (morphemes and idioms), on the other hand, is conventional; that is, speakers of a language implicitly agree on their meaning, and children acquiring the language must simply learn those meanings outright.

Although the agreed-upon meaning of a word may shift over time within a language community, we are not free as individuals to change the meanings of words at will; if we did, we would be unable to communicate with each other. Humpty Dumpty seems unwilling to accept this convention, though fortunately for us there are few such bad eggs among speakers. All the speakers of a language share a basic vocabulary—the sounds and meanings of thousands of morphemes and words. This linguistic knowledge permits us to use words to express our thoughts and to understand the thoughts of others. These meanings are stored in our mental lexicons.

## Theories of Word Meaning

Dictionaries are filled with words and give their meanings using other words rather than in terms of some more basic units of meaning, whatever they might be. In this sense, a dictionary really provides *paraphrases* rather than meanings. It relies on our *knowledge* of the language to understand the definitions. The meanings associated with words in our mental lexicon are not

*"There's nothing here under 'Superman'—is it possible you made the reservation under another name?"*

Michael Maslin / The New Yorker Collection/Cartoonbank.com

like what we find in a conventional dictionary, although it is a challenge to linguists to specify precisely how word meanings are represented in the mind.

## Reference

If the meaning of a word is not like a dictionary entry, what is it? This question has been debated by philosophers and linguists for centuries. One proposal is that the meaning of a word or expression is its **reference**, its association with the object it refers to. This real-world object is called the *referent*.

We have already determined that the meaning of a proper name like *Jack* is its reference: the link between the word *Jack* and the person named Jack, which is its referent. Proper names are noun phrases (NPs); you can substitute a proper name in any NP position in a sentence and preserve grammaticality. There are other NPs that refer to individuals as well. For instance, NPs such as *the happy swimmer, my friend*, and *that guy* can all be used to refer to Jack in the situation in which you've observed Jack swimming. The same is true for pronouns such as *I, you*, and *him*, which also function as NPs. In all these cases, the reference of the NP—which singles out the individual referred to under the circumstances—is part of the meaning of the NP.

On the other hand, not every NP refers to an individual. For instance, the sentence *No baby swims* contains the NP *no baby*, but your linguistic knowledge tells you that this NP does not refer to any specific individual. If *no baby* has no reference, but is not meaningless, there must be more to the meaning of NPs than reference alone.

In the fictional world of *Superman* and *Clark Kent*, they have the same reference—they are one and the same person. But there is more meaning to their names than that. If we substitute *Clark Kent* for *Superman* in the sentence *Lois Lane is in love with Superman* we alter its truth value from true to false. Again, we see that there must be a dimension of meaning beyond mere reference.

Similarly, *Barack Obama* and *the President* have (at this writing) the same reference, but the meaning of the NP *the President* is additionally "the head of state of the United States of America," which is an element of meaning separate from reference and more enduring.

## Sense

There must be something more to meaning than reference alone. This is also suggested by the fact that speakers know the meanings of many words that have no real-world referents (e.g., *hobbits, unicorns*, and *Harry Potter*). Similarly, what real-world entities would function words such as *of* and *by*, or modal verbs such as *will* or *may* refer to?

These additional elements of meaning are often termed **sense**. It is the extra something referred to earlier. *Unicorns, hobbits*, and *Harry Potter* have sense but no reference (with regard to objects in the real world). Conversely, proper names typically have only reference. A name such as *Clem Kadiddlehopper* may point out a certain person, its referent, but has little linguistic meaning beyond that.

Philosophers of language dating back to ancient Greece have suggested that part of the meaning of a word is the mental image it conjures up. This helps with the problem of unicorns, hobbits, and Harry Potter; we may have a clear image of these entities from books, movies, and so on, and that connection might serve as reference for those expressions. However, many meaningful expressions are not associated with any clear, unique image agreed on by most speakers of the language. For example, what image is evoked by the words *very*, *if*, and *every*? It's difficult to say, yet these expressions are certainly meaningful. What is the image of oxygen as distinct from nitrogen—both are colorless, odorless gases, yet they differ in meaning. What mental image would we have of *dog* that is general enough to include Yorkshire Terriers and Great Danes and yet excludes foxes and wolves? And the image of *no man* in *no man is an island* presents a riddle worthy of a Zen koan.

Although the idea that the meaning of a word corresponds to a mental image is intuitive (because many words do provoke imagery), it is clearly inadequate as a general explanation of what people know about word meanings.

Perhaps the best we can do is to note that the reference part of a word's meaning, if it has reference at all, is the association with its referent; and the sense part of a word's meaning contains the information needed to complete the association, and to suggest properties that the referent may have, whether it exists in the real world or in the world of imagination.

## Lexical Relations

Although we do not have a complete theory of word meaning, we know that speakers have considerable knowledge about the meaning relationships among different words in their mental lexicons, and any theory must account for that knowledge. Words are semantically related to one another in a variety of ways. Words that describe these relations often contain the bound morpheme *-nym*. The best-known lexical relation is synonymy, illustrated in the poem by Edward Lear, and antonymy, or opposites. Synonyms are words or expressions that have the same meaning in some or all contexts. There are dictionaries of synonyms that contain many hundreds of entries, such as:

apathetic/phlegmatic/passive/sluggish/indifferent
pedigree/ancestry/genealogy/descent/lineage

A sign in the San Diego Zoo Wild Animal Park states:

Please do not annoy, torment, pester, plague, molest, worry, badger, harry, harass, heckle, persecute, irk, bullyrag, vex, disquiet, grate, beset, bother, tease, nettle, tantalize, or ruffle the animals.

It has been said that there are no perfect synonyms—that is, no two words ever have *exactly* the same meaning. Still, the following two sentences have very similar meanings:

He's sitting on the sofa./He's sitting on the couch.

During the French Norman occupation of England that began in 1066 CE, many French words of Latin origin were imported into English. For this reason, English contains many synonymous pairs consisting of a word with an English (or Germanic) root, and another with a Latin root, such as:

| **English** | **Latin** |
|---|---|
| manly | virile |
| heal | recuperate |
| send | transmit |
| go down | descend |

Words that are opposite in meaning are **antonyms**. There are several kinds of antonymy. There are **complementary pairs**:

alive/dead    present/absent    awake/asleep

They are complementary in that *alive* = *not dead* and *dead* = *not alive*, and so on.

There are **gradable pairs** of antonyms:

big/small    hot/cold    fast/slow    happy/sad

The meaning of adjectives in gradable pairs is related to the objects they modify. The words do not provide an absolute scale. For example, we know that "a small elephant" is much bigger than "a large mouse." *Fast* is faster when applied to an airplane than to a car.

Another kind of opposition involves pairs such as

give/receive    buy/sell    teacher/pupil

They are called **relational opposites**, and they display symmetry in their meanings. If X *gives* Y to Z, then Z *receives* Y from X. If X is Y's *teacher*, then Y is X's *pupil*. Pairs of words ending in *-er* and *-ee* are usually relational opposites. If Mary is Bill's *employer*, then Bill is Mary's *employee*.

Other lexical relations include homonyms, polysemy, and hyponyms. Words like *bear* and *bare* are **homonyms** (also called **homophones**). Homonyms are words that are pronounced the same but have different meanings. Near nonsense sentences such as *Entre nous, the new gnu knew nu is a Greek letter* tease us with homonyms. Homonyms easily lead to ambiguity, as the confused goat in the cartoon confirms.

stephan Pastis (cartoonist)/Gocomics.com

When a word has multiple meanings that are related conceptually or historically, it is said to be **polysemous**. For example, the word *diamond* referring to a jewel and also to a baseball field is polysemous. Speakers of English know that the words *red*, *white*, and *blue* are color words. Similarly, *lion*, *tiger*, *leopard*, and *lynx* are all felines. *Hyponymy* is the relationship between the more general term such as *color* and the more specific instances of it, such as *red*. Thus, *red* is a hyponym of *color*, and *lion* is a hyponym of *feline*; or equivalently, *color* has the hyponym *red* and *feline* has the hyponym *lion*.

## Semantic Features

In Chapter 2, we observed that many words can be decomposed into morphemes, the most basic units of meaning. But, it is possible to find a more basic set of **semantic features** or properties that comprise some of the meaning of a word or morpheme and that clarify how certain words relate to other words. For example, two words can be antonyms only if they share a principal semantic feature in which they differ. The antonyms *wet* and *dry* share, but differ in, the feature "liquid." Similarly, *buy/sell* are relational opposites because both contain a semantic feature such as "change in possession," and differ only in the direction of the change. On the other hand, *big* and *red* are not antonyms because the principal feature of one is "size" and of the other "color."

Semantic features are among the conceptual elements that contribute to the meanings of words and sentences. Consider the sentence:

The assassin killed Thwacklehurst.

If the word *assassin* is in your mental dictionary, you know that it was some *person* who murdered some *important person* named Thwacklehurst. Your knowledge of the meaning of *assassin* tells you that an animal did not do the killing, and that Thwacklehurst was not an average citizen. Knowledge of *assassin* includes knowing that the individual to whom that word refers is human, is a murderer, and is a killer of important people. These bits of information are among the semantic features of the word that speakers agree on. The meaning of all nouns, verbs, adjectives, and adverbs—the content words—and even of some of the function words, such as *with* and *over*, can at least partially be specified by such features.

### Evidence for Semantic Features

Semantic features are not directly observable. Their existence must be inferred from linguistic evidence. Speech errors, or "slips of the tongue," provide one such source of evidence. The following are some unintentional word substitutions actually produced by speakers:

| Intended Utterance | Actual Utterance (Error) |
|---|---|
| bridge of the nose | bridge of the neck |
| when my gums bled | when my tongues bled |
| he came too late | he came too early |
| Mary was young | Mary was early |
| the lady with the Dachshund | the lady with the Volkswagen |
| that's a horse of another color | that's a horse of another race |

| | |
|---|---|
| his ancestors were farmers | his descendants were farmers |
| he has to pay her alimony | he has to pay her rent |

These errors, and thousands of others that have been collected and catalogued, reveal that the incorrectly substituted words are not random but share some semantic features with the intended words. *Nose, neck, gums,* and *tongues* are all "body parts" or "parts of the head." *Young, early,* and *late* are related to "time." *Dachshund* and *Volkswagen* are both "German" and "small." The shared semantic features of *color* and *race, ancestor* and *descendant,* and *alimony* and *rent* are apparent.

The semantic features that describe the linguistic meaning of a word should not be confused with other nonlinguistic properties, such as physical properties. Scientists know that water is composed of hydrogen and oxygen, but such knowledge is not part of a word's meaning. We know that water is an essential ingredient of lemonade and baths. However, we don't need to know any of these things to know what the word *water* means, and to be able to use and understand it in a sentence.

## Semantic Features and Grammar

King Features Syndicate

Further evidence that words are composed of smaller bits of meaning is that semantic features interact with different aspects of the grammar such as morphology or syntax. These effects show up in both nouns and verbs.

### Semantic Features of Nouns

Semantic features can be morphologically marked. In English, the feature "female" is sometimes indicated by the suffix *–ess*:

| | | |
|---|---|---|
| tigress | waitress | goddess |
| actress | princess | adulteress |
| poetess | hostess | baroness |

In some languages, though not English, nouns occur with **classifiers**, grammatical morphemes that indicate the semantic class of the noun. In Swahili, a noun that has the semantic feature "human" is prefixed with *m-* if singular and *wa-* if plural, as in *mtoto* (child) and *watoto* (children). A noun that has the feature "human artifact," such as *bed*, *chair*, or *knife*, is prefixed with the classifiers *ki-* if singular as in *kiti* (chair) and *vi-* if plural as in *viti* (chairs).

Semantic features may have syntactic and semantic effects, too. In English and many (though not all) languages, the kinds of determiners that a noun may occur with are controlled by whether it is a "count" noun or a "mass" noun. Consider these data:

| | |
|---|---|
| I have two dogs. | *I have two rice(s). |
| I have a dog. | *I have a rice. |
| *I have dog. | I have rice. |
| He has many dogs. | *He has many rice(s). |
| *He has much dogs. | He has much rice. |

**Count nouns** can be enumerated and pluralized—*one potato, two potatoes*. They may be preceded by the indefinite determiner *a*, and by the quantifier *many* as in *many potatoes*, but not by *much: *much potato*. They must also occur with a determiner of some kind. Nouns such as *rice*, *water*, and *milk*, which cannot be enumerated or pluralized, are **mass nouns**. They cannot be preceded by *a* or *many*, and they can occur with the quantifier *much* or without any determiner at all. The humor of the cartoon is based both on the ambiguity of *toast* and the fact that as a food *French toast* is a mass noun, but as an oration it is a count noun. The count/mass distinction captures the fact that speakers know the properties that govern which determiner types go with different nouns. Without it, we could not describe these differences.

Generally, the count/mass distinction corresponds to the difference between discrete objects and homogeneous substances. But it would be incorrect to say that this distinction is grounded in human perception because different languages may treat the same object differently. For example, in English, the words *hair, furniture,* and *spaghetti* are mass nouns. We say *Some hair is curly, Much furniture is poorly made, John loves spaghetti.* In Italian, however, these words are count nouns, as illustrated in the following sentences:

Ivano ha mangiato molti spaghetti ieri sera.
"Ivano ate many spaghettis last evening"
Piero ha comprato un mobile nuovo.
"Piero bought a new (piece of) furniture."
Luisella ha pettinato i suoi capelli.
"Luisella combed her hairs."

We would have to assume a radical form of linguistic determinism (remember the Sapir–Whorf hypothesis from Chapter 1) to say that Italian and English speakers have different perceptions of hair, furniture, and spaghetti. It is more reasonable to assume that languages can differ to some extent in the semantic or syntactic features they assign to words with the same referent, somewhat independently of the way their speakers conceptualize that referent. Even within a particular language, we can have different words—count and mass—to describe the same object or substance. For example, in English, we have *shoes* (count) and *footwear* (mass), *coins* (count), and *change* (mass).

## Semantic Features of Verbs

Verbs also have semantic features as part of their meaning. For example, "cause" is a feature of verbs such as *darken, kill, and uglify*.

| | |
|---|---|
| *darken* | cause to become dark |
| *kill* | cause to die |
| *uglify* | cause to become ugly |

"Go" is a feature of verbs that mean a change in location or possession, such as *swim, crawl, throw, fly, give*, or *buy*:

Jack swims.
The baby crawled under the table.
The boy threw the ball over the fence.
John gave Mary a beautiful engagement ring.

Words such as *swim* have an additional feature such as "in liquid," while *crawl* has "close to a surface."

"Become" is a feature expressing the end state of the action of certain verbs. For example, the verb *break* can be broken down into the following components of meaning: "cause" to "become" broken.

Semantic features of verbs, like features of nouns, may have syntactic consequences. For example, verbs can either describe **events**, such as *John kissed Mary/John ate oysters,* or **states**, such as *John knows Mary/John likes oysters.* The eventive/ stative difference is mirrored in the syntax. Eventive sentences still sound natural when passivized, when expressed progressively, when used as imperatives, and with certain adverbs:

**Eventives**

| | |
|---|---|
| Mary was kissed by John. | Oysters were eaten by John. |
| John is kissing Mary. | John is eating oysters. |
| Kiss Mary! | Eat oysters! |
| John deliberately kissed Mary. | John deliberately ate oysters. |

But stative sentences seem peculiar, if not ungrammatical or anomalous, when cast in the same form. (The preceding "?" indicates the strangeness.)

**Statives**

| | |
|---|---|
| ?Mary is known by John. | ?Oysters are liked by John. |
| ?John is knowing Mary. | ?John is liking oysters. |
| ?Know Mary! | ?Like oysters! |
| ?John deliberately knows Mary. | ?John deliberately likes oysters. |

Negation is a particularly interesting component of the meaning of some verbs. Expressions such as *ever, anymore, have a red cent,* are ungrammatical in certain simple affirmative sentences, but grammatical in corresponding negative ones.

*Mary will ever smile. (Cf. Mary will not ever smile.)
*I can visit you anymore. (Cf. I cannot visit you anymore.)
*It's worth a red cent. (Cf. It's not worth a red cent.)

Such expressions are called **negative polarity items** because they require a negative element such as "not" elsewhere in the sentence. Consider these data:

> *John thinks that he'll ever fly a plane again.
> *John hopes to ever fly a plane again.
> John doubts that he'll ever fly a plane again.
> John refuses to ever fly a plane again.

This suggests that verbs such as *doubt* and *refuse*, but not *think* and *hope*, have "negative" as a component of their meaning. *Doubt* may be analyzed as "think that not," and *refuse* as "intend not to." The negative feature in the verb provides the required support for the negative polarity item *ever* even without the overt presence of *not*.

Even rather subtle differences in a verb's semantic features can affect the syntactic operations that apply to sentences. For example, the verbs in (1) can take two objects—they're **ditransitive verbs**. Moreover, the arguments can be rearranged as it (2).

1. John threw/tossed/kicked/flung the ball to the boy.
2. John threw/tossed/kicked/flung the boy the ball.
3. John pushed/pulled/lifted/hauled the ball to the boy.
4. *John pushed/pulled/lifted/hauled the boy the ball.

The verbs in (3) are also ditransitive. However, these verbs do not allow the rearrangement of their arguments, as indicated by the ungrammatical examples in (4). Though the verbs in (1) and (3) are all verbs of motion, they differ in how the force of the motion is applied: the verbs in (1) involve a single quick motion whereas those in (3) involve a prolonged use of force. This semantic difference gives rise to different word order possibilities.

Similarly, the verbs in (5) and (7) are verbs of communication, but their meanings differ in the way the message is communicated; those in (5) involve an external apparatus whereas those in (7) involve the type of voice used. The verbs in (5) allow their arguments to be rearranged, as in (6), while the verbs in (7) do not.

5. Mary faxed/radioed/e-mailed/phoned the news to Helen.
6. Mary faxed/radioed/e-mailed/phoned Helen the news.
7. Mary murmured/mumbled/muttered/shrieked the news to Helen.
8. *Mary murmured/mumbled/muttered/shrieked Helen the news.

The verbs in (1)–(8) all have the feature "transfer." The to-be-transferred argument is the direct object, while the recipient of the transfer is the indirect object. In (1) the ball is transferred to the boy. In (5) the news is transferred, or leastwise transmitted, to Helen. Even when the transference is not overt, it may be inferred. In *John baked Mary a cake,* there is an implied transfer of the cake from John to Mary. A subtle difference in the manner of transfer affect the syntax of these verbs, and indeed, this connection between form and meaning may help children acquire the syntactic and semantic rules of their language.

## Argument Structure and Thematic roles

Verbs also differ in terms of the number and type of phrases they can take as complements. As we noted in Chapter 3, transitive verbs such as *find, hit,* and *chase* are subcategorized for (c-select) a direct object, whereas intransitive verbs such as *arrive* or *sleep* are not. Ditransitive verbs such as *give* or *throw* take two objects, as in *John threw Mary a ball.* In addition, most verbs take a subject.

The various NPs that occur with a verb are its **arguments**. Thus, intransitive verbs have one argument: the subject; transitive verbs have two arguments: the subject and direct object; ditransitive verbs have three arguments: the subject, direct object, and indirect object. The **argument structure** of a verb is part of its meaning and is included in its lexical entry.

The verb not only determines the number of arguments in a sentence, but it also determines the **thematic roles** of its arguments. Thematic roles express the kind of semantic relation that holds between the arguments of the verb and the type of situation that the verb describes. For example, in the following sentence the NP *the boy*

1. The boy rolled a red ball.
   agent theme

is the "doer" of the rolling action, also called the **agent**. The NP *a red ball* is the **theme** or the "undergoer" of the rolling action. Relations such as agent and theme are thematic roles.

A further example is the sentence:

2. The boy threw the red ball to the girl.
   agent theme goal

Here, *the girl* bears the thematic role of **goal**, that is, the endpoint of a change in location or possession. The verb phrase is interpreted to mean that the theme of *throw* ends up in the position of the *goal.*

Other thematic roles are **source**, where the action originates; **instrument**, the means used to accomplish the action; and **experiencer**, one receiving sensory input:

3. Professor Snape awakened Harry Potter with his wand.
   source experiencer instrument

The particular thematic roles assigned by a verb can be traced back to components of the verb's meaning. Verbs such as *throw, buy,* and *fly* contain a feature "go" expressing a change in location or possession. The feature "go" is thus linked to the presence of the thematic roles of theme, source, and goal. Verbs such as *awaken* or *frighten* have a feature "affects mental state" so that one of its arguments takes on the thematic role of experiencer.

Thematic role assignment, or **theta assignment**, is also connected to syntactic structure. In the sentence in (2), the role of theme is assigned to the direct object *the red ball* and the role of goal to the indirect object *the girl.* Verb pairs such as *sell* and *buy* as in the sentences in (4) and (5) both involve the feature "go." They are therefore linked to a thematic role of theme, which is assigned to the direct object:

**4.** John sold the book to Mary.

agent theme goal

**5.** Mary bought the book from John.

agent theme source

In addition, *sell* is linked to the presence of a goal (the recipient or endpoint of the transfer), and *buy* to the presence of a source (the initiator of the transfer). Thus, *buy/sell* are relational opposites because both contain the semantic feature "go" (the transfer of goods or services) and they differ only in the direction of transfer, that is, whether the indirect object is a source or goal. Thematic roles are not assigned to arguments randomly. There is a connection between the meaning of a verb and the syntactic structure of sentences containing the verb.

Our knowledge of verbs includes their syntactic category, which arguments they select, and the thematic roles they assign to their arguments. The thematic roles assigned by a particular verb to its arguments are constant even though the arguments may show up in different s-structure positions:

**6.** The dog bit the stick./The stick was bitten by the dog.
**7.** The trainer gave the dog a treat./The trainer gave a treat to the dog.

In both sentences in (6), *the dog* is the agent and *the stick* is the theme. Similarly in (7), *the treat* is the theme and *the dog* is the goal. This is because thematic roles are always assigned to the same d-structure position: for example, theme is assigned to the object of *bit/bitten*. The arguments then carry their theta roles with them when they move to a different s-structure position owing to syntactic rules. Our linguistic intuition that the two sentences in (6) and the two sentences in (7) are related to each other is due to the fact that *the stick* in the passive sentence *the stick was bitten by the dog* originated in object position in d-structure and moved to subject position in s-structure by a syntactic rule:

**8.** ___ was bitten the stick by the dog → the stick was bitten ___ by the dog

d-structure s-structure

Thus, the sentence pairs in (6) and (7) express the same semantic relationships between the verb and its arguments.

Even in cases in which not all the arguments of a verb are expressed, the theta roles for the realized NPs are constant, as the following examples illustrate:

**9.** The boy opened the door with the key.
**10.** The key opened the door.
**11.** The door opened.

In all three of these sentences, *the door* is the theme, the object that is opened. Thus, *the door* in (11) originates as the object of *open* in d-structure and undergoes a movement rule, much like in the passive example above.

___ opened the door → The door opened ___

Although the sentences in (9)–(11) are not strict paraphrases of one another, they are structurally and semantically related in that they have similar d-structure configurations. Indeed, sentence (9) entails (10) and (11), and (10) entails (11).

In the sentences in (9) and (10), *the key*, despite its different s-structure positions, has the thematic role of instrument, suggesting that these sentences also have a similar d-structure configuration. The semantics of the three sentences is determined by the meaning of the verb *open* and the rules that determine how thematic roles are assigned to the verb's NP arguments.

# Pragmatics

We've just discussed lexical semantics (the literal meanings of words) and compositional semantics (the literal meaning of sentences). We described the latter in terms of truth conditions. The idea is that you know what a sentence means if you know what the world would have to look like in order for that sentence to be true.

Literal meaning isn't the only sort of meaning we use when we use language to communicate with others. Some meaning is **extra-truth-conditional**: It comes about as a result of how a speaker uses the literal meaning in conversation, or as a part of a **discourse**. The study of extra-truth-conditional meaning is pragmatics.

Just as artists depict scenes with representations that aren't 100 percent explicit, like the sketch on page 159, language users describe states of affairs with sentences that aren't 100 percent explicit. And just as there are a number of reasons an artist might choose a sketch or an abstract painting to depict a scene (instead of a photograph), there are a number of reasons a speaker might choose a particular sentence or discourse to describe a state of affairs. In what follows, we'll discuss different ways in which speakers can convey meaning without expressing it literally.

## Pronouns and Other Deictic Words

One way in which context can supplement a less-than-explicit sentence meaning is through words that receive part of their meaning via context and the orientation of the speaker. Such words are referred to as **deictic** and include pronouns (*she, it, I*), demonstratives (*this, that*), adverbs (*here, there, now, today*), prepositions (*behind, before*) and complex expressions involving such words (*those towers over there*).

Imagine the sets of sentences in (1) and (2) being spoken by Taylor Swift in Venice on September 16, 2016.

1. Taylor Swift really likes it in Venice, Italy. On September 16, 2016, there was a boat parade in the canals in Venice, Italy. On September 17, 2016, an art festival will be held. The art festival on September 17, 2016 will be extremely fun. Italy is a great country to visit.
2. I really like it in Venice. Today there was a boat parade in the canals here. Tomorrow an art festival will be held. It will be extremely fun. This is a great country to visit.

The difference between (1) and (2) is that (1) is extremely explicit, while (2) relies on deictic terms to determine part of the meaning of the sentences, and real-world knowledge that Venice is in Italy and not Illinois. Because our use of language is relatively inexplicit we're used to interpreting such terms so that (2) sounds perfectly natural, far more natural than (1), as we are entirely accustomed to using these shortcuts.

And this is despite the fact that we often have to look to context to determine the reference of a pronoun. While proper nouns such as *September 16, 2016*, and *Taylor Swift* have context-independent meanings, that is they'll always pick out the same referents regardless of the context, other words such as *here, tomorrow*, and *this* have context-dependent meanings; their reference is determined in part by the context in which they're uttered.

We say "in part" because the particular deictic word itself helps provide restrictions on its own referent. *Here* and *there* have locations as referents; *then* and *now* are temporal referents, *this* and *that* refer to things already mentioned or known, *he* and *she* have human referents, and *I* is extremely restrictive: it can only refer to the speaker.

Even though the referent of a pronoun is lexically restricted, we need to look to the context in which the pronoun is uttered to determine the referent. This process is called **reference resolution**. There are two types of context relevant for the resolution of a pronoun: **linguistic** and **situational**. Linguistic context is anything that has been uttered in the discourse prior to or along with the pronoun. Situational context is anything nonlinguistic such as knowing that Venice is in Italy.

## Pronouns and Situational Context

Hank Ketcham/North America Syndicate/King Features Syndicate

Situational context often takes the form of a gesture, such as pointing or nodding, as in *He went that way!* or *Who IS that masked man?* Similarly, *next week* has a different reference when uttered today than a month from today. If you found an undated notice announcing a "BIG SALE NEXT WEEK," you would not know whether the sale had already taken place.

The "Dennis the Menace" cartoon illustrates the hilarity that may ensue if deictic words are misinterpreted.

Directional terms such as

before/behind  left/right  front/back

are deictic insofar as you need to know the orientation in space of the conversational participants to know their reference. In Japanese, the verb *kuru*, "come," can only be used for motion toward the speaker. A Japanese speaker cannot call up a friend and ask

May I *kuru* to your house?

as you might, in English, ask "May I come to your house?" The correct verb is *iku*, "go," which indicates motion away from the place of utterance. In Japanese, these verbs have a deictic aspect to their meaning. The verbs *come* and *go* have a similar effect in English. If someone says *A thief came into the house* versus *A thief went into the house*, you would assume the speaker to have been in the house in the first case, and not in the house in the second.

## Pronouns and Linguistic Context

There are two different ways in which the reference of a pronoun can be resolved by the linguistic context. The first is sentence-internal; the second is sentence-external. We'll illustrate the first way by discussing reflexive pronouns.

King Features Syndicate

A **reflexive pronoun** is a sort of pronoun that needs to receive its reference via linguistic context, and more specifically by sentence-internal linguistic context. In other words, it requires that the sentence contain another NP—an **antecedent**–that it can **co-refer** with. In English, reflexive pronouns end with *-self* or *-selves*, such as *himself* or *themselves*. (1a) shows that a reflexive pronoun requires an antecedent in the sentence. (1b) shows that a reflexive pronoun must match the person, gender, and number of its antecedent.

**1.** **(a)** I saw Mary. *Herself left.
**(b)** *John wrote herself/themselves a letter.

Interestingly, the restriction on reflexive pronouns is even stronger than (1) suggests. It's not enough that they have a matching antecedent in the sentence, but that antecedent must be in the right position with respect to the co-referring reflexive pronoun. (2a) shows that the antecedent cannot follow the reflexive pronoun; (2b) shows that there can't be another NP in between a reflexive pronoun and its antecedent.

**2.** **(a)** *Himself washed John.
**(b)** *Jane said the boy bit herself.

Thus, one of the things that you know when you know English is that pronouns can receive their reference from their linguistic context. You also know that some pronouns—reflexive pronouns—are particularly picky. Their reference can only be resolved if they have an antecedent which is nearby in the right sort of way.

Nonreflexive pronouns (which we'll refer to simply as *pronouns*) such as *he, she, him, her,* and *it* also have their reference resolved via linguistic context. These pronouns can have their antecedent in another, preceding sentence. This is demonstrated in (3).

**3.** Sue likes pizza. She thinks it is the perfect food.

Moreover, the antecedent doesn't even have to be in a sentence spoken by the same speaker. In the discourse in (4), Mary uses a pronoun (*there*) whose antecedent is in Sue's utterance.

**4.** SUE: I just got back from Rome.
MARY: I've always wanted to go there!

Depending on the context and the discourse, an antecedent can even be several sentences away from its co-referring pronoun. Language users are adroit at processing sentences with several different pronouns and their different antecedents. Consider the discourse in (5):

5. JOHN: It seems that the man loves the woman.
   BILL: Many people think he loves her.

A natural interpretation of Bill's utterance is one in which *he* co-refers with *the man* and *she* co-refers with *the woman.* This is a classic case of reference resolution via linguistic context.

But now read Bill's utterance (5) out loud, and put emphasis on her. When *her* is emphasized it seems more natural to fix its referent from the situational context. This utterance—with *her* emphasized—seems natural for a situation in which Bill is pointing at some other woman across the room.

Language users tend to use pronouns to refer to individuals in contexts—linguistic or situational—in which the referent of the pronoun is clear. The reference of the pronoun is constrained by a number of different factors, including the gender- and number-marking on the pronoun, whether or not the pronoun is reflexive, and what linguistic and situational contexts the pronoun is uttered in.

## Implicature

Pronouns are an example of how the context in which a sentence is uttered can help determine the meaning of that sentence. There is another way in which context can play a role in meaning: It can supplement the meaning of a sentence. Just as you were able to fill in the gaps in the sketch at the beginning of this chapter with extra details, you as a language user are able to fill in gaps in meaning. And just as there is a right and a wrong way to fill in the gaps in the sketch—Rembrandt probably didn't intend it to depict a sandwich—there is a right and a wrong way to fill in gaps in meaning.

We'll start with an example:

6. DAD: Very nice girl. What do you think, Hon?
   MOM: The turkey sure was moist.

From a semantic standpoint, (6) is very straightforward. With the right semantic theory, we can articulate the literal meanings of the parents' utterances. This semantic theory would summarize (6) literally as: Dad asked Mom whether she thinks the girl is nice and Mom asserts that the turkey was moist.

Of course, this summary already includes some extra-truth-conditional meaning. It assumes that *girl* gets its reference from the previous remark about Toni, and that the use of the definite article in *the turkey* assures that a turkey is known to the conversational participants. But there is still more meaning to attribute to (6). In many contexts, Dad (and the boy) will infer from Mom's statement that she doesn't particularly like Toni.

If this is right, Mom's answer is more of a sketch than a photograph. The most literal way Mom could have answered the question is "I do not like Toni." But instead of asserting this, Mom chooses to implicate it. An **implicature** is a great example of extra-truth-conditional meaning. An implicature is an inference based not only on an utterance, but also on what the speaker is trying to convey. An implicature is to an assertion what a sketch is to a photograph.

Just as there are a number of reasons to sketch something instead of photographing it, there are a number of reasons to implicate something as opposed to asserting it. Perhaps Mom is an adherent of Miss Manners and, being a good hostess, knows she mustn't disparage a guest. If Dad knows this about Mom then he might infer from the utterance *The turkey sure was moist*—which doesn't seem relevant—that Mom doesn't like Toni but is too polite to say so. Here are a few other examples of conversational implicatures:

7. SUE: Does Mary have a boyfriend?
   BILL: She's been driving to Santa Barbara every weekend.
8. JOHN: Do you know how to change a tire?
   JANE: I know how to call a tow truck.
9. DANA: Do these slacks make my butt look big?
   JAMIE: You look great in chartreuse.

In (7), Bill asserts that Mary has been driving to Santa Barbara every weekend. But he *implicates* that Mary has a boyfriend (and that the boyfriend lives in Santa Barbara). In (8), Jane asserts that she knows how to call a tow truck. But she *implicates* that she doesn't know how to change a tire. In (9), well, you figure it out.

These discourses should seem fairly natural to you. And it's likely that you calculated the same implicatures we did. That's what's interesting to linguists. Just as morphology, syntax, and semantics is rule-governed, as we have emphasized throughout this book, so is pragmatics (and, by extension, implication).

## Maxims of Discourse

The most notable effort made to formulate pragmatic rules is found in the work of the British philosopher H. Paul Grice. He attempted to formalize how we perceive implicature in a conversation. He concluded that language users can calculate implicatures because they are all following some implicit principles (and each language user can therefore assume that others are following those principles). Grice called these principles **"maxims" of discourse**, and used them to serve as the foundation of pragmatics, the study of extra-truth-conditional meaning. We'll list them and then provide examples of each.

**Maxim of Quality**: Truth

- Do not say what you believe to be false.
- Do not say that for which you lack adequate evidence.

**Maxim of Quantity**: Information

- Make your contribution as informative as is required for the current purposes of the exchange.
- Do not make your contribution more or less informative than is required.

**Maxim of Relation**: Relevance

- Be relevant to the matter under discussion.

**Maxim of Manner**: Clarity

- Avoid obscurity of expression.
- Avoid ambiguity.
- Avoid unnecessary wordiness.
- Be orderly.

These are not prescriptive rules but rather part of a strategy used by the community of language users to enable the use of conversational implicature. They tend to be violated only by uncooperative people. (The Maxims are sometimes referred to en masse as Grice's **cooperative principle**.) So, if John stops Mary on the street and asks her for directions to the library, and she responds "Walk up three streets and take a left," it's a successful discourse only because Mary is being cooperative (and John assumes Mary is being cooperative). In particular, John assumes that Mary is following the maxim of quality.

On the other hand, the following discourse (*Hamlet*, Act II, Scene II), which gave rise to Polonius's famous remark, does not seem quite right—it is not coherent, for reasons that Grice's maxims can explain.

POLONIUS: What do you read, my lord?
HAMLET: Words, words, words.
POLONIUS: What is the matter, my lord?
HAMLET: Between who?
POLONIUS: I mean, the matter that you read, my lord.
HAMLET: Slanders, sir: for the satirical rogue says here that old men have gray beards, that their faces are wrinkled, their eyes purging thick amber and plum-tree gum, and that they have a plentiful lack of wit, together with most weak hams: all which, sir, though I most powerfully and potently believe, yet I hold it not honesty to have it thus set down; for yourself, sir, should grow old as I am, if like a crab you could go backward.

Hamlet, who is feigning insanity, refuses to answer Polonius's questions "in good faith." He has violated the maxim of quantity, which states that a speaker's contribution to the discourse should be as informative as is required—neither more nor less. Hamlet has violated this maxim in both directions. In answering "Words, words, words" to the question of what he is reading, he is providing too little information. His final remark goes to the other extreme in providing too much information (this could also be seen as a violation of the maxim of manner). Hamlet also violates the maxim of relation when he "misinterprets" the question about the reading matter as a matter between two individuals.

A maxim is violated when a speaker chooses to be uncooperative for whatever reason. A maxim is obeyed in a literal discourse devoid of implicature, as in (10).

**10.** DAD: Very nice girl. What do you think, Hon?
MOM: Not really.

Implicatures can arise when a maxim is flouted. To flout a maxim is to choose not to follow that maxim in order to implicate something. In the Hamlet discourse above, Hamlet is violating the maxims in order to sound insane. But we can easily imagine a slightly different context, one in which Polonius and Hamlet have more or less the same exchange, but one in which Hamlet is not trying to be insane.

POLONIUS: What do you read, my lord?
HAMLET: Words, words, words.

In this context, Hamlet is still not obeying the maxim of quantity—he's not saying enough to really answer Polonius' question—but he is instead flouting the maxim to implicate that he doesn't want Polonius to know what he's reading.

The discourse in (6), repeated below, is an example of the maxim of relevance being flouted.

**11.** DAD: Very nice girl. What do you think, Hon?
MOM: The turkey sure was moist.

Because Mom knows that the quality of the turkey isn't relevant to being a "very nice girl"—and because Dad is assuming that Mom knows it, too—Dad can pick up on the fact that Mom is implicating that she doesn't like the girl.

Bereft of context, if one man says (truthfully) to another "I have never slept with your wife," that would be provocative because the very topic of conversation should be unnecessary, a violation of the maxims of quantity and relevance.

Asking an able-bodied person at the dinner table "Can you pass the salt?"—if answered literally—would force the responder into stating the obvious, also a violation of the maxim of quantity. To avoid this, the person asked seeks a reason for the question, and understands that the asker would like to have the salt shaker.

The maxim of relevance explains how saying "It's cold in here" to a person standing by an open window might be interpreted as a request to close it: or else why make the remark to that particular person in the first place?

Because implicatures may result from violations of one or more maxims, they can be easily cancelled by providing further, clarifying information. For example:

DAD: Very nice girl. What do you think, Hon?
MOM: The turkey sure was moist. *Toni basted it every ten minutes.*

The additional remark cancels, or at least weakens, the implicature that Mom dislikes Toni.

In this respect, implicatures are different from entailments and presuppositions. An entailment cannot be cancelled; it is logically necessary. The truth of

*Jon killed Jim* entails that Jim is dead and nothing anyone can say will resurrect him. But further world knowledge or verbal clarification may cancel an implicature.

## Presupposition

Nearly all utterances occur in context, and the context often contributes to the way the utterance is understood, and whether the utterance is appropriate. For example, *The present King of France is bald* is perfectly grammatical and meaningful except that it is inappropriate because nowadays France has no king. Situations that must exist for utterances to be appropriate are called **presuppositions**. *The present King of France is bald* has the presupposition that there is presently a king of France.

Questions such as *Have you stopped hugging your border collie?* presuppose that you hugged your border collie, and statements such as *The river Avon runs through Stratford* presuppose the existence of the river and the town. Presuppositions prevent utterances from being incongruous and when they are ignored, we get the confusion that Alice felt at the tea party. Statements such as *Take some more tea* or *Have another beer* carry the presupposition that one has already had some. The March Hare is oblivious to this aspect of language, of which the exasperated Alice is keenly aware.

Presuppositions hold up under negation. *I am **not** sorry that the team lost* still has the presupposition that the team lost. If a mad Mad Hatter said *Do **not** take any more tea* the presupposition of previous tea consumption would still be present.

Presuppositions are different from implicatures. Continuing with—*oh, the team didn't lose after all*—retracts the previous assertion *I'm sorry that the team lost.* No such incongruity arises when implicatures are cancelled.

Presuppositions also differ from entailments in that they are taken for granted by speakers. Unlike entailments, they remain when the sentence is negated. On the other hand, while *Jon killed Jim* entails *Jim died,* no such entailment follows from *Jon did not kill Jim.*

## Speech Acts

ZITS © 1998 ZITS PARTNERSHIP, KING FEATURES SYNDICATE

You can use language to do things. You can use language to make promises, lay bets, issue warnings, christen boats, place names in nomination, offer congratulations, or swear testimony. The theory of **speech acts** describes how this is done.

By saying *I warn you that there is a sheepdog in the closet*, you not only say something, you *warn* someone. Verbs such as *bet, promise, and warn* are **performative verbs**. Using them in a sentence (in the first person, present tense) adds something extra over and above the statement.

There are hundreds of performative verbs in every language. The following sentences illustrate their usage:

I *bet* you five dollars the Yankees win.
I *challenge* you to a match.
I *dare* you to step over this line.
I *fine* you $100 for possession of oregano.
I *move* that we adjourn.
I *nominate* Batman for mayor of Gotham City.
I *promise* to improve.
I *resign*!
I *pronounce* you husband and wife.

In all of these sentences, the speaker is the subject (i.e., the sentences are in first person), who by uttering the sentence is accomplishing some additional action, such as daring, nominating, or resigning. In addition, all of these sentences are affirmative, declarative, and in the present tense. They are typical **performative sentences**.

An informal test to see whether a sentence contains a performative verb is to begin it with the words *I hereby* .... Only performative sentences sound right when begun this way. Compare *I hereby apologize to you* with the somewhat strange *I hereby know you*. The first is generally taken as an act of apologizing. In all of the examples given, insertion of *hereby* would be acceptable.

In studying speech acts, the importance of context is evident. In some situations, *Band practice, my house, 6 to 8* is a reminder, but the same sentence may be a warning in a different context. We call this underlying purpose of the utterance—be it a reminder, a warning, a promise, a threat, or whatever—the **illocutionary force** of a speech act. Illocutionary force may accompany utterances without overt performative verbs, for example, *I've got five bucks that says you're wrong* has the illocutionary force of a bet under appropriate circumstances. Because the illocutionary force of a speech act depends on the context of the utterance, speech act theory is a part of pragmatics.

## Summary

Knowing a language means knowing how to produce and understand the meaning of infinitely many sentences. The study of linguistic meaning is called **semantics. Lexical semantics** is concerned with the meanings of morphemes and words. The study of how context affects meaning is called **pragmatics**.

There are cases when the meaning of larger units does not follow from the meaning of its parts. **Anomaly** is when the pieces do not fit sensibly together, as in *colorless green ideas sleep furiously*. **Metaphors** are sentences that appear to be anomalous, but to which a meaningful concept can be attached, such as *time is money*. **Idioms** are fixed expressions whose meaning is not compositional but rather must be learned as a whole unit, such as *kick the bucket* meaning "to die."

Part of the meaning of words may be the association with the objects the words refer to (if any), called **reference**, but often there is additional meaning beyond reference, which is called **sense**. The reference of *the President* is Barack Obama, and the sense of the expression is "highest executive office." Some expressions have reference but little sense, such as proper names, and some have sense but no reference, such as *the present King of France*.

Words are related in various ways. They may be **synonyms**, various kinds of **antonyms** such as **relational opposites**, or **homonyms**, words pronounced the same but with different meanings such as *bare* and *bear*.

Part of the meaning of words may be described by **semantic features** such as "female," "young," "cause," or "go." Nouns may have the feature "count," wherein they may be enumerated (one potato, two potatoes), or "mass," in which enumeration may require contextual interpretation (*one milk, *two milks, perhaps meaning "one glass or quart or portion of milk"). Some verbs have the feature "eventive" and others "stative." The semantic feature of negation is found in many words and is evidenced by the occurrence of *negative polarity* items (e.g., *John doubts that Mary gives a hoot*, but **John thinks that Mary gives a hoot*).

Verbs have various **argument structures**, which describe the NPs that may occur with particular verbs. For example, intransitive verbs take only an NP subject, whereas **ditransitive** verbs take an NP subject, an NP direct object, and an NP indirect object. **Thematic roles** describe the semantic relations between a verb and its NP arguments. Some thematic roles are: **agent**, the doer of an action; **theme**, the receiver of an action; **goal; source; instrument**; and **experiencer**. The assignment of thematic roles to the NP arguments of verbs occurs in d-structure. However, the positions of the NP arguments may differ in s-structure owing to the application of syntactic rules that move elements.

Some meaning is **extra-truth-conditional:** it comes about as a result of how a speaker uses the literal meaning in conversation, or as a part of a **discourse**. The study of extra-truth-conditional meaning is **pragmatics**.

Language users generally describe states of affairs with sentences that aren't 100 percent explicit. Context can be used to supplement linguistic meaning in various ways. Context may be *linguistic*—what was previously spoken or written—or *knowledge of the world*, including the speech situation: what we've called **situational context**.

Many pronouns rely on context for their reference to be resolved. Reflexive pronouns such as *himself* and *themselves* require a sentence-internal **antecedent**. Nonreflexive pronouns such as *he, she, him*, and *her* can have an antecedent in another sentence or earlier in the discourse or even determined by context. **Deictic** terms such as *you, there, now*, and *the other side* require knowledge of the situation (person spoken to, place, time, and spatial orientation) of the utterance to be interpreted referentially.

Speakers of all languages adhere to various **maxims of discourse**, which are instances of a general **cooperative principle** for communicating sincerely. Such maxims as "be relevant" or "say neither more nor less than the discourse requires" permit a person to interpret *It's cold in here* as "Shut the windows" or "Turn up the thermostat." **Implicatures** are the inferences that may be drawn from an utterance in context when one or another of the maxims is violated (either purposefully or naively). When Mary says *It's cold in here*, one of many possible implicatures may be "Mary wants the heat turned up." Implicatures are like entailments in that their truth follows from sentences of the discourse, but unlike entailments, which are necessarily true, implicatures may be cancelled by information added later. Mary might wave you away from the thermostat and ask you to hand her a sweater. **Presuppositions** are situations that must be true for utterances to be appropriate, so that *Take some more tea* has the presupposition "already had some tea."

The theory of **speech acts** tells us that people use language to do things such as lay bets, issue warnings, or nominate candidates. By using the words, "I nominate Bill Smith," you may accomplish an act of nomination that allows Bill Smith to run for office. Verbs that "do things" are called **performative verbs**. The speaker's intent in making an utterance is known as **illocutionary force**. In the case of performative verbs, the illocutionary force is mentioned overtly. In other cases, it must be determined from context.

## References for Further Reading

Austin, J. L. 1962. *How to do things with words*. Cambridge, MA: Harvard University Press.

Davidson, D., and G. Harman, eds. 1972. *Semantics of natural languages*. Dordrecht, The Netherlands: Reidel.

Grice, H. P. 1989. Logic and conversation. Reprinted in *Studies in the way of words*. Cambridge, MA: Harvard University Press.

Jackendoff, R. 1990. *Semantic Structures*, Cambridge, MA: MIT Press,

Lakoff, G., and M. Johnson. 2003. *Metaphors we live by, 2nd ed.* Chicago: University of Chicago Press.

Levinson, S. C. 2000. *Presumptive meanings: The theory of generalized conversational implicature*. Cambridge, MA: The MIT Press.

Saeed, J. 2009. *Semantics, 3rd ed.* Oxford, UK: Wiley-Blackwell.

Searle, J. R. 1969. *Speech acts: An essay in the philosophy of language*. Cambridge, UK: Cambridge University Press.

## Exercises

**1.** The following sentences are either tautologies (analytic), contradictions, or situationally true or false. Write T by the tautologies, C by the contradictions, and S by the other sentences.

**a.** Queens are monarchs.
**b.** Kings are female.
**c.** Kings are poor.

d. Queens are ugly.
e. Queens are mothers.
f. Kings are mothers.
g. Dogs are four-legged.
h. Cats are felines.
i. Cats are stupid.
j. Dogs are carnivores.
k. George Washington is George Washington.
l. George Washington is the first president.
m. George Washington is male.
n. Uncles are male.
o. My aunt is a man.
p. Witches are wicked.
q. My brother is a witch.
r. My sister is an only child.
s. The evening star isn't the evening star.
t. The evening star isn't Venus.
u. Babies are adults.
v. Babies can lift one ton.
w. Puppies are human.
x. My bachelor friends are all married.
y. My bachelor friends are all lonely.
z. Colorless ideas are green.

**2.** Here is a passage from *Alice's Adventures in Wonderland*:

"How is bread made?"
"I know *that*!" Alice cried eagerly.
"You take some flour—"
"Where do you pick the flower?" the White Queen asked.
"In a garden, or in the hedges?"
"Well, it isn't *picked* at all," Alice explained; "it's ground—"
"How many acres of ground?" said the White Queen.

On what kinds of pairs of words is the humor of this passage based? Identify each pair.

**3. Part One**

The following sentences may be lexically or structurally ambiguous, or both.

Provide paraphrases showing that you comprehend all the meanings.

*Example*: I saw him walking by the bank.

Meaning 1: I saw him and he was walking by the bank of the river.

Meaning 2: I saw him and he was walking by the financial institution.

Meaning 3: I was walking by the bank of the river when I saw him.

Meaning 4: I was walking by the financial institution when I saw him.

a. We laughed at the colorful ball.
b. He was knocked over by the punch.
c. The police were urged to stop drinking by the fifth.

**d.** I said I would file it on Thursday.
**e.** I cannot recommend visiting professors too highly.
**f.** The license fee for pets owned by senior citizens who have not been altered is $1.50. (Actual notice)
**g.** What looks better on a handsome man than a tux? Nothing! (Attributed to Mae West)
**h.** Wanted: Man to take care of cow that does not smoke or drink. (Actual notice)
**i.** For sale: Several old dresses from grandmother in beautiful condition. (Actual notice)
**j.** Time flies like an arrow. (*Hint*: There are at least four paraphrases, but some of them require imagination.)

**Part Two**

Do the same thing for the following newspaper headlines:

**a.** POLICE BEGIN CAMPAIGN TO RUN DOWN JAYWALKERS
**b.** DRUNK GETS NINE MONTHS IN VIOLIN CASE
**c.** FARMER BILL DIES IN HOUSE
**d.** STUD TIRES OUT
**e.** SQUAD HELPS DOG BITE VICTIM
**f.** LACK OF BRAINS HINDERS RESEARCH
**g.** MINERS REFUSE TO WORK AFTER DEATH
**h.** EYE DROPS OFF SHELF
**i.** JUVENILE COURT TO TRY SHOOTING DEFENDANT
**j.** QUEEN MARY HAVING BOTTOM SCRAPED
**k.** VOLUNTEERS NEEDED TO HELP TORTURE SURVIVORS
**l.** HOMICIDE VICTIMS RARELY TALK TO POLICE

**4.** Explain the semantic ambiguity of the following sentences by providing two or more sentences for each that paraphrase the multiple meanings. *Example*: "She can't bear children" can mean either "She can't give birth to children" or "She can't tolerate children."

**a.** He waited by the bank.
**b.** Is he really that kind?
**c.** The proprietor of the fish store was the sole owner.
**d.** The long drill was boring.
**e.** When he got the clear title to the land, it was a good deed.
**f.** It takes a good ruler to make a straight line.
**g.** He saw that gasoline can explode.
**h.** You should see her shop.
**i.** Every man loves a woman.
**j.** You get half off the cost of your hotel room if you make your own bed.
**k.** "It's his job to lose" (said the coach about his new player).
**l.** "We will change your oil in 10 minutes" (sign in front of a garage).
**m.** **Challenge exercise:** Bill wants to marry a Norwegian woman.

**5.** For each group of words given as follows, state what semantic feature or features distinguish between the classes of (a) words and (b) words.

If asked, also indicate a semantic property that the (a) words and the (b) words share.

*Example*: (a) widow, mother, sister, aunt, maid

(b) widower, father, brother, uncle, valet

The (a) and (b) words are "human."

The (a) words are "female" and the (b) words are "male."

**a.** (a) bachelor, man, son, paperboy, pope, chief
(b) bull, rooster, drake, ram

The (a) and (b) words are:

The (a) words are:

The (b) words are:

**b.** (a) table, stone, pencil, cup, house, ship, car
(b) milk, alcohol, rice, soup, mud

The (a) words are:

The (b) words are:

**c.** (a) book, temple, mountain, road, tractor
(b) idea, love, charity, sincerity, bravery, fear

The (a) words are:

The (b) words are:

**d.** (a) pine, elm, ash, weeping willow, sycamore
(b) rose, dandelion, aster, tulip, daisy

The (a) and (b) words are:

The (a) words are:

The (b) words are:

**e.** (a) book, letter, encyclopedia, novel, notebook, dictionary
(b) typewriter, pencil, pen, crayon, quill, charcoal, chalk

The (a) words are:

The (b) words are:

**f.** (a) walk, run, skip, jump, hop, swim
(b) fly, skate, ski, ride, cycle, canoe, hang glide

The (a) and (b) words are:

The (a) words are:

The (b) words are:

**g.** (a) ask, tell, say, talk, converse
(b) shout, whisper, mutter, drawl, holler

The (a) and (b) words are:

The (a) words are:

The (b) words are:

**h.** (a) absent/present, alive/dead, asleep/awake, married/single
(b) big/small, cold/hot, sad/happy, slow/fast

The (a) and (b) word pairs are:

The (a) words are:

The (b) words are:

**i.** (a) alleged, counterfeit, false, putative, accused
(b) red, large, cheerful, pretty, stupid

(*Hint*: Is an alleged murderer always a murderer? Is a pretty girl always a girl?)

The (a) words are:

The (b) words are:

6. **Research project:** There are many *-nym/-onym* words that describe classes of words with particular semantic properties. We mentioned a few in this chapter such as synonyms, antonyms, homonyms, and hyponyms. What is the etymology of *-onym?* What common English word is it related to? How many more *-nym* words and their meanings can you come up with? Try for five or ten on your own. With help from the Internet, dozens are possible. (*Hint*: One such *-nym* word was the winning word in the 1997 Scripps National Spelling Bee.)

7. There are several kinds of antonymy. By writing a *c*, *g*, or *r* in column C, indicate whether the pairs in columns A and B are complementary, gradable, or relational opposites.

| A | B | C |
|---|---|---|
| good | bad | ___ |
| expensive | cheap | ___ |
| parent | offspring | ___ |
| beautiful | ugly | ___ |
| false | true | ___ |
| lessor | lessee | ___ |
| pass | fail | ___ |
| hot | cold | ___ |
| legal | illegal | ___ |
| larger | smaller | ___ |
| poor | rich | ___ |
| fast | slow | ___ |
| asleep | awake | ___ |
| husband | wife | ___ |
| rude | polite | ___ |

8. For each definition, write in the first blank the word that has that meaning and in the second (and third if present) a differently spelled homonym that has a different meaning. The first letter of each of the words is provided.

   *Example*: “a pair”: t(*wo*) t(*oo*) t(*o*)

   **a.** “naked”: **b** ______ **b** ______

| | | | |
|---|---|---|---|
| **b.** "base metal": | l ______ | l ______ | |
| **c.** "worships": | p ______ | p ______ | p ______ |
| **d.** "eight bits": | b ______ | b ______ | b ______ |
| **e.** "one of five senses": | s ______ | s ______ | c ______ |
| **f.** "several couples": | p ______ | p ______ | p ______ |
| **g.** "not pretty": | p ______ | p ______ | |
| **h.** "purity of gold unit": | k ______ | c ______ | |
| **i.** "a horse's coiffure": | m ______ | m ______ | m ______ |
| **j.** "sets loose": | f ______ | f ______ | f ______ |

**9.** The following sentences consist of a verb, its noun phrase subject, and various noun phrases and prepositional phrases. Identify the thematic role of each NP by writing the letter *a, t, i, s, g,* or *e* above the noun, standing for *agent, theme, instrument, source, goal,* and *experiencer.*

a t s i
*Example*: The boy took the books from the cupboard with a handcart.

**a.** Mary found a ball.
**b.** The children ran from the playground to the wading pool.
**c.** One of the men unlocked all the doors with a paper clip.
**d.** John melted the ice with a blowtorch.
**e.** Helen looked for a cockroach.
**f.** Helen saw a cockroach.
**g.** Helen screamed.
**h.** The ice melted.
**i.** With a telescope, the boy saw the man.
**j.** The farmer loaded hay onto the truck.
**k.** The farmer loaded the hay with a pitchfork.
**l.** The hay was loaded on the truck by the farmer.
**m.** Helen heard music coming out of the speaker.

**10.** A criterion of a performative utterance is whether you can begin it with "I hereby." Notice that if you say sentence (i) aloud, it sounds like a genuine apology, but to say sentence (ii) aloud sounds funny because you cannot willfully perform an act of noticing:

**i.** I hereby apologize to you.
**ii.** ?I hereby notice you.

Determine which of the following are performative sentences by inserting "hereby" and seeing whether they sound right.

**a.** I testify that she met the agent.
**b.** I know that she met the agent.
**c.** I suppose the Yankees will win.
**d.** He bet her $2,500 that Trump would win.
**e.** I dismiss the class.
**f.** I teach the class.
**g.** We promise to leave early.
**h.** I owe the IRS $1 million.

i. I bequeath $1 million to the IRS.
j. I swore I didn't do it.
k. I swear I didn't do it.

**11.** **a.** Explain, in terms of Grice's Maxims, the humor or strangeness of the following exchange between mother and child. The child has just finished eating a cookie when the mother comes into the room.

MOTHER: What are these cookie crumbs doing in your bed?

CHILD: Nothing, they're just lying there.

**b.** Do the same for this "exchange" between an owner and her cat:

OWNER: If cats ruled the world, everyone would sleep on a pile of fresh laundry.

CAT: Cats *don't* rule the world??

**12.** **a.** Spend an hour or two observing conversations between people, including yourself if you wish. Record five (or more if you're having fun) utterances where the intended meaning is mediated by Grice's Maxims and cite the maxim or maxims involved. For example, someone says "I didn't quite catch that," with the possible meaning of "Please say it again," or "Please speak a little louder." In the above example, we would cite the maxims of relevance and quantity.

**b.** Here is a dialog excerpt from the 1945 motion picture *The Thin Man Goes Home*. The scene is in a shop that sells paintings and Nick Charles is leaving the shop.

| | |
|---|---|
| NICK CHARLES: | Well, thank you very much. Goodbye now. |
| SHOPKEEPER: | I beg your pardon? |
| NICK CHARLES: | I said, goodbye now. |
| SHOPKEEPER: | "Goodbye now?" There's no sense to that! Obviously it's now! I mean, you wouldn't say "goodbye tomorrow" or "goodbye two hours ago!" |
| NICK CHARLES: | You got hold of somethin' there, brother. |
| SHOPKEEPER: | I've got hold of some . . . I haven't got hold of anything . . . And I'm not your brother! |

Analyze this dialogue, intended to be humorous (one assumes), in light of Grice's maxims.

**13.** Consider the following "facts" and then answer the questions. Part A illustrates your ability to interpret meanings when syntactic rules have deleted parts of the sentence; Part B illustrates your knowledge of semantic features and entailment.

**a.** Roses are red and bralkions are too.
Booth shot Lincoln and Czolgosz, McKinley.

Casca stabbed Caesar and so did Cinna.

Frodo was exhausted, as was Sam.

**a.** What color are bralkions?
**b.** What did Czolgosz do to McKinley?
**c.** What did Cinna do to Caesar?
**d.** What did Sam feel?

**b.** Now consider these facts and answer the questions:
Black Beauty was a stallion.

Mary is a widow.

John pretended to send Martha a birthday card.

Jane didn't remember to send Tom a birthday card.

Tina taught her daughter to swim.

My boss managed to give me a raise last year.

Flipper is walking.

(T = true; F = false)

| | | |
|---|---|---|
| **a.** Black Beauty was male. | **T** __________ | **F** __________ |
| **b.** Mary was never married. | **T** __________ | **F** __________ |
| **c.** John sent Martha a card. | **T** __________ | **F** __________ |
| **d.** Jane sent Tom a card. | **T** __________ | **F** __________ |
| **e.** Tina's daughter can swim. | **T** __________ | **F** __________ |
| **f.** I didn't get a raise last year. | **T** __________ | **F** __________ |
| **g.** Flipper has legs. | **T** __________ | **F** __________ |

**14.** The following sentences have certain presuppositions that ensure their appropriateness. What are they?

*Example*: The minors promised the police to stop drinking.
Presupposition: The minors were drinking.

**a.** We went to the ballpark again.
**b.** Valerie regretted not receiving a new T-bird for Labor Day.
**c.** That her pet turtle ran away made Emily very sad.
**d.** The administration forgot that the professors support the students.
**e.** It is an atrocity that the World Trade Center was attacked on September 11, 2001.
**f.** It isn't tolerable that the World Trade Center was attacked on September 11, 2001.
**g.** Disa wants more popcorn.
**h.** Mary drank one more beer before leaving.
**i.** Jack knows who discovered Pluto in 1930.
**j.** Mary was horrified to find a cockroach in her bed.

**15.** Imagine that Alex and Bruce have a plan to throw Colleen a surprise party at work. It is Alex's job meet her for lunch at a local restaurant to get her out of the office, and Bruce's job to decorate as soon as she leaves. Alex phones Bruce and says, "The eagle has landed." What maxim is Alex flouting? What does his utterance implicate?

**16.** Each of the following single statements has at least one implicature in the situation described. What is it?

**a.** Statement: You make a better door than a window.
Situation: Someone is blocking your view.

**b.** Statement: It's getting late.
Situation: You're at a party and it's 4 a.m.

**c.** Statement: The restaurants are open until midnight.
Situation: It's 10 o'clock and you haven't eaten dinner.

**d.** Statement: If you'd diet, this wouldn't hurt so badly.
Situation: Someone is standing on your toe.

**e.** Statement: I thought I saw a fan in the closet.
Situation: It's sweltering in the room.

**f.** Statement: Mr. Smith dresses neatly, is well groomed, and is always on time to class.
Situation: The summary statement in a letter of recommendation to graduate school.

**g.** Statement: Most of the food is gone.
Situation: You arrived late at a cocktail party.

**h.** Statement: John or Mary made a mistake.
Situation: You're looking over some work done by John and Mary.

**17.** In each of the following dialogues between Jack and Laura, there is a conversational implicature. What is it?

**a.** Jack: Did you make a doctor's appointment?
Laura: Their line was busy.

**b.** Jack: Do you have the play tickets?
Laura: Didn't I give them to you?

**c.** Jack: Does your grandmother have a live-in boyfriend?
Laura: She's very traditional.

**d.** Jack: How did you like the string quartet?
Laura: I thought the violist was swell.

**e.** Laura: What are Boston's chances of winning the World Series?
Jack: Do bowling balls float?

**f.** Laura: Do you own a cat?
Jack: I'm allergic to everything.

**g.** Laura: Did you mow the grass and wash the car like I told you to?
Jack: I mowed the grass.

**h.** Laura: Do you want dessert?
Jack: Is the Pope Catholic?

5

# Phonetics: The Sounds of Language

When you know a language you know the *sounds* of that language, and you know how to combine those sounds into words. When you know English you know the sounds represented by the letters *b*, *s*, and *u*, and you are able to combine them to form the words *bus* and *sub*.

Although languages may contain different sounds, the sounds of all the languages of the world together constitute a class of sounds that the human vocal tract is designed to make. This chapter will discuss these speech sounds, how they are produced, and how they may be classified.

## Sound Segments

The study of speech sounds is called **phonetics**. To describe speech sounds, it is necessary to know what an individual sound is, and how each sound differs from all others. This is not as easy as it may seem, for when we speak, the sounds seem to run together and it isn't at all obvious where one sound ends and the next begins. But when we know the language being spoken, we hear the individual sounds in our "mind's ear" and are able to make sense of them, unlike the sign painter in the cartoon.

A speaker of English knows that there are three sounds in the word *bus*, yet physically the word is just one continuous sound. You can **segment** that continuous sound into individual pieces because you know English. And you recognize those pieces when they occur elsewhere, as *b* does in *b*et or ro*b*, as *u* does in *u*p, and as *s* does in *s*ister.

It is not possible to segment the sound of someone clearing their throat, not because throat-clearing is one continuous sound, but because such sounds are not speech and may not be decomposed into the sounds of speech.

Speakers of English can separate *keepout* into the two words *keep* and *out* because they know the language. We do not generally pause between words (except to take a breath), even though we may think we do. Children learning a language reveal this fact. A two-year-old child going down stairs heard his mother say, "hold on." He replied, "I'm holing don, I'm holing don," not knowing where the break between words occurred. In fact, word boundary misperceptions have changed the forms of words historically. At an earlier stage of English, the word *apron* was *napron*. However, the phrase *a napron* was so often misperceived as *an apron* that the word lost its initial *n*.

Some phrases and sentences that are clearly distinct when printed may be ambiguous when spoken. Read the following pairs aloud and see why we might misinterpret what we hear:

| | |
|---|---|
| grade A | gray day |
| I scream | ice cream |
| the sun's rays meet | the sons raise meat |

The lack of breaks between spoken words and individual sounds often makes us think that speakers of foreign languages run their words together, unaware that we do too. X-ray motion pictures of someone speaking make the absence of breaks very clear. One can see the tongue, jaw, and lips in continuous motion as the individual sounds are produced.

Yet, if you know a language, you have no difficulty segmenting the continuous sounds of speech. It doesn't matter whether there is an alphabet for the language or whether the listener can read and write. Everyone who knows a language knows how to segment sentences into words, and words into sounds. It is not a question of literacy; it is part of being human.

## Speech Sounds, Like Snowflakes

It is truly amazing, given the continuity of the speech signal, that we are able to understand the individual words in an utterance. This ability is more surprising because no two speakers ever say the same word identically. The speech signal produced when one speaker says *cat* is not absolutely the same as that of another speaker's *cat* due to differences in people's size, age, and gender, among other things. Even two utterances of *cat* by the same speaker will differ to some degree.

Our knowledge of a language determines when we judge physically different sounds to be the same. We know which aspects of pronunciation are linguistically important and which are not. If someone coughs in the middle of saying "How (cough) are you?" a listener will ignore the cough and interpret this simply as "How are you?" People speak at different pitch levels, at different rates of speed, and even with their head encased in a helmet, such as Darth Vader. However, such personal differences are not linguistically significant.

Our linguistic knowledge makes it possible to ignore nonlinguistic differences in speech. Furthermore, we are capable of making sounds that we know are not speech sounds in our language. Many English speakers can make a clicking sound of disapproval that writers sometimes represent as *tsk*. This sound never occurs as part of an English word. It is even difficult for many English speakers to combine this clicking sound with other sounds. Yet, clicks are speech sounds in Xhosa, Zulu, Sesotho, and Khoikhoi—languages spoken in southern Africa—just like the *k* and *t* in English. Speakers of those languages have no difficulty producing them as parts of words. Thus, *tsk* is a speech sound in Xhosa but not in English. The sound represented by the letters *th* in the word *think* is a speech sound in English but not in French. Languages differ to a greater or lesser degree in the inventory of speech sounds that words are built from.

The science of phonetics attempts to describe all of the sounds used in all languages of the world. **Acoustic phonetics** focuses on the physical properties of sounds; **auditory phonetics** is concerned with how listeners perceive these sounds; and **articulatory phonetics**—the primary concern of this chapter—is the study of how the vocal tract produces the sounds of language.

## The Phonetic Alphabet

**Orthography**, or "spelling," does not necessarily represent the sounds of a language in a consistent way. To be scientific—and phonetics *is* a science—we must devise a way for the same sound to be spelled with the same letter every time, and for the same letter to stand for the same sound every time.

To see that ordinary spelling with our Roman alphabet is woefully inadequate for the task, consider sentences such as:

Did h**e** bel**ie**ve that C**ae**sar could s**ee** the p**eo**ple s**ei**ze the s**ea**s?
The sill**y** am**oe**ba stole the k**ey** to the mach**i**ne.

The same sound is represented variously by **e, ie, ae, ee, eo, ei, ea, y, oe, ey**, and **i**. On the other hand, consider:

My f**a**ther w**a**nted m**a**ny **a** vill**a**ge d**a**me b**a**dly.

Here, the letter **a** represents the various sounds in *father, wanted, many*, and so on.

Making the spelling waters yet muddier, we find that a combination of letters may represent a single sound:

| | | | |
|---|---|---|---|
| **sh**oot | **ch**aracter | **Th**omas | **ph**ysics |
| ei**th**er | d**ea**l | rou**gh** | na**ti**on |
| c**oa**t | gla**ci**al | **th**eater | pl**ai**n |

Or, conversely, the single letter **x**, when not pronounced as **z**, usually stands for the *two* sounds **ks** as in sex (you may have to speak aloud to hear that *sex* is pronounced seks).

And some letters have no sound at all in certain words (so-called *silent* letters):

| | | | |
|---|---|---|---|
| **m**nemonic | autum**n** | as**th**ma | cor**ps** |
| **h**onest | **ch**thonic | hol**e** | Chris**t**mas |
| **p**sychology | s**w**ord | de**b**t | **g**naw |
| bou**gh** | **ph**thalate | i**s**land | **k**not |

**TABLE 5.1** | A Phonetic Alphabet for English Pronunciation

| Consonants | | | | | | Vowels | | | |
|---|---|---|---|---|---|---|---|---|---|
| p | **p**ill | t | **t**ill | k | **k**ill | i | b**ee**t | ɪ | b**i**t |
| b | **b**ill | d | **d**ill | g | **g**ill | e | b**ai**t | ɛ | b**e**t |
| m | **m**ill | n | **n**il | ŋ | ri**ng** | u | b**oo**t | ʊ | f**oo**t |
| f | **f**eel | s | **s**eal | h | **h**eal | o | b**oa**t | ɔ | b**o**re |
| v | **v**eal | z | **z**eal | l | **l**eaf | æ | b**a**t | a | p**o**t/b**a**r |
| θ | **th**igh | ʧ | **ch**ill | r | **r**eef | ʌ | b**u**tt | ə | sof**a** |
| ð | **th**y | ʤ | **g**in | j | **y**ou | aɪ | b**i**te | aʊ | b**ou**t |
| ʃ | **sh**ill | ʍ | **wh**ich | w | **w**itch | ɔɪ | b**oy** | | |
| ʒ | mea**s**ure | | | | | | | | |

English scholars of the past have advocated spelling reform. George Bernard Shaw complained that spelling was so inconsistent that *fish* could be spelled *ghoti*: *gh* as in *tough*, *o* as in *women*, and *ti* as in *nation*. Nonetheless, spelling reformers failed to significantly change our spelling habits. It took phoneticians to invent a **phonetic alphabet** that absolutely guaranteed a one-sound-to-one-symbol correspondence. There could be no other way to study the sounds of all human languages scientifically.

The **International Phonetic Alphabet (IPA)** uses both ordinary letters and invented symbols to represent all of the sounds across all of the world's languages. If you know this alphabet, you know how to pronounce a word written in it, and upon hearing a word pronounced, you would know how to write it using the alphabetic symbols.

Table 5.1 is a list of the IPA symbols that we will use to represent English speech sounds. The symbols do not tell us everything about the sounds, which may vary from person to person and which may depend on their position in a word. They are not all of the phonetic symbols needed for English, but they will suffice for our purposes. When we discuss the sounds in more detail later in the chapter, we will add appropriate symbols. From now on, we will enclose phonetic symbols in square brackets [ ] to distinguish them from ordinary letters.

The symbol [ə] in *sof**a*** toward the bottom right of the chart is called a *schwa*. We use it to represent vowels in syllables that are not emphasized in speaking and whose duration is very short, such as *general, **a**bout,* and *reader*. All other vowel symbols in the chart occur in syllables that receive at least some emphasis.

Some speakers of English pronounce *witch* and *which* with the same initial consonant, symbolized as [w] in the chart. Others pronounce them differently where the initial *w* in *which* has a little puff of air and is symbolized as [ʍ]. We have therefore listed both words in the chart of symbols.

It is difficult to include all the phonetic symbols needed to represent all differences in English. There may be sounds in your speech that are not represented, and vice versa, but that's okay. There are many varieties of English. The versions spoken in the United States, Canada, England, Australia, Ireland, India, and so on, and even within those countries, differ in their pronunciations.

The symbols in Table 5.1 are IPA symbols, with one small exception. The IPA uses an upside-down *r* ([ɹ]) for the English sound r. We, and many writers, prefer the right-side-up symbol [r] for clarity when writing for an English-reading audience. Using the IPA symbols, we can now unambiguously represent the pronunciation of words. For example, in the six words below, *ou* represents six distinct vowel sounds; the *gh* is silent in all but *rough*, where it is pronounced [f]; the *th* represents a single sound, either [θ] or [ð], and the *l* in *would* is silent. However, the phonetic transcription gives us the actual pronunciations.

| Spelling | Pronunciation |
|---|---|
| though | [ðo] |
| thought | [θɔt] |
| rough | [rʌf] |
| bough | [baʊ] |
| through | [θru] |
| would | [wʊd] |

# Articulatory Phonetics

The production of any sound involves the movement of air. Most speech sounds are produced by pushing lung air through the *vocal cords*, up the throat, into the mouth or nose, and finally out of the body.

A brief anatomy lesson is in order. The *opening* between the vocal cords is the **glottis** and is located in the voice box or **larynx**, pronounced "lair rinks." The tubular part of the throat above the larynx is the **pharynx** (rhymes with *larynx*). What sensible people call "the mouth," linguists call the **oral cavity** to distinguish it from the **nasal cavity**, which is the nose and the plumbing that connects it to the throat. Finally, we have the tongue and the lips, both of which are capable of rapid movement and shape changing. All of these together make up the **vocal tract**. By moving the different parts of the vocal tract, we change its shape, which results in the different sounds of language. Figure 5.1 should make these descriptions clearer. (The vocal cords and larynx are not specifically labeled in the figure.)

## Consonants

The sounds of all languages fall into two classes: consonants and vowels. Consonants are produced with some restriction or closure in the vocal tract that impedes the flow of air from the lungs. In phonetics, the terms *consonant* and *vowel* refer to types of *sounds*, not to the letters that represent them. In speaking of the alphabet, we may call *a* a vowel and *c* a consonant, but that means only

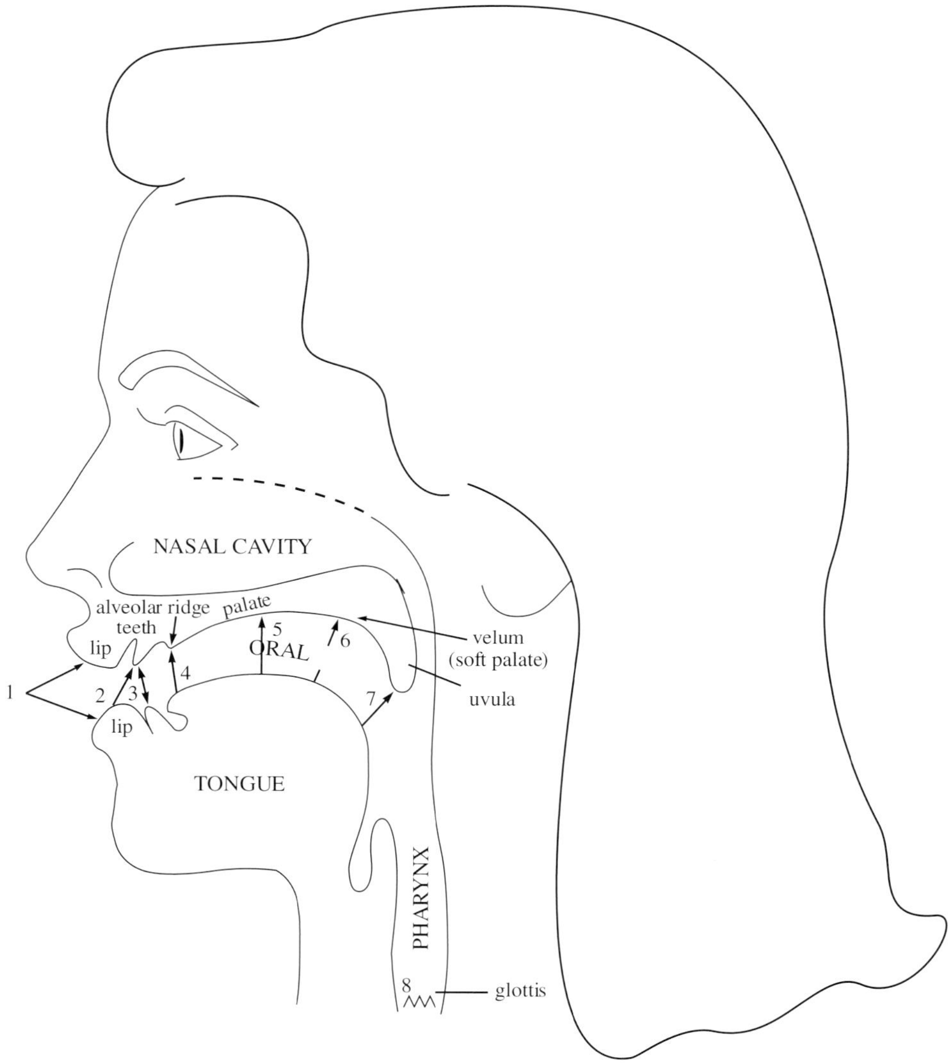


**FIGURE 5.1** | The vocal tract. Places of articulation: 1. bilabial; 2. labiodental; 3. interdental; 4. alveolar; 5. (alveo)palatal; 6. velar; 7. uvular; and 8. glottal.

that we use the letter *a* to represent vowel sounds and the letter *c* to represent consonant sounds.

## Place of Articulation

We classify consonants according to where in the vocal tract the airflow restriction occurs, called the **place of articulation**. Movement of the tongue and lips creates the constriction, reshaping the oral cavity in various ways to produce the various sounds. We are about to discuss the major places of articulation. As you read the description of each sound class, refer to

Table 5.1, which provides key words containing the sounds. As you pronounce these words, try to feel which articulators are moving. (Watching yourself in a mirror helps, too.) Look at Figure 5.1 for help with the terminology.

**Bilabials [p] [b] [m]** When we produce a [p], [b], or [m], we bring both lips together.

**Labiodentals [f] [v]** We also use our lips to form [f] and [v]. We make these sounds by touching the bottom lip to the upper teeth.

**Interdentals [θ] [ð]** These sounds, both spelled *th*, are pronounced by inserting the tip of the tongue between the teeth. However, for some speakers the tongue merely touches behind the teeth, making a sound more correctly called **dental**. Watch yourself in a mirror and say *think* or *these* and see where your tongue tip goes.

**Alveolars [t] [d] [n] [s] [z] [l] [r]** All seven of these sounds are pronounced with the tongue raised in various ways to the **alveolar ridge**.

- For [t], [d], and [n], the tongue tip is raised and touches the ridge, or slightly in front of it.
- For [s] and [z], the sides of the front of the tongue are raised, but the tip is lowered so that air escapes over it.
- For [l], the tongue tip is raised while the rest of the tongue remains down, permitting air to escape over its *sides*. Hence, [l] is called a **lateral** (meaning sideways) sound. You can feel this in the l's of *Lolita*.
- For [r] (IPA [ɹ]), the top of the tongue is curled back behind the alveolar ridge. As opposed to [l], when [r] is pronounced, air escapes through the central part of the mouth.

**Palatals [ʃ] [ʒ] [ʧ] [ʤ] [j]** For these sounds, which occur in *mission* [mɪʃən], *measure* [mɛʒər], *cheap* [ʧip], *judge* [**ʤ**ʌ**ʤ**], and *yoyo* [**j**o**j**o], the constriction occurs by raising the front part of the tongue to the palate.

**Velars [k] [g] [ŋ]** Another class of sounds is produced by raising the back of the tongue to the soft palate or **velum**. The initial and final sounds of the words *kick* [**k**ɪ**k**] and *gig* [**g**ɪ**g**], and the final sounds of the words *back* [bæ**k**], *bag* [bæ**g**], and *bang* [bæ**ŋ**], are all velar sounds.

**Uvulars [ʀ] [q] [ɢ] Uvular** sounds are produced by raising the back of the tongue to the **uvula**, the fleshy protuberance that hangs down in the back of our throats. The *r* in French is often a uvular **trill** symbolized by [ʀ]. The uvular sounds [q] and [ɢ] occur in Arabic. These sounds do not ordinarily occur in English.

**Glottals [h] [ʔ]** The sound of [h] is from the flow of air through the open **glottis** and past the tongue and lips as they prepare to pronounce a vowel sound, which always follows [h].

**TABLE 5.2** | Places of Articulation of English Consonants

| | | | | | | | |
|---|---|---|---|---|---|---|---|
| **Bilabial** | p | b | m | | | | |
| **Labiodental** | f | v | | | | | |
| **Interdental** | θ | ð | | | | | |
| **Alveolar** | t | d | n | s | z | l | r |
| **Palatal** | ʃ | ʒ | ʧ | ʤ | j | | |
| **Velar** | k | g | ŋ | | | | |
| **Glottal** | h | ʔ | | | | | |

If the air is stopped completely at the glottis by tightly closed vocal cords, the sound upon release of the cords is a **glottal stop [ʔ]**. The interjection *uh-oh*, which you hope never to hear your dentist utter, has two glottal stops and is spelled phonetically [ʔʌʔo]. The late singer Michael Jackson made free use of glottal stops in many of his most well-known songs.

Table 5.2 summarizes the classification of these English consonants by their place of articulation.

## Manner of Articulation

We have described several classes of consonants according to their places of articulation, yet we are still unable to distinguish the sounds within each class from one another. What distinguishes [p] from [b] or [b] from [m]? All are bilabial sounds. What is the difference between [t], [d], and [n], which are all alveolar sounds?

Speech sounds also vary in the way the airstream is affected as it flows from the lungs up and out of the mouth and nose. It may be blocked or partially blocked; the vocal cords may vibrate or not vibrate. We refer to this as the **manner of articulation**.

## Voiced and Voiceless Sounds

Sounds are **voiceless** when the vocal cords are apart so that air flows freely through the glottis into the oral cavity. [s] and [p] in *super* [supər] are two of the several voiceless sounds of English.

If the vocal cords are together, the airstream forces its way through and causes them to vibrate. Such sounds are **voiced**. [b] and [z] in *buzz* [bʌz] are two of the many voiced sounds of English. To get a sense of voicing, try putting a finger in each ear and say the voiced "z-z-z-z-z." You can feel the vibrations of the vocal cords. If you now say the voiceless "s-s-s-s-s," you will not sense these vibrations (although you might hear a hissing sound). When you whisper, you are making all the speech sounds voiceless. Try it! Whisper "Sue" and "zoo." No difference, right?

The voiced/voiceless distinction is very important in English. This phonetic property distinguishes the words in pairs like the following:

| | | | |
|---|---|---|---|
| ro**p**e/ro**b**e | fa**t**e/fa**d**e | ra**ck**/ra**g** | wrea**th**/wrea**the** |
| [ro**p**]/[ro**b**] | [fe**t**]/[fe**d**] | [ræ**k**]/[ræ**g**] | [ri**θ**]/[ri**ð**] |

The first word of each pair ends with a voiceless sound and the second word with a voiced sound. All other aspects of the sounds in each word pair are identical; the position of the lips and tongue is the same.

The voiced/voiceless distinction also occurs in the following pairs, where in each case the first word begins with a voiceless sound and the second with a voiced sound:

| | | |
|---|---|---|
| **f**ine/**v**ine | **s**eal/**z**eal | **ch**oke/**j**oke |
| [**f**aɪn]/[**v**aɪn] | [**s**il/**z**il] | [**tʃ**ok]/[**dʒ**ok] |
| **p**eat/**b**eat | **t**ote/**d**ote | **k**ale/**g**ale |
| [**p**it]/[**b**it] | [**t**ot]/[**d**ot] | [**k**el]/[**g**el] |

Though it is difficult to hear—for reasons explained in the next chapter—the initial sound in the word *pit* differs phonetically from the second sound in the word *spit*. During the production of the voiceless [p] (and [t] and [k]), the glottis is open and the air flows freely between the vocal cords. However, when a voiceless sound is followed by a voiced sound such as a vowel, the vocal cords must slam shut so they can vibrate.

Voiceless sounds fall into two classes depending on the timing of the vocal cord closure. When we say *pit*, the vocal cords remain open for a very short time after the lips come apart to release the *p*. We call this *p* **aspirated** because a brief puff of air escapes before the glottis closes.

When we pronounce the *p* in *spit*, however, the vocal cords start vibrating as soon as the lips open. That *p* is **unaspirated**. Hold your palm about two inches

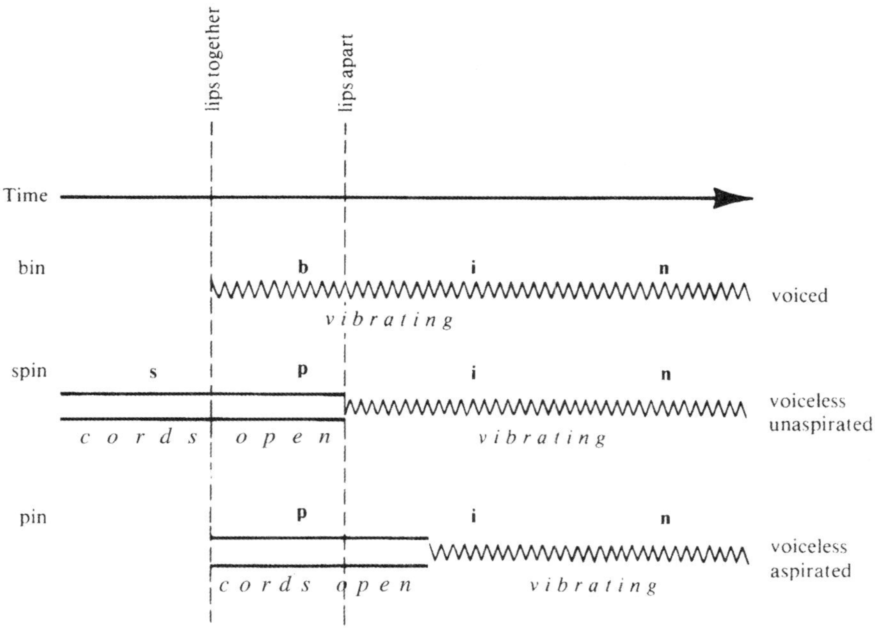


FIGURE 5.2 | Timing of lip closure and vocal-cord vibrations for voiced, voiceless unaspirated, and voiceless aspirated bilabial stops [b], [p] and [$p^h$].

in front of your lips and say *pit*. You will feel a puff of air, which you will not feel when you say *spit*. The *t* in *tick* and the *k* in *kin* are also aspirated voiceless stops, while the *t* in *stick* and the *k* in *skin* are unaspirated.

Finally, in the production of the voiced [b] (and [d] and [g]), the vocal cords are vibrating throughout the closure of the lips, and continue to vibrate during the vowel sound that follows after the lips part.

We indicate aspirated sounds by writing the phonetic symbol with a raised h, as in the following examples:

| | | | |
|---|---|---|---|
| pool | [pʰul] | spool | [spul] |
| tale | [tʰel] | stale | [stel] |
| kale | [kʰel] | scale | [skel] |

Figure 5.2 shows in diagrammatic form the timing of lip closure in relation to the state of the vocal cords.

## Nasal and Oral Sounds

The voiced/voiceless distinction differentiates the bilabials [b] and [p]. The sound [m] is also a bilabial, and it is voiced. What distinguishes it from [b]?

Figure 5.1 shows the roof of the mouth divided into the (hard) palate and the soft palate (or velum). The palate is a hard, bony structure at the front of the mouth. You can feel it with your thumb. First, wash your hands. Now, slide your thumb (nail down) along the hard palate back toward the throat; you will feel the velum, which is where the flesh becomes soft and pliable. Try not to throw up!

The velum terminates in the uvula, which you can see in a mirror if you open your mouth wide and say "aaah." The velum is movable, and when it is raised all the way to touch the back of the throat, the passage through the nose is cut off and air can escape only through the mouth.FIGURE 5.2 | Timing of lip closure and vocal-cord vibrations for voiced, voiceless unaspirated, and voiceless aspirated bilabial stops [b], [p] and [pʰ].

Sounds produced with the velum up, blocking the air from escaping through the nose, are **oral sounds**, because the air can escape only through the oral

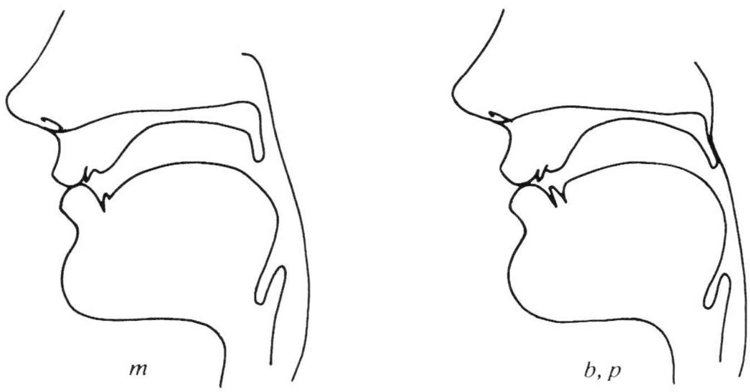


**FIGURE 5.3** | Position of lips and velum for *m* (lips together, velum down) and *b*, *p* (lips together, velum up).

TABLE 5.3 | Four Classes of Speech Sounds

| | Oral | Nasal |
|---|---|---|
| **Voiced** | b d g | m n ŋ |
| **Voiceless** | p t k | * |

*Nasal consonants in English are usually voiced. Both voiced and voiceless nasal sounds occur in other languages.

cavity. Most sounds in all languages are oral sounds. When the velum is lowered, air escapes through both the nose and the mouth. Sounds produced this way are **nasal sounds**. The sound [m] is a nasal consonant. Thus, [m] is distinguished from [b] because it is a nasal sound whereas [b] is an oral sound.

The diagrams in Figure 5.3 show the position of the lips and the velum when [m], [b], and [p] are articulated. The sounds [p], [b], and [m] are produced by stopping the airflow at the lips; [m] and [b] differ from [p] by being voiced; [m] differs from [b] by being nasal. (If you ever wondered why people sound "nasally" when they have a cold, it's because excessive mucus prevents the velum from closing properly during speech.)

The same oral/nasal difference occurs in ***raid*** [re**d**] and ***rain*** [re**n**], ***rug*** [rʌ**g**] and ***rung*** [rʌ**ŋ**]. The velum is raised in the production of [d] and [g], preventing the air from flowing through the nose, whereas for [n] and [ŋ] the velum is down, allowing the air out through both the nose and the mouth when the closure is released. The sounds [m], [n], and [ŋ] are therefore nasal sounds, and [b], [d], and [g] are oral sounds.

The presence or absence of these **phonetic features**—nasal and voiced—permit the division of all speech sounds into four classes: voiced, voiceless, nasal, and oral, as shown in Table 5.3.

We now have three ways of classifying consonants: by voicing, by place of articulation, and by nasalization. For example, [p] is a voiceless, bilabial, oral sound; [n] is a voiced, alveolar, nasal sound, and so on.

**Stops [p] [b] [m] [t] [d] [n] [k] [g] [ŋ] [ʧ] [ʤ] [ʔ]** We are seeing finer and finer distinctions of speech sounds. However, both [t] and [s] are voiceless, alveolar, and oral sounds. What distinguishes them? After all, *tack* and *sack* are different words.

Stops are consonants in which the airstream is completely blocked in the *oral* cavity for a short period (tens of milliseconds). All other sounds are **continuants**. The sound [t] is a stop, but the sound [s] is not, and that is what makes them different speech sounds.

- [p], [b], and [m] are *bilabial stops*, with the airstream stopped at the mouth by the complete closure of the lips.
- [t], [d], and [n] are *alveolar stops*; the airstream is stopped by the tongue, making a complete closure at or slightly behind the alveolar ridge.
- [k], [g], and [ŋ] are *velar stops*, with the complete closure at the velum.
- [ʧ] and [ʤ] are *palatal affricates* with complete stop closures. They will be further classified later.
- [ʔ] is a *glottal stop*; the air is completely stopped at the glottis.

We have been discussing the sounds that occur in English. A variety of stop consonants occur in other languages but not in English. For example, in Quechua, spoken in Bolivia and Peru, uvular stops occur, where the back of the tongue is raised and moved rearward to form a complete closure with the uvula. The phonetic symbol [q] denotes the voiceless version of this stop, which is the initial sound in the name of the language, *Quechua*. The voiced uvular stop [G] also occurs in Quechua.

**Fricatives [f] [v] [θ] [ð] [s] [z] [ʃ] [ʒ] [x] [ɣ] [h]** In the production of some continuants, the airflow is so severely obstructed that it causes friction, and the sounds are therefore called **fricatives**. The first of each of the following pairs of fricatives is voiceless; the second voiced.

- [f] and [v] are *labiodental fricatives;* the friction is created at the lips and teeth, where a narrow passage permits the air to escape.
- [θ] and [ð] are *interdental fricatives*, represented by *th* in *thin* and *then*. The friction occurs at the opening between the tongue and teeth.
- [s] and [z] are *alveolar fricatives*, with the friction created at the alveolar ridge.
- [ʃ] and [ʒ] are *palatal fricatives*, and contrast in such pairs as *mission* [mɪʃən] and *measure* [mɛʒər]. They are produced with friction created as the air passes between the tongue and the part of the palate behind the alveolar ridge. In English, the voiced palatal fricative never begins words except for foreign words such as *genre*. The voiceless palatal fricative begins the words *shoe* [ʃu] and *sure* [ʃur] and ends the words *rush* [rʌʃ] and *push* [pʊʃ].
- [x] and [ɣ] denote *velar fricatives*. They are produced by raising the back of the tongue toward, but not quite touching the velum. The friction is created as air passes through that narrow passage, and the sound is not unlike clearing your throat. These sounds do not commonly occur in English, though in some forms of Scottish English the final sound of *loch* meaning "lake" is [x]. In rapid speech, the *g* in *wagon* may be pronounced [ɣ]. The final sound of the composer J. S. Bach's name is also pronounced [x], which is a common sound in German.
- [h] is a glottal fricative. Its relatively weak sound comes from air passing through the open glottis and pharynx.

All fricatives are continuants. Although the airstream is obstructed as it passes through the oral cavity, it is not completely stopped.

**Affricates [ʧ] [ʤ]** These sounds are produced by a stop closure followed immediately by a gradual release of the closure that produces an effect characteristic of a fricative. The palatal sounds that begin and end the words *church* and *judge* are voiceless and voiced affricates, respectively. Affricates are not continuants because of the initial stop closure.

**Liquids [l] [r]** In the production of the sounds [l] and [r], there is some obstruction of the airstream in the mouth, but not enough to cause any real constriction or friction. These sounds are **liquids**. They are articulated differently, as described in the earlier alveolar section, but are grouped as a class because they are acoustically similar. Due to that similarity, foreign speakers of English may confuse the two sounds and substitute one for the other.

**Glides [j] [w]** The sounds [j] and [w], the initial sounds of *you* [ju] and *we* [wi], are produced with little obstruction of the airstream. They are always followed directly by a vowel and do not occur at the ends of words (don't be fooled by spelling; words ending in *y* or *w* like *say* and *saw* end in a vowel sound). After articulating [j] or [w] the tongue glides quickly into place for pronouncing the next vowel, hence the term **glide**.

The glide [j] is a palatal sound; the blade of the tongue (the front part minus the tip) is raised toward the hard palate in a position almost identical to that in producing the vowel sound in the word *beat*. The glide [w] is produced by both rounding the lips and simultaneously raising the back of the tongue toward the velum. It is thus a **labiovelar** glide. Where speakers of English have different pronunciations for the words *which* and *witch*, the labiovelar glide in the first word is voiceless, symbolized as [ʍ] (an upside-down w). The position of the tongue and the lips for [w] is similar to that for producing the vowel sound in *flute*.

**Approximants** The sounds [w], [j], [r], and [l] may also be called approximants because the articulators approximate a frictional closeness, but no actual friction occurs. The first three are central approximants, whereas [l] is a lateral approximant.

Although in this chapter we focus on the sounds of English, the IPA has symbols and classifications for all the sounds of the world's languages. For example, many languages have sounds that are referred to as trills, and others have clicks. These are described in the following sections.

**Trills and flaps** The r-sound of many languages may be different from the English [r]. A trilled *r* is produced by rapid vibrations of an articulator. An alveolar **trill**, as in the Spanish word for "dog," *perro*, is produced by vibrating the tongue tip against the alveolar ridge. Its IPA symbol is [r], strictly speaking, though we have co-opted [r] for the English r. Many French speakers articulate the initial sound of *rouge* as a uvular trill, produced by vibrating the uvula. Its IPA symbol is [ʀ].

Another *r*-sound is called a **flap** and is produced by a flick of the tongue against the alveolar ridge. It sounds like a very fast *d*. It occurs in Spanish in words such as *pero* meaning "but." It may also occur in British English in words such as *very*. Its IPA symbol is [ɾ]. Most American speakers produce a flap instead of a [t] or [d] in words like *writer* and *rider*, which then sound identical and are spelled phonetically as [raɪɾər].

**Clicks** These "exotic" sounds are made by moving air in the mouth between various articulators. The sound of disapproval often spelled *tsk* is an alveolar **click** that occurs in several languages of southern Africa such as Zulu. A lateral click, which is like the sound one makes to encourage a horse, occurs in Xhosa. In fact, the *X* in *Xhosa* stands for that particular speech sound.

## Phonetic Symbols for American English Consonants

We are now capable of distinguishing all of the consonant sounds of English via the properties of voicing, nasality, and place and manner of articulation. For

**TABLE 5.4** | Some Phonetic Symbols for American English Consonants

| | Bilabial | Labiodental | Interdental | Alveolar | Palatal | Velar | Glottal |
|---|---|---|---|---|---|---|---|
| **Stop** (oral) | | | | | | | |
| voiceless | p | | | t | | k | ʔ |
| voiced | b | | | d | | g | |
| **Nasal** (voiced) | m | | | n | | ŋ | |
| **Fricative** | | | | | | | |
| voiceless | | f | θ | s | ʃ | | h |
| voiced | | v | ð | z | ʒ | | |
| **Affricate** | | | | | | | |
| voiceless | | | | | ʧ | | |
| voiced | | | | | ʤ | | |
| **Glide** | | | | | | | |
| voiceless | ʍ | | | | | ʍ | |
| voiced | w | | | | j | w | |
| **Liquid** (voiced) | | | | | | | |
| (central) | | | | r | | | |
| (lateral) | | | | l | | | |

**TABLE 5.5** | Examples of Consonants in English Words

| | Bilabial | Labiodental | Interdental | Alveolar | Palatal | Velar | Glottal |
|---|---|---|---|---|---|---|---|
| **Stop** (oral) | | | | | | | |
| voiceless | *p*ie | | | *t*ie | | *k*ite | (**ʔ**)uh-(**ʔ**)oh |
| voiced | *b*uy | | | *d*ie | | *g*uy | |
| **Nasal** (voiced) | *m*y | | | *n*ight | | si*ng* | |
| **Fricative** | | | | | | | |
| voiceless | | *f*ine | *th*igh | *s*ue | *sh*oe | | *h*igh |
| voiced | | *v*ine | *th*y | *z*oo | mea*s*ure | | |
| **Affricate** | | | | | | | |
| voiceless | | | | | *ch*eese | | |
| voiced | | | | | *j*ump | | |
| **Glide** | | | | | | | |
| voiceless | *wh*ich | | | | | *wh*ich | |
| voiced | *w*ipe | | | | *y*ou | *w*ipe | |
| **Liquid** (voiced) | | | | | | | |
| (central) | | | | *r*ye | | | |
| (lateral) | | | | *l*ye | | | |

example, [f] is a voiceless, (oral), labiodental fricative; [n] is a (voiced), nasal, alveolar stop. The parenthesized features are usually not mentioned because they are redundant; all sounds are oral unless nasal is specifically mentioned, and all nasals are voiced in English.

Table 5.4 lists the consonants by their phonetic features. The rows stand for manner of articulation and the columns for place of articulation.

Examples of words in which these sounds occur are given in Table 5.5.

## Vowels

Vowels are produced with little restriction of the airflow from the lungs out through the mouth and/or the nose. The quality of a vowel depends on the shape of the vocal tract as the air passes through. Different parts of the tongue may be high or low in the mouth; the lips may be spread or pursed; the velum may be raised or lowered.

Vowel sounds carry pitch and loudness; you can sing vowels or shout vowels. They may be longer or shorter in duration. Vowels can stand alone—they can be produced without consonants before or after them. You can say the vowels of *beat* [bit], *bit* [bɪt], and *boot* [but] without the initial [b] or the final [t], but you cannot say a [b] or a [t] alone without at least a little bit of vowel sound.

We describe vowels by their articulatory features as we did with consonants. Just as we say a [d] is pronounced by raising the tongue tip to the alveolar ridge, we say an [i] is pronounced by raising the body of the tongue toward the palate. With a [b] the lips come together; for an [æ] (the vowel in *cat*) the tongue is low in the mouth with the tongue tip forward, behind the front teeth.

If you watch a side view of an X-ray (that's *-ray*, not *-rated*!) video of someone's tongue moving during speech, you will see various parts of the tongue rise up high and fall down low; at the same time you will see it move forward and backward in the mouth. These are the dimensions over which vowels are produced. We classify vowels according to three questions:

1. How high or low in the mouth is the tongue?
2. How forward or backward in the mouth is the tongue?
3. Are the lips rounded (pursed) or spread?

### Tongue Position

(In this section, we refer to the vowel symbols of Table 5.1 on page 140.) The upper two diagrams in Figure 5.4 show that the tongue is high in the mouth in the production of the vowels [i] and [u] in the words *he* [hi] and *who* [hu]. In *he* the front part (but not the tip) of the tongue is raised; in *who* it is the back of the tongue. (Prolong the vowels of these words and try to feel the raised part of your tongue.) These are both *high* vowels, and the [i] is a *high front* vowel while the [u] is a *high back* vowel.

To produce the vowel sound [a] of *hah* [ha], the tongue is low in the mouth, as the third diagram in Figure 5.4 shows. (The reason a doctor examining your throat may ask you to say *aah* is that the tongue is low and easy to see over.)

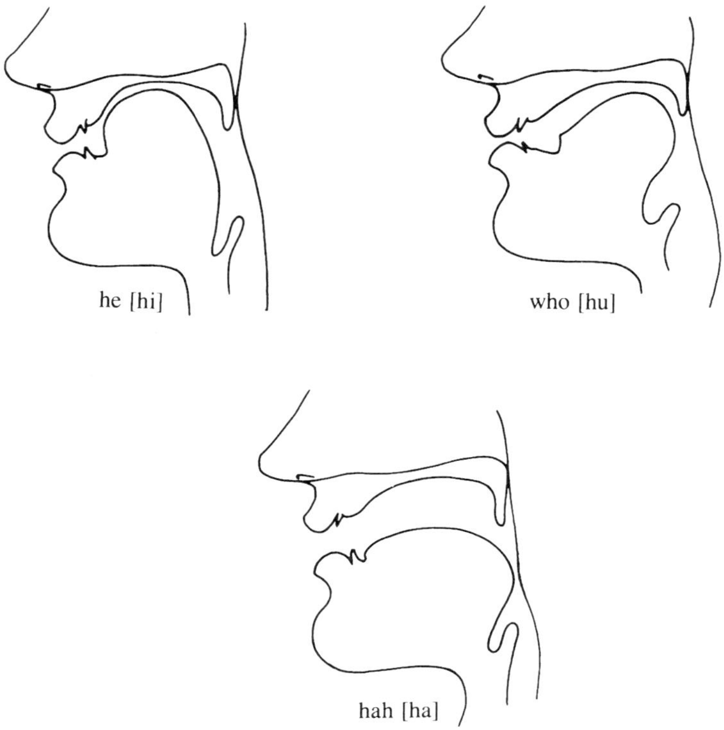


FIGURE 5.4 | Position of the tongue in producing the vowels in *he*, *who*, and *hah*.

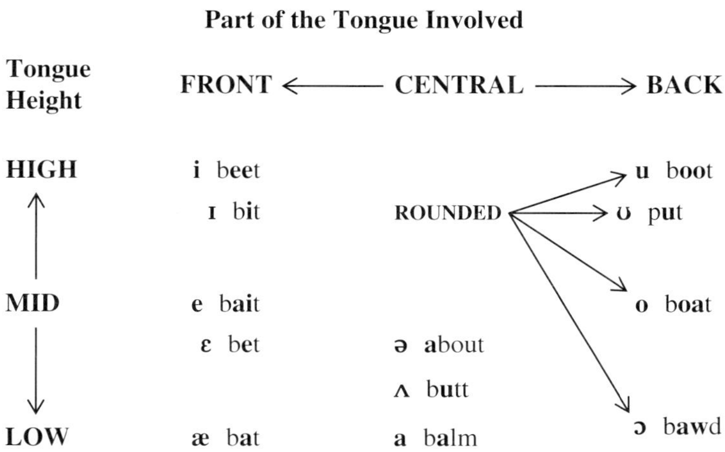


FIGURE 5.5 | Classification of American English vowels.

The vowels [ɪ] and [ʊ] in the words *hit* [hɪt] and *put* [pʰʊt] are similar to those in *heat* [hit] and *hoot* [hut] but with slightly lowered tongue positions.

The vowels [e] and [o] in *bait* [bet] and *boat* [bot] are *midvowels*—they are neither high nor low. [ɛ] in *bet* [bɛt] is also a midvowel, produced with a slightly lower tongue position than [e]. As well, [e] and [ɛ] are *front* vowels and [o] is a *back* vowel.

The vowel [æ] in *hack* [hæk] or *cat* [kʰæt] is produced with the front part of the tongue low in the mouth. Thus, [æ] is a *low front* vowel. The [ɔ] in *saw* [sɔ] is also a low vowel, but with the tongue back toward the throat. It is therefore a *low back* vowel.

The vowel [ʌ] in the word *luck* [lʌk] is a central vowel pronounced with the tongue low in the mouth though not as low as with [a]. Finally, the schwa [ə], which occurs as the first sound in *about* [əbaʊt], or the final sound of *sofa* [sofə], is articulated with the tongue in a neutral position between the extremes of high/low, front/back. The schwa is used mostly to represent unstressed vowels. (Figure 5.5 makes this vowel "geography" more apparent.)

## Lip Rounding

Vowels also differ as to whether the lips are rounded or spread. The back vowels [u], [ʊ], [o], and [ɔ] in *boot, put, boat,* and *bawd* are the only **rounded vowels** in (American) English. They are produced with pursed or rounded lips. You can get a feel for the rounding by prolonging the word *who*, as if you were an owl: *whoooooooooo*. Now pose for the camera and say *cheese*, only say it with a prolonged vowel: *cheeeeeeeeeeese*. The high front [i] in *cheese* is unrounded, with the lips in the shape of a smile, and you can feel it or see it in a mirror.

Other languages may differ in whether or not they have rounded vowels. French and Swedish, for example, have *front* rounded vowels, which English lacks. English also lacks a high back *unrounded* vowel, but this sound occurs in Mandarin Chinese, Japanese, and the Cameroonian language Feʔfeʔ, among others. The IPA symbol for this vowel is [ɯ]. The rounding distinction is important, as in Mandarin Chinese the unrounded [sɯ] means "four" but the round [su] (like sue) means "speed."

## Diphthongs

A **diphthong** is a sequence of two vowel sounds bonded together. Diphthongs occur in the phonetic inventory of many languages including English. The vowels we have studied so far are simple vowels, called **monophthongs**. The vowel sound in the word *bite* [baɪt], however, is the [a] of *father* joined to the [ɪ] of *fit*, resulting in the diphthong [aɪ]. Similarly, the vowel in *bout* [baʊt] is [a] joined to the [ʊ] of *put*, resulting in [aʊ]. Another diphthong that occurs in English is the vowel sound in *boy* [bɔɪ], which is the [ɔ] of *bore* joined to [ɪ], resulting in [ɔɪ]. The pronunciation of any of these diphthongs may vary from our description because of the diversity of English speakers.

To some extent, the midvowels [e] and [o] may be diphthongized, especially in American English, though not in other varieties such as Irish English. Many linguists therefore denote these sounds as [eɪ] and [oʊ] in a narrower transcription. [By "narrow transcription" we mean one that indicates all the phonetic details of a sound, even those that do not affect the words.] In this book, we will stay with [e] and [o] for these vowel sounds.

## Nasalization of Vowels

Vowels, like consonants, can be produced with a raised velum that prevents the air from escaping through the nose, or with a lowered velum that permits air to pass through the nasal passage. When the nasal passage is blocked, *oral* vowels result; when the nasal passage is open, *nasal* (or *nasalized*) vowels result. In English, nasal vowels occur for the most part before nasal consonants in the same syllable, and oral vowels occur in all other places.

The words *bean, bone, bingo, boom, bam,* and *bang* are examples of words that contain nasalized vowels. To show the nasalization of a vowel in a narrow phonetic transcription, an extra mark called a **diacritic**—the symbol ~ (tilde) in this case—is placed over the vowel, as in *bean* [bĩn] and *bone* [bõn].

In languages such as French, Polish, and Portuguese nasalized vowels occur without nasal consonants. The French word for "good" is *bon* [bõ]. The *n* in the spelling is not pronounced but indicates that the vowel is nasal.

## Tense and Lax Vowels

Figure 5.5 shows that the vowel [i] has a slightly higher tongue position than [ɪ]. This is also true for [e] and [ɛ]; and [u] and [ʊ]. The first vowel in each pair is generally produced with greater tension of the tongue muscles than its counterpart, and it is often a little longer in duration. These vowels are distinguished by the features **tense** and **lax** along with others:

| **Tense** | | **Lax** | |
|---|---|---|---|
| i | beat | ɪ | bit |
| e | bait | ɛ | bet |
| u | boot | ʊ | put |
| o | boat | ʌ | hut |
| ɔ | saw | æ | hat |
| a | pa | ə | about |
| aɪ | high | | |
| aʊ | how | | |
| ɔɪ | boy | | |

Tense vowels may occur at the ends of words: [si], [se], [su], [so], [pa], [saɪ], [haʊ], and [sɔɪ] represent the English words *see, say, sue, sew, pa, sigh, how,* and *soy*. Lax vowels do not ordinarily occur at the ends of words: [sɪ], [sɛ], [sʊ], [sʌ], [sæ], and [sə] are not possible words in English.

# Major Phonetic Classes

Biologists divide life forms into larger and smaller classes. They may distinguish between animals and plants; within animals, between vertebrates and invertebrates; and within vertebrates, between mammals and reptiles; and so on.

Linguists describe speech sounds similarly. All sounds are consonant sounds or vowel sounds, though some play dual roles. Within consonants, all are voiced or unvoiced, and so on. All the classes of sounds described so far in this chapter combine to form larger, more general classes that are important in the patterning of sounds in the world's languages.

## Noncontinuants and Continuants

Stops and affricates belong to the class of **noncontinuants**. There is a total obstruction of the airstream in the *oral cavity*. Nasal stops are included, although air does flow continuously out the nose. All other consonants, and all vowels, are continuants, in which the stream of air flows continuously out of the mouth.

## Obstruents and Sonorants

The non nasal stops, the fricatives, and the affricates form a major class of sounds called **obstruents**. The airstream may be fully obstructed, as in nonnasal stops and affricates, or nearly fully obstructed, as in the production of fricatives.

Sounds that are not obstruents are **sonorants**. Vowels, nasal stops [m], [n], and [ŋ], liquids [l] and [r], and glides [j] and [w] are all sonorants. They are produced with much less obstruction to the flow of air than the obstruents, which permits the air to resonate. Nasal stops are sonorants because, although the air is blocked in the mouth, it continues to resonate in the nasal cavity.

### Consonantal Sounds

Obstruents, nasal stops, liquids, and glides are all consonants. There is some degree of restriction to the airflow in articulating these sounds. With glides ([j], [w]), however, the restriction is minimal, and they are the most vowel-like, and the least consonant-like, of the consonants. Glides may even be referred to as "semivowels" or "semi-consonants." In recognition of this fact, linguists place the obstruents, nasal stops, and liquids in a subclass of consonants called **consonantal**, from which the glides are excluded.

Here are some other terms used to form subclasses of consonantal sounds. These are not exhaustive, nor are they mutually exclusive (e.g., the interdentals belong to two subclasses). A full course in phonetics would note further classes that we omit.

**Labials [p] [b] [m] [f] [v] [w] [ʍ]** Labial sounds are those articulated with the involvement of the lips. They include the class of *bilabial* sounds [p], [b], and [m], the *labiodentals* [f] and [v], and the *labiovelars* [w] and [ʍ].

**Coronals [θ] [ð] [t] [d] [n] [s] [z] [ʃ] [ʒ] [ʧ] [ʤ] [l] [r]** Coronal sounds are articulated by raising the tongue blade. Coronals include the *interdentals* [θ] and [ð], the *alveolars* [t], [d], [n], [s], and [z], the *palatals* [ʃ] and [ʒ], the *affricates* [ʧ] and [ʤ], and the *liquids* [l] and [r].

**Anteriors [p] [b] [m] [f] [v] [θ] [ð] [t] [d] [n] [s] [z]** Anterior sounds are consonants produced in the front part of the mouth, that is, from the alveolar area forward. They include the labials, the interdentals, and the alveolars.

**Sibilants [s] [z] [ʃ] [ʒ] [ʧ] [ʤ]** This class of consonantal sounds is characterized by an acoustic rather than an articulatory property of its members. The friction created by sibilants produces a hissing sound, which is a mixture of high-frequency sounds.

## Syllabic Sounds

Sounds that may function as the core of a syllable possess the feature **syllabic**. Clearly vowels are syllabic, but they are not the only sound class that anchors syllables.

Liquids and nasals may also be syllabic, as shown by the words *dazzle* [dæzl̩], *faker* [fekr̩], *rhythm* [rɪðm̩], and *wagon* [wægn̩]. (The diacritic mark under the [l̩], [r̩], [m̩], and [n̩] is the notation for syllabic.) Placing a schwa [ə] before the syllabic liquid or nasal also shows that these are separate syllables. The four words could be written as [dæzəl], [fekər], [rɪðəm], and [wægən]. We will use this transcription. Similarly, the vowel sound in words such as *bird* and *verb* are sometimes written as a syllabic *r*: [br̩d] and [vr̩b]. For consistency, we shall transcribe these words using the schwa—[bərd] and [vərb]—the only instances where a schwa represents a stressed vowel.

Obstruents and glides are never syllabic sounds because an obstruent or glide is always accompanied by a vowel that functions as the syllabic core.

# Prosodic Features

*Length, pitch,* and *stress* (or "accent") are **prosodic** or **suprasegmental** features. They are features *over and above* the segmental values such as place or manner of articulation, thus the *supra-* in *suprasegmental*. The term *prosodic* comes from poetry, where it refers to the metrical structure of verse. One of the essential characteristics of poetry is the placement of stress on particular syllables, which defines the versification of the poem.

Speech sounds that are identical in their place or manner features may differ in length (duration). Tense vowels are slightly longer than lax vowels, but only by a few milliseconds. However, in some languages when a vowel is prolonged to around twice its normal length, it can make a difference between words. In Japanese, the word *biru* [biru] with a regular *i* means "building," but with the *i* doubled in length as in *biiru*, spelled phonetically as [biːru], the meaning is "beer." (The colon-like ː is the IPA symbol for segment length or doubling.) In Japanese, vowel length can make the difference between two words.

Japanese, and many other languages such as Finnish and Italian, have long consonants that may contrast words. When a consonant is long, or doubled, either the closure or obstruction is prolonged. Pronounced with a short k, the word *saki* [saki] means "ahead" in Japanese; pronounced with a long *k*—prolonging the velar closure—the word *sakki* [sakːi] means "before." In effect, the extended silence of the prolonged closure is meaningful in these languages.

English is not a language in which vowel or consonant length can change a word. You might say "puleeeeeze" to emphasize your request, but the word is still *please*. You may also say in English "Whatttttt a dump!" to express your dismay at a hotel room, prolonging the t-closure, but the word *what* is not changed.

When we speak we also change the **pitch** of our voice. The pitch depends on how fast the vocal cords vibrate: the faster they vibrate, the higher the pitch. If the larynx is small, as in children, the shorter vocal cords vibrate faster and the pitch is higher, all other things being equal. If the larynx is larger, as in adults, the longer vocal cords vibrate more slowly and the pitch is lower. That is why men (being generally larger), women, and children have (to a greater or lesser degree) lower-, medium-, and higher-pitched voices.

In many languages including English, certain syllables in a word are louder, slightly higher in pitch, and somewhat longer in duration than other syllables in the word. They are **stressed** syllables. For example, in the adjective *PERfect* the first syllable is stressed, whereas in the verb *perFECT* the second syllable receives greater stress. Stress can be marked in several ways, as we did using capital letters or by using an accent mark as in *pérfect* versus *perféct*.

English is a "stress-timed" language, meaning that some syllables will be longer and some shorter and the intervals between stressed syllables are roughly equal in length. French, on the other hand, is a "syllable-timed" language, meaning that each syllable is more or less of equal length and equal (lack of) stress. When English speakers attempt to speak French, they cannot help but stress syllables, so their French is heard with "an English accent." When French speakers speak English, they often fail to stress syllables, and that contributes to what English speakers call "a French accent."

## Tone and Intonation

We have already seen how length and stress can make sounds perceptually different despite having the same segmental properties. In some languages, these differences make different words, such as the two *perfects* in English. The pitch with which a word or syllable is spoken can also make a difference in certain languages.

Speakers of all languages vary the pitch of their voice when they speak. The effect of pitch on a syllable differs from language to language. In English, it doesn't matter whether you say *cat* with a high pitch or a low pitch; it will still mean "cat." But, if you say [ba] with a relatively high pitch in Nupe (a language spoken in Nigeria), it will mean "to be sour," whereas if you say it with a relatively low pitch, it will mean "to count." Languages that use the pitch of individual vowels or syllables to contrast meanings of words are called **tone languages**. Rather than *pitch* we use the term *tone*.

Over half the world's languages are tone languages. There are more than one thousand tone languages spoken in Africa alone. Many languages of Asia, such as Mandarin Chinese, Burmese, and Thai, are tone languages. In Thai, for example, the same string of segmental sounds represented by [na:] will mean different things if one says the sounds with a low tone, a mid-tone, a high tone, a falling tone from high to low, or a rising tone from low to high. Thai therefore has five linguistic tones, illustrated as follows:

(Diacritics are used to represent distinctive tones in the phonetic transcriptions.)

| | | | | |
|---|---|---|---|---|
| [ˋ] | L | low tone | [nà:] | "a nickname" |
| [¯] | M | mid tone | [nā:] | "rice paddy" |
| [ˊ] | H | high tone | [ná:] | "young maternal uncle or aunt" |
| [ˆ] | HL | falling tone | [nâ:] | "face" |
| [ˇ] | LH | rising tone | [nǎ:] | "thick" |

There are two kinds of tones. If the pitch is level across the syllable, we have a **register tone**. If the pitch changes across the syllable, whether from high to low or vice versa, we have a **contour tone**. Thai has three level and two contour tones. Commonly, tone languages will have two or three register tones and possibly several contour tones.

In a tone language, it is not the absolute pitch that counts, but the relative pitch of adjacent syllables. Thus men, women and children with differently pitched voices communicate perfectly well.

**Intonation** is variation of pitch that does not distinguish words. Languages that are not tone languages, such as English or French, are called intonation languages. The **pitch contour** of an utterance may affect the meaning of the whole sentence, so that *The President is here* spoken with falling pitch is interpreted as a statement, but with rising pitch, as a question. We'll have more to say about intonation in the next chapter.

## Phonetic Symbols and Spelling Correspondences

Table 5.6 shows some but not all sound/spelling correspondences for American English. We have included the symbols for the voiceless aspirated stops to illustrate that what is spelled with one letter—for example *p*—may occur phonetically as two sounds: [p], [pʰ].

**TABLE 5.6** | Phonetic Symbol/English Spelling Correspondences

| | **Consonants** |
|---|---|
| **Symbol** | **Examples** |
| p | s**p**it, ti**p**, La**pp** |
| $p^h$ | **p**it, **p**rick, **p**laque, a**pp**ear |
| b | **b**it, ta**b**, **b**rat, **b**u**bb**le |
| m | **m**itt, ta**m**, s**m**ack, E**mm**y, co**mb**, Autu**mn** |
| t | s**t**ick, pi**t**, kiss**ed**, wri**t**e |
| $t^h$ | **t**ick, in**t**end, **pt**erodactyl, a**tt**ack |
| d | **D**ick, ca**d**, **d**rip, love**d**, ri**d**e |
| n | **n**ick, ki**n**, s**n**ow, **mn**emo**n**ic, **gn**ome, **pn**eumatic, **kn**ow |
| k | s**k**in, sti**ck**, s**c**at, criti**que**, el**k** |
| $k^h$ | **c**url, **k**in, **ch**arisma, **c**ritic, me**ch**anic, **c**lose |
| g | **g**irl, bur**g**, lon**g**er, Pittsbur**gh** |
| ŋ | si**ng**, thi**n**k, fi**n**ger |
| f | **f**at, **ph**iloso**ph**y, **f**lat, **ph**logiston, co**ff**ee, ree**f**, cou**gh** |
| v | **v**at, do**v**e, gra**v**el |
| s | **s**ip, **s**kip, **ps**ychology, pa**ss**, pat**s**, democra**c**y, **sc**issors, fa**s**ten, de**c**eive, de**sc**ent |
| z | **z**ip, ja**zz**, ra**z**or, pad**s**, kiss**es**, **X**erox, de**s**ign, la**z**y, sci**ss**ors, mai**z**e |
| θ | **th**igh, **th**rough, wra**th**, e**th**er, Ma**tth**ew |
| ð | **th**y, **th**eir, wea**th**er, la**the**, ei**th**er |
| ʃ | **sh**oe, mu**sh**, mi**ss**ion, na**t**ion, fi**sh**, gla**ci**al, **s**ure |
| ʒ | mea**s**ure, vi**s**ion, a**z**ure, ca**s**ual, **g**enre, rou**g**e |
| ʧ | ma**tch**, ri**ch**, righ**t**eous |
| $ʧ^h$ | **ch**oke, **Tch**aikovsky, dis**ch**arge |
| ʤ | ju**dg**e, mi**dg**et, **G**eor**g**e, ma**g**istrate, resi**d**ual |
| l | **l**eaf, fee**l**, ca**ll**, sing**l**e |
| r | **r**eef, fea**r**, Pa**r**is, singe**r** |
| j | **y**ou, **y**es, f**eu**d, **u**se |
| w | **w**itch, s**w**im, q**u**een |
| ʍ | **wh**ich, **wh**ere, **wh**ale (for speakers who pronounce *which* differently from *witch*) |
| h | **h**at, **wh**o, **wh**ole, re**h**ash |
| ʔ | bo**tt**le, bu**tt**on, glo**tt**al (for some speakers), (ʔ)uh-(ʔ)oh |
| ɾ | wri**t**er, ri**d**er, la**tt**er, la**dd**er |
| | **Vowels** |
| i | b**ee**t, b**ea**t, b**e**, rec**ei**ve, k**ey**, bel**ie**ve, am**oe**ba, p**eo**ple, C**ae**sar, Vasel**i**ne, ser**e**ne, Ral**eigh** |
| ɪ | b**i**t, cons**i**st, **i**njury, b**i**n, w**o**men, b**ui**ld |
| e | g**a**te, b**ai**t, r**ay**, gr**ea**t, **eigh**t, g**au**ge, gr**ey**hound, r**ei**n, f**eig**n |
| ɛ | b**e**t, ser**e**nity, s**ay**s, gu**e**st, d**ea**d, s**ai**d |
| æ | p**a**n, **a**ct, l**au**gh, comr**a**de |
| u | b**oo**t, l**u**te, wh**o**, s**ew**er, thr**ough**, t**o**, t**oo**, tw**o**, m**o**ve, L**ou**, tr**ue**, s**ui**t |
| ʊ | p**u**t, f**oo**t, b**u**tcher, c**ou**ld |
| ʌ | c**u**t, t**ou**gh, am**o**ng, **o**ven, d**oe**s, c**o**ver, fl**oo**d |
| o | c**oa**t, g**o**, b**eau**, gr**ow**, th**ough**, t**oe**, **ow**n, s**ew** |
| ɔ | c**augh**t, st**al**k, c**o**re, s**aw**, b**a**ll, **aw**e, **au**to |
| a | c**o**t, f**a**ther, p**al**m, s**e**rgeant, h**o**nor, h**o**spital, mel**o**dic |
| ə | sof**a**, **a**lone, symph**o**ny, s**u**ppose, mel**o**dy, b**i**rd, v**e**rb, th**e** |
| aɪ | b**i**te, s**igh**t, b**y**, b**uy**, d**ie**, d**ye**, **ai**sle, ch**oi**r, gu**i**de, **is**land, h**ei**ght, s**ig**n |
| aʊ | ab**ou**t, br**ow**n, d**oub**t, c**ow**ard, s**au**erkr**au**t |
| ɔɪ | b**oy**, **oi**l, R**eu**ters |

Some of these pronunciations may differ from your own. For example, you may (or may not) pronounce the words *cot* and *caught* identically. In the form of English described here, *cot* and *caught* are pronounced differently, *cot* with the vowel [a] as in *car*, and *caught* with the vowel [ɔ] as in *core*.

There will be other differences, too, because English is a worldwide language and is spoken in many forms in many countries. The English examples used in this book are most closely related to American English. However, our aim is to teach phonetics in general, and to show you how phonetics might describe the speech sounds of any of the world's languages. We merely use American English for illustration.

## Summary

The science of speech sounds is called **phonetics**. It aims to provide the set of properties necessary to describe and distinguish all the sounds in human languages throughout the world.

When we speak we produce continuous stretches of sound, which are the physical manifestations of strings of discrete linguistic **segments**. Knowledge of a language permits one to separate continuous speech into individual sounds and words.

The discrepancy between spelling and sounds motivated the development of phonetic alphabets in which one letter corresponds to one sound. The major **phonetic alphabet** in use is the **International Phonetic Alphabet (IPA),** by means of which the sounds of all human languages can be represented. To distinguish between **orthography** (spelling) and **phonetic transcriptions**, we write the latter between square brackets, as in [fənɛrɪk] for *phonetic*.

All English speech sounds come from the movement of lung air through the vocal tract. The air moves through the **glottis** (i.e., between the vocal cords), up the pharynx, through the oral (and possibly the nasal) cavity, and out the mouth or nose.

Human speech sounds fall into classes according to their phonetic properties. All speech sounds are either **consonants** or **vowels,** and all consonants are either **obstruents** or **sonorants.** Consonants have some obstruction of the airstream in the vocal tract, and the location of the obstruction defines their **place of articulation,** some of which are: **bilabial, labiodental, alveolar, palatal, velar, uvular,** and **glottal.**

Consonants are further classified according to their **manner of articulation.** They may be **voiced** or **voiceless, oral** or **nasal**, and long or short. They may be **stops, fricatives, affricates, liquids,** or **glides.** During the production of voiced sounds, the vocal cords are together and vibrating, whereas in voiceless sounds they are apart and not vibrating. Consonants may also be grouped according to certain features to form larger classes such as **labial, coronal, anterior,** and **sibilant.**

Vowels form the nucleus of syllables. They differ according to the position of the tongue and lips: high, mid, or low tongue; front, central, or back of the tongue; rounded or unrounded lips. The vowels in English may be **tense** or **lax.** Tense vowels are slightly longer in duration and slightly higher than lax vowels.

Vowels may also be **stressed** (longer, higher in pitch, and louder) or **unstressed.** Vowels, like consonants, may be nasal or oral, although most vowels in all languages are oral.

Length, pitch, loudness, and stress are **prosodic,** or **suprasegmental,** features. They are imposed over and above the segmental values of the sounds in a syllable. In many languages, the pitch or **tone** of the syllable is linguistically significant. For example, two words with identical segments may contrast in meaning if one has a high tone and the other a low tone. Such languages are **tone languages.** There are also **intonation** languages in which the rise and fall of pitch over an entire phrase may affect meaning.

English and other languages use stress to distinguish different words, such as *cóntent* and *contént.* In some languages, long vowels and long consonants contrast with their shorter counterparts. Thus, *biru* [biru] and *biiru* [bi:ru], *saki* [saki] and *sakki* [sak:i] are different words in Japanese.

**Diacritics** to specify such properties as nasalization, length, stress, and tone may be combined with the phonetic symbols for more detailed (narrow) phonetic transcriptions. A phonetic transcription of *man* would use a tilde diacritic to indicate the nasalization of the vowel: [mæ̃n].

## References for Further Reading

Grayson, G. 2003. *Talking with your hands, listening with your eyes: A complete photographic guide to American sign language.* Garden City Park, New York: Square One Publishers.

International Phonetic Association. 1999. *Handbook of the International Phonetic Association.* Cambridge, UK: Cambridge University Press.

Ladefoged, P. 2005. *Vowels and consonants, 2nd ed.* Oxford, UK: Blackwell Publishers.

Ladefoged, P., and Johnson, K. 2011. *A course in phonetics, 6th ed.* Boston, MA: Wadsworth, Cengage Learning.

Ladefoged, P., and I. Maddieson. 1995. *The sounds of the world's languages.* Oxford, UK: Blackwell Publishers.

Ogden, R. 2010. *An introduction to English phonetics.* Edinburgh, UK: Edinburgh University Press.

Pullum, G.K., and W. A. Ladusaw. 2013. *Phonetic symbol guide, 2nd ed.* Chicago: University of Chicago Press.

## Exercises

**1.** Write the phonetic symbol for the first sound in each of the following words according to the way you pronounce it.

*Example*: ooze [u]

**a.** judge [ ]
**b.** Thomas [ ]
**c.** though [ ]
**d.** easy [ ]
**e.** pneumonia [ ]

psycho [s]

**f.** thought [ ]
**g.** contact [ ]
**h.** phone [ ]
**i.** civic [ ]
**j.** usual [ ]

**2.** Write the phonetic symbol for the *last* sound in each of the following words.

*Example*: boy [ɔɪ] (Diphthongs should be treated as one sound.)

**a.** fleece [ ]
**b.** neigh [ ]
**c.** long [ ]
**d.** health [ ]
**e.** watch [ ]
**f.** cow [ ]
**g.** rough [ ]
**h.** cheese [ ]
**i.** bleached [ ]
**j.** rags [ ]

**3.** Write the following words in phonetic transcription, according to your pronunciation.

*Examples: knot* [nat]; *delightful* [dilaɪtfəl] or [dəlaɪtfəl]. Some of you may pronounce some of these words the same.

**a.** physics
**b.** merry
**c.** marry
**d.** Mary
**e.** yellow
**f.** sticky
**g.** transcription
**h.** Fromkin
**i.** tease
**j.** weather
**k.** coat
**l.** Rodman
**m.** heath
**n.** "your name"
**o.** touch
**p.** cough
**q.** larynx
**r.** through
**s.** beautiful
**t.** honest
**u.** president

**4.** Following is a **narrow** phonetic transcription of a verse in the poem "The Walrus and the Carpenter" by Lewis Carroll. There is *one major error* in each line that is a mispronunciation or incorrect phonetic symbol. Write the word in which the error occurs in the correct phonetic transcription.

| | *Corrected Word* |
|---|---|
| **a.** ðə t$^{h}$ãɪm hæz cʌ̃m | [k$^{h}$ʌ̃m] |
| **b.** ðə wɔlrəs sed | |
| **c.** t$^{h}$u t$^{h}$ɔlk əv mɛ̃ni θĩŋz | |
| **d.** əv ʃuz ãnd ʃɪps | |
| **e.** æ̃nd silĩŋ wæx | |
| **f.** əv k$^{h}$æbəgəz æ̃nd k$^{h}$ĩŋz | |
| g. æ̃nd waɪ ðə si ɪs bɔɪlĩŋ hat | |
| **h.** æ̃nd wɛθər p$^{h}$ɪgz hæv wĩŋz | |

**5.** The following are all English words written in a broad phonetic transcription (omitting details such as nasalization and aspiration). Write the words using ordinary spelling.

**a.** [hit]
**b.** [strok]
**c.** [fez]
**d.** [ton]
**e.** [boni]
**f.** [skrim]
**g.** [frut]
**h.** [pritʃər]
**i.** [krak]
**j.** [baks]
**k.** [θæŋks]
**l.** [wɛnzde]
**m.** [krɔld]
**n.** [kantʃiɛntʃəs]
**o.** [parləmɛntæriən]
**p.** [kwəbɛk]
**q.** [pitsə]
**r.** [bərak obamə]
**s.** [mɪt ramni]
**t.** [tu θaʊzənd ænd twɛlv]

**6.** Write the symbol that corresponds to each of the following phonetic descriptions, then give an English word that contains this sound.

*Example*: voiced alveolar stop [d] *dough*

**a.** voiceless bilabial unaspirated stop [ ]
**b.** low front vowel [ ]
**c.** lateral liquid [ ]
**d.** velar nasal [ ]
**e.** voiced interdental fricative [ ]
**f.** voiceless affricate [ ]
**g.** palatal glide [ ]
**h.** mid lax front vowel [ ]
**i.** high back tense vowel [ ]
**j.** voiceless aspirated alveolar stop [ ]

**7.** In each of the following pairs of words, the **boldfaced** sounds differ by one or more phonetic properties (features). Give the IPA symbol for each of the boldfaced sounds, state their differences and, in addition, state what properties they have in common.

*Example*: cl**ea**n—cl**ea**nse [i]-[ɛ]

The *ea* in cl**ea**n is high and tense.

The *ea* in cl**ea**nse is mid and lax.

Both are front vowels.

**a.** ba*th*—ba*th*e
**b.** redu*c*e—redu*c*tion
**c.** c*oo*l—c*o*ld
**d.** wi*f*e—wi*v*es
**e.** cat*s*—dog*s*
**f.** i*m*polite—i*n*decent

**8.** Write a phonetic transcription for each of the words in the following sets. Note that the words in each set are <u>written</u> with the same vowel.

| **a** | **ea** |
|---|---|
| swam | hear |
| swan | heart |
| | heard |

| **o** | **ou** |
|---|---|
| bone | shout |
| done | should |
| gone | shoulder |
| one | trouble |
| both | you |
| bother | |
| brother | |

**9.** For each group of sounds listed, state the phonetic feature(s) they all share.

*Example*: [p] [b] [m] Features: bilabial, stop, consonant

**a.** [g] [p] [t] [d] [k] [b]
**b.** [u] [ʊ] [o] [ɔ]
**c.** [i] [ɪ] [e] [ɛ] [æ]
**d.** [t] [s] [ʃ] [p] [k] [ʧ] [f] [h]
**e.** [v] [z] [ʒ] [ʤ] [n] [g] [d] [b] [l] [r] [w] [j]
**f.** [t] [d] [s] [ʃ] [n] [ʧ] [ʤ]

**10.** Write the following broad phonetic transcriptions in regular English spelling.

**a.** nom ʧamski ɪz e lɪngwɪst hu tiʧəz æt ɛm aɪ ti
**b.** fənɛtɪks ɪz ðə stʌdi əv spiʧ saʊndz
**c.** ɔl spokən læŋgwɪʤəz juz saʊndz prədust baɪ ðə ʌpər rɛspərətɔri sɪstəm
**d.** ɪn wʌn daɪəlɛkt əv ɪnglɪʃ kat ðə naʊn ænd kɔt ðə vərb ar prənaʊnst ðə sem
**e.** sʌm pipəl θɪŋk fənɛtɪks ɪz vɛri ɪntərɛstɪŋ
**f.** vɪktɔrijə framkən rabərt radmən ænd ninə haɪəmz ar ðə ɔθərz əv ðɪs bʊk

**11.** What phonetic property or feature distinguishes the sets of sounds in column A from those in column B?

| | A | B |
|---|---|---|
| **a.** | [i] [ɪ] | [u] [ʊ] |
| **b.** | [p] [t] [k] [s] [f] | [b] [d] [g] [z] [v] |
| **c.** | [p] [b] [m] | [t] [d] [n] [k] [g] [ŋ] |
| **d.** | [i] [ɪ] [u] [ʊ] | [e] [ɛ] [o] [ɔ] [æ] [a] |

| | A | B |
|---|---|---|
| e. | [f] [v] [s] [z] [ʃ] [ʒ] | [ʧ] [ʤ] |
| f. | [i] [ɪ] [e] [ə] [ɛ] [æ] | [u] [ʊ] [o] [ɔ] |

**12.** Which of the following sound pairs have the same manner of articulation, and what is that manner of articulation?

a. [h] [ʔ]
b. [r] [w]
c. [m] [ŋ]
d. [ð] [v]
e. [r] [t]
f. [f] [ʃ]
g. [k] [θ]
h. [s] [g]
i. [j] [w]
j. [j] [ʤ]

**13. Part One**

Which of the following vowels are lax and which are tense?

a. [i]
b. [ɪ]
c. [u]
d. [ʌ]
e. [ʊ]
f. [e]
g. [ɛ]
h. [o]
i. [ɔ]
j. [æ]
k. [a]
l. [ə]
m. [aɪ]
n. [aʊ]
o. [ɔɪ]

**Part Two**

Think of ordinary, nonexclamatory one-syllable English words that end in [ʃ] preceded directly by each of the vowels in Part One. Which are possible (or actual) words? Are any such words impossible in English?

*Example: push* [pʊʃ] is an actual word; *nish* [nɪʃ] is a possible word; but words ending in [-aɪʃ] are not possible in English.

**Part Three**

In terms of tense/lax, which vowel type is found in most such words?

**14.** Write a made-up sentence in narrow phonetic transcription that contains at least six different vowels and two different diphthongs.

**15.** The front vowels of English, [i], [ɪ], [e], [ɛ], and [æ], are all unrounded. However, many languages have rounded front vowels, such as French. Here are three words in French with rounded front vowels. Transcribe them phonetically by finding out the correct IPA symbols for front rounded vowels: (Hint: Try one of the books given in the references, or Google around.)

**a.** *tu,* "you," has a high front rounded vowel and is transcribed phonetically as [ ]

**b.** *bleu,* "blue," has a midfront rounded vowel and is transcribed phonetically as [ ]

**c.** *heure,* "hour," has a low midfront rounded vowel and is transcribed phonetically as [ ]

**16. Challenge exercise:**

**a.** Take all of the vowels from Exercise 13, Part One, except the schwa and for each find a monosyllabic word containing that vowel followed directly by [t], and give both the spelling and the phonetic transcription.

*Example: beat* [bit], *foot* [fʊt]

**b.** Now do the same thing for monosyllabic words ending in [r]. Indicate when such a word appears not to occur in the way you speak English.

**c.** And do the same thing for monosyllabic words ending in [g].

**d.** Is there a quantitative difference in the number of examples found as you went from Part One to Part Three in Exercise 13?

**e.** Are most vowels that "work" in B tense or lax? How about in C?

**f.** Write a brief summary of the difficulties you encountered in trying to do this exercise.

**17.** In the first column are the last names of well-known authors. In the second column are their best-known works (one for each). Match each work to its author and write the author's name and work in conventional spelling.

*Example*: **a. 1.**

| | | |
|---|---|---|
| *Example*: | **a.** [dɪkə̃nz] | **1.** [ɔləvər $t^h$wɪst] |
| Answer: | a—1 (Dickens, Oliver Twist) | |
| | **b.** [sɛrvãntɛs] | **2.** [ə fɛrwɛl $t^h$u armz] |
| | **c.** [dãnte] | **3.** [æ̃nə̃məl farm] |
| | **d.** [dɪkə̃nz] | **4.** [dõn kihote] |
| | **e.** [ɛliət] | **5.** [greps ʌv ræθ] |
| | **f.** [hɛ̃mĩŋwe] | **6.** [gret ɛkspɛk$t^h$eʃə̃nz] |
| | **g.** [hõmər] | **7.** [gʌləvərz $t^h$rævəlz] |
| | **h.** [mɛlvɪl] | **8.** [hæ̃mlət] |
| | **i.** [ɔrwɛl] | **9.** [mobi-dɪk] |

**j.** [ʃekspir]
**k.** [staĩnbɛk]
**l.** [swɪft]
**m.** [t$^{h}$ɔlstɔɪ]
**n.** [t$^{h}$wẽn]

**10.** [saɪləs marnər]
**11.** [ðə dɪvaĩn k$^{h}$ãmədi]
**12.** [ðə ɪliəd]
**13.** [t$^{h}$ãm sɔɪjər]
**14.** [wɔr ǣnd p$^{h}$is]

6

# Phonology: The Sound Patterns of Language

What do you think is greater: the number of languages in the world, or the number of speech sounds in all those languages? Well, there are thousands of languages, but only hundreds of speech sounds, some of which we examined in the previous chapter. Even more remarkable, only a few dozen features, such as *voicing* and *bilabial*, are needed to describe every speech sound that occurs in every human language.

That being the case, why, you may ask, do languages sound so different? One reason is that the sounds form different patterns in different languages. English has nasalized vowels, but only in syllables with nasal consonants. Portuguese puts nasal vowels anywhere it pleases, with or without nasal consonants. The speech sound that ends the word *song*—the velar nasal [ŋ]—cannot begin a word in English, but it can in Vietnamese. The common Vietnamese name spelled *Nguyen* begins with this sound, and the reason few of us can pronounce this name correctly is that it doesn't follow the English pattern. The ability to pronounce particular sounds depends on the speaker's knowledge of the sound patterns of his or her own language or languages.

The study of how speech sounds form patterns is **phonology**. These patterns may be as simple as the fact that the velar nasal cannot begin a syllable in English, or as complex as why *g* is silent in *sign* but is pronounced in the related word *signal*. To see that this is a pattern and not a one-time exception, just consider the slippery *n* in *autumn* and *autumnal*, or the illusive *b* in *bomb* and *bombard*.

The word *phonology* refers both to the linguistic knowledge that speakers have about the sound patterns of their language and to the description of that knowledge that linguists try to produce. It's like the way we defined *grammar*: your mental knowledge of your language, or a linguist's description of that knowledge.

Phonology tells you what sounds are in your language and which ones are foreign; it tells you what combinations of sounds comprise a possible word in your language, whether it is an actual word like *black*, or a nonword (in English) like *blick*; and it tells you what combination of sounds is not a possible word in your language like *mbick. It also explains why certain phonetic features are important to identifying a word, for example, voicing in English, as in *pat* versus *bat*, while other features such as vowel nasality in English are not crucial to identifying a word—though it is in Portuguese where the word *pão* with a nasalized vowel means "bread" and *pao* without the nasalization means "stick." Finally, it allows us to adjust our pronunciation of morphemes, for example, the past and plural morphemes, to suit the different phonological contexts in which they occur.

# The Pronunciation of Morphemes

Knowledge of phonology determines how we pronounce words and the parts of words or morphemes (Chapter 2). Often, certain morphemes are pronounced differently depending on their contexts, and we will introduce a way of describing this variation with (usually unconscious) phonological rules. We begin with some examples from English, and then move on to examples from other languages.

## The Pronunciation of Plurals

Nearly all English nouns have a plural form: *cat/cats, dog/dogs, fox/foxes*. But have you ever paid attention to how plural forms are *pronounced?* Listen to a native speaker of English (or yourself if you are one) pronounce the plurals of the following nouns.

| A | B | C | D |
|---|---|---|---|
| cab | cap | bus | child |
| cad | cat | bush | ox |
| bag | back | buzz | mouse |
| love | cuff | garage | criterion |
| lathe | faith | match | sheep |
| cam | | badge | |
| can | | | |
| call | | | |
| bar | | | |
| spa | | | |
| boy | | | |

The final sound of the plural nouns from Column A is a [z]—a *voiced* alveolar fricative. For column B the plural ending is an [s]—a *voiceless* alveolar fricative. And for Column C it's [əz]. Here is our first example of a morpheme with different pronunciations. Note also that there is a regularity in columns A, B, and C that does not exist in D. The plural forms in D—*children, oxen, mice, criteria,* and *sheep*—are a hodge-podge of special cases that are memorized individually when you acquire English, whether natively or as a second language. This is because there is no way to predict the plural forms of these words.

How do we know how to pronounce this plural morpheme? The spelling, which adds *s* or *es*, is misleading—not a *z* in sight—yet if you know English, you pronounce it as we indicated. When faced with this type of question, it's useful to make a chart that records the phonological environments in which each variant of the morpheme is known to occur. (The more technical term for a variant of a morpheme is **allomorph**.) Writing the words from the first three columns in broad phonetic transcription, we have our first chart for the plural morpheme. (And our first example of "phonological analysis.")

| Allomorph | Environment |
|---|---|
| [z] | After [kæb], [kæd], [bæg], [lʌv], [leð], [kæm], [kæn], [bæŋ], [kɔl], [bar], [spa], [bɔɪ], e.g., [kæbz], [kædz] . . . [bɔɪz] |
| [s] | After [kæp], [kæt], [bæk], [kʌf], [feθ], e.g., [kæps], [kæts] . . . [feθs] |
| [əz] | After [bʌs], [bʊʃ], [bʌz], [gəraʒ], [mæʧ], [bæʤ], e.g., [bʌsəz], [bʊʃəz] . . . [bæʤəz] |

To discover the pattern behind the way plurals are pronounced, we look for some property of the environment associated with each group of allomorphs. For example, what is it about [kæb] or [lʌv] that determines that the plural morpheme will take the form [z] rather than [s] or [əz]?

To guide our search, we look for **minimal pairs** in our list of words. A minimal pair is two words with different meanings that are identical except for one sound segment that occurs in the same place in each word. For example, *cab* [kæb] and *cad* [kæd] are a minimal pair that differ only in their final segments, whereas *cat* [kæt] and *mat* [mæt] are a minimal pair that differ only in their initial segments. Other minimal pairs in our list include *cap/cab, bag/back,* and *bag/badge.*

Minimal pairs whose members take different allomorphs are particularly useful for our search. For example, consider *cab* [kæb] and *cap* [kæp], which respectively take the allomorphs [z] and [s] to form the plural. Clearly, the final segment is responsible, because that is where the two words differ. The same for *bag* [bæg] and *badge* [bæʤ]: their final segments determine the different plural allomorphs [z] and [əz].

Apparently, the distribution of plural allomorphs in English is conditioned by the final segment of the singular form. We can make our chart more concise by considering just the final segment. (We treat diphthongs such as [ɔɪ] as single segments.)

| Allomorph | Environment |
|---|---|
| [z] | After [b], [d], [g], [v], [ð], [m], [n], [ŋ], [l], [r], [a], [ɔɪ] |
| [s] | After [p], [t], [k], [f], [θ] |
| [az] | After [s], [ʃ], [z], [ʒ], [ʧ], [ʤ] |

We now want to understand *why* the English plural follows this pattern. We *always* answer questions of this type by inspecting the *phonetic properties* of the conditioning segments. Such an inspection reveals that the segments that trigger the [əz] plural have in common the property of being *sibilants*. Of the nonsibilants, the *voiceless* segments take the [s] plural, and the *voiced* segments take the [z] plural. Now the rules can be stated in more general terms:

| Allomorph | Environment |
|---|---|
| [z] | After voiced nonsibilant segments |
| [s] | After voiceless nonsibilant segments |
| [əz] | After sibilant segments |

An even more concise way to express these rules is to assume that the basic or underlying form of the plural morpheme is /z/, with the meaning "plural." This is the "default" pronunciation. The rules tell us when the default does *not* apply:

1. Insert a [ə] before the plural morpheme /z/ when a regular noun ends in a sibilant, giving [əz].
2. Change the plural morpheme /z/ to a voiceless [s] when preceded by a voiceless sound. (It's crucial that this rule apply after rule 1, as we'll see.)

These rules will derive the phonetic forms—that is, the pronunciations—of plurals for all regular nouns. Because the basic form of the plural is /z/, if no rule applies, then the plural morpheme will be realized as [z]. The following chart shows how the plurals of *bus, butt,* and *bug* are formed. At the top are the basic forms. The two rules apply or not as appropriate as one moves downward. The output of rule 1 becomes the input of rule 2. At the bottom are the phonetic realizations—the way the words are pronounced.

| | *bus* + pl. | *butt* + pl. | *bug* + pl. |
|---|---|---|---|
| *Basic representation* | /bʌs + z/ | /bʌt + z/ | /bʌg + z/ |
| Apply rule (1) | ↓ ə | NA* ↓ | NA |
| Apply rule (2) | NA | s | NA |
| *Phonetic representation* | [bʌsəz] | [bʌts] | [bʌgz] |

*NA means "not applicable."

As we have formulated these rules, (1) must apply before (2). (See Exercise 2 at the end of the chapter.) If we applied the rules in reverse order, we would derive an incorrect phonetic form for the plural of *bus*, as a diagram similar to the previous one illustrates:

| *Basic representation* | /bʌs + z/ |
|---|---|
| Apply rule (2) | s |
| Apply rule (1) | ə |
| *Phonetic representation* | *[bʌsəs] |

The particular phonological rules that determine the phonetic form of the plural morpheme and other morphemes of the language are **morphophonemic rules**. Such rules concern the pronunciation of specific morphemes. The pronunciation of a word like *horse* /hɔrs/ is with a final [s] because there is no morpheme boundary between the /s/ and the voiced /r/ that precedes it.

## Additional Examples of Allomorphs

The formation of the regular past tense of English verbs parallels the formation of regular plurals. Like plurals, some irregular past tenses conform to no particular rule and must be learned individually, such as *go/went, sing/sang,* and *hit/hit.* And like plurals, there are three *phonetic* past-tense morphemes for regular verbs: [d], [t], and [əd]. Study example sets A, B, and C and try to see the regularity before reading further:

Set A: *gloat* [glot], *gloated* [glotəd]; *raid* [red], *raided* [redəd]

Set B: *grab* [græb], *grabbed* [grabd]; *hug* [hʌg], *hugged* [hʌgd]; *faze* [fez], *fazed* [fezd]; *plan* [plæn], *planned* [plænd]

Set C: *reap* [rip], *reaped* [ript]; *poke* [pok], *poked* [pokt]; *kiss* [kɪs], *kissed* [kɪst]; *fish* [fɪʃ], *fished* [fɪʃt]; *patch* [pæʧ], *patched* [pæʧt]

Set A suggests that if the verb ends in a [t] or a [d] (i.e., non-nasal alveolar stops), [əd] is added to form the past tense, similar to the insertion of [əz] to form the plural of nouns that end in sibilants. Set B suggests that if the verb ends in a voiced segment other than [d], you add a voiced [d]. Set C shows us that if the verb ends in a voiceless segment other than [t], you add a voiceless [t].

Just as /z/ was the basic form of the plural morpheme, /d/ is the basic form of the past-tense morpheme, and the rules for past-tense formation of regular verbs are much like the rules for the plural formation of regular nouns. These are also *morphophonemic* rules as they apply specifically to the past-tense morpheme /d/. As with the plural rules, the output of rule 1, if any, provides the input to rule 2, and the rules must be applied in order.

1. Insert a [ə] before the past-tense morpheme when a regular verb ends in a non-nasal alveolar stop, giving [əd].
2. Change the past-tense morpheme to a voiceless [t] when a voiceless sound precedes it.

Two further allomorphs in English are the possessive morpheme and the third-person singular morpheme, spelled *s* or *es*. These morphemes take on the same phonetic form as the plural morpheme *according to the same rules*! Add [s] to *ship* to get *ship's*; add [z] to *woman* to get *woman's*; and add [əz] to *judge* to get *judge's*. Similarly, for the verbs *eat, need,* and *rush,* the third-person singular forms are *eats* with a final [s], *needs* with a final [z], and *rushes* with a final [əz].

That the rules of phonology are based on properties of segments rather than on individual words is one of the factors that make it possible for young children to learn their native language in a relatively short period. The young child doesn't need to learn each plural, each past tense, each possessive form, and each verb ending, on a noun-by-noun or verb-by-verb basis. Once the rule is learned, thousands of word forms are automatically known. As we will see when we discuss language acquisition in Chapter 9, children give clear evidence of learning morphophonemic rules such as the plural rules by applying the rule too broadly and producing forms such as *mouses and mans*, which are ungrammatical in the adult language.

## Phonemes: The Phonological Units of Language

The phonological rules discussed in the preceding section apply only to particular morphemes. However, other phonological rules apply to sounds as they occur in any morpheme in the language. These rules express our knowledge about the sound patterns of the entire language.

This section introduces the notions of **phoneme** and **allophone**. Phonemes are the abstract basic form of a sound as sensed mentally rather than spoken or heard. Phonemes distinguish one word or morpheme from another in our mental lexicon. Each phoneme is manifested physically by one or more actual sounds, called allophones, which are the perceptible sounds corresponding to the phoneme in various environments. For example, the phoneme /p/ is pronounced with the aspirated allophone [p$^h$] in *pit* but without aspiration [p] in *spit*. Phonological rules operate on phonemes to make explicit which allophones are pronounced in which environments.

### Illustration of Allophones

English contains a general phonological rule that determines the contexts in which vowels are nasalized. In Chapter 5, we noted that both oral and nasal vowels occur *phonetically* in English. The following examples show this:

| | | | |
|---|---|---|---|
| bean | [bĩn] | bead | [bid] |
| roam | [rõm] | robe | [rob] |

Taking oral vowels as the "default", we have a phonological rule that states:

Vowels are nasalized before a nasal consonant within the same syllable.

**TABLE 6.1** | Nasal and Oral Vowels: Words and Nonwords

| Words | | | | | | Nonwords | | |
|---|---|---|---|---|---|---|---|---|
| be | [bi] | bead | [bid] | bean | [bĩn] | *[bĩ] | *[bĩd] | *[bin] |
| lay | [le] | lace | [les] | lame | [lẽm] | *[lẽ] | *[lẽs] | *[lem] |

This rule expresses your knowledge of English pronunciation: nasalized vowels occur only before nasal consonants and never elsewhere. The effect of this rule is seen in Table 6.1.

As the table shows, oral vowels in English occur in final position and before non-nasal consonants; nasalized vowels occur only before nasal consonants. The nonwords (starred) show us that nasalized vowels do not occur finally or before non-nasal consonants, nor do oral vowels occur before nasal consonants.

You may be unaware of this variation in your vowel production, but this is to be expected because whether or not the vowel in *bean* is nasalized the meaning of the word is the same. Without nasalization, it might sound a bit strange, as if you had a foreign accent, but *bean* pronounced [bĩn] and *bean* pronounced [bin] would convey the same word. Likewise, if you pronounced *bead* as [bĩd], with a nasalized vowel, someone might suspect you had a cold, or that you spoke nasally, but the word would remain *bead*. Because nasalization is an *inessential difference* insofar as what the vowel actually is, we tend to be unaware of it.

Contrast this situation with a change in vowel height. If you intend to say *bead* but say *bed* instead, that makes a difference. The [i] in *bead* and the [ɛ] in *bed* are sounds from *different* phonemes. Substitute one for another and you get a different word (or no word). The [i] in *bead* and the [ĩ] in the nasalized *bead* do not make a difference in meaning. These two sounds, then, belong to the same phoneme, an abstract high front vowel that we denote between slashes as /i/.

Similarly, English also contains a phonological rule that determines the context in which voiceless stops—/p/, /t/, and /k/—are aspirated:

Voiceless stops are aspirated when they occur initially in a stressed syllable.

Table 6.2 illustrates the distribution of aspirated stops versus unaspirated stops.

**TABLE 6.2** | Distribution of Aspirated Voiceless Stops

| Syllable-Initial before a Stressed Vowel | | | After a Syllable Initial /s/ | | | Nonword* | | |
|---|---|---|---|---|---|---|---|---|
| [pʰ] | [tʰ] | [kʰ] | [p] | [t] | [k] | | | |
| *pill* | *till* | *kill* | *spill* | *still* | *skill* | [pɪl]* | [tɪl]* | [kɪl]* |
| [pʰɪl] | [tʰɪl] | [kʰɪl] | [spɪl] | [stɪl] | [skɪl] | [spʰɪl]* | [stʰɪl]* | [skʰɪl]* |
| *par* | *tar* | *car* | *spar* | *star* | *scar* | [par]* | [tar]* | [kar]* |
| [pʰar] | [tʰar] | [kʰar] | [spar] | [star] | [skar] | [spʰar]* | [stʰar]* | [skʰar]* |

Where the unaspirated stops occur, the aspirated ones do not, and vice versa. You could pronounce *spit* with an aspirated [pʰ], as [spʰɪt], and it would be understood as *spit*, even though listeners would probably think you were spitting out your words. Because aspiration is an *inessential difference* in English, we do not notice it (unless we're linguists or students of linguistics). Thus, there is one phoneme /p/—an abstract voiceless bilabial stop—which may be pronounced [pʰ] or [p] depending on the phonetic context.

As a third illustration of allophones, consider the voiceless alveolar stop /t/ along with the following examples:

| **Spelling** | **Phonemic representation** | **Phonetic representation** |
|---|---|---|
| tick | /tɪk/ | [tʰɪk] |
| stick | /stɪk/ | [stɪk] |
| blitz | /blɪts/ | [blɪts] |
| bitter | /bɪtər/ | [bɪɾər] |

In *tick* we normally find an aspirated [tʰ], whereas in *stick* and *blitz* we find an unaspirated [t], and in *bitter* we find the flap [ɾ]. Swapping these sounds around will not change word meaning. If we pronounce *bitter* with a [tʰ], it will not change the word; it will simply sound unnatural (to most Americans).

We account for this knowledge of how *t* is pronounced by positing a phoneme /t/ with three allophones [tʰ], [t], and [ɾ]. We also note phonological rules that specify that the aspirated voiceless stop [tʰ] occurs initially in a stressed syllable, the unaspirated [t] occurs directly before or after /s/, and the flap [ɾ ] occurs between a stressed vowel and an unstressed vowel.

## Phonemes and How to Find Them

Phonemes are the dark matter of phonology; they are not physical sounds or directly observable. They are abstract mental representations of the phonological units of a language, the units used to represent words in our mental lexicon. The phonological rules of the language apply to phonemes to determine the actual pronunciation of words.

The process of substituting one sound for another in a word to see if it makes a difference is a good way to identify the phonemes of a language. Here are twelve words differing only in their vowels:

| | | | | | |
|---|---|---|---|---|---|
| *beat* | [bit] | [i] | *boot* | [but] | [u] |
| *bit* | [bɪt] | [ɪ] | *but* | [bʌt] | [ʌ] |
| *bait* | [bet] | [e] | *boat* | [bot] | [o] |
| *bet* | [bɛt] | [ɛ] | *bought* | [bɔt] | [ɔ] |
| *bat* | [bæt] | [æ] | *bout* | [baʊt] | [aʊ] |
| *bite* | [baɪt] | [aɪ] | *bot* | [bat] | [a] |

Any two of these words form a *minimal pair*: two *different* words that differ in one sound in the same position. The two sounds that cause the word difference belong to different phonemes.

From the minimal set of [b_t] words, we can infer that English has at least twelve vowel phonemes. (We consider diphthongs to function as single vowel sounds.) To that total we can add a phoneme corresponding to [ʊ] resulting from minimal pairs such as *book* [bʊk] and *beak* [bik]; and we can add one for [ɔɪ] resulting from minimal pairs such as *boy* [bɔɪ] and *buy* [baɪ].

Our minimal pair analysis has revealed eleven monophthongal and three diphthongal vowel phonemes, namely, /i/, /ɪ/, /e/, /ɛ/, /æ/, /u/, /ʊ/, /o/, /ɔ/, /a/, /ʌ/, and /aɪ/, /aʊ/, and /ɔɪ/. (This set may differ somewhat in other variants of English.) Importantly, each of these vowel phonemes has (at least) two allophones (i.e., two ways of being pronounced): orally as [e] or [o] or [a], etc., and nasally as [ẽ] or [õ] or [ã], etc., when they occur in the context of a nasal consonant.

A particular realization (pronunciation) of a phoneme is called a **phone**. The aggregate of phones that are the realizations of the same phoneme are called the *allophones* of that phoneme. In English, each vowel phoneme has both an oral and a nasalized allophone. The choice of the allophone is not random or haphazard; it is *rule-governed*.

To distinguish graphically between a phoneme and its allophones, we use slashes / / to enclose phonemes and continue to use square brackets [ ] for allophones or phones. For example, [o] and [õ] are allophones of the phoneme /o/; thus, we will represent *bode* and *bone* phonemically as /bod/ and /bon/. We refer to these as *phonemic* transcriptions. The rule for the distribution of oral and nasal vowels in English shows that phonetically these words will be pronounced as [bod] and [bõn].

## Complementary Distribution

Minimal pairs illustrate that some speech sounds in a language are contrastive and can be used to make different words such as *big* and *dig*. These contrastive sounds constitute the phonemes of that language. Some sounds are noncontrastive and cannot be used to make different words. The sounds [tʰ] and [ɾ] were cited as examples that do not contrast in English, so [raɪtʰər] and [raɪɾər] are not a minimal pair, but rather alternate ways in which *writer* may be pronounced.

Oral and nasal vowels in English are also noncontrastive sounds. Because their distribution is rule-governed, the oral and nasal allophones of each vowel phoneme never occur in the same phonological context, as Table 6.3 illustrates.

**TABLE 6.3** | Distribution of Oral and Nasal Vowels in English Syllables

| | In Final Position | Before Nasal Consonants | Before Oral Consonants |
|---|---|---|---|
| Oral vowels | Yes | No | Yes |
| Nasal vowels | No | Yes | No |

Where oral vowels occur, nasal vowels do not occur, and vice versa. In this sense, the phones are said to complement each other or to be in **complementary distribution**. Table 6.2 also shows that aspirated and unaspirated voiceless stop consonants are in complementary distribution. In general, then, the allophones of a phoneme are in complementary distribution—never occurring in identical environments. We can understand why this is so when we consider that the choice of one or another allophone is determined by its phonetic environment. Vowels are nasalized when they occur before nasal consonants, and otherwise they are not nasalized. Phonological rules of this sort give rise to the complementary distribution of allophones.

Complementary distribution is a fundamental concept of phonology, and interestingly enough, it shows up in everyday life. Here are a couple of examples that draw on the common experience of reading and writing English.

The first example focuses on *printed* letters such as those that appear on the pages of this book. Each printed letter of English has two main variants: lowercase and uppercase (or capital). If we restrict our attention to words that are not proper names or acronyms (such as Ron or UNICEF), we can formulate a simple rule that does a fair job of determining how letters will be printed:

> A letter is printed in uppercase if it is the first letter of a sentence; otherwise, it is printed in lowercase.

Even ignoring names and acronyms, this rule is only approximately right, but let's go with it anyway. It helps to explain why written sentences such as the following appear so strange:

> phonology is the study of the sound patterns of human languageS.
> pHONOLOGY iS tHE sTUDY oF tHE sOUND pATTERNS oF hUMAN lANGUAGES.

These "sentences" violate the rule in funny ways. Despite that, they are comprehensible, just as the pronunciation of *cold* with a nasal [õ] as [cõld] would sound, well, like you had a cold but it would be understood.

To the extent that the rule is correct, the lowercase and uppercase variants of an English letter *are in complementary distribution*. The uppercase variant occurs in one particular context (namely, at the beginning of the sentence), and the lowercase variant occurs in every other context (or elsewhere). Therefore, just as every English vowel phoneme has an oral and a nasalized allophone that occur in different spoken contexts, every letter of the English alphabet has two variants, or allographs, that occur in different written contexts.

Our next example turns to *cursive* handwriting, which you are likely to have learned in elementary school. Writing in cursive is more similar to the act of speaking than printing because in cursive writing each letter of a word (usually) connects to the following letter—just as adjacent sounds connect during speech. The following figure illustrates that the connections between the letters of a word in cursive writing create different variants of a letter in different environments:

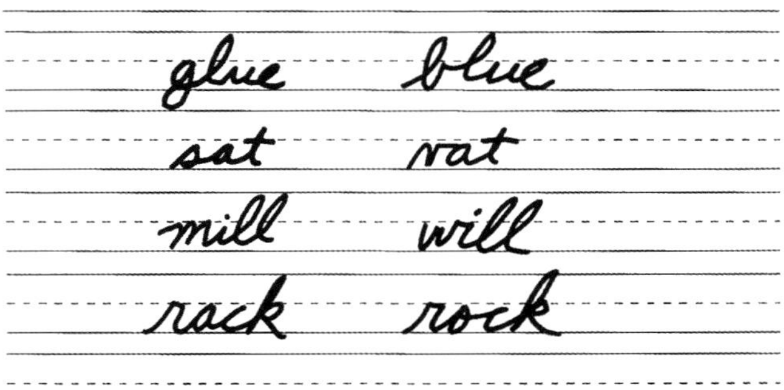


Compare how the letter *l* appears after a *g* (as in *glue*) and after a *b* (as in *blue*). In the first case, the *l* begins near the bottom of the line, but in the second case, the *l* begins near the middle of the line (which is indicated by the dashes). In other words, the same letter *l* has two variants. Meaning is unaffected by the position of *l*: wherever the *l* begins, it's still an *l*. Likewise, whether a vowel in English is nasalized or not does not affect meaning, it's still that same vowel. Which *l* variant occurs in a particular word is determined by the immediately preceding letter. The variant that begins near the bottom of the line appears after letters like *g* that end near the bottom of the line. The variant that begins near the middle of the line appears after letters like *b* that end near the middle of the line. The two variants of *l* are therefore in complementary distribution.

This pattern of complementary distribution is not specific to *l* but occurs for other cursive letters in English. By examining the pairs *sat* and *vat*, *mill* and *will*, and *rack* and *rock*, you can see the complementary distribution of the variants of *a*, *i*, and *c*, respectively. In each case, the immediately preceding letter determines which variant occurs, with the consequence that the variants of a given letter are in complementary distribution.

Finally, Superman and Clark Kent, Batman and Bruce Wayne, and Dr. Jekyll and Mr. Hyde—for those of you familiar with these fictional characters—are in complementary distribution *with respect to time*. At a given moment in time, the individual is either one or another of his alter egos.

## The Need for Similarity

When sounds are in complementary distribution, they do not contrast with each other. The replacement of one sound for the other will not change the meaning of a word, although it might not sound like typical English pronunciation. Given these facts about the patterning of sounds in a language, a phoneme can be viewed as a set of phonetically similar sounds that are in complementary distribution. The phonetic environment determines which sound is chosen for pronunciation. A set may consist of as few as a single sound so that all occurrences of the phoneme are pronounced the same. In such a case, the phoneme has one allophone.

Complementary distribution alone is not sufficient to determine the allophones of a phoneme. The phones must also be *phonetically similar,* that is, share most phonetic features. In English, the velar nasal [ŋ] and the glottal fricative [h] are in complementary distribution; [ŋ] does not occur word-initially and [h] does not occur word-finally. But they share very few phonetic features; [ŋ] is a voiced velar nasal stop; [h] is a voiceless glottal fricative. Therefore, they are not allophones of the same phoneme; [ŋ] and [h] are allophones of different phonemes.

Speakers of a language generally perceive the different allophones of a single phoneme as the same sound or phone. For example, most speakers of English are unaware that the vowels in *bead* and *bean* are different phones because mentally, speakers produce and hear phonemes, not phones.

## Distinctive Features of Phonemes

We are generally not aware of the phonetic properties or features that distinguish the phonemes of our language. *Phonetics* provides the means to describe the phones (sounds) of language, showing how they are produced and how they vary. *Phonology* tells us how various sounds form patterns to create phonemes and their allophones.

The minimal pairs *seal* [sil] and *zeal* [zil] show that [s] and [z] represent two contrasting phonemes in English. They cannot be allophones of one phoneme because one cannot replace the [s] with the [z] without changing the meaning of the word. The fact that you can find a minimal pair also means they are not in complementary distribution as both occur word initially before the vowel [i]. They are therefore allophones of the two different phonemes /s/ and /z/. From the discussion of phonetics in Chapter 5, we know that [s] and [z] differ in voicing: [s] is voiceless and [z] is voiced. The phonetic feature of voicing therefore distinguishes the two words. Voicing also distinguishes *feel* and *veal* [f]/[v] and *cap* and *cab* [p]/[b]. When a feature distinguishes one phoneme from another, hence one word from another, it is a **distinctive feature** or, equivalently, a **phonemic feature**.

## Feature Values

One can think of voicing and voicelessness as the presence or absence of a single feature, *voiced*. This single feature may have two values: plus (+), which signifies its presence, and minus (–), which signifies its absence. For example, [b] is [+voiced] and [p] is [–voiced].

The presence or absence of nasality can similarly be designated as [+nasal] or [–nasal], with [m] being [+nasal] and [b] and [p] being [-nasal]. A [–nasal] sound is an *oral* sound.

We consider the phonetic and phonemic symbols to be *cover symbols* for sets of distinctive features. They are a shorthand method of specifying the phonetic properties of segments. Phones and phonemes are not indissoluble units; they are composed of phonetic features, similar to the way that molecules are composed of atoms. A more explicit description of the phonemes /p/, /b/, and /m/ may thus be given in a feature matrix of the following sort.

| | p | b | m |
|---|---|---|---|
| **Labial** | + | + | + |
| **Voiced** | – | + | + |
| **Nasal** | – | – | + |

Aspiration is not listed as a phonemic feature in the specification of these units for English (but is for Thai, say, as we shall see), because [p] and [pʰ] do not represent different phonemes in English. In a *phonetic* transcription, however, the aspiration feature would be specified where it occurs.

A phonetic feature is distinctive when the + and – values of that feature in certain words result in words with different meanings, for example [+voiced] on [z] in [zɪp] and [–voiced] on [s] in [sɪp].

At least one feature value difference must distinguish each phoneme from all the other phonemes in a language. Because the phonemes /b/, /d/, and /g/ contrast in English by virtue of the place of articulation features—*labial, alveolar,* and *velar*—these place features are also distinctive in English. The distinctive features of the voiced stops in English are shown in the following:

| | b | m | d | n | g | ŋ |
|---|---|---|---|---|---|---|
| **Voiced** | + | + | + | + | + | + |
| **Labial** | + | + | – | – | – | – |
| **Alveolar** | – | – | + | + | – | – |
| **Velar** | – | – | – | – | + | + |
| **Nasal** | – | + | – | + | – | + |

Each phoneme in this chart differs from all the other phonemes by at least one distinctive feature.

Vowels, too, have distinctive features. For example, the feature [±back] distinguishes the vowel in *look* [lʊk] ([+back]) from the vowel in *lick* [lɪk] ([–back]) and is therefore distinctive in English. Similarly, [±tense] distinguishes [i] from [ɪ] (*beat* versus *bit*) and is also a distinctive feature of the English vowel system.

## Nondistinctive Features

As we saw, aspiration is not a distinctive feature of English consonants. It is a **nondistinctive** or **redundant** or **predictable feature** (all equivalent terms). "Predictable" means predictable by rule. Some features may be distinctive for one class of sounds but predictable for another. For example, nasality is a distinctive feature of English consonants but not for English vowels. There is no way to predict when an /m/ or an /n/ will occur in an English word. You learn this when you learn the word. On the other hand, the nasality feature value of the vowels in *bean, mean, comb,* and *sing* is predictable because the nasalized vowels occur before nasal consonants. Thus, the feature nasal is **nondistinctive** *for vowels.*

This is not the case in all languages. As we noted above, nasality on vowels is phonemic in Portuguese. Nasalization is also a distinctive feature for vowels in Akan (spoken in Ghana), as the following examples illustrate:

| | | | |
|---|---|---|---|
| [ka] | "bite" | [kã] | "speak" |
| [fi] | "come from" | [fĩ] | "dirty" |
| [tu] | "pull" | [tũ] | "den" |
| [nsa] | "hand" | [nsã] | "liquor" |
| [ʧi] | "hate" | [ʧĩ] | "squeeze" |
| [pam] | "sew" | [pãm] | "confederate" |

Nasalization is not predictable in Akan, as it is in English. There is no nasalization rule in Akan, as shown by the minimal pair [pam] and [pãm], or in Portuguese, as shown by the minimal pair [pão], "bread," and [pao], "stick." If you substitute an oral vowel for a nasal vowel, or vice versa, you will change the word.

Two languages may have the same phonetic segments (phones) but have two different phonemic systems. Phonetically, both oral and nasalized vowels exist in English, Portuguese, and Akan. However, English does not have nasalized vowel phonemes, but Akan and Portuguese do. The same phonetic segments function differently in English and the other two languages. Nasalization of vowels in English is redundant and nondistinctive; nasalization of vowels in Akan and Portuguese is nonredundant and distinctive.

Another nondistinctive feature in English is aspiration for voiceless stops. The voiceless aspirated stops [pʰ], [tʰ], and [kʰ] and the voiceless unaspirated stops [p], [t], and [k] are in complementary distribution. The presence of this feature is predicted by rule and therefore does not have to be learned by speakers when acquiring words.

## Natural Classes of Speech Sounds

We show what speakers know about the predictable aspects of speech through phonological rules. In English, these rules determine the environments in which vowels are nasalized or voiceless stops aspirated. These rules apply to *all* the words in the language, and even apply to made-up words such as *sint*, *peeg*, and *sparg*, which would be /sɪnt/, /pig/, and /sparg/ phonemically and [sɪ̃nt], [pʰig], and [sparg] phonetically.

As linguists examine more and more of the world's languages, they see similar rules affecting the same classes of sounds such as nasals and voiceless stops. For example, many languages besides English have a rule that nasalizes vowels before nasal consonants:

> Nasalize a vowel when it precedes a nasal consonant in the same syllable.

The rule will apply to all vowel phonemes when they occur in a context preceding any segment marked [+nasal] in the same syllable, and will add the feature [+nasal] to the feature matrix of the vowel. Our description of vowel nasalization in English needs only this rule. It need not include a list of the individual vowels to which the rule applies or a list of the sounds that result from its application.

Many languages have rules that refer to [+voiced] and [–voiced] sounds. For example, the aspiration rule in English applies to the class of [–voiced] noncontinuant sounds in word-initial position. As in the vowel nasality rule, we do not

TABLE 6.4 | Feature Specification of Major Natural Classes of Sounds

| Features | Obstruents | Nasals | Liquids | Glides | Vowels |
|---|---|---|---|---|---|
| Consonantal | + | + | + | – | – |
| Sonorant | – | + | + | + | + |
| Syllabic | – | +/– | +/– | – | + |
| Nasal | – | + | – | – | +/– |

need to consider individual segments. The rule automatically applies to initial /p/, /t/, /k/, and /ʧ/.

Phonological rules often apply to **natural classes** of sounds. A natural class is a group of sounds described by a small number of distinctive features such as [–voiced], [–continuant], which describe /p/, /t/, /k/, and /ʧ/. Any individual member of a natural class would require more features in its description than the class itself, so /p/ is not only [–voiced], [–continuant], but also [+labial].

The relationships among phonological rules and natural classes illustrate why segments are to be regarded as bundles of features. If segments were not specified as feature matrices, the similarities among /p/, /t/, and /k/ or /m/, /n/, and /ŋ/ would be lost. It would be just as likely for a language to have a rule such as

**1.** Nasalize vowels before *p*, *i*, or *z*.

as to have a rule such as

**2.** Nasalize vowels before *m*, *n*, or *ŋ*.

Rule 1 has no phonetic explanation, whereas rule 2 does: the lowering of the velum in anticipation of a following nasal consonant causes the vowel to be nasalized. In rule 1, the environment is a motley collection of unrelated sounds that cannot be described with a few features. Rule 2 applies to the natural class of nasal consonants, namely sounds that are [+nasal], [+consonantal].

The various classes of sounds discussed in Chapter 5 also define natural classes to which the phonological rules of all languages may refer. They also can be specified by + and – feature values. Table 6.4 illustrates how these feature values combine to define some major classes of phonemes. The presence of +/– indicates that the sound may or may not possess a feature depending on its context. For example, word-initial nasals are [–syllabic] but some word-final nasals can be [+syllabic], as in *wagon* [wægn̩], where the diacritic ˌ below the [n̩] indicates its syllabicity.

## Feature Specifications for American English Consonants and Vowels

Here are feature matrices for vowels and consonants in English. By selecting all segments marked the same for one or more features, you can identify natural classes. For example, the natural class of high vowels /i/, /ɪ/, /u/, /ʊ/ is marked

TABLE 6.5 | Features of Some American English Vowels

| Features | i | ɪ | e | ɛ | æ | u | ʊ | o | ɔ | a | ʌ | ə |
|---|---|---|---|---|---|---|---|---|---|---|---|---|
| High | + | + | – | – | – | + | + | – | – | – | – | – |
| Low | – | – | – | – | + | – | – | – | + | + | + | – |
| Back | – | – | – | – | – | + | + | + | + | – | – | – |
| Central | – | – | – | – | – | – | – | – | – | + | + | + |
| Round | – | – | – | – | – | + | + | + | + | – | – | – |
| Tense | + | – | + | – | – | + | – | + | + | + | – | – |

[+high] in the vowel feature chart of Table 6.5; the natural class of voiced stops /b, m, d, n, g, ŋ, ʤ/ are the ones marked [+voice] [–continuant] in the consonant chart of Table 6.6.

# The Rules of Phonology

Throughout this chapter, we have emphasized that the relationship between the *phonemic* representation of a word and its *phonetic* representation, or how it is pronounced, is *rule-governed*. Phonological rules are part of a speaker's knowledge of the language.

The phonemic representations are *minimally specified* because some features or feature values are predictable. For example, in English all nasal consonants are voiced, so we don't need to specify voicing in the phonemic feature matrix for nasals. Similarly, we don't need to specify the feature *round* for back vowels. If Table 6.6 was strictly phonemic, then instead of a + in the *voice* row for *m*, *n*, and *ŋ*, the cells would be left blank, as would the cells in the *round* row of Table 6.5 for *u*, *ʊ*, *o*, and *ɔ*. Such underspecification reflects the redundancy in the phonology, which is also part of a speaker's knowledge of the sound system. The phonemic representation should include only the nonpredictable, distinctive features of the phonemes in a word. The phonetic representation, derived by applying the phonological rules, includes all of the linguistically relevant phonetic aspects of the sounds. It does not include all of the physical properties of the sounds of an utterance, however, because the physical signal may vary in many ways that have little to do with the phonological system.

The absolute pitch of the sound, the rate of speech, or its loudness is not linguistically significant. The phonetic transcription is therefore also an abstraction from the physical signal; it includes the nonvariant phonetic aspects of the utterances, those features that remain relatively constant from speaker to speaker and from one time to another.

Although the specific rules of phonology differ from language to language, the kinds of rules, what they do, and the natural classes they refer to are universal.

**TABLE 6.6** | Features of Some American English Consonants

| **Features** | p | b | m | t | d | n | k | g | ŋ | f | v | θ | ð | s | z | ʃ | ʒ | ʧ | ʤ | l | r | j | w | h |
|---|---|---|---|---|---|---|---|---|---|---|---|---|---|---|---|---|---|---|---|---|---|---|---|---|
| Consonantal | + | + | + | + | + | + | + | + | + | + | + | + | + | + | + | + | + | + | + | + | + | – | – | – |
| Sonorant | – | – | + | – | – | + | – | – | + | – | – | – | – | – | – | – | – | – | – | + | + | + | + | – |
| Syllabic | – | – | –/+ | – | – | –/+ | – | – | –/+ | – | – | – | – | – | – | – | – | – | – | –/+ | –/+ | – | – | – |
| Nasal | – | – | + | – | – | + | – | – | + | – | – | – | – | – | – | – | – | – | – | – | – | – | – | – |
| Voiced | – | + | + | – | + | + | – | + | + | – | + | – | + | – | + | – | + | – | + | + | + | + | + | – |
| Continuant | – | – | – | – | – | – | – | – | – | + | + | + | + | + | + | + | + | – | – | + | + | + | + | + |
| Labial | + | + | + | – | – | – | – | – | – | + | + | – | – | – | – | – | – | – | – | – | – | – | + | – |
| Alveolar | – | – | – | + | + | + | – | – | – | – | – | – | – | + | + | – | – | – | – | + | + | – | – | – |
| Palatal | – | – | – | – | – | – | – | – | – | – | – | – | – | – | – | + | + | + | + | – | – | + | – | – |
| Anterior | + | + | + | + | + | + | – | – | – | + | + | + | + | + | + | – | – | – | – | + | + | – | – | – |
| Velar | – | – | – | – | – | – | + | + | + | – | – | – | – | – | – | – | – | – | – | – | – | – | + | – |
| Coronal | – | – | – | + | + | + | – | – | – | – | – | + | + | + | + | + | + | + | + | + | + | + | – | – |
| Sibilant | – | – | – | – | – | – | – | – | – | – | – | – | – | + | + | + | + | + | + | – | – | – | – | – |

*Note*: The phonemes /r/ and /l/ are distinguished by the feature [lateral], not shown here. /l/ is the only phoneme that would be [+lateral].

## Feature-Changing Rules

Many rules change features from one value to its opposite or even add features not present in the phonemic representation. In English, the /z/ plural morpheme has its voicing value changed from plus to minus when it follows a voiceless sound. Similarly, the /n/ in the phonemic negative prefix morpheme /ɪn/ undergoes a change in its place of articulation feature when preceding bilabials or velars.

The rule in English that aspirates voiceless stops at the beginning of a syllable simply adds a nondistinctive feature. Generally, aspiration occurs only if the following vowel is stressed. The /p/ in *pit* and *repeat* is an aspirated [pʰ], but the /p/ in *inspect* or *compass* is an unaspirated [p]. We also note that even with an intervening consonant, the aspiration takes place so that words such as *crib, clip,* and *quip* ([kʰrɪb], [kʰlɪp], and [kʰwɪp]) all begin with an aspirated [kʰ]. And finally, the affricate /ʧ/ is subject to the rule, so *chip* is phonetically [ʧʰɪp]. We can now state the rule:

> A voiceless noncontinuant has [+aspirated] added to its feature matrix at the beginning of a syllable when followed by a stressed vowel with an optional intervening consonant.

Aspiration is not specified in any phonemic feature matrix of English, as Table 6.6 shows. The aspiration rule adds this feature for reasons having to do with the timing of the closure release.

### Assimilation Rules

A particular kind of feature-changing rule is assimilation. We have seen that nasalization of vowels in English is nonphonemic because it is predictable by rule. The vowel nasalization rule is an *assimilation rule* that makes neighboring segments more similar by adding the feature [+nasal] to the vowel.

For the most part, assimilation rules stem from articulatory processes. There is a tendency when we speak to make articulation easier. It is easier to lower the velum while a vowel is being pronounced before a nasal stop than to wait for the completion of the vowel and then require the velum to move suddenly.

We now wish to look more closely at the phonological rules we have been discussing. Previously, we stated the vowel nasalization rule:

> *Vowels are nasalized before a nasal consonant within the same syllable.*

This rule specifies the class of sounds affected by the rule:

> *Vowels*

It states what phonetic change will occur by applying the rule:

> *Change phonemic oral vowels to phonetic nasal vowels.*

And it specifies the context or phonological environment.

> *Before a nasal consonant within the same syllable.*

A shorthand notation to write rules, similar to the way scientists and mathematicians use symbols, makes the rule statements more concise. Every physicist knows that $E = mc^2$ means "Energy equals mass times the square of the speed of light." We can use similar notations to state the nasalization rule as:

V → [+nasal] / _ [+nasal] $

Let's look at the rule piece by piece.

| V | → | [+nasal] | / | _ | [+nasal] | $ |
|---|---|---|---|---|---|---|
| Vowels | become | nasalized | in the environment | before | nasal segments | within a syllable |

To the left of the arrow is the class of sounds that is affected. To the right of the arrow is the phonetic change that occurs. The phonological environment follows the slash. The underscore _ is the relative position of the sound to be changed within the environment, in this case *before* a nasal segment. The dollar sign denotes a syllable boundary and guarantees that the environment does not cross over to the next syllable.

This rule tells us that the vowels in such words as *den* /dɛn/ will become nasalized to [dɛ̃n], but *deck* /dɛk/ will not be affected and is pronounced [dɛk] because /k/ is not a nasal consonant. As well, a word such as *dental* /dɛn$təl/ will be pronounced [dɛ̃n$təl]: we have showed the syllable boundary explicitly. However, the first vowel in *denote*, /di$not/, will not be nasalized, because the nasal segment does not precede the syllable boundary, so the "within a syllable" condition is not met.

Any rule written in formal notation can be stated in words. The use of formal notation is a shorthand way of presenting the information, and also a way of eliminating ambiguity and making sure the intended meaning of the rule is completely clear. Notation also reveals the *function* of the rule more explicitly than words. It is easy to see in the formal statement of the rule that this is an assimilation rule because the change to [+nasal] occurs before [+nasal] segments. Assimilation rules in languages reflect **coarticulation**—the spreading of phonetic features either in the anticipation or in the perseveration (the "hanging on") of articulatory processes. The auditory effect is that words sound smoother.

The following example illustrates how the English vowel nasalization rule applies. It also shows the assimilatory nature of the rule, that is, the change to [+nasal] before a [+nasal] segment:

| | "bob" | | | "boom" | | |
|---|---|---|---|---|---|---|
| Phonemic representation | /b | a | b/ | /b | u | m/ |
| Nasality: phonemic feature value | – | 0* | – | – | 0* | + |
| Apply nasal rule | | NA | | | ↓ | |
| Nasality: phonetic feature value | – | – | – | – | + | + |
| Phonetic representation | [b | a | b] | [b | ũ | m] |

*The 0 means not present on the phonemic level.

There are many assimilation rules in English and other languages. Recall that the voiced /z/ of the English regular plural suffix is changed to [s] after a voiceless sound, and that similarly the voiced /d/ of the English regular past tense suffix is changed to [t] after a voiceless sound. These are instances of voicing assimilation. In these cases, the value of the voicing feature goes from [+voice] to [–voice] because of assimilation to the [–voice] feature of the final consonant of the stem, as in the derivation of *cats*:

/kæt + z/ → [kæts]

We saw a different kind of assimilation rule in Akan, where we observed that the nasal negative morpheme was expressed as [m] before /p/, [n] before /t/, and [ŋ] before /k/. (This is the homorganic nasal rule.) In this case, the place of articulation—bilabial, alveolar, velar—of the nasal assimilates to the place of articulation of the following consonant. The same process occurs in English: the negative morpheme prefix spelled *in-* or *im-* agrees in place of articulation with the word to which it is prefixed, so we have *impossible* [ĩ**m**pʰasəbəl], *intolerant* [ĩ**n**tʰalərə̃nt], and *incongruous* [ĩ**ŋ**kʰãŋgruəs]. In effect, the rule makes two consonants that appear next to each other more similar.

## Dissimilation Rules

It is understandable that so many languages have assimilation rules; they permit greater ease of articulation. It might seem strange, then, to learn that languages also have feature-changing rules called **dissimilation rules**, in which certain segments becomes less similar to other segments. Ironically, such rules have the same explanation: it is sometimes easier to articulate dissimilar sounds. The difficulty of tongue twisters like "the sixth sheik's sixth sheep is sick" is based on the repeated similarity of sounds. If one were to make some sounds less similar, as in "the second sheik's tenth sheep is sick," it would be easier to say. The cartoon makes the same point, with *toy boat* being more difficult to articulate repeatedly than *sail boat*, because the [ɔɪ] of *toy* is more similar to the [o] of *boat* than to the [e] of *sail*.

An example of easing pronunciation through dissimilation is found in some varieties of English, in which there is a fricative dissimilation rule. This rule applies to sequences /fθ/ and /sθ/, changing them to [ft] and [st]. Here the fricative /θ/ becomes dissimilar to the preceding fricative by becoming a stop. For example, the words *fifth* and *sixth* come to be pronounced as if they were spelled *fift* and *sikst*.

A classic example of the same kind of dissimilation occurred in Latin, and the results of this process show up in the derivational morpheme /-ar/ in English. In Latin, a derivational suffix *-alis* was added to nouns to form adjectives. When the suffix was added to a noun that contained the liquid /l/, the suffix was changed to *-aris;* that is, the liquid /l/ was changed to the dissimilar liquid /r/. These words came into English either as adjectives ending in *-al* or in its dissimilated form *–ar*. In the following examples, all of the *-ar* adjectives contain /l/ in the root, and as *columnar* illustrates, the /l/ need not be the consonant directly preceding the dissimilated segment.

Dennis the Menace, Hank Ketcham. Reprinted with permission of North America Syndicate.

| **-al** | **-ar** |
|---|---|
| anecdot-al | angul-ar |
| annu-al | annul-ar |
| ment-al | column-ar |
| pen-al | perpendicul-ar |
| spiritu-al | simil-ar |
| ven-al | vel-ar |

Assimilation rules, dissimilation rules, and other kinds of feature-changing rules are part of Universal Grammar (UG) and are found throughout the world's languages.

## Segment Insertion and Deletion Rules

Phonological rules may add or delete entire segments. These are different from the feature-changing rules we have seen so far, which affect only parts of segments. The process of inserting a consonant or vowel is called **epenthesis**.

The rules for forming regular plurals, possessive forms, and third-person singular verb agreement in English all require an epenthesis rule. Here is the first part of that rule that we gave earlier for plural formation:

> Insert a [ə] before the plural morpheme /z/ when a regular noun ends in a sibilant, giving [əz].

Letting the symbol Ø stand for "null," we can write this *morphophonemic* epenthesis rule more formally as "null becomes schwa between two sibilants," or like this:

Ø → ə / [+sibilant] ___ [+sibilant]

There is a plausible explanation for insertion of a [ə]. If we merely added a [z] to *squeeze* to form its plural, we would get [skwiz:], which would be hard for English speakers to distinguish from [skwiz] because in English we do not contrast long and short consonants. This and other examples suggest that the morphological patterns in a language are closely related to other generalizations about the phonology of that language.

Segment deletion rules are commonly found in many languages and are far more common than segment insertion rules. One such rule in English occurs in casual or rapid speech. We often delete the unstressed vowels in words such as the following:

myst***e***ry gen***e***ral mem***o***ry fun***e***ral vig***o***rous Barb***a***ra

These words in casual speech can sound as if they were written:

mystry genral memry funral vigrous Barbra

The silent *g* that torments spellers in such words as *sign* and *design* is actually the result of a segment deletion rule. Consider the following examples:

| **A** | | **B** | |
|---|---|---|---|
| sign | [sãɪn] | signature | [sɪgnətʃər] |
| design | [dəzãɪn] | designation | [dɛzɪgneʃə̃n] |
| paradigm | [pʰærədãɪm] | paradigmatic | [pʰærədɪgmærək] |

None of the words in column A have a phonetic [g], but a [g] occurs in each corresponding word in column B. Our knowledge of English phonology accounts for these phonetic differences. The "[g]—no [g]" alternation is regular and is

**Tumbleweeds**

"Tumbleweeds." Tom K. Ryan. Reprinted with permission of North America Syndicate.

also seen in pairs such as *gnostic* [nastɪk] and *agnostic* [ægnastɪk], and by the silent g's in the cartoon:
This rule may be stated as:

> Delete a /g/ word-initially before a nasal consonant or before a syllable-final nasal consonant.

Given this rule, the phonemic representations of the stems in *sign/signature, design/designation, malign/malignant, phlegm/phlegmatic, paradigm/paradigmatic, gnostic/agnostic,* and so on will include a /g/ that will be deleted by the regular rule if a prefix or suffix is not added. By stating the class of sounds that follow the /g/ (nasal consonants) rather than any specific nasal consonant, the rule deletes the /g/ before both /m/ and /n/.

## From One to Many and from Many to One

As we've seen, phonological rules that relate phonemic to phonetic representations have several functions, among which are the following:

| **Function** | **Example** |
|---|---|
| **1.** Change feature values | Nasal consonant assimilation rules in Akan and English |
| **2.** Add new features | Aspiration in English |
| **3.** Delete segments | *g*-deletion before nasals in English |
| **4.** Add segments | Schwa insertion in English plural and past tense |

The relationship between the phonemes and phones of a language is complex and varied. Rarely is a phoneme realized as one and only one phone. We often find a phoneme realized as several phones, as in the case with English voiceless stops that may be realized as aspirated or unaspirated, among other possibilities. And we find the same phone may be the realization of several different phonemes. Here is a dramatic example of that many-to-one relationship.

Consider the vowels in the following pairs of words:

| | A | | B | |
|---|---|---|---|---|
| /i/ | comp**e**te | [i] | comp**e**tition | [ə] |
| /ɪ/ | med**i**cinal | [ɪ] | med**i**cine | [ə] |
| /e/ | maint**ai**n | [e] | maint**e**nance | [ə] |
| /ɛ/ | t**e**legraph | [ɛ] | t**e**legraphy | [ə] |
| /æ/ | an**a**lysis | [æ] | an**a**lytic | [ə] |
| /a/ | s**o**lid | [a] | s**o**lidity | [ə] |
| /o/ | ph**o**ne | [o] | ph**o**netic | [ə] |

In column A, all the various stressed vowels are boldfaced; in column B the corresponding boldfaced vowels are without stress, or **reduced**, and are pronounced as schwa [ə]. In these cases, the stress pattern of the word varies because of the different suffixes. The vowel that is stressed in one form becomes unstressed in a different form and is therefore pronounced as [ə]. In their phonemic representations all of the root morphemes contain a stressed vowel such as /i/ or /e/ that becomes phonetically [ə] when it is destressed. We can conclude, then, that [ə] is an allophone of all English vowel phonemes. The rule to derive the schwa is simple to state:

Change a vowel to a [ə] when the vowel is unstressed.

In the phonological description of a language, it is not always straightforward to determine phonemic representations from phonetic transcriptions. How would we deduce the /o/ in *phonetic* from its pronunciation as [fənɛrɪk] without a complete phonological analysis? However, given a phonemic representation and the phonological rules, we can always derive the correct phonetic representation. Because words in the mental lexicon occur in their phonemic forms and speakers know the rules of their language they have no trouble deriving the correct phonetic representations.

Similar rules exist in other languages that show that there is no one-to-one relationship between phonemes and phones. For example, in German both voiced and voiceless obstruents occur as phonemes, as is shown by the following minimal pair:

*Tier* [tiːr] "animal"   *dir* [diːr] "to you"

However, when voiced obstruents occur at the end of a word or syllable, they become voiceless. The words meaning "bundle," *Bund* /bʊnd/, and "colorful," *bunt* /bʊnt/, are phonetically identical and pronounced [bʊ̃nt] with a final [t]. Obstruent voicing is noncontrastive in syllable-final position.

The German devoicing rule changes feature specifications. The phonemic representation of the final stop in *Bund* is the [+voiced] /d/; it is changed by rule to [–voiced] to derive the phonetic [t] in word-final position. German presents us with this picture:

The devoicing rule in German provides a further illustration that we cannot discern the phonemic representation of a word given only the phonetic form: [bʊ̃nt] can be derived from either /bʊnd/ or /bʊnt/. The phonemic representations and the phonological rules together determine the phonetic forms.

## The Function of Phonological Rules

The function of the phonological rules (P-rules) in a grammar is to provide the phonetic information necessary for the pronunciation of utterances. We may illustrate this point in the following way:

Input: *Phonemic (Mental Lexicon) Representation of Words in a Sentence*

↓

Phonological rules (P-rules)

↓

Output: *Phonetic Representation of Words in a Sentence*

The input to the P-rules is the phonemic representation. The P-rules apply to the phonemic strings and produce as output the phonetic representation.

The application of rules in this way is called a **derivation**. We have given examples of derivations that show how plurals are derived, how phonemically oral vowels become nasalized, and how /t/ and /d/ become flaps in certain environments. A derivation is an explicit way of showing both the effects and the function of phonological rules in a grammar.

All the examples of derivations we have so far considered show the application of just one phonological rule, except the plural and past-tense rules, which are actually one rule with two parts. In any event, it is common for more than one rule to apply to a word. For example, the word *tempest* is phonemically /tɛmpɛst/ (as shown by the pronunciation of *tempestuous* [tʰɛ̃mpʰɛstʃuəs]) but phonetically [tʰɛ̃mpəst]. Three rules apply to it: the aspiration rule, the vowel nasalization rule, and the schwa rule. We can derive the phonetic form from the phonemic representation as follows:

| | | | | | | | | | |
|---|---|---|---|---|---|---|---|---|---|
| Underlying phonemic representation | / | t | ɛ | m | p | ɛ | s | t | / |
| Aspiration rule | | tʰ | | | | | | | |
| Nasalization rule | | | ɛ̃ | | | | | | |
| Schwa rule | | | | | | ə | | | |
| Surface phonetic representation | [ | tʰ | ɛ̃ | m | p | ə | s | t | ] |

# Prosodic Phonology

## Syllable Structure

Baby Blues. Baby Blues Partnership. King Features Syndic

Words are composed of one or more syllables. A **syllable** is a phonological unit composed of one or more phonemes. Every syllable has a **nucleus**, which is usually a vowel (but can be a syllabic liquid or nasal). The nucleus may be preceded and/or followed by one or more phonemes called the syllable **onset** and **coda**. In rhyming words, the nucleus and the coda of the final syllable of both words are identical, as in the following jingle:

Jack and J**ill**
Went up the h**ill**
To fetch a pail of water.
Jack fell d**own**
And broke his cr**own**
And Jill came tumbling after.

For this reason, the nucleus + coda constitute the subsyllabic unit called a **rime** (note the spelling).

A syllable thus has a hierarchical structure. Using the IPA symbol σ (lowercase Greek letter "sigma") for the phonological syllable, the hierarchical structure of the monosyllabic word *splints* can be shown:

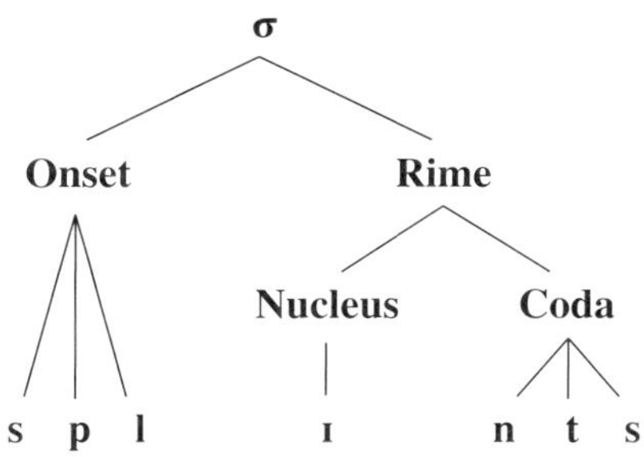

## Word Stress

In many languages, including English, one or more of the syllables in every content word are stressed. A stressed syllable, which can be marked by an acute accent (´), is perceived as more prominent than an unstressed syllable, as shown in the following examples:

| | | | |
|---|---|---|---|
| pérvert | (noun) | as in | "My neighbor is a pervert." |
| pervért | (verb) | as in | "Don't pervert the idea." |
| súbject | (noun) | as in | "Let's change the subject." |
| subjéct | (verb) | as in | "He'll subject us to criticism." |

These pairs show that stress can be contrastive in English. In these cases, it distinguishes between nouns and verbs. It may also distinguish between words of other categories, such as the adjective inválid (not valid) and the noun ínvalid (a sickly person).

Some words may contain more than one stressed vowel, but exactly one of the stressed vowels is more prominent than the others. The vowel that receives primary stress is marked by an acute accent (´). The other stressed vowels are indicated by grave accents (`) over the vowels (these vowels receive secondary stress).

| | | |
|---|---|---|
| rèsignátion | lìnguístics | sỳstemátic |
| fùndaméntal | ìntrodúctory | rèvolútion |

Generally, speakers of a stress-timed language like English (as opposed to French, say) know which syllable receives primary stress, which ones receive secondary stress, and which ones are unstressed. It is part of their implicit knowledge of the language. It's usually easy to distinguish between stressed and unstressed syllables because the vowels in unstressed syllables are pronounced as schwa [ə] in English except at the ends of certain words such as *confetti, laboratory,* and *motto*. It may be harder to distinguish between primary and secondary stress. If you are unsure of where the primary stress is in a word (and you are a native or near-native speaker of English), try shouting the word as if talking to a person across a busy street. Often, the difference in stress becomes more apparent.

The stress pattern of a word may differ among English-speaking people. For example, in most varieties of American English the word *láboratòry* [lǽbərətʰɔ̀ri] has two stressed syllables, but in most varieties of British English it receives only one stress [ləbɔ́rətri]. Because English vowels generally reduce to schwa or delete when they are not stressed, the British and American vowels differ in this word. In fact, in the British version the fourth vowel is deleted because it is not stressed.

Stress is a property of the syllable rather than a segment; it is a **prosodic** or **suprasegmental feature**. To produce a stressed syllable, one can change the pitch (usually by raising it), make the syllable louder, or make it longer. We often use all three of these phonetic means to stress a syllable.

## Sentence and Phrase Stress

When words are combined into phrases and sentences, one syllable receives greater stress than all others. Just as there is only one primary stress in a word spoken in isolation, only one of the vowels in a phrase (or sentence) receives primary stress or accent. All of the other stressed vowels are demoted to secondary stress. As noted in Chapter 3, in English we place primary stress on the adjectival part of a compound noun (which may be written as one word, two words separated by a hyphen, or two separate words), but we place the stress on the noun when the words are a noun phrase consisting of an adjective followed by a noun. The differences between the following pairs are therefore predictable:

| **Compound Noun** | **Adjective + Noun** |
|---|---|
| tíghtròpe ("a rope for acrobatics") | tìght rópe ("a rope drawn taut") |
| Rédcòat ("a British soldier") | rèd cóat ("a coat that is red") |
| hótdòg ("a frankfurter") | hòt dóg ("an overheated dog") |
| Whíte Hòuse ("the President's house") | whìte hóuse ("a house painted white") |

Say these examples out loud, speaking naturally, and at the same time listen or feel the stress pattern. If English is not your native language, listen to a native speaker say them.

These pairs show that stress may be predictable from the morphology and syntax. The phonology interacts with the other components of the grammar. The stress differences between the noun and verb pairs discussed in the previous section (*subject* as noun or verb) are also predictable from the syntactic word category.

## Intonation

In Chapter 5, we discussed pitch as a phonetic feature in reference to tone languages and intonation languages and noted its role in determining meaning. We can now see that pitch is also a *phonemic* feature in tone languages such as Chinese, Thai, and Akan. We refer to these relative pitches as **contrasting tones**. In non-tone languages, such as English, pitch still plays an important role, but only in the form of the **pitch contour** or **intonation** of the phrase or sentence.

In English, intonation may reflect syntactic or semantic differences. If we ask, "What is your middle name, David?" with falling pitch at the end it is a request to someone named David to reveal his middle name. With rising pitch at the end, it is a query as to whether the addressee's middle name is David.

A sentence that is ambiguous in writing may be unambiguous when spoken because of differences in the pitch contour. Written, the following sentence is unclear as to whether Tristram intended for Isolde to read and follow directions, or merely to follow him:

Tristram left directions for Isolde to follow.

Spoken, if Tristram wanted Isolde to follow him, the sentence would be pronounced with a rise in pitch on the first syllable of *follow*, followed by a fall in pitch:

Tristram left directions for Isolde to follow.

In this pronunciation of the sentence, the primary stress is on the word *follow*.

If the meaning is to read and follow a set of directions, the highest pitch comes on the second syllable of *directions*:

Tristram left directions for Isolde to follow.

The primary stress in this pronunciation is on the word *directions*.

Pitch plays an important role in both tone and non-tone languages, but in different ways depending on the phonological systems of the respective languages.

# Sequential Constraints of Phonemes

Suppose you were given the following four phonemes and asked to arrange them to form all possible English words:

/b/ /ɪ/ /k/ /l/

You would most likely produce the following:

/blɪk/

/klɪb/

/bɪlk/

/kɪlb/

These are the only permissible arrangements of these phonemes in English. */lbkɪ/, */ɪlbk/, */bkɪl/, and */ɪlkb/ are not possible English words. Although /blɪk/ and /klɪb/ are not now existing words, if you heard someone say:

"I just bought a beautiful new blick."

you might ask: "What's a blick?"

If, on the other hand, you heard someone say:

"I just bought a beautiful new lbɪk."

you might reply, "You just bought a new *what*?"

Your knowledge of English phonology includes information about what sequences of phonemes are permissible, and what sequences are not. After a consonant such as /b/, /g/, /k/, or /p/, another stop consonant in the same syllable is not permitted by the phonology. If a word begins with an /l/ or an /r/, the next segment must be a vowel. That is why */lbɪk/ does not sound like an English word. It violates the restrictions on the sequencing of phonemes. People who like to work crossword puzzles are often more aware of these constraints than the ordinary speaker, whose knowledge, as we have emphasized, may not be conscious.

Other such constraints exist in English. If the initial sounds of *chill* or *Jill* begin a word, the next sound must be a vowel. The words /ʧʌt/ and /ʧon/ and /ʧæk/ are possible in English (*chut, chone, chack*), as are / ʤæl/ and /ʤil/ and /ʤalɪk/ (*jal, jeel, jolick*), but */ʧlɔt/ and */ʤpurz/ are not. No more than three sequential consonants can occur at the beginning of a word, and these three are restricted:

| | | | | | | | |
|---|---|---|---|---|---|---|---|
| /**spl**/ | *splay* | /**spr**/ | *spruce* | *spw | — | /**spj**/ | *spew* |
| /**skl**/ | *sclerosis* | /**skr**/ | *screen* | /**skw**/ | *squat* | /**skj**/ | *skew* |
| *stl | — | /**str**/ | *streak* | *stw | — | *stj | — |

Other languages have different sequential restrictions. In Polish, *zl* and *kt* are permissible syllable-initial combinations, as in /zlev/, "a sink," and /kto/, "who." Croatian permits words such as the name *Mladen*. Japanese has severe constraints on what may begin a syllable; most combinations of consonants (e.g., /br/, /sp/) are impermissible. In Twi, a word may end only in a vowel or a nasal consonant. The sequence /pik/ is not a possible Twi word because it breaks the sequencing rules of the language, whereas /mba/ is not a possible word in English, although it is a word in Twi.

The limitations on sequences of segments are called **phonotactic constraints**. Phonotactic constraints have as their basis the syllable, rather than the word. That is, only the clusters that can begin a syllable can begin a word, and only a cluster that can end a syllable can end a word.

In multisyllabic words, clusters that seem illegal may occur, for example, the /kspl/ in *explicit* /ɛksplɪsɪt/. However, there is a syllable boundary between the /k/ and /spl/, which we can make explicit using $: /ɛk $ splɪs $ it/. Thus, we have a permitted syllable coda /k/ that ends a syllable adjoined to a permitted onset /spl/ that begins a syllable. On the other hand, English speakers know that "condstluct" is not a possible word because the second syllable would have to start with an impermissible onset, either /stl/ or /tl/.

## Lexical Gaps

The words *bot* [bat] and *crake* [kʰrek] are not known to all speakers of English, but they are words. On the other hand [bʊt] (rhymes with *put*), *creck* [kʰrɛk], *cruke* [kʰruk], *cruk* [kʰrʌk], and *crike* [kʰraɪk] are not words in English now, although they are possible words.

Advertising professionals often use possible but nonoccurring words for the names of new products. Although we would hardly expect a new product or company to come on the market with the name *Zhleet* [ʒlit]—an impossible word in English—we do not bat an eye at *Bic, Xerox* /ziraks/, *Kodak, Glaxo,* or *Spam* (a meat product, not junk mail), because those once nonoccurring words obey the phonotactic constraints of English.

A *possible word* contains phonemes in sequences that obey the phonotactic constraints of the language. An actual, occurring word is the union of a possible word with a meaning. Possible words without meaning are sometimes called nonsense words and are also referred to as **accidental gaps** in the lexicon, or

**lexical gaps**. Thus, "words" such as *creck* and *cruck* are nonsense words and represent accidental gaps in the lexicon of English.

## Why Do Phonological Rules Exist?

A very important question that we have not addressed thus far is: Why do grammars have phonological rules at all? In other words, why don't underlying or phonemic forms surface intact rather than undergoing various changes?

In the previous section, we discussed *phonotactic constraints*, which are part of our knowledge of phonology. As we saw, phonotactic constraints specify which sound sequences are permissible in a particular language, so that in English *blick* is a possible word but **lbick* isn't. Many linguists believe that phonological rules exist to ensure that the surface or phonetic forms of words do not violate phonotactic constraints. If underlying forms remained unmodified, they would often violate the phonotactics of the language.

Consider, for example, the English past-tense rule and recall that it has two subrules. The first inserts a schwa when a regular verb ends in an alveolar stop (/t/ or /d/), as in *mated* [met**ə**d]. The second devoices the past-tense morpheme /d/ when it occurs after a voiceless sound, as in *reaped* [rip**t**] or *peaked* [pʰik**t**]. Notice that the part of the rule that devoices /d/ reflects the constraint that English words may not end in a sequence consisting of a voiceless stop *-d*. Words such as [lɪpd] and [mɪkd] do not exist, nor could they exist. They are impossible words of English, just as [bkɪl] is.

More generally, there are no words that end in a sequence of obstruents whose voicing features do not match. Thus, words such as [kasb], where the final two obstruents are [–voice] [+voice] are not possible, nor are words such as [kabs], whose final two obstruents are [+voice] [–voice]. On the other hand, [kasp] and [kɛbz] are judged to be possible words because the final two segments agree in voicing. Thus, there appears to be a phonotactic constraint in English, stated as follows:

**(A)** Obstruent sequences may not differ with respect to their voice feature at the end of a syllable.

We can see then that the devoicing part of the past-tense rule changes the underlying form of the past-tense morpheme to create a surface form that conforms to this general constraint.

Similarly, the schwa insertion part of the past-tense rule creates possible sound sequences from impossible ones. English does not generally permit sequences of sounds within a single syllable that are very similar to each other, such as [kk], [kg], [gk], [gg], [pp], [sz], and [zs]. (The words spelled *egg* and *puppy* are phonetically [ɛg] and [pʌpi].) Thus, the schwa insertion rule separates sequences of sounds that are otherwise not permitted in the language because they are too similar to each other: for example, the sequence of /d/ and /d/ in /mɛnd + d/, which becomes [mɛndəd] *mended*, and /t/ and /d/ in /vent + d/, which becomes [vɛntəd] *vented*. The relevant constraint is stated as follows:

**(B)** Sequences of obstruents that are alike with the possible exception of voicing are not permitted within a syllable.

Constraints such as (A) and (B) are far more general than any particular rule like the past-tense rule. For example, constraint B might also explain why an adjective such as *smooth* turns into the abstract noun *smoothness*, rather than taking the affix *-th* [θ], as in *wide/width, broad/breadth,* and *deep/depth.* Suffixing *smooth* with *-th* would result in a sequence of too-similar obstruents, smoo[ðθ], which differ only in their voicing feature. This suggests that languages may satisfy constraints in various grammatical situations.

Thus, phonological rules exist because languages have general principles that constrain possible sequences of sounds. The rules specify minimal modifications of the underlying forms that bring them in line with the surface constraints. Therefore, we find different variants of a particular underlying form depending on the phonological context.

# Phonological Analysis

Children recognize phonemes at an early age without being taught, as we shall see in Chapter 9. Before reading this book, or learning anything about phonology, you knew a *p* sound was a phoneme in English because it contrasts words like *pat* and *cat, pat* and *sat, pat* and *mat.* But you probably did not know that the *p* in *pat* and the *p* in *spit* are different sounds. There is only one /p/ phoneme in English, but that phoneme has more than one allophone (pronunciation), including an aspirated one and an unaspirated one.

If a non-English-speaking linguist analyzed English, how could this fact about the sound *p* be discovered? More generally, how do linguists discover the phonological system of a language?

To do a phonological analysis, the words to be analyzed must be transcribed in great phonetic detail because we do not know in advance which phonetic features are distinctive and which are not.

Consider the following Finnish words:

| | | | | | |
|---|---|---|---|---|---|
| **1.** | [kudot] | "failures" | **5.** | [madon] | "of a worm" |
| **2.** | [kate] | "cover" | **6.** | [maton] | "of a rug" |
| **3.** | [katot] | "roofs" | **7.** | [ratas] | "wheel" |
| **4.** | [kade] | "envious" | **8.** | [radon] | "of a track" |

Given these words, do the voiceless/voiced alveolar stops [t] and [d] represent different phonemes, or are they allophones of the same phone?

Here are a few hints as to how a phonologist might proceed:

1. Check to see whether there are any minimal pairs.
2. Items (2) and (4) are minimal pairs: [kate] "cover" and [kade] "envious." Items (5) and (6) are minimal pairs: [madon] "of a worm" and [maton] "of a rug."
3. Conclude that [t] and [d] in Finnish represent the distinct phonemes /t/ and /d/.

That was an easy problem. Now consider the following data from English, again focusing on [t] and [d] together with the alveolar flap [ɾ] and primary stress ′:

| | | | |
|---|---|---|---|
| [ráɪt] | "write" | [ráɪɾər] | "writer" |
| [déɾə] | "data" | [dét] | "date" |
| [mǽd] | "mad" | [mǽt] | "mat" |
| [bətróð] | "betroth" | [lǽɾər] | "ladder" |
| [lǽɾər] | "latter" | [dístə̃ns] | "distance" |
| [ráɪɾər] | "rider" | [ráɪd] | "ride" |
| [déɾĩŋ] | "dating" | [bɛ́dsaɪd] | "bedside" |
| [mʌ́ɾər] | "mutter" | [túɾər] | "tutor" |
| [mǽɾər] | "madder" | [mǽdnɪs] | "madness" |

A broad examination of the data reveals minimal pairs involving [t] and [d], so clearly /t/ and /d/ are phonemes. We also see some interesting homophones, such as *ladder* and *latter*, and *writer* and *rider*. And the flap [ɾ]? Is it a phoneme? Or is it predictable somehow? At this point, the linguist undertakes the tedious task of identifying *all* of the immediate environments for [t], [d], and [ɾ], using # for a word boundary:

[t]: áɪ_#, é_#, ǽ_#, ə_r, s_ə, #_ú
[d]: #_é (3 times), ǽ_#, #_í, áɪ_#, ɛ́_s, ǽ_n
[ɾ]: áɪ_ə (2 times), é_ə, ǽ_ə (3 times), é_ɪ, ú_ə, ʌ́_ə

It does not appear at this point that anything systematic is going on with vowel or consonant quality, so we abstract the data a little, using v for an unstressed vowel, v́ for a stressed vowel, C for a consonant, and # for a word boundary:

[t]: v́_#, #_v́, C_v, v_C
[d]: #_v́, v́_#, v́_C
[ɾ]: v́_v

Now we see clearly that [ɾ] is in complementary distribution with both [t] and [d]. It occurs only when preceded by a stressed vowel and followed by an unstressed vowel, and neither [t] nor [d] ever do. We may conclude, based on these data, that [ɾ] is an allophone of both /t/ and /d/. We tentatively propose the "alveolar flap rule":

> An alveolar stop becomes a flap in the environment between a stressed and unstressed vowel.

The phonemic forms lack a flap, so that *writer* is phonemically /raɪtər/ and *rider* is /raɪdər/, based on [raɪt] and [raɪd]. Similarly, we can propose /mædər/ for *madder* based on [mæd] and [mædnɪs], and /detɪŋ/ for *dating* based on [det]. But we don't have enough information to determine phonemic forms of *data*, *latter*, and *tutor*. This is typically the case in actual analyses. Rarely is there sufficient evidence to provide all the answers.

## Summary

Part of our knowledge of a language is knowledge of the **phonology** or sound system of that language. It includes the inventory of **phones**—which are the phonetic sounds that occur in the language—and the ways in which they pattern. This patterning determines the inventory of **phonemes**—the abstract basic units that differentiate words.

When similar phones occur in **complementary distribution**, they are **allophones**—predictable phonetic variants—of one phoneme. Thus, the aspirated [pʰ] and the unaspirated [p] are allophones of the phoneme /p/ because they occur in different phonetic environments.

Some phones may be allophones of more than one phoneme. There is no one-to-one correspondence between the phonemes of a language and their allophones. In English, for example, stressed vowels become unstressed according to regular rules, and ultimately reduce to schwa [ə], which is an allophone of each English vowel.

Phonological segments—phonemes and phones—are composed of **phonetic features** such as *voiced, nasal, labial,* and *continuant,* whose presence or absence is indicated by + or − signs. The set of features is universal but languages can differ with respect to which of the features are distinctive (or phonemic) and which are non-distinctive (redundant, predictable). *Voiced, continuant,* and many others are **distinctive features** in English—they can contrast phonemes. Other features like *aspiration* are **nondistinctive** in English and are predictable from phonetic context. Some features like *nasal* may be distinctive for one class of sounds (e.g., English consonants) but nondistinctive for a different class of sounds (e.g., English vowels). Phonetic features that are nondistinctive in one language may be distinctive in another. Nasalization is distinctive in Akan and nondistinctive in English.

When two distinct words are distinguished by a single phone occurring in the same position, they constitute a **minimal pair** (e.g., *fine* /faɪn/and *vine* /vaɪn/). Minimal pairs also occur in sign languages. Signs may contrast by handshape, location, and movement.

Words in some languages may also be phonemically distinguished by **prosodic** or **suprasegmental** features, such as pitch, stress, and segment length. Languages in which syllables or words are contrasted by pitch are called **tone languages**. Non-tone languages may still use pitch variations to distinguish meanings of phrases and sentences.

The relationship between phonemic representation and phonetic representation (pronunciation) is determined by phonological rules. Phonological rules apply to phonemic strings and alter them in various ways to derive their phonetic pronunciation, or in the case of signed languages, their hand configuration. They may be **assimilation rules, dissimilation rules,** rules that *add* **nondistinctive features, epenthetic** rules that *insert* segments, and **deletion** rules that *delete* segments.

Phonological rules generally refer to entire classes of sound. These are **natural classes,** characterized by a small set of phonetic features shared by all the members of the class, for example, [−continuant], [−voiced], to designate the natural class of voiceless stops.

Linguists may use a mathematical-like formulation to express phonological rules in a concise way. For example, the rule that nasalizes vowels when they occur before a nasal consonant within the same syllable may be written as: V → [+nasal] / _ [+nasal]$

**Morphophonemic rules** apply to specific morphemes such as the past tense morpheme /d/, which is phonetically [d], [t], or [əd] depending on the final phoneme of the verb to which it is attached.

The phonology of a language also includes sequential constraints **(phonotactics)** that determine which sounds may be adjacent within the syllable. These determine what words are possible in a language, and what phonetic strings are impermissible. Possible but nonoccurring words constitute **accidental gaps** and are **nonsense words,** for example, *blick* [blɪk]. Phonological rules exist in part to enforce phonotactic constraints.

To discover the phonemes of a language, linguists (or students of linguistics) can use a methodology such as looking for minimal pairs of words, or for sounds that are in complementary distribution.

The phonological rules in a language show that the phonemic shape of words is not identical with their phonetic form. The phonemes are not the actual phonetic sounds, but are abstract mental constructs that are realized as sounds by the operation of rules such as those described in this chapter. No one is taught these rules, yet everyone knows them subconsciously.

## References for Further Reading

Gussenhoven, C., and Jacobs, H. 2014. *Understanding phonology, 3rd ed.* New York: Routledge.

Hayes, B. 2009. *Introductory phonology.* Oxford, UK: Wiley-Blackwell.

Odden, D. 2013. *Introducing phonology, 2nd ed.* New York: Cambridge University Press.

## Exercises

Data in languages other than English are given in phonetic transcription without square brackets unless otherwise stated. The phonetic transcriptions of English words are given within square brackets.

**1.** The following sets of minimal pairs show that English /p/ and /b/ contrast in initial, medial, and final positions.

| **Initial** | **Medial** | **Final** |
|---|---|---|
| **p**it/**b**it | ra**p**id/ra**b**id | ca**p**/ca**b** |

Find similar sets of minimal pairs for each pair of consonants given:

**a.** /k/—/g/
**b.** /m/—/n/
**c.** /l/—/r/
**d.** /b/—/v/
**e.** /b/—/m/
**f.** /p/—/f/
**g.** /s/—/ʃ/

**h.** /tʃ/—/ʤ/
**i.** /s/—/z/

**2.** Reconsider the two rules for the plural morpheme /z/:

**a.** Insert a [ə] before the plural morpheme /z/ when a regular noun ends in a sibilant, giving [əz].
**b.** Change the plural morpheme /z/ to a voiceless [s] when preceded by a voiceless sound.

Reformulate these two rules so that their order of application doesn't matter. (This shows that the necessity for rule ordering depends on how the rules are formulated, but that if we make the rules very specific to avoid rule ordering, we may sacrifice a degree of simplicity.) How is your reformulation somehow less simple than the one that requires rule ordering?

**3.** In some dialects of English, the following words have different vowels, as is shown by the phonetic transcriptions:

| A | | B | | C | |
|---|---|---|---|---|---|
| bite | [bʌɪt] | bide | [baɪd] | die | [daɪ] |
| rice | [rʌɪs] | rise | [raɪz] | by | [baɪ] |
| ripe | [rʌɪp] | bribe | [braɪb] | sigh | [saɪ] |
| wife | [wʌɪf] | wives | [waɪvz] | rye | [raɪ] |
| dike | [dʌɪk] | dime | [dãɪm] | guy | [gaɪ] |
| | | nine | [nãɪn] | | |
| | | rile | [raɪl] | | |
| | | dire | [daɪr] | | |
| | | writhe | [raɪð] | | |

**a.** How may the classes of sounds that end the words in columns A and B be characterized? That is, what feature specifies all the final segments in A and all the final segments in B?
**b.** How do the words in column C differ from those in columns A and B?
**c.** Are [ʌɪ] and [aɪ] in complementary distribution? Give your reasons.
**d.** If [ʌɪ] and [aɪ] are allophones of one phoneme, should they be derived from /ʌɪ/ or /aɪ/? Why?
**e.** Give the phonetic representations of the following words as they would be spoken in the dialect described here:

life ______ lives ______ lie ______
file ______ bike ______ lice ______

**f.** Formulate a rule that will relate the phonemic representations to the phonetic representations of the words given above.

**4.** Pairs such as *top* and *chop, dunk* and *junk, so* and *show,* and *Caesar* and *seizure* reveal that /t/ and /ʧ/, /d/ and /ʤ/, /s/ and /ʃ/, and /z/ and /ʒ/ are distinct phonemes in English. Consider these same pairs of nonpalatalized and palatalized consonants in the following data. (The palatal forms are optional forms that often occur in casual speech.)

| **Nonpalatalized** | | **Palatalized** | |
|---|---|---|---|
| [hɪt mi] | "hit me" | [hɪʧ ju] | "hit you" |
| [lid hĩm] | "lead him" | [liʤ ju] | "lead you" |
| [pʰæs ʌs] | "pass us" | [pʰæʃ ju] | "pass you" |
| [luz ðem] | "lose them" | [luʒ ju] | "lose you" |

Formulate the rule that specifies when /t/, /d/, /s/, and /z/ become palatalized as [ʧ], [ʤ], [ʃ], and [ʒ]. Restate the rule using feature notations. Does the formal statement reveal the generalizations?

**5.** Consider the following English verbs. Those in column A have stress on the penultimate (next-to-last) syllable, whereas the verbs in column B and C have their last syllables stressed.

| **A** | **B** | **C** |
|---|---|---|
| astónish | collápse | amáze |
| éxit | exíst | impróve |
| imágine | resént | surpríse |
| cáncel | revólt | combíne |
| elícit | adópt | belíeve |
| práctice | insíst | atóne |

**a.** Transcribe the words under columns A, B, and C phonemically. (Use a schwa for the unstressed vowels even if they can be derived from different phonemic vowels. This should make it easier for you.)

Examples: *astonish* /əstanɪʃ/, *collapse* /kəlæps/, *amaze* /əmez/

**b.** Consider the phonemic structure of the stressed syllables in these verbs. What is the difference between the final syllables of the verbs in columns A and B? Formulate a rule that predicts where stress occurs in the verbs in columns A and B.

**c.** In the verbs in column C, stress also occurs on the final syllable. What must you add to the rule to account for this fact? (Hint: for the forms in columns A and B, the final consonants had to be considered; for the forms in column C, consider the vowels.)

**6.** Following are listed the phonetic transcriptions of ten "words." Some are English words, some are not words now but are possible or nonsense words, and others are not possible because they violate English sequential constraints.

Write the English words in regular spelling. Mark the other words as *possible* or *not possible*. For each word that you mark as "not possible," state your reason.

| | **Word** | **Possible** | **Not Possible** | **Reason** |
|---|---|---|---|---|
| *Example*: | | | | |
| [θrot] | throat | | | |
| [slig] | | X | | |

| | | | |
|---|---|---|---|
| [lsig] | | X | No English word can begin with a liquid followed by an obstruent. |

| | Word | Possible | Not Possible | Reason |
|---|---|---|---|---|
| a. | [pʰril] | | | |
| b. | [skriʧ] | | | |
| c. | [kʰno] | | | |
| d. | [maɪ] | | | |
| e. | [gnostɪk] | | | |
| f. | [jũnəkʰɔrn] | | | |
| g. | [fruit] | | | |
| h. | [blaft] | | | |
| i. | [ŋar] | | | |
| j. | [æpəpʰlɛksi] | | | |

7. Consider these pairs of semantically related phonetic forms and meanings (+ indicates a morpheme boundary):

| Phonetic | Gloss | Phonetic | Gloss |
|---|---|---|---|
| [bãm] | explosive device | [bãmb+ard] | to attack with explosive devices |
| [kʰrʌ̃m] | a morsel or bit | [kʰrʌ̃mb+əl] | to break into bits |
| [aɪæ̃m] | a metrical foot | [aɪæ̃mb+ɪk] | consisting of metrical feet |
| [θʌ̃m] | an opposable digit | [θʌ̃mb+əlĩnə] | a tiny woman of fairy tales |
| [rãm] | a rhombus | [rãmb+ɔɪd] | shaped like a rhombus |
| [tũm] | a burial chamber | [tũmb+əl] | like a burial chamber |

a. What are the two allomorphs of the root morpheme in each line of data?
b. What is the phonemic form of the underlying root morpheme? (Hint: Consider pairs such as *atom/atomic* and *form/formal* before you decide.)
c. State a rule that derives the allomorphs.
d. Spell these words using the English alphabet.

8. With regard to English plural and past-tense rules, we observed that the two parts of the rules must be carried out in the proper order. If we reverse the order, we would get *[bʌsəs] instead of [bʌsəz] for the plural of *bus* (as illustrated in the text), and *[stetət] instead of [stetəd] for the past tense of *state*. Although constraints A and B (given below) are the motivation for the plural and past-tense rules, both the correct and incorrect plural and past-tense forms are consistent with those constraints. What additional constraint is needed to prevent [bʌsəs] and [stetət] from being generated?

a. Obstruent sequences may not differ with respect to their voice features at the end of a syllable.
b. Sequences of obstruents that are alike with the possible exception of voicing are not permitted within a syllable.

9. Slips of the tongue, or **speech errors,** in which we deviate in some way from an intended utterance, show phonological rules in action. We all make speech errors, and they tell us interesting things about language and its use. Consider the following speech errors:

| Intended Utterance | Actual Utterance |
|---|---|
| 1. gone to seed | god to seen |
| [gɑ̃n tə sid] | [gad tə sĩn] |
| 2. stick in the mud | smuck in the tid |
| [stɪk ĩn ðə mʌd] | [smʌk ĩn ðə tʰɪd] |
| 3. speech production | preach seduction |
| [spitʃ pʰrədʌkʃə̃n] | [pʰritʃ sədʌkʃə̃n] |

In each example, explain the phonetic form of the slip in terms of segment swapping and the phonological rules of nasalization and aspiration.

7

# Language in Society

## Dialects

All speakers of English can talk to each other and pretty much understand each other. Yet, no two of us speak exactly alike. Some differences are the result of age, sex, social situation, and where and when the language was learned. These differences are reflected in word choices, the pronunciation of words, and grammatical rules. The language of an individual speaker with its unique characteristics is referred to as the speaker's **idiolect**. English may then be said to consist of anywhere from 450 million to upwards of two billion idiolects (or speakers) according to the most generous estimates.

Differences may also exist among different groups of people who speak the same language. Bostonians, New Yorkers, Texans, blacks in Chicago, whites in Denver, and Hispanics in Albuquerque all show variation in the way they speak English. When there are systematic differences in the way groups speak a language, we say that each group speaks a **dialect** of that language. Dialects are *mutually intelligible* forms of a language that *differ in systematic ways. Every* speaker, whether rich or poor, regardless of region or racial origin, speaks at least one dialect, just as each individual speaks an idiolect. A dialect is *not* an inferior or degraded form of a language, and logically could not be so because all dialects are rule-governed and have limitless expressive power.

It is not always easy to decide whether the differences between two speech communities reflect two dialects or two languages. Sometimes this rule-of-thumb definition is used: When dialects become mutually unintelligible—when the speakers of one dialect group can no longer understand the speakers of another dialect group—these dialects become different languages.

However, this rule of thumb does not always jibe with how languages are officially recognized, which is determined by political and social considerations. For example, despite regular differences in their grammars, Danish speakers, Norwegian speakers, and Swedish speakers can converse with each other. Nevertheless, Danish, Norwegian, and Swedish are considered separate languages because they are spoken in separate countries. Hindi and Urdu, spoken in India and Pakistan, are considered different "languages" even though they are as mutually intelligible as American and Australian English. The fact that the two countries have contentious cultural and religious issues and use different writing systems contributes to the impression that they are different languages.

On the other hand, linguistically distinct languages in China, such as Mandarin and Cantonese, which are not mutually intelligible when spoken, are nevertheless referred to as dialects of Chinese in the media and elsewhere because they have a common writing system that can be read by all speakers (because it's ideographic—see Chapter 8), and because they are spoken in a single country.

It is also not easy to draw a distinction between dialects and languages on strictly linguistic grounds. Dialects and languages reflect the underlying grammars and lexicons of their speakers. It would be completely arbitrary to say, for example, that grammars that differ from one another by, say, twenty rules represent different languages whereas grammars that differ by fewer than twenty rules are dialects. Why not ten rules or thirty rules? In reality, there is no sudden major break between dialects. Rather, dialects merge into each other, forming a **dialect continuum**.

Imagine a traveler journeying from Vienna to Amsterdam by bicycle. She would notice small changes in the German spoken as she bicycled from village to village, and the people in adjacent villages would have no trouble communicating with one another. Yet, by the time our traveler reached Dutch-speaking Amsterdam, she would realize that the accumulated differences made the German of Vienna and the Dutch of Amsterdam nearly mutually unintelligible.

Because neither mutual intelligibility, nor degree of grammatical difference, nor the existence of political or social boundaries is decisive, it is not possible to precisely define the difference between a language and a dialect. We shall, however, use the rule-of-thumb definition and refer to dialects of one language as mutually intelligible linguistic systems, with systematic differences among them.

As we will discuss in the next chapter, languages change continually but these changes occur gradually. They may originate in one geographic region or in one social group and spread slowly to others, and often over several generations of speakers. Dialect diversity develops when the changes that occur in one region or group do not spread. When speakers are in regular contact with one another, linguistic properties spread and are acquired by children. However, when some communication barrier separates groups of speakers—be it a physical barrier such as an ocean or a mountain range, or social barriers of a political, racial, class, educational, or religious kind—linguistic changes do not spread so readily, and the differences between groups are reinforced and grow in number.

**Dialect leveling** is movement toward greater uniformity and less variation among dialects. Though one might expect dialect leveling to occur as a result of the ease of travel and mass media, this is not generally the case. Dialect variation in the United Kingdom is maintained although only a few major dialects are spoken on national radio and television. There may actually be greater dialect variation in urban areas, where different groups attempt to maintain their distinctness and group identity.

## Regional Dialects

When various linguistic differences accumulate in a geographic region (e.g., the city of Boston or the southern United States), the language spoken has its own character. Each version of the language is referred to as a **regional dialect**. The hypothetical journey from Vienna to Amsterdam discussed previously crossed regional dialects. In the United States, dialectal differences are based primarily though not entirely on geographic region.

The origins of many regional dialects of American English can be traced to the people who settled in North America in the seventeenth and eighteenth centuries. Because they came from different parts of England, these early settlers already spoke different dialects of English, and these differences were carried to the original thirteen American colonies. By the time of the American Revolution, there were three major dialect regions in the British colonies: the Northern dialect spoken in New England and around the Hudson River, the Midland dialect spoken in Pennsylvania, and the Southern dialect. (There were, of course, a number of minor dialect areas as well.) These dialects differed from one another and from the English spoken in England in systematic ways. Some of the changes that occurred in British English spread to the colonies; others did not.

How dialects develop is illustrated by the pronunciation of words with an *r* in different parts of United States. As early as the eighteenth century, the British in southern England were dropping their *r*'s before consonants and at the ends of words. Words such as *farm, farther,* and *father* were pronounced as [faːm], [faːðə] and [faːðə] and as the cartoon suggests, *card* and *cod* are homophones in the Bostonian version of that dialect, namely [kad].

© 2015 Grimmy, Inc. Distributed by King Features Syndicate, Inc.

By the end of the eighteenth century, *r*-drop was a general rule among many of the early settlers in New England and the southern Atlantic seaboard. Close commercial ties were maintained between the New England colonies and London, and Southerners sent their children to England to be educated, which reinforced the *r*-drop rule. The *r*-less dialect is still spoken today in Boston, New York, and

Savannah, Georgia. Later settlers, however, came from northern England, where the *r* had been retained; as the frontier moved westward, so did the *r*. Pioneers from all three dialect areas spread westward. The mingling of their dialects leveled many of their dialect differences, which is why the English used in large sections of the Midwest and the West is similar.

Regional phonological or phonetic distinctions are often referred to as different **accents**. We typically use the term *accent* to refer to characteristics of speech that convey information about what country or in what part of the country the speaker grew up, or to which sociolinguistic group the speaker belongs. A person is said to have a Boston or Brooklyn or Midwestern accent, a Southern drawl, an Irish brogue, and so on. Thus, people in the United States often refer to someone as having a British accent or an Australian accent; in Britain they refer to an American accent.

The term *accent* is also used to refer to the speech of non-native speakers, who have learned a language as a second language. For example, a native French speaker's English is described as having a French accent and vice versa. In this sense, *accent* refers to phonological differences caused by one's native language. Unlike regional accents, such foreign accents do not reflect differences in the speech of the community where the language was learned.

Regional dialects may differ not only in their pronunciation but also in their lexical choices and grammatical rules. A comedian once remarked that "the Mason–Dixon line is the dividing line between *you-all* and *youse-guys*." In the following sections, we discuss the different linguistic levels at which dialects may vary.

## Phonological Differences

Most dialect differences in American English involve differences in pronunciation (phonology). These variations created difficulties for us in writing Chapter 5 (phonetics), where we wished to illustrate the different sounds of English by using key words in which the sounds occur. As mentioned, some people pronounce *caught* [kɔt] with the vowel [ɔ] and *cot* [kat] with [a], whereas others pronounce them both [kat]. Some pronounce *Mary, merry,* and *marry* the same; others pronounce the three words differently as [meri], [mɛri], and [mæri]; and still others pronounce just two of them the same. In the south and northeast *pajamas* is pronounced [pəʤãməz] with tense [a] but as [pəʤæ̃məz] with a lax [æ] in the Midlands. Many speakers of American English pronounce *pin* and *pen* identically, whereas others pronounce the first [pĩn] and the second [pɛ̃n].

The pronunciation of British English (or many dialects of it) differs in systematic ways from many dialects of American English. In a survey of hundreds of American and British speakers conducted via the Internet, 48 percent of the Americans pronounced the mid consonants in *luxury* as voiceless [lʌkʃəri], whereas 96 percent of the British pronounced them as voiced [lʌgʒəri]. Sixty-four percent of the Americans pronounced the first vowel in *data* as [e] and 35 percent as [æ], as opposed to 92 percent of the British pronouncing it with an [e] and only 2 percent with [æ]. The most consistent difference occurred in the placement of primary stress, with most Americans putting stress on the first syllable and most British on the second or third in polysyllabic words such as *cigarette, applicable, formidable,* and *laboratory*.

The United Kingdom also has many regional dialects. The British vowels described in the phonetics chapter are used by speakers of the dialect called RP for "received pronunciation" because it is "received" (accepted) in the court of the monarch. In this dialect, *h* is pronounced at the beginning of both *head* and *herb*, whereas in most American English dialects *h* is not pronounced in *herb*. In some British English dialects, the *h* is regularly dropped from most words in which it is pronounced in American, such as *house*, pronounced [aʊs], and *hero*, pronounced [iro].

As is true of the origin of certain American dialects, many of the regional dialects of British English, such as the West Country dialect, the East Anglia dialect, and the Yorkshire dialect, are not deviations from the "standard" dialect spoken in London, but are direct descendants of earlier varieties that existed alongside London English as far back as the eleventh century. (Watch old Harry Potter movies to hear some of what we've been discussing vis-à-vis British English.)

English is the most widely spoken language in the world (as a first or second language). It is the national language of several countries, including the United States, large parts of Canada, the British Isles, Australia, and New Zealand. For many years, it was the official language in countries that were once colonies of Britain, including India, Nigeria, Ghana, Kenya, and the other "anglophone" countries of Africa. There are many other phonological differences in the various dialects of English used around the globe.

## Lexical Differences

Mort Walker (11/27/12). Copyright 2012 by King Features Syndicate

Regional dialects may differ in the words people use for the same object, as well as in phonology. Hans Kurath, an eminent dialectologist, in his paper "What Do You Call It?" asked:

> Do you call it a *pail* or a *bucket*? Do you draw water from a *faucet* or from a *spigot?* Do you pull down the *blinds*, the *shades*, or the *curtains* when it gets dark? Do you *wheel* the baby, or do you *ride* it or *roll* it? In a *baby carriage*, a *buggy*, a *coach*, or a *cab*?

People take a *lift* to the *first floor* (our *second floor*) in England, but an *elevator* in the United States; English drivers needn't mind pedestrians on the *pavement* (our *sidewalks*) and they fill up with *petrol* (not *gas*) in London; in Britain a *public school* is "private" (you have to pay), and if a student showed up there wearing *pants* ("underpants") instead of *trousers* ("pants"), he would be sent home to get dressed.

If you ask for a *tonic* in Boston, you will get a drink called *soda* or *soda-pop* in Los Angeles; ice cream cones can be covered in *jimmies* in Boston and *sprinkles* in New York; and a *freeway* in Los Angeles is a *thruway* in New York, a *parkway* in New Jersey, a *motorway* in England, and an *expressway* or *turnpike* in other dialect areas.

## Syntactic Differences

Dialects can also be distinguished by systematic syntactic differences. In most American dialects, sentences may be conjoined as follows:

1. John will eat and Mary will eat. → John and Mary will eat.

In the Ozark dialect of southern Missouri, the following conjunction is also possible:

2. John will eat and Mary will eat. → John will eat and Mary.

In (1) the VP *will eat* in the first conjunct is deleted, while in (2) the VP in the second conjunct is deleted. Most dialects of English allow deletion of only the first conjunct and in those dialects *John will eat and Mary* is ungrammatical. The Ozark dialect differs in allowing the second VP to delete.

Speakers of some American dialects say *Have them come early!* where others would say *Have them* ***to*** *come early!* Many speakers of the latter dialect also exhibit double modal auxiliary verbs, so that expressions such as *He* ***might could*** *do it* or *You* ***might should*** *go home* are grammatical. Most dialects of English allow only one modal.

Some of the dialects that permit double modals (e.g., Appalachian English) also allow expressions such as *I caught me a fish*; and *a*-prefixing with progressives such as *He came a-runnin'*. In some American English dialects, the pronoun *I* occurs when *me* would be used in other dialects. This difference is a syntactically conditioned morphological difference.

| **Dialect 1** | **Dialect 2** |
|---|---|
| between you and I | between you and me |
| Won't he let you and I swim? | Won't he let you and me swim? |
| *Won't he let I swim? | |

The use of *I* in these structures is only permitted in a conjoined NP, as the starred (ungrammatical) sentence shows. *Won't he let me swim?*, however, is grammatical in both dialects. Dialect 1 is growing, and these forms are becoming Standard English, spoken by TV announcers, political leaders, and university professors, although language purists still frown on this usage.

In British English, the pronoun *it* in the sentence *I could have done it* can be deleted. British speakers say *I could have done*, which is not in accordance with the syntactic rules of American English. American English, however, permits the deletion of *done it*, and Americans say *I could have*, which does not accord with the British syntactic rules.

Despite such differences, we are still able to understand speakers of other English dialects. Although regional dialects differ in pronunciation, vocabulary, and syntactic rules, the differences are minor when compared with the totality of the grammar. Dialects typically share most rules and vocabulary, which explains why the dialects of a language are mutually intelligible.

If you speak American English and you would like fairly good guess at the actual dialect you speak, we encourage you to take the New York Times on-line interactive dialect quiz: http://www.nytimes.com/interactive/2013/12/20/sunday-review/dialect-quiz-map.html?_r=0

## Social Dialects

Social boundaries and class differences can be as confining as the physical barriers that often define regional dialects. It is therefore not surprising that different dialects of a language evolve within social groups.

The social boundaries that give rise to dialect variation are numerous. They may be based on socioeconomic status, religious, ethnic, and racial differences, country of origin, and even gender. Middle-class American and British speakers are often distinguishable from working-class speakers; in Baghdad the Christian, Muslim, and Jewish groups all speak different varieties of Arabic; in India people often use different dialects of a standard regional language such as Hindi, Gujarati, or Bengali depending on the social *caste* they belong to; in America, many speakers of African descent speak a different dialect than those of European, Asian, or Hispanic descent; and, as we shall see, women and men each have their own distinguishing speech characteristics.

Dialect differences that seem to come about because of social factors are called **social dialects**, as opposed to *regional dialects*, which are due to geographical factors. However, there are regional aspects to social dialects and, clearly, social aspects to regional dialects, so the distinction is not entirely cut and dried.

### The "Standard"

Every language is a composite of dialects. But it is a widespread misconception that a language is a well-defined fixed system with various dialects diverging from this norm. One "language pundit" accused the editors of *Webster's Third New International Dictionary*, published in 1961, of confusing "to the point of obliteration the older distinction between standard, substandard, colloquial, vulgar, and slang," attributing to them the view that "good and bad, right and wrong, correct and incorrect no longer exist." In the next section, we argue that such criticisms are ill-founded.

### Language Purists

Prescriptive grammarians, or language purists, usually consider the dialect used by political leaders and national newscasters as the correct form of the language. (See Chapter 1 for a discussion of prescriptive grammars.) This is the dialect taught in "English" or "grammar" classes in school, and it is closer to the written form of the language than many other dialects, which also lends it an air of superiority.

Otto Jespersen, the great Danish linguist, ridiculed the view that a particular dialect is better than any other when he wrote: "We set up as the best language that which is found in the best writers, and count as the best writers those that best write the language. We are therefore no further advanced than before."

The dominant, or **prestige**, dialect is often called the standard dialect. **Standard American English (SAE)** is a dialect of English that many Americans *nearly* speak; divergences from this "norm" are labeled "Philadelphia dialect," "Chicago dialect," "African American English," and so on.

SAE is an idealization. Nobody speaks this dialect; and if somebody did, we would not know it, because SAE is not defined precisely (like most dialects, none of which are easy to clarify). Teachers and linguists held a conference in the 1990s that attempted to come up with a precise definition of SAE. This meeting did not succeed in satisfying everyone's view of SAE. SAE was once represented by the language used by national news broadcasters, but today many of them speak a regional dialect or a style of English that is not universally accepted as "standard." For example, the British Broadcasting Corporation (BBC) once used mostly speakers of RP English, but today speakers of Irish, Welsh, Scottish, and other regional dialects of English are commonly heard on BBC programs. The BBC describes its English as "the speech of educated professionals."

A standard dialect (or prestige dialect) of a particular language may have social functions. Its use in a group may bind people together or provide a common written form for multidialectal speakers. If it is the dialect of the wealthy, influential, and powerful members of society, this may have important implications for the entire society. All speakers who aspire to become successful may be required to speak that dialect even if it isn't their own.

Or they may desire it. For example, in 1954 the British scholar Alan Ross published *Linguistic Class-Indicators in Present-Day English* in which he compared the language of the English upper class, whom he labeled "U," with the speech habits of "non-U" speakers. Ross concluded that although the upper class has words and pronunciations peculiar to it, the main characteristic of U speech is the avoidance of non-U speech; and the main characteristic of non-U speech is, ironically, the effort to sound U. "They've a lovely home," for example, is pure non-U, because it is an attempt to be refined. Non-U speakers say "wealthy" and "ever so"; U speakers say "rich" and "very." Non-U speakers "recall"; U-speakers simply "remember."

Non-U language often includes **hypercorrections**, deviations from the norm *thought* to be "proper English," such as pronouncing *often* with a [t], or saying *between you and I*, while U speakers, who are generally more secure about their dialect, say [ɔfən] and *between you and me*. Ironically, in some cases non-U speech is so pervasive it eventually becomes part of the prestige dialect, as we are seeing today with *often* and *between you and I/me*.

No dialect, however, is more expressive, less corrupt, more logical, more complex, or more regular than any other dialect or language. They are simply different. More precisely, dialects reflect a different set of rules or lexical items represented in the minds of their speakers. Any judgments, therefore, as to the superiority or inferiority of a particular dialect or language are social judgments, which have no linguistic or scientific basis.

To illustrate the arbitrariness of "standard usage," consider the English *r*-drop rule discussed earlier. Britain's prestigious RP accent omits the *r* in words such as *car, far,* and *barn*. Thus, an *r*-less pronunciation is more prestigious than dialects that maintain the *r*. So much for England. In America, however, *r*-drop is generally considered substandard versus dialects that preserve the *r*. This shows that there is nothing inherently better or worse about one pronunciation over another, but simply that one variant is perceived as better or worse depending on a variety of social factors.

## Banned Languages

Language purists wish to prevent language or dialect differentiation because of their false belief that some languages are better than others, or that change leads to corruption. Languages and dialects have also been banned as a means of political control. Russian was the only legal language permitted by the Russian tsars, who banned the use of Ukrainian, Lithuanian, Georgian, Armenian, Azeri, and all the other languages spoken by national groups under the rule of Russia.

Cajun English and French were once banned in southern Louisiana by practice if not by law. Even as recently as August 8, 2006, Mary Tutwiler writes in a blog entitled "The French Connection," "Many local French speakers were so traumatized by the experience of being punished for speaking their mother tongue in school that they suppress their linguistic knowledge in public."

For many years, American Indian languages were banned in federal and state schools on reservations. Speaking Faroese was formerly forbidden in the Faroe Islands. A proscription against speaking Korean was imposed by the Japanese during their occupation of Korea between 1910 and 1945. Throughout history many languages and dialects have been banned to various degrees.

In France, a notion of the "standard" (the dialect spoken in Paris) as the only correct form of the language is promoted by the French Academy, an official panel of "scholars" who determine what usage constitutes the "official French language." Some years ago, the Academy enacted a law forbidding the use of "Franglais," which are words of English origin such as *le parking, le weekend,* and *le hotdog*. The French, of course, continue to use them, and because such words are notorious, they are widely used in advertising, where being noticed is more important than being correct. Only in government documents can these proscriptions be enforced.

In the past (and to some extent in the present), a French citizen from the provinces who wished to succeed in French society nearly always had to learn the prestigious Parisian French dialect. Then, several decades ago, members of regional autonomy movements demanded the right to use their own languages in their schools and for official business. In the section of France known as l'Occitanie, the popular singers sing in Langue d'oc, a Romance language of the region, both as a protest against the official language policy and as part of the cultural revival movement.

## African American English

Most regional dialects of the United States are largely free from stigma. Some regional dialects, like the *r*-less New Yorkese, are the victims of so-called humor, and speakers of one dialect may ridicule the "drawl" (vowel diphthongization) of southerners or the "twang" (excessive nasality) of Texans, even though not all speakers of southern dialects drawl, nor do all Texans twang.

There is, however, a *social* dialect of North American English that has been a victim of prejudicial ignorance. This dialect, **African American English (AAE)**,[1] is spoken by a large population of Americans of African descent. The distinguishing features of this English dialect persist for social, educational, and economic reasons. The historical discrimination against African Americans has created the social boundaries that permit this dialect to thrive. In addition, particularly in recent years, many blacks have embraced their dialect as a means of positive group identification. AAE is generally used in casual and informal situations, and is much more common among working-class people. African Americans from middle- or upper-class backgrounds and with higher levels of education are now more likely to be speakers of SAE. Former U.S. President Barack Obama and First Lady Michelle Obama are cases in point.

Since the onset of the civil rights movement in the 1960s AAE has been the focus of national attention. Some critics claim that AAE is a "deficient, illogical, and incomplete" language. Such descriptions cannot be applied to any language, and they are as unscientific in reference to AAE as to Russian, Chinese, or Standard American English.

Some people, white and black, think they can identify the race of a person by speech alone, believing that different races inherently speak differently. This belief is patently false. A black child raised in Britain will speak the British dialect of the household. A white child raised in an environment where AAE is spoken will speak AAE. Children learn the language they hear around them.

AAE is an especially interesting American dialect because it has a range of morphological and syntactic regularities that differ systematically from the so-called standard dialects. A vast body of research shows that linguistic differences between AAE and SAE are similar to those that occur between many of the world's major dialects.

### Phonological Differences between African American English and SAE

Because AAE is not a single, monolithic dialect, but rather refers to a collection of tightly related dialects, not everything discussed in this section applies to all speakers of AAE.

#### *r-Deletion*

Similar to several dialects of both British and American English, some speakers of AAE have a rule of *r-deletion* that deletes /r/ everywhere except before a vowel. Pairs of words like *guard* and *god*, *nor* and *gnaw*, *sore* and *saw*, *poor*

[1] AAE is actually a group of closely related dialects also variously called African American Vernacular English (AAVE), Black English (BE), Inner City English (ICE), and Ebonics.

and *Poe, fort* and *fought,* and *court* and *caught* may be pronounced identically by those speakers of AAE because of this phonological rule. There is also an *l-deletion* rule for some speakers of AAE, creating identically pronounced pairs like *toll* and *toe*, *all* and *awe*.

A *consonant cluster reduction* rule in AAE simplifies consonant clusters, particularly at the ends of words and when one of the two consonants is an alveolar (/t/, /d/, /s/, or /z/). The application of this rule may delete the past-tense morpheme so that *meant* and *mend* are both pronounced as *men*, and *past* and *passed (pass + ed)* may both be pronounced like *pass*. When speakers of this dialect say *I pass the test yesterday,* they are not showing an ignorance of past and present-tense forms of the verb, but are pronouncing the past tense according to this phonological rule in their grammar.

The deletion rule is optional; it does not always apply, and studies have shown that it is more likely to apply in nouns like *paste* [pest], where the final [t] does not represent the past-tense morpheme, than in verbs like *chased* [ʧest] where it does. This has also been observed with final [s] and [z], which are more likely to be omitted by speakers of AAE in words like *Keats* /kits/ to yield a surface form /kit/, than in words where /s/ represents a plural morpheme, as in *seats* /sit + s/.

Consonant cluster reduction is not unique to AAE. It exists optionally for speakers of many other dialects including SAE. For example, in SAE the medial [d] in *didn't* is often deleted, producing [dĩnt]. Furthermore, nasals are commonly deleted before final voiceless stops, to result in [hĩt] versus [hĩnt]. The *r*-deletion rule mentioned above is also a feature of some dialects spoken in New York City.

### *Neutralization of [ɪ] and [ɛ] before Nasal Consonants*

AAE shares with many regional dialects a lack of distinction between /ɪ/ and /ɛ/ before nasal consonants, producing identical pronunciations of *pin* and *pen*, *bin* and *Ben*, *tin* and *ten*, *him* and *hem*, and so on. The vowel sound in these words is roughly between the [ɪ] of *pit* and the [ɛ] of *pet*.

### *Diphthong Reduction*

AAE has a rule that reduces the diphthong /ɔɪ/ to the simple vowel [ɔ] without the glide, so that *boil* and *boy* are pronounced [bɔ].

/ɔɪ/ → [ɔ]

This rule is common throughout the regional dialects of the South irrespective of race and social class.

### *Loss of Interdental Fricatives*

A regular feature is the change of /θ/ to /f/ and /ð/ to /v/ at the ends of syllables so that *Ruth* is pronounced [ruf] and *brother* is pronounced [brʌvər]. This [θ]–[f] correspondence also holds in some dialects of British English, in which /θ/ is not even a phoneme. *Think* is regularly [fĩŋk] in Cockney English.

Initial /ð/ in such words as *this, that, these,* and *those* are pronounced as [d]. This is again not unique to AAE, but a common characteristic of certain regional, nonethnic dialects of English, many of which are found in the state of New Jersey as well as in New York City and Boston.

Another regular feature found in many varieties of AAE (and non-AAE) is the substitution of a glottal stop for /d/ at the end of non-word-final syllables; thus the name *Rodman* is pronounced [raʔmə̃n], but the word *rod* is pronounced [rad]. In fact, we observed in Chapter 5 on phonetics that the glottal stop [ʔ] is a common allophone of /t/ in many dialects of English.

All of these differences are rule-governed and similar to the kinds of phonological variation that is found in languages all over the world, including Standard American English.

## Syntactic Differences between AAE and SAE

Syntactic differences also exist between dialects. They have often been used to illustrate that AAE is illogical, and yet these differences are evidence that AAE is as syntactically complex and as logical as any language.

### *Multiple Negatives*

Constructions with multiple negatives akin to AAE *He don't know nothing* are commonly found in languages of the world, including French, Italian, and the English of Chaucer, as illustrated in the epigraph from *The Canterbury Tales*. The multiple negatives of AAE are governed by rules of syntax and are not illogical.

### *Deletion of the Verb Be*

In most cases, if in Standard American English the verb can be contracted, in African American English sentences it is deleted; where it can't be contracted in SAE, it can't be deleted in AAE, as shown in the following sentences:

| SAE | AAE |
|---|---|
| He is nice/He's nice. | He nice. |
| They are mine/They're mine. | They mine. |
| She is going to do it/She's gonna do it. | She gonna do it. |
| He is/he's as nice as he says he is. | He as nice as he say he is. |
| *He's as nice as he says he's | *He as nice as he say he. |
| How beautiful you are. | How beautiful you are. |
| *How beautiful you're. | *How beautiful you. |
| Here I am. | Here I am. |
| *Here I'm. | *Here I. |

These examples show that syntactic reduction rules operate in both dialects although they show small systematic differences.

### *Habitual Be*

In SAE, the sentence *John is happy* can be interpreted to mean *John is happy now* or *John is generally happy*. One can make the distinction clear in SAE only by lexical means, that is, the addition of words. One would have to say *John is generally happy* or *John is a happy person* to disambiguate the meaning from *John is presently happy*.

In AAE, this distinction is made syntactically; an uninflected form of *be* is used if the speaker is referring to *habitual* state.

| | |
|---|---|
| John be happy. | "John is usually happy." |
| John happy. | "John is happy now." |
| *John be happy at the moment. | |
| He be late. | "He is habitually late." |
| He late. | "He is late this time." |
| *He be late this time. | |
| Do you be tired? | "Are you generally tired?" |
| You tired? | "Are you tired now?" |
| *Do you be tired today? | |

The ungrammatical sentences are caused by a conflict between the habitual meaning of *be* with the momentary meaning conveyed by *at the moment, this time*, and *today*. The syntactic distinction between habitual and nonhabitual aspect also occurs in SAE, but with verbs other than *be*. In SAE eventive verbs (see Chapter 4) such as *walk*, when marked with the present tense *-s* morpheme, have only a habitual meaning and cannot refer to an ongoing situation: *Susan walks to school* is habitual, and **Susan walks to school now* is ungrammatical if the intended meaning is *Susan is walking to school* as a description of a presently observed event. On the other hand, with a stative verb such as *love, John loves Mary* refers to an ongoing or habitual situation and **John is loving Mary* is ungrammatical with that meaning though it may be interpretable as something like "John is presently *making* love to Mary."

#### *There Replacement*

Some AAE dialects replace SAE *there* with *it's* in positive sentences, and *don't* or *ain't* in negative sentences.

| | |
|---|---|
| It's a fly messing with me. | "There's a fly messing with me." |
| Ain't no one going to help you. | |
| Don't no one going to help you. | "There's no one going to help you." |

Combined with multiple negatives, consonant cluster simplification, and complement deletion, speakers produce highly condemned, but clear, logically sound, even colorful sentences like *Ain't no hard worker never get no good payin' job*: "There isn't a hard worker who never gets a good paying job."

## Genderlects

Dialects are defined in terms of groups of speakers, and speakers are most readily grouped by geography. Thus, regional dialects are the most apparent and generally are what people mean when they use the word *dialect*. Social groups are more amorphous, and social dialects correspondingly less well delineated and, until recently, less well studied. Surprisingly, the most obvious division of humankind into groups—women and men—has not engendered (if you'll pardon the expression) as much dialectal attention as regional and social divisions.

In the earliest work on women and language a number of features were identified that occurred more frequently in women's speech than in men's. For example, women "hedge" their speech more often than men do, with expressions such as *I suppose, I would imagine, This is probably wrong, sort of, and*

*but*. . . . Women also use tag questions more frequently to qualify their statements *(He's not a very good actor, is he?)*, as well as words of politeness (e.g., *please, thank you*) and intensifying adjectives such as *really* and *so (It's a really good film, It's so nice of you)*. It was claimed that the use of these devices was due to uncertainty and a lack of confidence on the part of women.

Since this early work, an increasing number of scholars have been conducting research on language, gender, and sexism, investigating the differences between male and female speech and their underlying causes. Many sociolinguists studying gender differences in speech now believe that women use hedges and other, similar devices not because they lack confidence but in order to express friendliness and solidarity, a sharing of attitudes and values, with their listeners.

There is a widespread belief that when men and women converse, women talk more and that they tend to interrupt more than men in conversation. This is a frequent theme in sitcoms and the subject of jokes and sayings in various cultures, such as the Irish proverb: "Where there are women there is talk, and where there are geese there is cackling," or the Native American "A squaw's tongue runs faster than the wind's legs." However, serious studies of mixed-sex conversations show that in a number of different contexts men dominate the talking, particularly in non-private conversation such as television interviews, business meetings, and conference discussions where talking can increase one's status.

This dominance of males in mixed speech situations seems to develop at an early age. It occurs in classroom situations in which boys dominate talk time with the teachers. One study found that boys were eight times more likely to call out answers than girls. There is also evidence that teachers encourage this dominant behavior, reprimanding girls more often than boys when they call out.

It has also been observed that women typically have a more standard speech style. For example, they are less likely to use vernacular forms such as the reduction of *-ing* to *-in'* or *him* to *'im* as in *I was walkin' down the street when I saw 'im.* Some dialects of British English drop word-initial [h] in casual speech as in *'arf an hour* (half an hour), *'enry* (Henry), *'appy* (happy). This *h*-less pronunciation happens more frequently in the speech of men than women. The tendency for women to speak more "properly" than men has been confirmed in many studies and appears to develop at an early age. Children as young as six show this pattern, with girls avoiding the vernacular forms used more commonly by boys from the same background.

The general view among sociolinguists is that women speak more "proper" English than men because of an insecurity caused by sexism in society. Among the more specific reasons that have been suggested are that women use more standard language to gain access to senior-level jobs that are often less available to them, that society tends to expect "better" behavior in general from women than men, that people who find themselves in subordinate roles (as women do in many societies) must be more polite, and that men prefer to use more vernacular forms because it helps to identify them as tough and strong. It has also been suggested that most sociolinguistic experiments are conducted by middle-class, well-educated academics and it is possible that the women who are interviewed "accommodate" to the interviewer, changing their speech to be more like the interviewer's or simply in response to the more formal nature of the interview situation. Men, on the other hand, may be less responsive to these perceived pressures.

The different variants of English used by men and women are sometimes called "genderlects" (a blend of *gender* and *dialect*). Variations in the language of men and women occur in many, if not all, languages. In Japanese, women may choose to speak a distinct female dialect, although they know the standard dialect used by both men and women. The Japanese language has many *honorific* words—words intended to convey politeness, respect, humility, and lesser social status in addition to their regular meaning. As noted earlier, women tend to use polite forms more often than men. Japanese has formal and informal verbal inflections, and again, women use the formal forms more frequently. There are also different words in Japanese used in male and female speech: For example,

| | **Women's Word** | **Men's Word** |
|---|---|---|
| stomach | onaka | hara |
| delicious | oishii | umai |
| I/me | watashi | boku |

and phrases such as:

| | | |
|---|---|---|
| eat a meal | gohan-o taberu | meshi-o kuu |
| be hungry | onaka-ga suita | hara-ga hetta |
| | "stomach become empty" | "stomach decrease" |

One effect of the different genderlects of Japanese shows up in the training of guide and helper dogs. The animals learn their commands in English because the sex of the owner is not known in advance, and it is easier for an impaired person to use English commands than it is for trainers to train the dog in both language styles.

# Languages in Contact

Human beings are great travelers and traders and colonizers. The mythical tales of nearly all cultures tell of the trials and tribulations of travel and exploration, such as those of Odysseus (Ulysses) in Homer's *Odyssey*. Surely one of the tribulations of ranging outward from your home is that sooner or later you will encounter people who do not speak your language, nor you theirs. In some parts of the world, for example, in bilingual communities, you may not have to travel very far at all to find the language disconnect, and in other parts you may have to cross an ocean. Because this situation is so common in human history and society, several solutions for bridging this communication gap have arisen.

## Lingua Francas

Many areas of the world are populated by people who speak diverse languages. In such areas, where groups desire social or commercial communication, one language is often used by common agreement. Such a language is called a **lingua franca**.

In medieval times, a trade language based largely on the languages that became modern Italian and Provençal came into use in the Mediterranean ports. That language was called Lingua Franca, "Frankish language." The term *lingua franca* was generalized to other languages similarly used. Thus, any language can be a lingua franca.

English has been called "the lingua franca of the whole world" and is standardly used at international business meetings and academic conferences. French, at one time, was "the lingua franca of diplomacy." Russian serves as the lingua franca in the countries of the former Soviet Union, where many different local languages are spoken. Latin was a lingua franca of the Roman Empire and of western Christendom for a millennium, just as Greek served eastern Christendom as its lingua franca. Yiddish has long served as a lingua franca among Jewish people, permitting Jews of different nationalities to communicate with one another.

More frequently, lingua francas serve as trade languages. East Africa is populated by hundreds of villages, each speaking its own language, but most Africans of this area learn at least some Swahili as a second language, and this lingua franca is used and understood in nearly every marketplace. A similar situation exists in Nigeria, where Hausa is the lingua franca.

Hindi and Urdu are the lingua francas of India and Pakistan. The linguistic situation of this area of the world is so complex that there are often regional lingua francas—usually local languages surrounding commercial centers. The Dravidian language Kannada is a lingua franca for the area surrounding the southwestern Indian city of Mysore. A similar situation existed in Imperial China.

In modern China, 94 percent of the people speak Han languages, which can be divided into eight major language groups that for the most part are mutually unintelligible. Within each language group there are hundreds of dialects. In addition to the Han languages, there are more than fifty "national minority" languages, including the five principal ones: Mongolian, Uighur, Tibetan, Zhuang, and Korean.

The situation is complex, and therefore the government inaugurated an extensive language reform policy to establish as a lingua franca the Beijing dialect of Mandarin, with elements of grammar from northern Chinese dialects, and enriched with the vocabulary of modern colloquial Chinese. They called this dialect *Putonghua*, meaning "common speech." The native languages and dialects are not considered inferior. Rather, the approach is to spread the "common speech" so that all may communicate with one another in this lingua franca.

Certain lingua francas arise naturally; others are instituted by government policy and intervention. In many parts of the world, however, people still cannot speak with their neighbors only a few miles away.

## Contact Languages: Pidgins and Creoles

A lingua franca is typically a language with a broad base of native speakers, likely to be used and learned by persons with different native languages (usually in the same language family). Often in history, however, speakers of mutually unintelligible languages have been brought into contact under specific socioeconomic and political conditions and have developed a language to communicate with one another that is not native to anyone. Such a language is called a **pidgin**.

Many pidgins developed during the seventeenth, eighteenth, and nineteenth centuries, in trade colonies along the coasts of China, Africa, and the New World. These pidgins arose through contact between speakers of colonial European languages such as English, French, Portuguese, and Dutch, and the indigenous, non-European languages. Some pidgins arose among extended groups of slaves and slave owners in the United States and the Caribbean in the nineteenth century. Other cases include Hawaiian Pidgin English, which was established on the pineapple plantations of Hawaii among immigrant workers from Japan, China, Portugal, and the Philippines; Chinook Jargon, which evolved among the Indian tribes of the Pacific Northwest as a lingua franca among the tribes themselves as well as between the tribes and European traders; and various pidgins that arose during the Korean and Vietnam Wars for use between foreign soldiers and local civilians.

In all these cases, the contact is too specialized and the cultures too widely separated for the native language of any one group to function effectively as a lingua franca. Instead, the two or more groups use their native languages as a basis for developing a rudimentary lingua franca with reduced grammatical structures and small lexicons. Also in these situations, it is generally the case that one linguistic group is in a more powerful position, economically or otherwise, such as the relationship of plantation owner to worker or slave owner to slave. Most of the lexical items of the pidgin come from the language of the dominant group. This language is called the **superstrate** or **lexifier language**. For example, English (the language of the plantation owners) is the superstrate language for Hawaiian Pidgin English, Swahili for the various forms of Pidgin Swahili spoken in East and Central Africa, and Bazaar Malay for pidgins spoken in Malaysia, Singapore, and Indonesia. The other language or languages also contribute to the lexicon and grammar, but in a less obvious way. These are called **substrate languages**. Japanese, Chinese, Tagalog, and Portuguese were the substrate languages of Hawaiian Pidgin English and all contributed to its grammar. Chinook Jargon had features both from indigenous languages of the area such as Chinook and Nootka and from French and English.

Many linguists believe that pidgins form part of a linguistic "life cycle." In the very early stage of development the pidgin has no native speakers and is strictly a contact language. Its use is reserved for specialized functions, such as trading or work-oriented tasks, and its speakers speak their (respective) native languages in all other social contexts. In this early stage the pidgin has little in the way of clear grammatical rules and few (usually specialized) words. Later, however, if the language continues to exist and be necessary, a much more regular and complex form of pidgin evolves—what is sometimes called a "stabilized pidgin"—and this allows it to be used more effectively in a variety of situations. Further development leads to the creation of a **creole**, which most linguists believe has all the grammatical complexity of an ordinary language. **Pidginization** (the creation of a pidgin) thus involves a *simplification* of languages and a reduction in the number of domains of use. **Creolization**, in contrast, involves the linguistic *expansion* in the lexicon and grammar of existing pidgins, and an increase in the contexts of use. We discuss creoles and creolization further in the next section.

Although pidgins are in some sense rudimentary, they are not devoid of rules. The phonology is rule-governed, as in any human language. The inventory of phonemes is generally small. English dialects, for example, have forty-four phonemes more or less whereas pidgins commonly have half that number, and each phoneme may have an uncommon number of allophonic pronunciations. In one English-based pidgin, for example, [s], [ʃ] and [tʃ] are all possible pronunciations of the phoneme /s/; [masin], [maʃin], and [matʃin] all mean "machine." Sounds that occur in both the superstrate and substrate languages will generally be maintained, but if a sound occurs in the superstrate but not in the substrates, it will tend to be eliminated. For example, the English sounds [ð] and [θ] as in *this* and *thing* are usually converted to [d] and [t] so that "this thing" is pronounced *dis ting*.

Typically, pidgins have fewer grammatical words such as auxiliary verbs, prepositions, and articles, and inflectional morphology, including tense and case endings, as in:

| | |
|---|---|
| He bad man. | "He is a bad man." |
| I no go bazaar. | "I'm not going to the market." |

Bound morphology is largely absent. For example, some English pidgins have the word *sus* from the English *shoes*, but *sus* does not include a plural morpheme as it is used to refer to both a single shoe and multiple shoes. Note that this has happened in the development of English, too. Originally, the ending *-a* was a plural marker for Latinate words such as *agenda* but has come to have a singular meaning and the plural of agenda is now *agendas*.

Verbs and nouns usually have a single shape and are not altered to mark tense, number, gender, or case. The set of pronouns is often simpler in pidgins. In Kamtok, an English-based pidgin spoken in Cameroon, the pronoun system does not show gender or all the case differences that exist in Standard English (SE).

| | **Kamtok** | | | **SE** | |
|---|---|---|---|---|---|
| a | mi | ma | I | me | my |
| yu | yu | yu | you | you | your |
| i | i/am | i | he | him | his |
| i | i/am | i | she | her | her |
| wi | wi | wi | we | us | our |
| wuna | wuna | wuna | you | you | your |
| dem | dem/am | dem | they | them | their |

Pidgins also may have fewer prepositions than the languages on which they are based. In Kamtok, for example, *fɔ* means "to," "at," "in," "for," and "from," as shown in the following examples:

| | |
|---|---|
| Gif di buk fɔ mi. | "Give the book to me." |
| I dei fɔ fam. | "She is at the farm." |
| Dɛm dei fɔ chɔs. | "They are in the church." |
| Du dis wan fɔ mi, a bɛg. | "Do this for me, please." |
| Di mɔni dei fɔ tebul. | "The money is on the table." |
| You fit muf tɛn frank fɔ ma kwa. | "You can take ten francs from my bag." |

Other morphological processes are more productive in pidgins. Reduplication is common, often to indicate emphasis. For example, in Kamtok, *big* means "big" and *big-big* means "enormous"; *luk* means "look" and *luk-luk* means "stare at." Compounding is also productive and serves to increase the otherwise small lexicons.

| | |
|---|---|
| big ai | greedy |
| drai ai | brave |
| gras bilong fes | beard |
| gras antap long ai | eyebrow |
| gras bilong head | hair |
| han bilong pisin | wing (of a bird) |
| fella bilong Mrs. Queen | husband of the queen |

Most words in pidgin languages also function as if they belong to several syntactic categories. For example, the Kamtok word *bad* can function as an adjective, noun, or adverb:

| | | |
|---|---|---|
| **Adjective** | tu bad pikin | two bad children |
| **Noun** | We no laik dis kain bad. | We don't like this kind of badness. |
| **Adverb** | A liakam bad. | I liked it very much. |

In terms of syntax, early pidgins have a simple clausal structure, lacking embedded sentences and other complex complements. And word order may be variable so that speakers from different linguistic backgrounds can adopt the word order of their native language and still be understood. For example, Japanese is an SOV (verb final) language, and a Japanese speaker of an English-based pidgin may put the verb last, as in *The poor people all potato eat.* On the other hand, a Filipino speaker of Tagalog, a VSO language, may put the verb first, as in *Work hard these people.* Word order eventually becomes more established in pidgins and creoles, which over time become more like other languages with respect to the range of clause types.

*Pidgin* has come to have negative connotations, perhaps because many pidgins were associated with European colonial empires. The *Encyclopedia Britannica* once described a pidgin as "an unruly bastard jargon, filled with nursery imbecilities, vulgarisms and corruptions." It no longer uses such a definition. In recent times, there is greater recognition that pidgins reflect human creative linguistic ability and show many of the defining characteristics of language in general.

Pidgins also serve a useful function. For example, it is possible to learn an English-based pidgin well enough in six months to begin many kinds of semiprofessional training. Learning English for the same purpose might take ten times as long. In areas with many mutually unintelligible languages, a pidgin can play a vital role in unifying people of different cultures and ethnicities.

In general, pidgins are short-lived, perhaps spanning several human generations, though a few have lasted much longer. Pidgins may die out because the speakers all come to share a common language. This was the fate of Chinook Jargon, whose speakers all learned English. In addition, because pidgins are often disdained, there is social pressure for speakers to learn a "standard" language, usually the one on which the pidgin is based. For example, through massive education, English replaced a pidgin spoken on New Zealand by the Maoris. Though it failed to succumb to years of government interdiction, Chinese Pidgin English could not resist the onslaught of English that fueled its demise by the close of the nineteenth century. Finally, and ironically, the death of a pidgin language may come about because of its success in uniting diverse communities; the pidgin proves so useful and becomes so widespread that successive generations in the communities in which it is spoken adopt it as their native tongue, elaborating its lexicon and grammar to become a creole.

## Creoles and Creolization

A creole is defined as a language that has evolved in a contact situation to become the native language of a generation of speakers. The traditional view is that creoles are the creation of children who, exposed to an impoverished and unstable pidgin, develop a far richer and more complex language that shares the fundamental characteristics of a "regular" human language and allows speakers to use the language in all domains of daily life.

In contrast to pidgins, creoles may have inflectional morphology for tense, plurality, and so on. For example, in creoles spoken in the South Pacific the affix *-im* is added to transitive verbs, but when the verb has no object the *-im* ending does not occur:

man i pairip**im** masket.
man be fired-him musket
"The man fired the musket."

masket i pairip.
musket be fired
"The gun was fired."

The same affix *-im* is used derivationally to convert adjectives into verbs like English *-en* in *redden*:

| | | | |
|---|---|---|---|
| bik | big | bikim | to enlarge; to make something bigger |
| daun | down | daunim | to lower; to make something go down |
| nogut | no good | nogutim | to spoil, damage; to make something no good |

Creoles typically develop more complex pronoun systems. For example, in the creoles of the South Pacific there are two forms of the pronoun we: inclusive *we* referring to speaker and listener, and exclusive *we* referring to the speaker and other people but not the listener. The Portuguese-based Cape Verdean Creole has three classes of pronouns: strong, weak, and clitic (meaning affixed to another word, like the possessive *'s* of English), as illustrated in Table 7.1.

The compounds of pidgins often reduce in creoles: for example, *wara bilong skin* (water belong skin) meaning "sweat" becomes *skinwara*. The compound *baimbai* (by and by), used to indicate future time, becomes a tense inflection *ba* in the creole. Thus, the sentence *baimbai yu go* ("you will go") becomes *yu bago*. The phrasal structure of creoles is also vastly enriched, including embedded and relative clauses, among many other features of "regular" languages.

How are children able to construct a creole based on the rudimentary input of the pidgin? One answer is that they use their innate linguistic capacities to rapidly transform the pidgin into a full-fledged language. This would account for the many grammatical properties that creoles have in common: for example, SVO word order and tense and aspect distinctions.

**TABLE 7.1** | Cape Verdean Creole Pronouns

| | Emphatic (Strong) Forms | Free (Weak) Forms | Subject Clitics | Object Clitics |
|---|---|---|---|---|
| 1sg | ami | mi | N- | -m |
| 2sg (informal) | abo | bo | bu- | -bu/-u |
| 2sg (formal, masc.) | anho | nho | nhu- | |
| 2sg (formal, fem.) | anha | nha | | |
| 3sg | ael | el | e- | -l |
| 1pl | anos | nos | nu- | -nu |
| 2pl | anhos | nhos | | |
| 3pl | aes | es | -s | |

It should be noted that defining pidgins and creoles in terms of whether they are native (creoles) versus non-native second languages (pidgins) is not without problems. There are languages such as Tok Pisin, widely spoken in New Guinea, which are first languages to many speakers, but also used as second contact languages by other speakers. Some linguists have also rejected the idea that creoles derive from pidgins, claiming that the geographic areas and social conditions under which they develop are different.

Moreover, the view that children are the creators of creoles is not universally accepted. Various linguists believe that creoles are the result of imperfect second language learning of the lexifier or dominant language by adults and the "transfer" of grammatical properties from their native non-European languages. This hypothesis would account for some of the characteristics that creoles share with L2 "interlanguages": for example, invariant verb forms, lack of determiners, and the use of adverbs rather than verbs and auxiliaries to express tense and modality.

Although some linguists believe that creoles are simpler systems than "regular" languages, most researchers who have closely examined the grammatical properties of various creoles argue that they are not structurally different from non-creole languages and that the only exceptional property of creoles is the sociohistorical conditions under which they evolve.

Creoles often arose on slave plantations where Africans of many different tribes spoke mutually incomprehensible African languages. Haitian Creole, based on French, developed in this way, as did the "English" spoken in parts of Jamaica. Gullah is an English-based creole spoken by the descendants of African slaves on islands off the coast of Georgia and South Carolina. Louisiana Creole, related to Haitian Creole, is spoken by large numbers of blacks and whites in Louisiana. Krio, the language spoken by as many as a million Sierra Leoneans, and illustrated in the epigraph to this section, developed at least in part from an English-based pidgin.

One of the theories concerning the origins of African American English is that it derives from an earlier English-based creole that developed when Africans slaves had no common language other than the English spoken by their colonial masters. Proponents of this hypothesis point out that at least some of the unique features of AAE are traceable to influences of the West African languages once spoken by the slaves, or their parents/grandparents in any case. In addition, several of the features of AAE, such as aspect marking (distinct from that which occurs in Standard English), are typical of creole languages.

The alternative view is that AAE formed directly from English without any pidgin/creole stage. It is apparent that AAE is closer to Southern dialects of American English than to other dialects. It is possible that the African slaves learned the English of white Southerners as a second language. It is also possible that many of the distinguishing features of Southern dialects were acquired from AAE during the many decades in which a large number of Southern white children were raised by black women and played with black children.

Tok Pisin, originally a pidgin, was gradually creolized throughout the twentieth century. It evolved from Melanesian Pidgin English, once a widely-spoken lingua franca of Papua New Guinea used by English-speaking traders and the native population. Because New Guinea is so linguistically diverse—more than eight hundred different languages were once spoken on the island—the pidgin came to be used as a lingua franca among the indigenous population as well.

Tok Pisin has its own writing system, its own literature, and its own newspapers and radio programs; it has even been used to address a United Nations meeting. Papers in (not on!) Tok Pisin have been presented at linguistics conferences in Papua New Guinea, and it is commonly used for debates in the parliament of the country. Today, Tok Pisin is one of the three recognized national languages of The Independent State of Papua New Guinea, alongside English and Kiri Motu, another creole.

The study of pidgins and creoles has contributed a great deal to our understanding of the nature of human language and the processes involved in language creation and language change, and of the sociohistorical conditions under which these instances of language contact occurred.

## Bilingualism

The term **bilingualism** refers to the ability to speak two (or more) languages, either by an individual speaker, **individual bilingualism**, or within a society, **societal bilingualism**. There are various degrees of individual bilingualism. Some people have native-like control of two languages, whereas others make regular use of two languages with a high degree of proficiency but lack the linguistic competence of a native or near-native speaker in one or the other language. In addition, some bilinguals may have oral competence but cannot read or write one or more of their languages.

The situations under which people become bilingual may vary. Some people grow up in a household in which more than one language is spoken; others move to a new country where they acquire the local language, usually from people outside the home. Still others learn second languages in school. In communities with rich linguistic diversity, contact between speakers of different languages may also lead to bilingualism.

Bilingualism (or multilingualism) also refers to the situation in which two (or more) languages are spoken and recognized as official or national languages of a particular nation. Societal bilingualism exists in many countries, including Canada, where English and French are both official languages, and Switzerland, where French, German, Italian, and Romansch all have official status.

Interestingly, research shows that there are fewer bilingual individuals in bilingual countries than in so-called "unilingual" countries. This makes sense when you consider that in unilingual countries such as the United States, Italy, and France, people who do not speak the dominant language must learn some amount of it to function. In addition, the main concern of multilingual states has been the maintenance and use of two or more languages, rather than the promotion of individual bilingualism among its citizens.

The United States is broadly perceived as a monolingual English-speaking society even though there is no reference to a national language in the Constitution. However, there are numerous bilingual communities with long histories throughout the country. English-Spanish bilinguals are measurably more numerous than any other combination according to the 2010 census, but the variety of languages found among bilingual and multilingual people living in the United States is far too numerous to mention and perhaps not even known to its fullest extent.

Recent studies reveal that a shift to monolingual English is growing rapidly and that knowledge of Spanish and other common bilingual partners of English (e.g., Tagalog, Vietnamese, and various languages of China) is being lost faster in the twenty-first century than at any other period of history.

## Codeswitching

Codeswitching is a speech style unique to bilinguals in which fluent speakers switch languages between or within sentences, as illustrated by the following sentence:

Sometimes I'll start a sentence in English and termino en español.
Sometimes I'll start a sentence in English and finish it in Spanish.

Codeswitching is a universal language-contact phenomenon that reflects the grammars of both languages working simultaneously. Bilingual Spanish-English speakers may switch between English and Spanish as in the above example, whereas Quebecois in Canada switch between French and English:

I mean, c'est un idiot, ce mec-là.
I mean, he's an idiot, that guy.

The following examples are from German-English, Korean-English, and Mandarin-English bilinguals:

Johan hat mir gesagt that you were going to leave.
Johan told me you were going to leave.

Chigum ton-uls ops-nunde, I can't buy it.
As I don't have money now, I can't buy it.

Women zuotian qu kan de movie was really amazing.
The movie we went to see yesterday was really amazing.

Codeswitching occurs wherever groups of bilinguals speak the same two languages. Furthermore, codeswitching occurs in specific social situations, enriching the repertoire of the speakers.

A common misconception is that codeswitching is indicative of a language disability of some kind, for example, that bilinguals use codeswitching as a coping strategy for incomplete mastery of both languages, or that they are speaking "broken" English. These characterizations are completely inaccurate. Recent studies of the social and linguistic properties of codeswitching indicate that it is a marker of bilingual identity, and has its own internal grammatical structure. For example, bilinguals will commonly codeswitch between a subject and a verb, as in:

Mis amigos finished first.        My friends finished first.

but would judge ungrammatical a switch between a subject pronoun and a verb as in:

*Ellos finished first. They finished first.

Codeswitchers also follow the word order rules of the languages. For example, in a Spanish noun phrase, the adjective usually follows the noun, as opposed to the English NP in which it precedes, as shown by the following:

English: My mom fixes **green tamales**. (Adj N)
Spanish: Mi mamà hace **tamales verdes**. (N Adj)

A speaker might codeswitch as follows:

My mom fixes **tamales verdes**.
or Mi mamà hace **green tamales**.

but would not accept or produce such utterances as

*My mom fixes **verdes tamales**.
or *Mi mamà hace **tamales green**.

because the word order within the NPs violates the rules of the language.

Codeswitching is to be distinguished from (bilingual) **borrowing**, which occurs when a word or short expression from one language occurs embedded among the words of a second language and adapts to the regular phonology, morphology, and syntax of the second language. In codeswitching, in contrast, the two languages that are interwoven preserve their own phonological and other grammatical properties. Borrowing can be easily distinguished from codeswitching by the pronunciation of an element. Sentence (1) involves borrowing, and (2) codeswitching.

(1) I love biscottis [bɪskaɾiz] with my coffee.
(2) I love biscotti [biskɔt:i] with my coffee.

In sentence (1) *biscotti* takes on an (American) English pronunciation and plural *-s* morphology, while in (2) it preserves the Italian pronunciation and plural morpheme *-i* (plural for *biscotto*, "cookie").

What needs to be emphasized is that people who codeswitch have knowledge not of one but of two (or more) languages and that codeswitching, like linguistic knowledge in general, is highly structured and rule-governed.

# Language in Use

## Styles

Most speakers of a language speak one way with friends, another on a job interview or presenting a report in class, another talking to small children, another with their parents, and so on. These "situation dialects" are called **styles**, or **registers**.

Nearly everybody has at least an informal and a formal style. In an informal style, the rules of contraction are used more often, the syntactic rules of negation and agreement may be altered, and many words are used that do not occur in the formal style.

Informal styles, although permitting certain abbreviations and deletions not permitted in formal speech, are also rule-governed. For example, questions are often shortened with the subject *you* and the auxiliary verb deleted. You can ask *Running the marathon?* or *You running the marathon?* instead of the more formal *Are you running the marathon?* but you cannot shorten the question to **Are running the marathon?* Informal talk is not anarchy. It is rule-governed, but the rules of deletion, contraction, and word choice are different from those of the formal language.

It is common for speakers to have competence in several styles, ranging between the two extremes of formal and informal. The use of styles is often a means of identification with a particular group (e.g., family, gang, church, and team), or a means of excluding groups believed to be hostile or undesirable (cops, teachers, parents).

Many cultures have rules of social behavior that govern style. Some Indo-European languages distinguish between *you* (familiar) and *you* (polite). German *du* and French *tu* are to be used only with "intimates"; *Sie* and *vous* are more formal and used with nonintimates. Thai has three words meaning "eat" depending on the social status of who is speaking with whom.

Social situations affect the details of language usage, but the core grammar remains intact, with a few superficial variations that lend a particular flavor to the speech.

## Slang

One mark of an informal style is the frequent occurrence of **slang**. Slang is something that nearly everyone uses and recognizes, but nobody can define precisely. It is more metaphorical, playful, elliptical, vivid, and shorter-lived than ordinary language.

The use of slang has introduced many new words into the language by re-combining old words into new meanings. *Spaced out, right on, hang-up, drill down,* and *rip-off* have all gained a degree of acceptance. Slang also introduces entirely new words such as *barf, flub, hoodie,* and *dis*. Finally, slang often consists of ascribing entirely new meanings to old words. *Rave* has broadened its meaning to "an all-night dance party," where people take *ecstasy* (slang for a kind of drug) to get *high; crib* refers to one's home and *posse* to one's cohorts. *Weed* and *pot* widened their meaning to "marijuana"; *pig* and *fuzz* are derogatory terms for "police officer"; *rap, cool, dig, stoned, split,* and *suck* have all extended their semantic domains.

The words we have cited may sound slangy because they have not gained total acceptability. Words such as *dwindle, freshman, glib,* and *mob* are former slang words that in time overcame their "unsavory" origin. It is not always easy to know where to draw the line between slang words and regular words. The borderland between slang and formal language is ill-defined and is more of a continuum than a strict boundary.

There are scads (another slang word) of sources of slang. It comes from the underworld: *crack, payola,* to *hang paper*. It comes from college campuses: *crash, wicked, peace*. It even comes from the White House: *pencil* (writer), *still* (photographer), and *football* (black box of security secrets).

Slang is universal. It is found in all languages and all time periods. It varies from region to region, and from past to present. Slang meets a variety of social needs and rather than a corruption of the language, it is yet further evidence of the creativity of the human language user. If you are a lover of "crazy" words, you need to know about the online Urban Dictionary at http://www.urbandictionary.com/

## Jargon and Argot

Practically every conceivable science, profession, trade, and occupation uses specific slang terms called **jargon**, or **argot**. Linguistic jargon, some of which is used in this book, consists of terms such as *phoneme*, *morpheme*, *case*, *lexicon*, *phrase structure rule*, and *X-bar schema*. Part of the reason for specialized terminology is for clarity of communication, but part is also for speakers to identify themselves with persons with whom they share interests.

Because the jargon used by different professional and social groups is so extensive (and so obscure in meaning), court reporters in the Los Angeles Criminal Courts Building have a library that includes books on medical terms, guns, trade names, and computer jargon, as well as street slang.

The computer age not only ushered in a technological revolution, it also introduced a slew of jargon, called slangily, *computerese*, used by computer "hackers" and others. So vast is this specialized vocabulary that *Webster's New World Computer Dictionary* has four hundred pages and contains thousands of computer terms as entries. A few such words that are familiar to most people are *modem* (from ***mo**dulator-**dem**odulator), bit* (from ***bi**nary digi**t***), and *byte* ("eight *bits"*). Acronyms and alphabetic abbreviations abound in computer jargon. *ROM* ("read-only memory"), *RAM* ("random-access memory"), *CPU* ("central processing unit"), and *DVD* ("digital video disk") are a small fraction of what's out there.

Some jargon may over time pass into the standard language. Jargon, like all types of slang, spreads from a narrow group that originally embraced it until it is used and understood by a large segment of the population.

## Taboo or Not Taboo?

An item in a newspaper once included the following paragraph:

> "This is not a Sunday school, but it is a school of law," the judge said in warning the defendants he would not tolerate the "use of expletives during jury selection." "I'm not going to have my fellow citizens and prospective jurors subjected to filthy language," the judge added.

How can language be filthy? In fact, how can it be clean? The filth or beauty of language must be in the ear of the listener, or in the collective ear of society. The writer Paul Theroux points this out:

> A foreign swear-word is practically inoffensive except to the person who has learned it early in life and knows its social limits.

Nothing about a particular string of sounds makes it intrinsically clean or dirty, ugly or beautiful. If you say that you *pricked* your finger when sewing, no one would raise an eyebrow, but if you refer to your professor as a *prick*, the judge quoted previously would undoubtedly censure this "dirty" word.

You know the obscene words of your language, and you know the social situations in which they are desirable, acceptable, forbidden, and downright dangerous to utter. This is true of all speakers of all languages. All societies have their taboo words. (*Taboo* is a Tongan word meaning "forbidden.") People everywhere seem to have a need for undeleted expletives to express their emotions or attitudes.

Forbidden acts or words reflect the particular customs and views of the society. Among the Zuni Indians, it is improper to use the word *takka*, meaning "frogs," during a religious ceremony. In the world of Harry Potter, the evil Voldemort is not to be named but is referred to as "You-Know-Who." In some religions, believers are forbidden to "take the Lord's name in vain," and this prohibition often extends to other religious jargon. Thus, the taboo words *hell* and *damn* are changed to *heck* and *darn*, though the results are sometimes not euphonious. Imagine the last two lines of Act II, Scene 1, of *Macbeth* if they were "cleaned up":

> Hear it not, Duncan; for it is a knell
> That summons thee to heaven, or to *heck*

Words relating to sex, sex organs, and natural bodily functions make up a large part of the set of taboo words of many cultures. Often, two or more words or expressions can have the same linguistic meaning, with one acceptable and the other taboo. In English, words borrowed from Latin sound "scientific" and therefore appear to be technical and "clean," whereas native Anglo-Saxon counterparts are taboo. Such pairs of words are illustrated as follows:

| Anglo-Saxon Taboo Words | Latinate Acceptable Words |
|---|---|
| cunt | vagina |
| cock | penis |
| prick | penis |
| tits | mammaries |
| shit | feces, defecate |

There is no grammatical reason why the word *vagina* is "clean" whereas *cunt* is "dirty," or why *balls* is taboo but *testicles* acceptable. Although there is no grammatical basis for such preferences, there certainly are sociolinguistic reasons to embrace or eschew such usages, just as there are sociolinguistic reasons for speaking formally, respectfully, disrespectfully, informally, in jargon, and so on.

## Euphemisms

As we noted in Chapter 1, the existence of taboo words and ideas motivates the creation of **euphemisms**. A euphemism is a word or phrase that replaces a taboo word or serves to avoid frightening or unpleasant subjects. In many societies, because death is feared, there are many euphemisms related to this subject.

People are less apt to *die* and more apt to *pass on* or *pass away*. Those who take care of your loved ones who have passed away are more likely to be *funeral directors* than *morticians* or *undertakers*. And then there's *feminine protection* . . .

The use of euphemisms is not new. It is reported that the Greek historian Plutarch in the first century CE wrote that "the ancient Athenians . . . used to cover up the ugliness of things with auspicious and kindly terms, giving them polite and endearing names. Thus, they called harlots *companions,* taxes *contributions,* and prison a *chamber.*"

Just as surely as all languages and societies have taboo words, they have euphemisms. The aforementioned taboo word *takka,* meaning "frogs," is replaced during a Zuni religious ceremony by a complex compound word that literally translates as "several-are-sitting-in-a-shallow-basin-where-they-are-in-liquid." The euphemisms for bodily excretions and sexual activity are legion, and lists of them may be found in online dictionaries of slang. There you will find such gems for urination as *siphon the python* and *point Percy at the porcelain,* and for intercourse *shag, hide the ferret (salami, sausage),* and *stuffin' the muffin,* among a gazillion others.

These euphemisms, as well as the difference between the accepted Latinate "genteel" terms and the "dirty" Anglo-Saxon terms, show that a word or phrase has not only a linguistic **denotative meaning** but also a **connotative meaning** that reflects attitudes, emotions, value judgments, and so on. In learning a language, children learn which words are taboo, and these taboo words differ from one child to another, depending on the value system accepted in the family or group in which the child grows up.

## Racial and National Epithets

The use of epithets for people of different religions, nationalities, or races tells us something about the speakers. Words such as *kike* (for Jew), *wop* (for Italian), *nigger* or *coon* (for African American), *slant* (for Asian), and *towelhead* (for Middle Eastern Arab) reflect racist and chauvinist views of society.

Even words that sound like epithets are perhaps to be avoided. An administrator in Washington, D.C., described a fund he administers as "niggardly," meaning stingy. He resigned his position under fire for using a word "so close to a degrading word."

Language, however, is creative, malleable, and ever-changing. The epithets used by a majority to demean a minority may be reclaimed as terms of bonding and friendship among members of the minority. Thus, for *some*—we emphasize *some*—African Americans, the word *nigger* is used to show affection. Similarly, the ordinarily degrading word *queer* is used among *some* gay people as a term of endearment, as is *cripple* or *crip* among *some* individuals who share a disability.

## Language and Sexism

The discussion of obscenities, blasphemies, taboo words, and euphemisms showed that words of a language are not intrinsically good or bad but reflect individual or societal values. This is also seen in references to a woman as a *castrating female, ballsy women's libber,* or *courageous feminist advocate,* depending on who is talking.

Early dictionaries often gave clues to the social attitudes of that time. In some twentieth-century dictionaries, examples used to illustrate the meaning of words include "manly courage" and "masculine charm," as opposed to "womanish tears" and "feminine wiles." Contemporary dictionaries are far more enlightened and try to be scrupulous in avoiding sexist language.

Until recently, most people who heard "My cousin is a professor (or a doctor, or the chancellor of the university, or a steelworker)" would assume that the cousin is a man; if they heard "My cousin is a nurse (or elementary school teacher, or clerk-typist, or house worker)," they would conclude that the cousin is a woman. This is changing because society is changing and increasingly, both women and men hold jobs once held primarily by one sex.

Despite flashes of enlightenment, words for women with abusive or sexual overtones abound: *dish, piece, piece of ass, piece of tail, bunny, chick, pussy, bitch, doll, slut, cow, cougar*—to name just a few. Far fewer such sexual terms exist for men, and those that do, such as *boy toy, stud muffin, hunk, and jock,* are not pejorative in the same way.

It's clear that language reflects sexism. It reflects any societal attitude, positive or negative. Languages are infinitely flexible and expressive, but is language itself amoral and neutral? Or is there something about language, or a particular language, that abets sexism? Before we attempt to answer that question, let's look more deeply into the subject, using English as the illustrative language.

## Marked and Unmarked Forms

There is an asymmetry between male and female terms in which there are male/female pairs of words. The male form is *unmarked*, and is the more generally used term, whereas the female term is *marked* and often created by adding a bound morpheme or making a compound. We have many such examples in English:

| Male | Female |
|---|---|
| heir | heir**ess** |
| major | major**ette** |
| hero | hero**ine** |
| Robert | Robert**a** |
| equestrian | equestri**enne** |
| aviator | aviat**rix** |
| wolf | **she**wolf |
| scout | **Girl** Scout |
| cop | **lady** cop |

When referring in general to the profession of acting, or flying, or riding horseback, the unmarked terms *actor, aviator,* and *equestrian* are used. The marked terms are used to emphasize the female gender. (Rare exceptions to this is the unmarked word *widow* for a woman with a deceased husband but *widow***er** for a man with a deceased wife; and *escort* meaning a female prostitute but ***male*** *escort* for its gender opposite.)

The unmarked third person pronoun in English is male *(he, him, his). Everybody had better pay* ***his*** *fee next time* allows for the clients to be male or female, but *Everybody had better pay* ***her*** *fee next time* presupposes a female client. Attempts to find a suitable genderless third person pronoun have included forms such as *e, hesh, po, tey, co, jhe, ve, xe, he'er, thon,* and *na,* none of which speakers have the least inclination to adopt. The use of the gender neutral pronoun *they,* as in *Every teenager loves their first car,* is close to becoming standard usage (except perhaps in your English class where you should probably stick to *he* and *she*).

With women occupying more and varied roles in society (from combat military to "Wichita Linemen"), many of the marked female forms have been replaced by the male forms, which are used to refer to either sex. Thus women, as well as men, are authors, actors, poets, heroes, heirs, postal carriers, firefighters, and police officers. Women, however, remain countesses, duchesses, and princesses, if they are among this small group of female aristocrats.

The Sapir–Whorf hypothesis, discussed in Chapter 1, proposes that the way a language encodes—puts into words—different categories like male and female subtly affects the way speakers of the language think about those categories. Thus, it may be argued that because English speakers are often taught to choose *he* as the unmarked pronoun *(Everyone should respect* ***him****self),* and to choose *she* only when the referent is specifically female, they tend to think of the male sex as predominant. Likewise, the fact that nouns require special affixes to make them feminine forces people to think in terms of male and female, with the female somehow more derivative because of affixing or compounding. The different titles, Mr., Mrs., Miss, and Ms., also emphasize the male/female distinction. Finally, the preponderance of words denigrating females in English and in many other languages may promote a climate that is more tolerant of sexist behavior.

## Summary

Every person has a unique way of speaking, called an **idiolect**. The language used by a group of speakers is a **dialect**. The dialects of a language are the mutually intelligible forms of that language that differ in systematic ways from each other. Dialects develop because languages change, and the changes that occur in one group or area may differ from those that occur in another. **Regional dialects** and **social dialects** develop for this reason. Some differences in U.S. regional dialects may be traced to the dialects spoken by colonial settlers from England. Those from southern England spoke one dialect and those from the north spoke another. In addition, the colonists who maintained close contact with England reflected the changes occurring in British English, while earlier forms were preserved among Americans who spread westward and broke communication with the Atlantic coast.

Social dialects arise when groups are isolated socially, such as Americans of African descent in the United States, many of whom speak dialects collectively called African American (Vernacular) English, which are distinct from the dialects spoken by non-Africans.

Dialect differences include phonological or pronunciation differences (often called **accents**), vocabulary distinctions, and syntactic rule differences.

The grammar differences among dialects are not as great as the similarities, thus permitting speakers of different dialects to communicate.

In many countries, one dialect or dialect group is viewed as the **standard**, such as **Standard American English (SAE).** Although this particular dialect is not linguistically superior, some language purists consider it the only correct form of the language. Such a view has led to the idea that some non-standard dialects are deficient. Studies of minority dialects show them to be as logical, complete, rule-governed, and expressive as any other dialect. This is true of **African American English (AAE). Codeswitching** is shifting between languages within a single sentence or discourse by a bilingual speaker. It reflects both grammars working simultaneously and does not represent a form of "broken" English or Spanish or whatever language.

Attempts to legislate the use of a particular dialect or language have been made throughout history and exist today, even extending to banning the use of languages other than the preferred one.

In areas where many languages are spoken, one language may become a **lingua franca** to ease communication among people. In other cases, where traders, missionaries, or travelers need to communicate with people who speak a language unknown to them, a **pidgin** may develop. A pidgin is a simplified system with properties of both the **superstrate (lexifier)** and **substrate** languages. When a pidgin is widely used, and constitutes the primary linguistic input to children, it is *creolized*. The grammars of **creole** languages are similar to those of other languages, and languages of creole origin now exist in many parts of the world.

Besides regional and social dialects, speakers may use different **styles**, or **registers**, depending on the context. **Slang** is not often used in formal situations or writing but is widely used in speech; **argot** and **jargon** refer to the unique vocabularies used by particular groups of people to facilitate communication, provide a means of bonding, and exclude outsiders.

In all societies, certain acts or behaviors are frowned on, forbidden, or considered **taboo**. The words or expressions referring to these taboo acts are then also avoided or considered "dirty." Language cannot be obscene or clean; attitudes toward specific words or linguistic expressions reflect the views of a culture or society toward the behaviors and actions of the language users. At times, slang words may be taboo while scientific or standard terms with the same meaning are acceptable in "polite society." Taboo words and acts give rise to **euphemisms**, which are words or phrases that replace the expressions to be avoided. Thus, *powder room* is a euphemism for *toilet*, which started as a euphemism for *lavatory*, which is now more acceptable than its replacement.

Just as the use of some words may indicate society's views toward sex, natural bodily functions, or religious beliefs, some words may also indicate racist, chauvinist, or sexist attitudes. Language is not intrinsically racist or sexist but reflects the views of various sectors of a society. However, the availability of offensive terms, and particular grammatical peculiarities such as the lack of a genderless third-person singular pronoun, may perpetuate and reinforce biased views and be demeaning and insulting to those addressed. Thus, culture influences language, and, arguably, language may have an influence on the culture in which it is spoken.

## References for Further Reading

Carver, C. M. 1987. *American regional dialects: A word geography*. Ann Arbor, MI: University of Michigan Press.

Cassidy, F. G. (chief ed.). 1985, 1991, 1996, 2002, 2012. *Dictionary of American regional English*, Volumes 1, 2, 3, 4, 5. Cambridge, MA: Harvard University Press.

Chambers, J., and P. Trudgill. 1998. *Dialectology, 2nd ed*. Cambridge, UK: Cambridge University Press.

Holm, J. 2000. *An introduction to pidgins and creoles*.Cambridge, UK: Cambridge University Press.

Labov, W. 1972. *Sociolinguistic patterns*. Philadelphia: University of Pennsylvania Press.

________. 1969. The logic of nonstandard English. *Georgetown University 20th Annual Round Table, Monograph Series on Languages and Linguistics,* No. 22.

________. 1966. The social stratification of English in New York City. Washington, DC: Center for Applied Linguistics.

Lakoff, R. 1990. *Talking power: The politics of language*. New York: Basic Books.

Tannen, D. 1994. *Gender and discourse*. New York: Oxford University Press.

________. 1990. *You just don't understand: Women and men in conversation*. New York: Ballantine.

Velupillai V. 2015. *Pidgins, Creoles and Mixed Languages: An Introduction*. Amsterdam, The Netherlands: John Benjamins Publishing Company

Wardhaugh, R. 2015. *An introduction to sociolinguistics, 7th ed*. London: Wiley-Blackwell Publishers.

Wolfram, W., and N. Schilling-Estes. 2006. *American English dialects and variation, 2nd ed*. London: Wiley-Blackwell Publishers.

## Exercises

**1.** Each pair of words is pronounced as shown phonetically in at least one American English dialect. Write in phonetic transcription your pronunciation of each word that you pronounce differently.

| | | | | |
|---|---|---|---|---|
| **a.** | horse | [hɔrs] | hoarse | [hors] |
| **b.** | morning | [mɔrnĩŋ] | mourning | [mornĩŋ] |
| **c.** | for | [fɔr] | four | [for] |
| **d.** | ice | [ʌɪs] | eyes | [aɪz] |
| **e.** | knife | [nʌɪf] | knives | [naɪvz] |
| **f.** | mute | [mjut] | nude | [njud] |
| **g.** | din | [dĩn] | den | [dɛ̃n] |
| **h.** | hog | [hɔg] | hot | [hat] |
| **i.** | marry | [mæri] | Mary | [meri] |
| **j.** | merry | [mɛri] | marry | [mæri] |
| **k.** | rot | [rat] | wrought | [rɔt] |
| **l.** | lease | [lis] | grease (v.) | [griz] |
| **m.** | what | [ʍat] | watt | [wat] |

| | | | |
|---|---|---|---|
| **n.** ant | [æ̃nt] | aunt | [ãnt] |
| **o.** creek | [$k^h$rɪk] | creak | [$k^h$rik] |

2. In the period from 1890 to 1904, *Slang and Its Analogues,* by J. S. Farmer and W. E. Henley, was published in seven volumes. The following entries are included in this dictionary. For each item (1) state whether the word or phrase still exists; (2) if not, state what the modern slang term would be; and (3) if the word remains but its meaning has changed, provide the modern meaning.

*all out*: completely, as in "All out the best" (The expression goes back to as early as 1300.)
*to have apartments to let*: be an idiot; one who is empty-headed
*been there*: in "Oh, yes, I've been there." (Applied to a man who is shrewd and who has had many experiences.)
*belly-button*: the navel
*berkeleys*: a woman's breasts
*bitch*: most offensive appellation that can be given to a woman, even more provoking than *whore*
*once in a blue moon*: seldom
*boss*: master; one who directs
*bread*: employment. (1785—"out of bread" = "out of work")
*claim*: to steal
*cut dirt*: to escape
*dog cheap*: of little worth (Used in 1616 by Dekker: "Three things there are dog-cheap, learning, poorman's sweat, and oathes.")
*funeral*: as in "It's not my funeral." "It's no business of mine."
*to get over*: to seduce, to fascinate
*groovy*: settled in habit; limited in mind
*grub*: food
*head*: toilet (nautical use only)
*hook*: to marry
*hump*: to spoil
*hush money*: money paid for silence; blackmail
*itch*: to be sexually excited
*jam*: a sweetheart or a mistress
*leg bags*: stockings
*to lie low*: to keep quiet; to bide one's time
*to lift a leg on*: to have sexual intercourse
*looby*: a fool
*malady of France*: syphilis (Used by Shakespeare in 1599.)
*nix*: nothing
*noddle*: the head
*old*: money (1900—"Perhaps it's somebody you owe a bit of the old to, Jack.")
*to pill*: talk platitudes
*pipe layer*: a political intriguer; a schemer
*poky*: cramped, stuffy, stupid
*pot*: a quart; a large sum; a prize; a urinal; to excel

*puny*: a freshman
*puss-gentleman*: an effeminate

3. Suppose someone asked you to help compile items for a new dictionary of slang. List ten slang words, and provide a short definition for each.

4. Below are some words used in British English for which different words are usually used in American English. See whether you can match the British and American equivalents.

| | British | American |
|---|---|---|
| a. | clothes peg | candy |
| b. | braces | truck |
| c. | lift | line |
| d. | pram | main street |
| e. | waistcoat | crackers |
| f. | shop assistant | suspenders |
| g. | sweets | wrench |
| h. | boot (of car) | flashlight |
| i. | bobby | potato chips |
| j. | spanner | vacation |
| k. | biscuits | baby buggy |
| l. | queue | elevator |
| m. | torch | can |
| n. | underground | cop |
| o. | high street | wake up |
| p. | crisps | trunk |
| q. | lorry | vest |
| r. | holiday | subway |
| s. | tin | clothes pin |
| t. | knock up | clerk |

5. Below are sentences that might be spoken between two friends chatting informally. For each, state what the nonabbreviated full sentence in SAE would be. In addition, state in your own words (or formally if you wish) the rule or rules that derived the informal sentences from the formal ones.

   a. Where've ya been today?
   b. Watcha gonna do for fun?
   c. Him go to church?
   d. There's four books there.
   e. Who ya wanna go with?

6. Column A lists euphemisms for words in Column B. Match each item in A with its appropriate B word.

| | A | B |
|---|---|---|
| a. | Montezuma's revenge | condom |
| b. | joy stick | genocide |
| c. | friggin' | fire |

| | |
|---|---|
| **d.** ethnic cleansing | diarrhea |
| **e.** French letter (old) | masturbate |
| **f.** diddle oneself | kill |
| **g.** holy of holies | urinate |
| **h.** spend a penny (British) | penis |
| **i.** ladies' cloak room | die |
| **j.** knock off (from 1919) | waging war |
| **k.** vertically challenged | vagina |
| **l.** hand in one's dinner pail | women's toilet |
| **m.** sanitation engineer | short |
| **n.** downsize | fuckin' |
| **o.** peace keeping | garbage collector |

**7.** Write a thoughtful essay that grapples with one or more the following questions (review the discussion of the Sapir–Whorf hypothesis in Chapter 1):

Although people can undoubtedly be sexist, and even cultures can be sexist, can language be sexist?
Can language mold us into being something that we do not want to be?
Can language magnify any natural inclinations that we may have?
Can language be free of societal values?

**8.** One aspect of different English genderlects is lexical choice. For example, women say *darling* and *lovely* more frequently than men; men use sports metaphors such as *homerun* and *slam dunk* more than women. Think of other lexical usages that appear to be asymmetric between the sexes.

**9.** **Research project:** Throughout history many regimes have banned languages. Write a report in which you mention several such regimes, the languages they banned, and possible reasons for banning them (e.g., you might have discovered that the Basque language was banned in Spain under the regime of Francisco Franco (1936–1975) owing in part to the separatist desires of the Basque people and because the Basques opposed his dictatorship).

**10.** Abbreviated English (AE) is a register of written English used in newspaper headlines and elsewhere. Some examples follow:

CLINTON IN BULGARIA THIS WEEK
OLD MAN FINDS RARE COIN
BUSH HIRES WIFE AS SECRETARY
POPE DIES IN VATICAN

AE does not involve an arbitrary omission of parts of the sentence but is regulated by grammatical rules.

**a.** Translate each of these headlines into Standard American English (SAE).
**b.** What features or rules distinguish AE from SAE?
**c.** Are there other contexts (besides headlines) in which we find AE? If so, provide examples.

d. **Challenge exercise:** What is the time reference of the above headlines (e.g., present, recent past, remote past, and future)?
e. **Challenge exercise:** Is there a difference in possible tense interpretations when the predicate is eventive (e.g., *dies*) and when it is stative (e.g., *in Bulgaria*)? (You may have to review these terms in Chapter 4.)

8

# Language Change: The Syllables of Time

All living languages change with time. It is fortunate that they do so rather slowly compared to the human life span. It would be inconvenient to have to relearn our native language every twenty years. As years pass, we hardly notice any change. Yet, if we were to turn on a radio and miraculously receive a broadcast in our "native language" from the year 1000, we would probably think we had tuned into a foreign language station.

Bereft of spoken recordings, we must consult written records to achieve a sense of language change. We know a great deal of the history of English because it has been a written language for more than one thousand three-hundred years. Old English, spoken in England during the first millennium, is scarcely recognizable as English. (Of course, our linguistic ancestors did not call their language Old English!) A speaker of Modern English would find the language unintelligible. There are college courses in which Old English is studied as a foreign language.

A line from *Beowulf* illustrates why Old English must be translated:[1]

Wolde guman findan þone þe him on sweofote sare geteode.
"He wanted to find the man who harmed him while he slept."

Approximately five hundred years after *Beowulf*, Chaucer wrote *The Canterbury Tales* in what is now called Middle English, spoken from around 1100 to 1500. It is more easily understood by present-day readers, as seen by reading the opening of the *Tales*:

Whan that Aprille with his shoures soote
The droght of March hath perced to the roote . . .
"When April with its sweet showers
The drought of March has pierced to the root . . ."

[1]The letter þ is called *thorn* and is pronounced [θ] in this example.

Two hundred years after Chaucer, in a language that is considered an early form of Modern English, Shakespeare's Hamlet says:

> A man may fish with the worm that hath eat of a king, and eat of the fish that hath fed of that worm.

The stages of English are Old English (449–1100 CE), Middle English (1100–1500), and Modern English (1500–present). This division is somewhat arbitrary, being marked by important dates in English history, such as the Norman Conquest of 1066, the results of which profoundly influenced the English language.

The branch of linguistics that deals with how languages change, what kinds of changes occur, and why they occurred is called **historical and comparative linguistics**. It is "historical" because it deals with the history of particular languages; it is "comparative" because it deals with relations among languages.

Changes in a language are changes in the grammar and lexicon of speakers and are carried forward as new generations of children acquire the altered grammars. All components of the grammar are subject to change over the course of time. Although most of the examples in this chapter are from English, all languages change over time. This is true of sign languages, too, which change in ways similar to spoken languages.

# The Regularity of Sound Change

The southern United States represents a major dialect area of American English. For example, words pronounced with the diphthong [aɪ] in non-Southern English will usually be pronounced with the monophthong [a:] in the South. Local radio and TV announcers at the 1996 Olympics in Atlanta called athletes to the [ha:] "high" jump, and local natives invited visitors to try Georgia's famous pecan [pa:] "pie." The [aɪ]-[a:] correspondence of these two dialects is an example of a **regular sound correspondence**. When [aɪ] occurs in a word in non-Southern dialects, [a:] occurs in the Southern dialect, and *this is true for all such words*.

The different pronunciations of *I, my, high, pie,* and so on did not always exist in English. In this chapter, we will discuss how such dialect differences arose and why the sound differences are usually regular and not confined to just a few words. We will also consider changes that occur in other parts of the grammar and in the lexicon.

## Sound Correspondences

In Middle English a *mouse* [maʊs] was called a *mūs* [mu:s], and this *mūs* may have lived in someone's *hūs* [hu:s], as *house* was pronounced at that time. In general, Middle English speakers pronounced [u:] where we now pronounce [aʊ]. This is a regular correspondence like the one between [aɪ] and [a:]. Thus *out* [aʊt] was pronounced [u:t], *south* [saʊθ] was pronounced [su:θ], and so on. Many such regular correspondences show the relation of older and newer forms of English, just as they show the relation of different regional pronunciations of current forms of English.

The regular sound correspondences we observe are the result of phonological changes that affect certain sounds, or classes of sounds, rather than individual words. Centuries ago English underwent a phonological change called a **sound shift** in which [uː] became [aʊ].

Phonological changes can also account for dialect or regional differences. At an earlier stage of American English a sound shift of [aɪ] to [aː] took place among certain speakers in the southern region of the United States. The change did not spread beyond the South because the region was somewhat isolated. Many pronunciation differences among dialects result from sound shifts whose spread is limited.

Regional dialect differences may also arise when innovative changes occur everywhere but in a particular region. One regional dialect may be conservative relative to others. The pronunciation of *it* as *hit*, found in the Appalachian region of the United States, was standard in older forms of English. The dropping of the [h] was the innovation that affected many other dialects.

## Ancestral Protolanguages

Many modern languages developed from regional dialects that became widely spoken and highly differentiated, finally becoming separate languages. The Romance languages—French, Spanish, Italian, and so on—were once dialects of Latin spoken in the Roman Empire. There is nothing degenerate about regional pronunciations. They are the result of natural sound changes that occur wherever human language is spoken.

In a sense, the Romance languages are the offspring of Latin, their metaphorical parent. Because of their common ancestry, the Romance languages are **genetically related**. Early forms of English and German, too, were once dialects of a common ancestor called **Proto-Germanic**. A **protolanguage** is the ancestral language from which related languages have developed. Both Latin and Proto-Germanic were descendants of an older language called **Indo-European** or **Proto-Indo-European**.

Protolanguages are not actually attested languages, but are hypothesized by linguists to explain the relationships between existing languages. Thus, Germanic languages such as English and German are genetically related to the Romance languages such as French and Spanish. All these national languages were once regional dialects. Proto-Indo-European explains these genetic relationships.

How do we know that the Germanic and Romance languages have a common ancestor? One clue is the large number of sound correspondences. If you have studied a Romance language such as French or Spanish, you may have noticed that where an English word begins with *f*, the corresponding word in a Romance language often begins with *p*, as shown in the following examples:

| English /f/ | French /p/ | Spanish /p/ | Italian /p/ |
|---|---|---|---|
| **f**ather | **p**ère | **p**adre | **p**adre |
| **f**ish | **p**oisson | **p**escado | **p**esce |

This /f/-/p/ correspondence is just one example of many such regular sound correspondences between the Germanic and Romance languages, and their prevalence cannot be explained by chance. What then accounts for them? A reasonable guess is that a common ancestor language used a *p* in words for *fish, father,* and so on. We posit a /p/ rather than an /f/ because more languages show a /p/ in these words.

At some point speakers of this language separated into two groups that lost contact with each other. In one of the groups a sound change of *p* → *f* took place. The language spoken by this group eventually became the ancestor of the Germanic languages. This ancient sound change left its trace in the *f-p* sound correspondence that we observe today, as illustrated in the diagram.

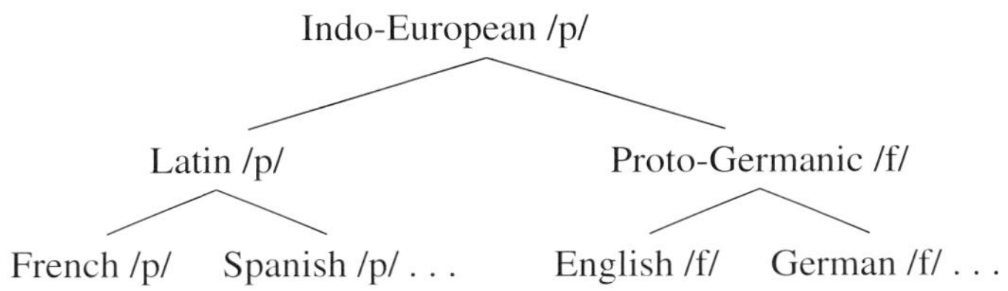


# Phonological Change

Regular sound correspondences illustrate changes in the phonological system of a language. In earlier chapters, we discussed speakers' knowledge of phonology, including knowledge of the phonemes and phonological rules of the language. Both aspects of the phonology are subject to change.

The velar fricative /x/ is no longer part of the phonemic inventory of most Modern English dialects. *Night* used to be pronounced [nɪxt] and *drought* was pronounced [druxt]. This phonological change—the loss of /x/—took place between the times of Chaucer and Shakespeare. All words that were once pronounced with an /x/ no longer include this sound. In some cases, it disappeared altogether, as in *night* and *light*. In other cases, the /x/ became a /k/, as in *elk* (Old English *eolh* [ɛɔlx]). In yet other cases, it disappeared to be replaced by a vowel, as in *hollow* (Old English *holh* [hɔlx]). Dialects of Modern English spoken in Scotland have retained the /x/ sound in some words, such as *loch* [lɔx] meaning "lake."

These examples show that languages can lose phonemes over time. They can also add phonemes. Old English did not have the phoneme /ʒ/ of *leisure* [liʒər]. Through a process of palatalization—a change in place of articulation to the palatal region—certain occurrences of /z/ were pronounced [ʒ]. Eventually the [ʒ] sound became a phoneme in its own right. Similarly, occurrences of /f/ between vowels were once pronounced [v], which eventually became the additional phoneme /v/.

## Phonological Rules

An interaction of phonological rules may result in changes in the lexicon. The nouns *house* and *bath* were once differentiated from the verbs *house* [haʊz] and *bathe* [beð] by the fact that the verbs once ended with a short vowel sound, namely /huːsə/ and /baːθə/. Furthermore, the same rule that realized /f/ as [v] between vowels also realized /s/ and /θ/ as [z] and [ð] between vowels. This general rule added voicing to voiceless intervocalic fricatives. Thus, the /s/ in the verb /huːsə/ was pronounced [z], and the /θ/ in the verb /baːθə/ was pronounced [ð].

Later, a rule was added to the grammar of English deleting unstressed short vowels at the end of words (even though the final vowel still appears in the written words). A contrast between the voiced and voiceless fricatives resulted, and new phonemes /z/ and /ð/ were added to the phonemic inventory. The verbs *house* [haʊz] and *bathe* [beð] were now represented in the mental lexicon with final voiced consonants.

Eventually, both the unstressed vowel deletion rule and the intervocalic-voicing rule were lost from the grammar of English. The set of phonological rules can change both by addition and by loss of rules.

Changes in phonological rules can, and often do, result in dialect differences. In the previous chapter, we discussed the addition of an *r*-dropping rule in English (/r/ is not pronounced unless followed by a vowel) that did not spread throughout the language. Today, we see the effect of that rule in the *r*-less pronunciation of British English, and of American English dialects spoken in the northeastern and the southern United States.

From the standpoint of the language as a whole, phonological changes occur gradually over the course of many generations of speakers, although any given speaker's grammar may or may not reflect the change. The changes are not planned any more than we are presently planning what changes will take place in English by the year 2300. In a single generation, changes are evident only through dialect differences.

# The Great Vowel Shift

Between 1400 and 1600 a major change took place in English that resulted in new phonemic representations of words and morphemes. This phonological restructuring is known as the **Great Vowel Shift**. The seven long, or tense, vowels of Middle English underwent the following change:

| Shift | | | Example | | | |
|---|---|---|---|---|---|---|
| **Middle English** | | **Modern English** | **Middle English** | | **Modern English** | |
| [iː] | → | [aɪ] | [miːs] | → | [maɪs] | mice |
| [uː] | → | [aʊ] | [muːs] | → | [maʊs] | mouse |
| [eː] | → | [iː] | [geːs] | → | [giːs] | geese |
| [oː] | → | [uː] | [goːs] | → | [guːs] | goose |
| [ɛː] | → | [eː] | [brɛːken] | → | [breːk] | break |

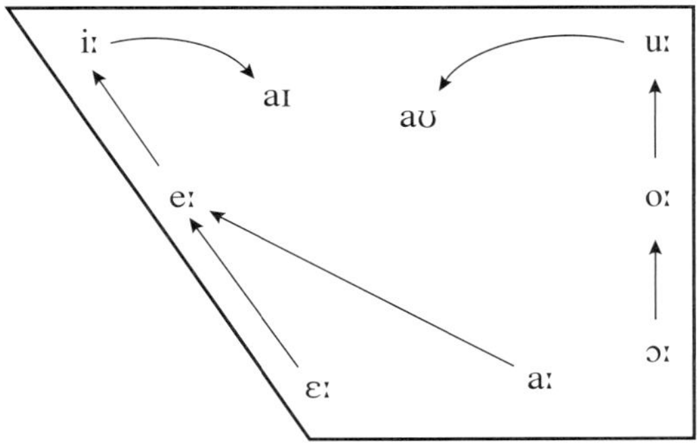


FIGURE 8.1 | The Great Vowel Shift.

| **Shift** | | | **Example** | | | |
|---|---|---|---|---|---|---|
| **Middle English** | | **Modern English** | **Middle English** | | **Modern English** | |
| [ɔː] | → | [oː] | [brɔːken] | → | [broːk] | broke |
| [aː] | → | [eː] | [naːmə] | → | [neːm] | name |

By diagramming the Great Vowel Shift on a vowel chart (Figure 8.1), we can see that the high vowels [iː] and [uː] became the diphthongs [aɪ] and [aʊ], while the long vowels underwent an increase in tongue height, as if to fill in the space vacated by the high vowels. In addition, [aː] was fronted to become [eː].

These changes are among the most dramatic examples of regular sound shift. The phonemic representation of many thousands of words changed. Today, some reflection of this vowel shift is seen in the alternating forms of morphemes in English: *please—pleasant, serene—serenity; sane—sanity; crime—criminal; sign—signal;* and so on. Before the Great Vowel Shift, the vowels in each pair were pronounced the same. Then the vowels in the second word of each pair were shortened by the **Early Middle English Vowel Shortening** rule. As a result, the Great Vowel Shift, which occurred later and applied only to long vowels, affected only the first word in each pair. This is why the vowels in the morphologically related words are pronounced differently today, as shown in Table 8.1.

TABLE 8.1 | Effect of Vowel Shift on Modern English

| Middle English Vowel | Shifted Vowel | Short Vowel | Word with Shifted Vowel | Word with Short Vowel |
|---|---|---|---|---|
| ī | aɪ | ɪ | divine | divinity |
| ū | aʊ | ʌ | abound | abundant |
| ē | i | ɛ | serene | serenity |
| ō | u | a | fool | folly |
| ā | e | æ | sane | sanity |

Many spelling inconsistencies of English are due to the Great Vowel Shift because our spelling system still reflects the way words were pronounced before it occurred. In general, the written language changes more slowly than the spoken language.

## Morphological Change

Like phonological rules, rules of morphology may be lost, added, or changed. We can observe some of these changes by comparing older and newer forms of the language and by looking at different dialects.

Extensive changes in morphology have occurred in the history of the Indo-European languages. Latin had **case endings**, suffixes on nouns based on their thematic role or grammatical relationship to the verb. These are no longer found in the Romance languages except on pronouns. (See Chapter 4 for a more extensive discussion of thematic roles; the terms used by historical linguists are somewhat different than those used by modern semanticists.) The following is a **declension**, or list of cases, for the Latin noun *lupus,* "wolf":

| Noun | Noun Stem | | Case Ending | Case | Example |
|---|---|---|---|---|---|
| lupus | lup | + | us | nominative | The *wolf* runs. |
| lupī | lup | + | ī | genitive | A sheep in *wolf's* clothing. |
| lupō | lup | + | ō | dative | Give food *to the wolf.* |
| lupum | lup | + | um | accusative | I love *the wolf.* |
| lupō | lup | + | ō | ablative | She walked *with the wolf.* |
| lupe | lup | + | e | vocative | *Wolf,* come here! |

In *Alice's Adventures in Wonderland,* Lewis Carroll has Alice give us a brief lesson in grammatical case. Alice has become very small and is swimming around in a pool of her own tears with a mouse that she wishes to befriend:

> "Would it be of any use, now," thought Alice, "to speak to this mouse? Everything is so out-of-the-way down here, that I should think very likely it can talk: at any rate, there's no harm in trying." So she began: "O Mouse, do you know the way out of this pool? I am very tired of swimming about here, O Mouse!" (Alice thought this must be the right way of speaking to a mouse: she had never done such a thing before, but she remembered having seen in her brother's Latin Grammar, "A mouse-of a mouse-to a mouse-a mouse-O mouse!")

Alice's examples are the English equivalents of the nominative, genitive, dative, accusative, and vocative cases, which existed in Latin and in Old English but not in Modern English, where word order and prepositions convey the same information.

Ancient Greek and Sanskrit also had extensive case systems expressed through noun suffixing, as did Old English, as illustrated by the following noun forms:

| Case | OE Singular | | OE Plural | |
|---|---|---|---|---|
| nominative | stān | "stone" | stānas | "stones" |
| genitive | stānes | "stone's" | stāna | "stones'" |
| dative | stāne | "stone" | stānum | "stones" |
| accusative | stān | "stone" | stānas | "stones" |

Lithuanian and Russian retain much of the early Indo-European case system, but it is nearly obliterated in most modern Indo-European languages.

English retains traces of the genitive case, which is written with an apostrophe *s*, as in *Robert's dog*, but nothing more remains as far as possessives are concerned. Pronouns retain a few more case distinctions: *he/she* are nominative, *him/her* accusative and dative, and *his/hers* genitive. And of course English (barely) retains the *who/whom* distinction, much beloved by English teachers, reflecting nominative and non-nominative cases. English has replaced its depleted case system with an equally expressive system of prepositions, as shown in Alice's examples. For example, the dative case is often indicated by the preposition *to*, the genitive case by the preposition *of*, and the accusative case by the word order verb-noun phrase (V NP) with no intervening preposition.

# Syntactic Change

When we see a word-for-word translation of older forms of English, we are most struck by the differences in word order. Consider again the opening lines of *The Canterbury Tales*, this time translated word-for-word:

> Whan that Aprille with his shoures soote
> "When that April with its showers sweet"
> The droght of March hath perced to the roote . . .
> "The drought of March has pierced to the root . . ."

In Modern English, adjectives generally precede the nouns they modify. Thus, we would say *sweet showers* in place of *showers sweet*. Moreover, a direct object now generally follows its verb, so *has pierced the drought of March to the root* would be a modern rendering of the second line. Thus, the rules of syntax that govern these word orders, even taking "poetic license" into account, appear to have changed. It is safe to say that syntactic change in English and other languages is most evident in the changes of permitted word orders.

Syntactic change in English is a good illustration of the interrelationship of the various parts of the grammar. Changes in syntax were often influenced by changes in morphology, and these in turn by changes in the phonology of the language. And conversely, there is evidence that changes in syntax may very well have precipitated changes in the other two systems. These interrelations between the different components of grammar are complex. It is not always easy for historical linguists to determine which part of the grammar affected which other part and when. As in nearly all subfields of linguistics, much more research is needed to solve the many outstanding questions.

When the rich system of case endings of Old English became simplified, due in part to phonological changes and in part to syntactic changes that were underway, speakers of English were forced to rely more heavily on word order to convey the function of noun phrases. A sentence such as

| sē | man | þone | kyning | sloh |
|---|---|---|---|---|
| "the (nominative) | man | the (accusative) | king | slew" |

was understood to mean "the man slew the king." Because of the case of the noun phrases, there would have been no confusion as to who did what to whom.

In addition, in earlier stages of English the verb had a richer system of subject–verb agreement. For example, the verb *to sing* had the following forms: *singe* (I sing), *singest* (you sing), *singeth* (he sings), and *singen* (we, plural you, they sing). It was therefore possible to identify the subject on the basis of verb inflection even if it was not apparent from word order, which was already evolving from the subject–object–verb (SOV) word order of the example to the now more usual subject–verb–object (SVO).

In Modern English, *the man the king slew* is only grammatical as a relative clause meaning "the man that the king slew," with the subject and object of *slew* reversed. To convey the meaning "the man slew the king," Modern English speakers *must* rely on word order—subject–verb–object—or other syntactic devices such as the ones that generate sentences like *It was the king that the man slew*.

The change in English word order reflects a change in grammatical structure. In Old English, the verb came last in the basic verb phrase as it does today in Dutch and German. But English alone underwent a change that made the verb come first in the verb phrase. As a result, Modern English has a basic SVO word order whereas Old English (and modern Dutch and German) have a basic SOV word order.

However, Modern English still has remnants of the original SOV word order in "old-fashioned" kinds of expressions such as *I thee wed*. Word order and morphological distinctions, dancing as partners through time, affected each other: word order became more rigid at the same time that morphological distinctions were vanishing.

As discussed in Chapter 3, in Modern English we form questions by moving an auxiliary verb, if there is one, before the NP subject:

Can the girl kiss the boy?
Will the girl kiss the boy?
Has the girl kissed the boy yet?
Was the girl kissing the boy when you arrived?

However, if an auxiliary verb is absent, Modern English requires the word *do* to spell out the tense of the sentence:

Does the girl kiss the boy often?
*Kisses the girl the boy often?

Older forms of English had a more general rule that moved the first verbal element, which meant that if no auxiliary occurred in the sentence, then the main verb moved. The question

Kisses the girl the boy often?

was grammatical in English through the time of Shakespeare (e.g., *Goes Fleance with you?,* Macbeth, III, 1). This more general verb movement rule still exists in languages such as Dutch and German. In English, however, the rule of question formation changed, as indicated above: now only auxiliary verbs move and if no auxiliary verb is present, a *do* fills its role. This rule change interacted with the English case system. In Old English, *the girl* and *the boy* would have been marked for case, so there was no confusion over who was kissing whom. In effect, the sentence would be:

Kisses the (nominative) girl the (accusative) boy often?

Old English provides another example of how syntax influences morphology with its case endings on nouns that follow prepositions. In Old English, certain prepositions "governed" certain cases:

| **Old English** | **Modern English** |
|---|---|
| in þæt hūs (accusative, singular) | "into that house" |
| fram þæm hūse (dative, singular) | "from that house" |
| til þæs hūses (genitive, singular) | "up to/as far as that house" |

Since the meaning was already conveyed by the preposition, the case endings on *that* and *house* became redundant and therefore, over generations, no longer were pronounced.

Another syntactic change in English affected the rules of comparative and superlative constructions. Today we form the comparative by adding *-er* to the adjective or by inserting *more* before it; the superlative is formed by adding *-est* or by inserting *most.* In Malory's *Tales of King Arthur,* written in 1470, double comparatives and double superlatives occur, which today are ungrammatical: *more gladder, more lower, moost royallest,* and *moost shamefullest.*

Here is another interesting little change in syntactic rules. Both Old English and Middle English permitted split genitives, that is, possessive constructs in which the words that describe the possessor occur on both sides of the head noun:

Inwæres broþur ond Healfdenes (Old English)
"Inwær's brother and Healfden's"
"Inwær's and Healfden's brother"

The Wife's tale of Bath (Middle English)
"The Wife of Bath's tale"

Modern English does not allow such structures, but English does permit rather complex genitive expressions to precede the head noun:

The man with the two small children's hat
The girl whose sister I'm dating's roommate
When does you guys's party begin? (Cf. When does your (pl.) party begin?)

Because they do not occur in written records, we can infer that expressions like *the Queen of England's crown* were ungrammatical in earlier periods of English. The title *The Wife's Tale of Bath* (rather than *The Wife of Bath's Tale*) in *The Canterbury Tales* supports this inference.

# Lexical Change

Changes in the lexicon also occur, among which are changes in the syntactic categories of words (i.e., their "parts of speech"), addition of new words, the "borrowing" of words from other languages, the loss of words, the shift in the meanings of words over time, and even the faux back formations (see Chapter 2) that create new bound morphemes such as *–tini* noted above (and, by the way, if you are a teetotaler you can always order a virgintini).

## Change in Category

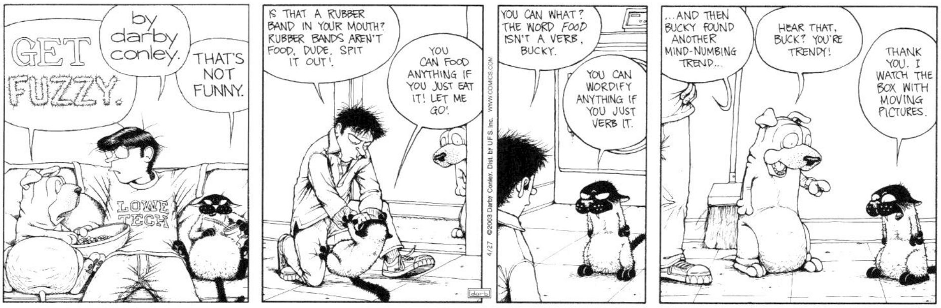




The words *food* and *verb* are ordinarily used as nouns, but Bucky the cat refuses to be so restricted and "wordifies" them into verbs. If we speakers of English adopt Bucky's usage, then *food* and *verb* will become verbs in addition to nouns. Recently, a radio announcer said that Congress was *to-ing and fro-ing* on a certain issue, to mean "wavering." This strange compound verb is derived from the adverb *to and fro*. Now when we search on the Internet, we *google*, a verb derived from the company name *Google*. American police *Mirandize* arrested persons, meaning "read them their rights according to the Miranda rule." The judicial ruling was made in 1966, so we have a complete history of how a proper name became a verb. More recently the noun *text* has been "verbed" and means "to communicate by text message," and even more recent is the hijacking of the verb *twitter* and "Proper Noun-ing" it as the name of a social networking and micro-blogging service.

## Addition of New Words

One of the most obvious ways a language changes is through the addition of new words. Unlike grammatical change, which may take generations to notice, new words are readily apparent. Societies often require new words to describe changes in technology, sports, entertainment, and so on. Languages are accommodating and inventive in meeting these needs.

In Chapter 2, we discussed some ways in which new words are born, such as through derivational processes, back-formations, and compounding. There are other ways that words may enter the vocabulary of a language. These include out-and-out word coinage, deriving words from names, blending words to form new words, shortening old words to form new ones, creating acronyms and borrowing words from other languages.

### Word Coinage

Words may be created outright to fit some purpose. The advertising industry has added many words to English, such as *Kodak, nylon, Orlon*, and *Dacron*. Specific brand names such as *Xerox, Band-Aid, Kleenex, Jell-O, Brillo*, and *Vaseline* are now sometimes used as the generic names for different brands of these types of products. Some of these words were actually created from existing words (e.g., *Kleenex* from the word *clean* and *Jell-O* from *gel*).

The sciences have given us a raft of newly coined words over the ages. Words such as *asteroid, neutron, genome, krypton, pterodactyl*, and *vaccine* were created to describe the objects or processes arising from scientific investigation.

A word so (relatively) new that its spelling is still in doubt is *dot-com*, also seen in magazines as *.com, dot.com*, and even *dot com* without the hyphen. It means "a company whose primary business centers on the Internet."

Greek roots borrowed into English have also provided a means for coining new words. *Thermos*, "hot," plus *metron*, "measure," gave us *thermometer*. If you have an intense and all-consuming horror of cats you have *ailurophobia* from *aílouros* "cat" and *phóbos* "fear."

Latin, like Greek, has also provided prefixes and suffixes that are used productively with both native and nonnative roots. The prefix *ex-* comes from Latin:

ex-husband ex-wife ex-sister-in-law ex-teacher

The suffix *-able/-ible* is also Latin and can be attached to almost any English verb:

writable readable answerable movable learnable

Even new bound morphemes may enter the language. The prefix *e-*, as in *e-commerce, e-mail*, and *e-trade*, meaning "electronic," is barely two decades old, and most interestingly has given rise to the prefix *s-* as in *s-mail* to contrast with *e-mail*. The suffix *-gate*, meaning "scandal," which was derived from the Watergate scandal of the 1970s, may now be suffixed to a word to convey that meaning. Thus, *Dianagate*, a British usage, refers to a scandal involving wire-tapped conversations of the then Princess of Wales, and *Qatar-gate*, a reference to unethical practices in the awarding of the soccer (football) world cup locale in 2022.

Finally, there are occasions when signers need to represent a word or concept for which there is no sign. For such cases, ASL may conceive a series of new hand shapes and movements, but absent this possibility, letters of the English alphabet may be expressed through *finger spelling* to convey any meaning that might be written.

## Words from Names

**Eponyms** are words that are coined from proper names and are another way that the vocabulary of a language expands. For example, our favorite lunch food was named for the fourth Earl of *Sandwich*, who put his food between two slices of bread so that he could eat while he gambled. And the favorite material of our work clothes is *denim*, named for a kind of cloth originally imported *de Nîmes* ("from Nîmes") a city in France. If you like olives, be sure and get the *jumbo* size, the name of an elephant brought to the United States for a circus. ("Jumbo olives" need not be as big as an elephant, however.)

## Blends

**Blends** are similar to compounds in that they are produced by combining two words, but in blends parts of the words that are combined are deleted. *Smog*, from *smoke* + *fog; brunch*, from *breakfast* and *lunch; motel*, from *motor* + *hotel; infomercial*, from *info* + *commercial*; and *urinalysis*, from *urine* + *analysis* are examples of blends that have attained full lexical status in English. *Podcast (podcasting, podcaster)* is a relatively new word meaning "Internet audio broadcast" and recently joined the English language as a blend of *iPod* and *broadcast*. Some more recent blends that are younger than most of our readers include *bromance* (a blend of "brother" and "romance" meaning a nonsexual relationship between two men), *locavore* (someone who eats locally sourced foods), *frenemy* (an enemy who pretends to be a friend), *staycation* (a vacation at home), *chillax* (be calm and relaxed), and *sexting* (sending text messages with sexual content).

Lewis Carroll's *chortle*, from *chuckle* + *snort*, has achieved limited acceptance in English. Carroll is famous for both coining and blending words. In *Through the Looking-Glass*, he describes the "meanings" of the made-up words in "Jabberwocky" as follows:

> "Brillig" means four o'clock in the afternoon—the time when you begin broiling things for dinner . . . "Slithy" means "lithe and slimy" . . . You see it's like a portmanteau—there are two meanings packed up into one word. . . . "Toves" are something like badgers—they're something like lizards—and they're something like corkscrews . . . also they make their nests under sun-dials—also they live on cheese. . . . To "gyre" is to go round and round like a gyroscope. To "gimble" is to make holes like a gimlet. And "the wabe" is the grass-plot round a sun-dial . . . It's called "wabe" . . . because it goes a long way before it and a long way behind it. . . . "Mimsy" is "flimsy and miserable" (there's another portmanteau . . . for you).

Carroll's "portmanteaus" are what we have called blends, and such words can become part of the regular lexicon.

### Reduced Words

Speakers tend to abbreviate words in various ways to shorten the messages they convey. Texting has turned this skill into a national pastime. However, we will concern ourselves with *spoken* language and observe three reduction phenomena: *clipping, acronyms,* and *alphabetic abbreviations.*

**Clipping** is the abbreviation of longer words into shorter ones by leaving out one or more syllables such as *fax* for *facsimile*, the British word *telly* for *television*, *flu* for *influenza, porn* for *pornography*, and *droid* for *android*. Once marginalized as slang, and despite Jonathan Swift's contempt, many of these words have over time become lexicalized, that is, bona fide members of the English vocabulary. Clippings may clip the beginning of a word (*phone* for *telephone*), the end of a word (*auto* for *automobile*), or both ends (*fridge* for *refrigerator*).

There are two possible semantic outcomes of clipping. The most common by far is that the clipped word has the same meaning as its source. All of the examples in the previous paragraph are of that ilk. In a minority of instances, the clipped word takes on a different meaning. *Fan, van,* and *rad* are clipped from *fanatic*, *caravan*, and *radical*, but fans are not (generally) fanatics except at English football matches. Van is a single vehicle not a cavalcade, and something that is rad is marvelous though not necessarily radical. The use of *droid* to mean a certain kind of smartphone (itself a recent word) has a different meaning than *android*, though the use of the word is intended to convey robotic intelligence.

Clippings continue to come into existence. *Dis*, once rapper slang for *disrespect*, is gaining acceptance with the meaning "show contempt for." *Blog* (from *weblog*, another new word!) is perhaps the most successful clip of the current millennium, being today both a noun and a verb with all the related morphology (*blogs, blogging, blogged, blogger*, etc.)

**Acronyms** are words derived from the initials of several words. Such words are pronounced as the spelling indicates: *Radar* from *ra*dio *d*etecting *a*nd *r*anging, *laser* from *l*ight *a*mplification by *s*timulated *e*mission of *r*adiation, *scuba* from *s*elf-*c*ontained *u*nderwater *b*reathing *a*pparatus and *AIDS* from *a*cquired *i*mmunity *d*eficiency *s*yndrome are beacons to the creative aspect of language.

When the string of letters is not easily pronounced as a word, the "acronym" becomes an **alphabetic abbreviation**, produced by sounding out each letter, as in *NFL* for *N*ational *F*ootball *L*eague, *UCLA* for *U*niversity of *C*alifornia at *L*os *A*ngeles, and *MRI* for *m*agnetic *r*esonance *i*maging and let us not forget *OMG* (Oh my God).

Unbelievable though it may seem, acronyms in use somewhere in the English-speaking world number more than one million according to the online Acronym Finder, about the same number as English words if we look back four centuries, a dramatic nod to the creativity and changeability of human language.

## Borrowings or Loan Words

Languages pay little attention to Polonius's admonition quoted above, and many are avid borrowers and lenders, and poor ones at that, for the borrowers rarely return the borrowed items, and the lenders nearly never demand the return of the loans.

**Borrowing** words from other languages is an important source of new words, which are called **loan words**. Borrowing occurs when one language adds a word or morpheme from another language to its own lexicon. This often happens in situations of language contact, when speakers of different languages regularly interact with one another, and especially where there are many bilingual or multilingual speakers.

The pronunciation of loan words is often (but not always) altered to fit the phonological rules of the borrowing language. For example, English borrowed *ensemble* [ãsãblə] from French but pronounce it [ãnsãmbəl], with [n] and [m] inserted, because English doesn't ordinarily have syllables centered on nasal vowels alone. Other borrowed words such as the composer's name *Bach* will often be pronounced as the original German [bax], with a final velar fricative, even though such a pronunciation does not conform to the rules of English.

When an expression is borrowed and then translated into the borrowing language it is called a **loan translation**. *It goes without saying* from French *il va sans dire* is a loan translation from French. On the other hand, Spanish speakers eat *perros calientes*, a loan translation of *hot dogs* with an adjustment reversing the order of the adjective and noun as required by the rules of Spanish syntax.

The lexicons of most languages can be divided into native words and loan words. A native word is one whose history or **etymology** can be traced back to the earliest known stages of the language.

A language may borrow a word directly or indirectly. A direct borrowing means that the borrowed item is a native word in the language from which it is borrowed. For example, *feast* was borrowed directly from French, along with a host of terms, as a result of the Norman Conquest. By contrast, the word *algebra* was borrowed from Spanish, which in turn had borrowed it from Arabic. Thus, *algebra* was indirectly borrowed from Arabic, with Spanish as an intermediary. Some languages are heavy borrowers. Albanian has borrowed so heavily that few native words are retained. On the other hand, most Native American languages borrowed little from their neighbors.

English has borrowed extensively. Of the 20,000 or so words in common use, about three-fifths are borrowed. But of the 500 most frequently used words, only two-sevenths are borrowed, and because these words are used repeatedly in sentences—they are mostly function words—the actual frequency of appearance of native words is about 80 percent. The frequently used function words *and, be, have, it, of, the, to, will, you, on, that*, and *is* are all native to English.

Languages may borrow not only words and phrases but other linguistic units as well. The bound morpheme suffixes *ible/able* were borrowed from French, arriving in English by hitchhiking on French words such as *incredible* but soon attaching themselves to native words such as *drinkable*.

## History through Loan Words

We may trace the history of the English-speaking peoples by studying the kinds of loan words in their language and when they were borrowed. Until the Norman Conquest in 1066, the Angles, the Saxons, and the Jutes inhabited England. They were of Germanic origin and they spoke Germanic dialects from which Old English developed. These dialects contained some Latin borrowings but few foreign elements beyond that. These Germanic tribes had displaced the earlier Celtic-speaking inhabitants, whose influence on Old English was confined mostly to a few Celtic place names. (The modern languages Welsh, Irish, and Scots Gaelic are descended from the Celtic dialects.)

The conquering Normans spoke French and French was used for all affairs of state and for most commercial, social, and cultural matters. Nevertheless, regional varieties of English continued to be used in homes, churches and the marketplace. This was a situation of language contact between French, the culturally dominant language, and English, the "language of the people." For three centuries vast numbers of French words entered English, of which the following are representative:

| | | | | |
|---|---|---|---|---|
| government | crown | prince | estate | parliament |
| nation | jury | judge | crime | sue |
| attorney | saint | miracle | charity | court |
| lechery | virgin | value | pray | mercy |
| religion | chapel | royal | money | society |

Until the Normans came, when an Englishman slaughtered an ox for food, he ate *ox*. If it was a pig, he ate *pig*. If it was a sheep, he ate *sheep*. However, "*ox*" served at the Norman tables was *beef (boeuf)*, "pig" was *pork (porc)*, and "sheep" was *mutton (mouton)*. These words were borrowed from French into English, as were the food-preparation words *boil, fry, stew,* and *roast*. Over the years, French foods have given English a flood of borrowed words for menu preparers:

| | | | | |
|---|---|---|---|---|
| aspic | bisque | bouillon | brie | brioche |
| canapé | caviar | consommé | coq au vin | coupe |
| crêpe | croissant | croquette | crouton | escargot |
| fondue | mousse | pâté | quiche | ragout |

English borrowed many "learned" words from foreign sources during the Renaissance. In 1475, William Caxton introduced the printing press in England. By 1640, 55,000 books had been printed in English. The authors of these books used many Greek and Latin words, which consequently entered the language.

From Greek came *drama, comedy, tragedy, scene, botany, physics, zoology,* and *atomic*. Latin loan words in English are numerous. They include:

| | | | | | |
|---|---|---|---|---|---|
| bonus | scientific | exit | alumnus | quorum | describe |

*Bin, flannel, clan, slogan,* and *whisky* are all words of Celtic origin, borrowed at various times from Welsh, Scots Gaelic, or Irish. Dutch was a source of borrowed words, too, many of which are related to shipping: *buoy, freight, leak, pump, yacht*. From German came *quartz, cobalt,* and—as we might guess—*sauerkraut*. From Italian, many musical terms, including words describing opera houses, have been borrowed: *opera, piano, virtuoso, balcony,* and *mezzanine*. Italian also gave us *influenza*, which was derived from the Italian word for "influence" because the Italians were convinced that the disease was *influenced* by the stars. And more recently, courtesy of Starbucks, *barista*, referring to preparers of espresso (another Italian loan) drinks, from the Italian word for "bartender."

Many scientific words were borrowed indirectly from Arabic, because early Arab scholarship in these fields was quite advanced. *Alcohol, algebra, cipher,* and *zero* are a small sample. Spanish has loaned us (directly) *barbecue, cockroach,* and *ranch*, as well as *California*, literally "hot furnace." In America, the English-speaking colonists borrowed from Native American languages, another situation of language contact, but in which English is the culturally dominant language. Native American languages provided us with *hickory, chipmunk, opossum,* and *squash*, to mention only a few. Nearly half the names of U.S. states are borrowed from one American Indian language or another.

English has borrowed from Yiddish. Many non-Jews as well as non-Yiddish-speaking Jews use Yiddish words. There was once even a bumper sticker proclaiming: "Marcel Proust is a yenta." *Yenta* is a Yiddish word meaning "gossipy woman." *Lox*, meaning "smoked salmon," and *bagel*, "a doughnut dipped in cement," now belong to English, as well as Yiddish expressions such as *chutzpah, schmaltz, schlemiel, schmuck, schmo, schlep,* and *kibitz*.

English is a lender of many words to other languages, especially in the areas of technology, sports, and entertainment. Words and expressions such as *jazz, whisky, blue jeans, rock music, supermarket, baseball, picnic,* and *computer* have been borrowed from English into languages as diverse as Twi, Hungarian, Russian, and Japanese.

## Loss of Words

RED ROVER © 2012 Brian Basset Dist. By UNIVERSAL UCLICK. Reprinted with permission. 

Languages may be said to lose words in the sense that the frequency of usage falls below a certain threshold. Such words may still be counted when tallying up the size of the lexicon, but they are lost to the general population. The departure of an old word is never as striking as the arrival of a new one. When a new word comes into vogue, its unusual presence draws attention, but a word is lost through inattention—nobody thinks of it, nobody uses it, and its usage fades away to nothing.

A reading of Shakespeare's works shows that English has lost many words, such as these taken from *Romeo and Juliet: beseem*, "to be suitable," *mammet*, "a doll or puppet," *wot*, "to know," *gyve*, "a fetter," *fain*, "gladly," and *wherefore*, "why," as in Juliet's plaintive cry: "O Romeo, Romeo! wherefore art thou Romeo," in which she is questioning why he is so named, not his current whereabouts.

More recently, there are expressions used by your grandparents that have already been lost. *Two bits*, meaning "twenty-five cents," is rarely used nowadays and the same for *lickety-split* and *pell-mell,* meaning "very fast" and "recklessly hurried." Even words used by your parents (and us) sound dated, like *groovy* ("excellent"), *davenport* ("sofa"), and *grass* and *pot*, now called *weed*, referring to "marijuana." The word *stile*, meaning "steps crossing a fence or gate," is no longer widely understood. Other similar words for describing rural objects are fading out of the language as a result of urbanization. *Pease*, from which *pea* is a back-formation, is rare, and *porridge*, meaning "boiled cereal grain," is falling out of usage, although it is sustained by a discussion of its ideal serving temperature in the children's story *Goldilocks and the Three Bears* and its appearance on Harry Potter's breakfast table.

Technological change may also be the cause for the loss of words. *Acutiator* once meant "sharpener of weapons," and *tormentum* once meant "siege engine." Advances in warfare have put these terms out of business but given us *cruise missile* and an extension of the word *drone*, a pilotless aircraft. *Whiteboard* is in and *blackboard* is out insofar as classroom teaching is concerned. Although one still finds the words *buckboard, buggy, dogcart, hansom, surrey*, and *tumbrel* in the dictionary—all of them referring to subtly different kinds of horse-drawn carriages—progress in transportation is likely to render these terms obsolete and eventually they will be lost.

## Semantic Change

We have seen that a language may gain or lose lexical items. Additionally, the meaning or semantic representation of words may change, by becoming broader or narrower, or by shifting.

## Broadening

When the meaning of a word becomes broader, it means everything it used to mean and more. The Middle English word *dogge* referred to a specific breed of dog, but was eventually **broadened** to encompass all members of the species *canis familiaris*. The word *holiday* originally meant a day of religious significance, from "holy day." Today the word refers to any day that we do not have to work. *Quarantine* once meant "forty days' isolation," but has broadened to mean any period of isolation. More recent broadenings, spurred by the computer age, are *mouse, cookie, cache, virus, worm,* and *hacker*. *Footage* used to refer to a certain length of film or videotape, but nowadays it means any excerpt from the electronic video media irrespective of whether its length can be measured in feet. *Twitter* and *tweet* were once words about birds—need we say more.

### Narrowing

In the King James Version of the Bible (1611 CE), God says of the herbs and trees, "to you they shall be for meat" (Genesis 1:29). To a speaker of seventeenth-century English, *meat* meant "food," and *flesh* meant "meat." Since that time, semantic change has narrowed the meaning of *meat* to what it is in Modern English. The word *deer* once meant "beast" or "animal," as its German cognate *Tier* still does. The meaning of *deer* has been narrowed to a particular kind of animal. Similarly, the word *hound* used to be the general term for "dog," like German *Hund*. Today *hound* refers to a certain class of hunting dogs. *Skyline* once meant "horizon" but has been narrowed to mean "the outline of a city at the horizon."

### Meaning Shifts

The third kind of semantic change that a lexical item may undergo is a shift in meaning. The word *knight* once meant "youth" but shifted to "mounted man-at-arms." *Lust* used to mean simply "pleasure," with no negative or sexual overtones. *Lewd* was merely "ignorant," and *immoral* meant "not customary." *Silly* used to mean "happy" in Old English. By the Middle English period, it had come to mean "naive," and only in Modern English does it mean "foolish." The overworked Modern English word *nice* meant "ignorant" a thousand years ago. When Juliet tells Romeo, "I am too *fond*," she is not claiming she likes Romeo too much. She means "I am too *foolish*." And if a drone has you in its sights, look forward to something rather worse than a bee sting.

# The History of Writing

The creation and development of writing systems is one of humanity's greatest achievements. Unlike spoken/sign languages, which are biologically innate and need not be purposefully learned, writing is a result of human ingenuity, more like the wheel than the ability to walk upright on two legs.

There are many stories about the invention of writing. Greek legend has it that Cadmus, Prince of Phoenicia and founder of the city of Thebes, invented the alphabet and brought it with him to Greece. In one Chinese fable, the four-eyed dragon-god Cang Jie invented writing, but in another, writing first appeared as markings on the back of the chi-lin, a white unicorn of Chinese legend. In other myths, the Babylonian god Nebo and the Egyptian god Thoth gave writing as well as speech to humans. The Talmudic scholar Rabbi Akiba believed that the alphabet existed before humans were created, and according to Hindu tradition the Goddess Saraswati, wife of Brahma, invented writing.

Although these are delightful stories it is evident that uncountable billions of words were spoken before a single word was written. The invention of writing comes relatively late in human history and its development was gradual. It is doubtful that a gifted ancestor bounded naked from his bath one fine morning shouting "Eureka, I have invented writing."

## Pictograms and Ideograms

The roots of writing were the early drawings made by ancient humans. Cave art, called **petroglyphs**, have been found in such places as the Chauvet-Pont-d'Arc cave in southern France, the so-called "Cave of Forgotten Dreams." These

**FIGURE 8.2** | Six of seventy-seven symbols developed by the National Park Service for use as signs indicating activities and facilities in parks and recreation areas. These symbols denote, from left to right: "environmental study area," "grocery store," "men's restroom," "women's restroom," "fishing," and "amphitheater." Certain symbols are available with a prohibiting slash—a diagonal red bar across the symbol that means that the activity is forbidden.
National Park Service, U.S. Department of the Interior

can be "read" today although they were created by humans living 30,000 or more years ago. They are literal portrayals of life at that time. We don't know why they were produced; they may be esthetic expressions rather than pictorial communications.

Later drawings, however, are clearly "picture writings," or **pictograms**. Unlike modern writing systems each pictogram is an image of the object it represents. There is an explicit relationship between the shape of the symbol and its meaning. Comic strips, minus captions, are pictographic—literal representations of the ideas to be conveyed. This early form of writing represented objects in the world directly rather than through their linguistic names. Thus, they did not represent the words and sounds of spoken language.

Pictographic writing has been found throughout the ancient and modern world, from Africa to Oceania to the contemporary world of Internet communications. Email, Instant Messaging, Twittering, texting and other forms of electronic communication make copious use of **emoticons** and **emoji** (a Japanese loanword), which are pictographic symbols such as :-) and ☹, which convey specific meanings independent of any language. Pictograms are also found today in international road signs, where the native language of a region might not be understood by all travelers. You do not need to know English to understand the signs used by the U.S. National Park Service (Figure 8.2).

Once a pictogram was accepted as the representation of an object, its meaning was extended to attributes of that object, or concepts associated with it. A picture of the sun could represent warmth, heat, light, daytime, and so on. Pictograms began to represent ideas rather than objects. Such generalized pictograms are called **ideograms** ("idea pictures" or "idea writing").

The difference between pictograms and ideograms is not always clear. Ideograms tend to be less direct representations, and one may have to learn what a particular ideogram means. Pictograms tend to be more literal. For example, the no parking symbol  is an ideogram. It represents the idea of no parking abstractly. A sign like  meaning "no bicycles" is more like a pictogram.

Inevitably, pictograms and ideograms became highly stylized and difficult to interpret without learning the words of the language that the ideograms represented. Thus, the ideograms became linguistic symbols. They stood for the words, both the meanings and sounds that represented the ideas. This stage was a revolutionary step in the development of writing systems.

## Cuneiform Writing

Much of what we know about writing stems from the records left by the Sumerians, an ancient people of unknown origin who built a civilization in southern Mesopotamia (modern Iraq) more than six thousand years ago. They left tens of thousands of inscribed clay tablets containing business documents, epics, prayers, poems, proverbs, and so on, written in an elaborate pictography. Some examples are shown here:

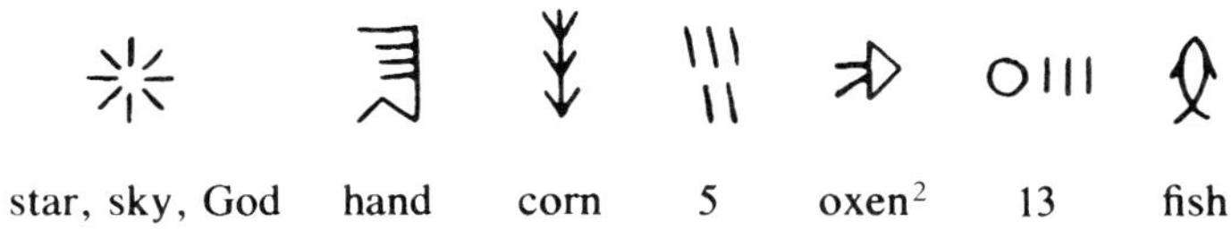


Over the centuries the Sumerians simplified their pictographs and began to write them by pressing a wedge-shaped stylus into soft clay tablets, which the desert sun baked hard to produce enduring records. This form of writing is called **cuneiform**—literally, "wedge-shaped" (from Latin *cuneus*, "wedge"). Here is an illustration of the evolution of Sumerian pictograms to cuneiform:

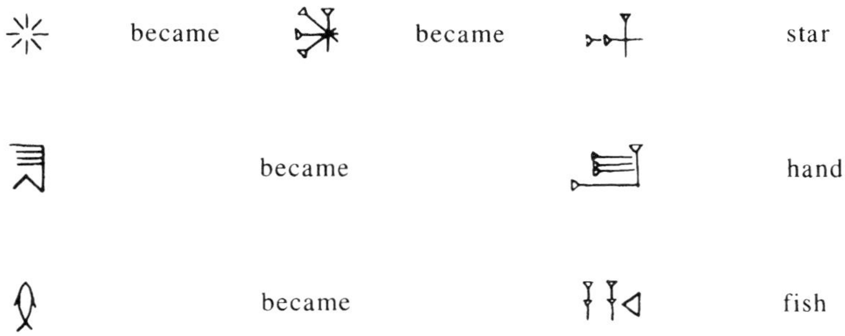


The cuneiform symbols in the third column do little to remind us (or the Sumerians) of the meaning represented. As cuneiform evolved its users began to think of the symbols more in terms of the name of the objects represented than of the object itself. Eventually cuneiform script came to represent words of the language directly, and through them the meaning. Such a system is called **logographic**, or **word writing**, and the symbols themselves are called **logograms**.

Cuneiform writing spread throughout the Middle East and Asia Minor. The Babylonians, Assyrians, and Persians made use of it by adapting the cuneiform characters to represent the sounds of the syllables in their own languages. In this way, cuneiform evolved into a **syllabic writing** system or **syllabary**.

[2]The pictograph for 'ox' evolved, much later, into the letter *A*.

In a syllabic writing system, each syllable in the language is represented by its own symbol, and words are written syllable by syllable. Cuneiform was never purely syllabic as many symbols remained that stood for whole words. The Assyrians retained many word symbols even though every word in their language could be written out syllabically. Thus, they could write  *mātu* "country" as:

ma + a + tu

The Persians (ca. 600–400 BCE) devised a greatly simplified syllabic alphabet for their language, which was in wide use by the reign of Darius I (521–486 BCE). The following characters illustrate it:

 da

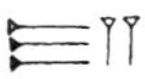 di

 fa

 ma

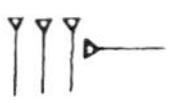 tu

## The Rebus Principle

When a graphic sign no longer has a visual relationship to the word it represents, it becomes a **phonographic symbol**, standing for the sounds that represent the word. A single sign can then be used to represent all words that sound alike. If, for example, the symbol ⊙ stood for *sun* in English, it could then be used in a sentence like *My* ⊙ *is a doctor*. This sentence is an example of the **rebus principle**.

A rebus is a representation of words by pictures of objects whose names sound like the word. Thus,  might represent *eye* or the pronoun *I*. The sounds of the two words are identical, even though the meanings are not. Similarly,  could represent *belief* (*be* + *lief* = *bee* + *leaf*), and  could be *believes*.

This system has drawbacks because words cannot always be divided into sequences of sounds that have meaning by themselves. It would be difficult, for example, to represent the word *English* (/ɪŋ/ + /glɪʃ/) in English according to the rebus principle. *Eng* by itself does not mean anything, nor does *glish*.

## From Hieroglyphics to the Alphabet

At the time that Sumerian pictography was flourishing (around 4000 BCE), the Egyptians were using a similar system called **hieroglyphics** from Greek *hiero*, "sacred," + *glyphikos*, "carvings". These sacred carvings originated as pictography as shown by the following:

''eye'' ''giraffe'' ''to rule''[3] ''fresh'' or ''cool''[4]

Eventually, these pictograms came to represent both the concept and the word for the concept. Once this happened hieroglyphics became a bona fide logographic writing system. Through the rebus principle, hieroglyphics also became a syllabic writing system.

The Phoenicians, a Semitic people who lived in what is today Lebanon, were aware of hieroglyphics as well as the offshoots of Sumerian writing. By 1500 BCE they had developed a writing system of twenty-two characters, the West Semitic Syllabary. Mostly, the characters stood for consonants alone. The reader provided the vowels, and hence the rest of the syllable, through knowledge of the language. (Cn y rd ths?) Thus the West Semitic Syllabary was both a syllabary and a **consonantal alphabet** (also called **abjad**).

The ancient Greeks tried to borrow the Phoenician writing system, but it was unsatisfactory as a syllabary because Greek has too complex a syllable structure. In Greek, unlike in Phoenician, vowels cannot be determined by context so they had to be specifically written. Fortuitously, Phoenician had more consonants than Greek, so when the Greeks borrowed the system they used the leftover consonant symbols to represent vowel sounds. The result was **alphabetic writing**, a system in which both consonants and vowels are symbolized. (The word *alphabet* is derived from *alpha* and *beta*, the first two letters of the Greek alphabet.)

Most alphabetic systems are based on the Greek system. The Etruscans knew the Greek alphabet and through them it became known to the Romans, who used it for Latin. The alphabet spread with Western civilization, and today most nations of the world are able to use alphabetic writing.

Readers of this book will understand that if language did not consist of discrete individual sounds, no one could have invented alphabetic letters to represent them. When humans started to use one symbol for one phoneme, they were revealing their intuitive knowledge of the phonological system of their language.

[3]The symbol portrays the Pharaoh's staff.

[4]Water trickling out of a vase.

## Summary

All living languages change. Linguistic change such as **sound shift** is found in the history of all languages, as evidenced by the **regular sound correspondences** that exist between different stages of the same language, different dialects of the same language, and different languages. Languages that evolve from a common source are **genetically related**. Genetically related languages were once dialects of the same language. For example, English, German, and Swedish were dialects of a postulated earlier form of Germanic called **Proto-Germanic**, whereas earlier forms of Romance languages, such as Spanish, French, and Italian, were dialects of Latin. Going back even further in time, earlier forms of Proto-Germanic, Latin, and other languages were dialects of **(Proto-)Indo-European**, a postulated ancestor.

All components of the grammar may change. Phonological, morphological, syntactic, lexical, and semantic changes occur. Words, morphemes, phonemes, and rules of all types may be added, lost, or altered. The meanings of words and morphemes may **broaden, narrow**, or shift. The lexicon may expand by **borrowing**, which results in **loan words** in the vocabulary. This is very common in **language contact** situations. It also grows through word coinage, blends, compounding, acronyms, and other processes of word formation. On the other hand, the contemporary lexicon may shrink as the frequency of usage of words like *typewriter, blackboard, record player,* and *phone booth* fall below a threshold level.

No one knows all the causes of linguistic change. Some sound changes result from assimilation, a fundamentally physiological process of ease of articulation. Others, like the **Great Vowel Shift**, are more difficult to explain. Some grammatical changes are **analogic changes**, generalizations that lead to more regularity, such as *cows* instead of *kine* and *waked* instead of *woke*.

Writing is a basic tool of civilization. Without it, the world as we know it could not exist. The precursor of writing was "picture writing," which used **pictograms** to represent objects directly and literally. Pictograms are called **ideograms** when the drawings become less literal, and the meanings extend to concepts associated with the objects originally pictured. When ideograms become associated with the words for the concepts they signify they are called **logograms**. Logographic systems are true writing systems in the sense that the symbols stand for words of a language.

The Sumerians first developed a pictographic writing system to keep track of commercial transactions. It was later expanded for other uses and eventually evolved into the highly stylized (and stylus-ized) **cuneiform** writing. Cuneiform was generalized to other writing systems by application of the **rebus principle**, which uses the symbol of one word or syllable to represent another word or syllable pronounced the same.

A different pictographic system known as **hieroglyphics** arose in ancient Egypt. Under its influence the Phoenicians developed the West Semitic Syllabary which was borrowed by the Greeks who used the symbols to represent both consonants and vowels, thus inventing the first alphabet.

## References for Further Reading


Algeo, J. 2010. *The origins and development of the English language, 6th ed.* Boston: Wadsworth/Cengage.

Bybee, J. L. 2015. *Language change.* New York: Cambridge University Press.

Campbell, L. 2004. *Historical linguistics: An introduction, 2nd ed.* Cambridge, MA: MIT Press.

Comrie, B. (ed.). 1990. *The world's major languages.* New York: Oxford University Press.

Fischer, R. S., 2004. *A history of writing.* London: Reaktion Books.

Lewis, M. Paul (ed.), 2009. *Ethnologue: Languages of the world, 16th ed.* Dallas, TX.: SIL International. (http://www.ethnologue.com/)

Michel, J-B, et al. "Quantitative analysis of culture using millions of digitized books." *Science,* v. 331, pp 176–182, Jan 14, 2011.

Normile, D. "Experiments probe language's origins and development." *Science,* v. 336, pp 408–411, Apr 27, 2012.

Wolfram, W. 2001. Language death and dying. In Chambers, J. K., Trudgill, P., and Schilling-Estes, N. (eds.), *The handbook on language variation and change.* Oxford, UK: Basil Blackwell.


## Exercises

**1.** Many changes in the phonological system have occurred in English since 449 CE. Below are some Old English words (given in their spelling and phonetic forms) and the same words as we pronounce them today. They are typical of regular sound changes that took place in English. What sound change or changes have occurred in each case?

*Example*: OE hlud [xlu:d] → Mod. Eng. loud

**Changes:** (1) The [x] was lost.
(2) The long vowel [u:] became [aʊ].

| | OE | | Mod E |
|---|---|---|---|
| **a.** | crabba [kraba] | → | crab |
| | Changes: | | |
| **b.** | fisc [fɪsk] | → | fish |
| | Changes: | | |
| **c.** | fūl [fu:l] | → | foul |
| | Changes: | | |
| **d.** | gāt [ga:t] | → | goat |
| | Changes: | | |
| **e.** | lǣfan [læ:van] | → | leave |
| | Changes: | | |
| **f.** | tēþ [te:θ] | → | teeth |
| | Changes: | | |

**2.** The Great Vowel Shift left its traces in Modern English in such meaning-related pairs as:

**(1)** ser**e**ne/ser**e**nity [i]/[ɛ]
**(2)** div**i**ne/div**i**nity [aɪ]/[ɪ]

**(3)** sane/sanity [e]/[æ]

List five such meaning-related pairs that relate [i] and [ɛ] as in example (1), five that relate [aɪ] and [ɪ] as in example (2), and five that relate [e] and [æ] as in example (3).

| | **[i]/[ɛ]** | **[aɪ]/[ɪ]** | **[e]/[æ]** |
|---|---|---|---|
| **a.** | | | |
| **b.** | | | |
| **c.** | | | |
| **d.** | | | |
| **e.** | | | |

**3.** Sentences a–g, taken from Old English, Middle English, and early Modern English texts, illustrate some changes that have occurred in the syntactic rules of English grammar. (Note: In the sentences, the earlier spelling forms and words have been changed to conform to the spelling of Modern English. That is, the OE sentence *His suna twegen mon brohte to þæm cynige* would be written as *His sons two one brought to that king,* which in Modern English would be *His two sons were brought to the king.*) Underline the parts of each sentence that differ from Modern English. Rewrite the sentence in Modern English. State what changes must have occurred.

*Example*: It not belongs to you. (Shakespeare, *Henry IV*)
Mod. Eng.: It does not belong to you.

Change: At one time a negative sentence simply had a *not* before the verb. Today, the word *do,* in its proper morphological form, must appear before the *not.*

**a.** It nothing pleased his master.
**b.** He hath said that we would lift them whom that him please.
**c.** I have a brother is condemned to die.
**d.** I bade them take away you.
**e.** I wish you was still more a Tartar.
**f.** Christ slept and his apostles.
**g.** Me was told.

**4.** There are some exceptions to the Adj-Noun order in Modern English, as the examples in column A and B illustrate:

| **A** | **B** | **C** |
|---|---|---|
| A man alone | *an alone man | a lone man |
| No man alive | *no alive man | no living man |
| A lion asleep | *an asleep lion | a sleeping lion |

**a.** Can you identify a common feature of the adjectives that are grammatical in post-noun position?
**b.** Provide some other examples like those in column A.

c. The expressions in column C have the normal Adj-N order. Do they have the same meaning as their respective items in column A? If not, say how they are different.

5. A *rebus* is a written representation of words or syllables that uses pictures of objects whose names resemble the sounds of the intended words or syllables. For example,  might be the symbol for “eye” or “I” or the first syllable in “idea.”

   Part One: Using the rebus principle, “write” the following words:

   **a.** tearing
   **b.** icicle
   **c.** bareback
   **d.** cookies

   Part Two: Why would such a system be a difficult system in which to represent all words in English? Illustrate with an example.

9

# Language Acquisition

As we have seen in preceding chapters, language is extremely complex. Yet very young children—before the age of five—already know most of the intricate system that is the grammar of their language. Before they can add small numbers or tie their shoes, children are inflecting verbs and nouns, forming questions, negating sentences, using pronouns appropriately, embedding clauses and effortlessly producing and understanding a limitless number of sentences they never heard before. How children accomplish this prodigious task is the subject of this chapter.

## The Linguistic Capacity of Children

Clearly, children do not learn a language simply by memorizing sentences. Rather, they acquire a system of grammatical rules of the sort we have discussed in previous chapters. They are not taught these rules explicitly, but must extract the rules from the language they hear around them, in effect "reinventing" the grammar of mature speakers. No specific kind of environment is required for them to do this. Children exposed to different languages under different cultural and social circumstances all develop their native language during a narrow window of time, going through similar, possibly universal, developmental stages. Even deaf children of deaf signing parents acquire signed languages in stages that parallel those of children acquiring spoken languages.

The uniformity of language development in the face of varying environments and (as we will see) impoverished input leads many linguists to believe that children are equipped with an innate template or blueprint for language—which we have referred to as Universal Grammar (UG)—and that this blueprint aids the child in the task of constructing a grammar for her language.

## What's Learned, What's Not?

"WHAT'S THE BIG SURPRISE? ALL THE LATEST THEORIES OF LINGUISTICS SAY WE'RE BORN WITH THE INNATE CAPACITY FOR GENERATING SENTENCES."

ScienceCartoonsPlus.com

The **innateness** hypothesis receives its strongest support from the observation that the grammars people ultimately end up with contain many abstract rules and structures that are not directly represented in the linguistic input they receive. In this sense, the input to the child is said to be **impoverished** and this argument for the innateness of UG is called the **poverty of the stimulus**.

The principle of structure dependency illustrates one way in which the linguistic input is impoverished. Structure dependency, discussed in Chapter 3, refers to the fact that grammatical rules are dependent on hierarchical structure and not on serial order. For example, the rule that moves the auxiliary in English questions, illustrated in (1), must refer to the *main* auxiliary of the sentence and not merely to the *first* auxiliary.

1. The boy is sleeping. → Is the boy sleeping?

This is clearly shown by introducing a more complex sentence containing a relative clause. We see that moving the main auxiliary, as in (2), produces a grammatical output, while moving the first auxiliary, as in (3), leads to ungrammaticality:

The boy who is sleeping was dreaming.

2. Was the boy who is sleeping ________ dreaming?
3. *Is the boy who ________ sleeping was dreaming?

Naturalistic and experimental studies show that young children do not produce sentences such as (3). Presented with simple declarative-question pairs such as (1), children infer the structure-dependent rule, and when tested on the more complex cases, they correctly invert the *main* auxiliary and not the *first* auxiliary. The fact that children come up with a structure-dependent rule means that they know that sentences are organized hierarchically, and this is not information that is provided in the input.

Many grammatical rules rely on the structural difference between main and subordinate clauses. For example, a pronoun can sometimes refer to a following NP as in (1) where *he* can refer to *Billie*. But sometimes pronouns cannot co-refer in this way, as in (2).

1. When *he* lost the race *Billie* was sad.
2. **He* was sad when *Billie* lost the race. (ungrammatical with *he* = *Billie*)

The linear relationship between the pronoun and the NP is the same in both sentences, so this cannot be the reason for the difference in grammaticality. Rather, the rule that permits co-reference in (1) but not (2) is structure-dependent (and it is also universal): it states (roughly) that a pronoun in hierarchically higher position (e.g. root subject) cannot refer to a name in lower position (e.g. embedded subject). As in the case of the question formation rule, when tested on sentences such as (1) and (2) children allow co-reference in (1), but not in (2), showing that they are sensitive to the structural difference between the two sentences and to the structure-dependent pronoun rule.

Children are not provided with information about structure dependency, constituent structure or indeed about any other abstract property of grammar. Their language input consists of sequences of sounds (or signs), not sets of phrase structure trees. Yet, children formulate rules that are sensitive to structure. According to the innateness hypothesis, the child does not need to learn structure dependency or the pronoun rule or any other universal principle of sentence formation, such as the rule that heads of categories can take complements. These aspects of grammar are part of the innate blueprint for language.

At the same time, it is clear that some aspects of language are learned. Children exposed to English acquire English, not some other language, and similarly for all other languages. The specific sounds and words of a language, as well as the language-specific ordering and movement rules, must be learned by the child based on the linguistic input. For example, children acquiring English must learn that it is an SVO language while Japanese children learn that their language is SOV. These orderings are clearly demonstrated in the language they hear spoken around them.

English-speaking children must also learn that yes–no questions are formed by moving the auxiliary while Japanese children learn that to form a yes–no question, the morpheme *-ka* is suffixed to a verb stem.

| | |
|---|---|
| Tanaka ga sushi o tabete iru. | "Tanaka is eating sushi." |
| Tanaka ga sushi o tabete iru**ka?** | "Is Tanaka eating sushi?" |

As in the case of word order, this information is provided in the linguistic input. The process of acquiring language is rooted in human biology and supported by linguistic input from the environment.

One of the central goals of linguistic theory is to solve *the logical problem of language acquisition*:

> What accounts for the ease, rapidity, and uniformity of language acquisition in the face of impoverished data?

A partial answer is that children are able to acquire a complex grammar quickly and easily without any particular help beyond exposure to the language because they do not start from scratch. Innate principles of UG such as structure dependency and X-bar theory, among many others, provide them with a significant head start. UG constrains the kinds of grammatical rules children formulate. It predisposes them to follow a restricted course of development that avoids many grammatical errors and that gives rise to uniform developmental stages, as we will discuss in the next section.

The innateness hypothesis also predicts that all languages will conform to UG principles. While we are still far from understanding the full structure of UG, research on different languages provides a way to test any principles that linguists propose. Hypotheses may be revised based on new evidence, as is the case in any science. But there is little doubt that human languages conform to abstract universal principles and that the human brain is specially equipped for acquisition of human language grammars, as we will discuss in the following chapter.

## Stages in Language Acquisition

Children do not wake up one morning with a fully formed grammar in their heads. In moving from first words to adult competence children pass through linguistic stages. They begin by babbling, they then acquire their first words, and in just a few months they begin to put words together into sentences.

Studies of language acquisition are based on various sources including tape recordings and videotapes of children's spontaneous language, usually in interactions with adults, as well as controlled experiments that test both their productive abilities and their comprehension of language. Researchers have also invented ingenious experimental techniques for studying the linguistic abilities of infants, who are not yet speaking.

Children's early utterances may not look exactly like adult sentences, but child language is not just a degenerate form of adult language. The words and sentences that the children produce at each stage of development reflect the set of grammatical rules they have developed to that point. Children's "errors" can therefore provide researchers with a window into their grammars.

Although child grammars and adult grammars differ in certain respects, they also share many formal properties. Like adults, children have grammatical categories such as NP and VP, rules for building phrase structures and for moving constituents, as well as phonological, morphological, and semantic rules, and they adhere to universal principles such as structure dependency.

Children are biologically equipped to acquire all aspects of grammar. In the following sections, we will look at development in each of the components of language, and we will illustrate the role that Universal Grammar and other factors play in this development.

## The Perception and Production of Speech Sounds

Any notion that a person is born with a mind like a blank slate is belied by a wealth of evidence showing that newborns react to some subtle distinctions in their environment and not to others. Infants will respond to visual depth and distance distinctions, to differences between rigid and flexible physical properties of objects, and to human faces rather than to other visual stimuli. Infants also show a very early response to different properties of language. Experiments demonstrate that infants will increase their sucking rate—as measured by ingeniously designed pacifiers—when the stimuli (visual or auditory) presented to them are varied, but will decrease the sucking rate when the same stimuli are presented repeatedly. When tested with a preferential listening technique, slightly older infants will turn their heads toward and listen longer to sounds, stress patterns, and words that are familiar to them. On the other hand, they will also respond to novel patterns, showing that they can distinguish the different linguistic elements being tested. These instinctive responses can be used to measure a baby's ability to discriminate and recognize different linguistic stimuli.

A newborn will respond to phonetic contrasts found in human languages even when these differences are not phonemic in the language spoken in the baby's home. A baby hearing a human voice over a loudspeaker saying [pa] [pa] [pa] will slowly decrease her rate of sucking. If the sound changes to [ba] or even [pʰa], the sucking rate increases dramatically. Adults find it difficult to differentiate between the allophones of a phoneme, but for infants it comes naturally. Japanese infants can distinguish between [r] and [l] whereas their parents cannot; babies can hear the difference between aspirated and unaspirated stops even if students in an introductory linguistics course cannot. Babies can discriminate between sounds that are phonemic in other languages and nonexistent in the language of their parents. For example, in Hindi, there is a phonemic contrast between a retroflex *t* [ʈ] (made with the tongue curled back) and the alveolar [t]. To English-speaking adults, these may sound the same; to their infants, they do not. However, babies will not react to distinctions that do not correspond to phonemic contrasts in any human language, such as sounds spoken more or less loudly or by speakers of different ages and genders.

Because infants are born with the ability to perceive just those sounds that are phonemic in some language, it is possible for them to learn any human language they are exposed to. During the first year of life, the infant's job is to uncover the sounds of the ambient language. From around six months, he begins to lose the ability to discriminate between sounds that are not phonemic in his own language as his linguistic environment begins to shape his initial perceptions. Japanese infants can no longer hear the difference between [r] and [l], which do not contrast in Japanese, whereas babies in English-speaking homes retain this perception. They have begun to learn the sounds of the language of their parents. Before that, they appear to know the sounds of human language in general.

## Babbling

"Hi & Lois"/King Features Syndicate

The child's linguistic environment shapes not only the child's perceptions of speech sounds but also his productions. Babbling illustrates the readiness of the human mind to respond to linguistic input from a very early stage.

At around six months, the infant begins to babble. The sounds produced in this period include many sounds that do not occur in the language of the household, but belong to the set of possible human speech sounds. By the end of the first year the babbles come to include only those sounds and sound combinations that occur in the target language, and also conform to the specific intonation pattern of the language. At around nine months old children's babbles consist mainly of repeated consonant-vowel sequences, like *mama, gaga,* and *dada*. Later babbles are more varied and begin to sound like words, although they may not have any specific meaning attached to them. At this point English-speaking adults can distinguish the babbles of an English-babbling infant from those of an infant babbling in Cantonese or Arabic. Deaf children exposed to sign language also babble–on their hands. They produce repetitive hand motions consisting of elements of the sign languages used in deaf communities around the world. During the first year of life, the infant's perceptions and productions are being fine-tuned to the surrounding language(s).

## First Words

Some time after the age of one, children begin to use the same string of sounds repeatedly to mean the same thing, thereby producing their first words. The age at which first words appear can vary and has nothing to do with the child's intelligence.

The child's first words may not sound exactly like the adult versions. The following words of one child, J. P., at the age of sixteen months, illustrate the point:

[ʔaʊ] "not," "no," "don't"
[bʌʔ]/[mʌʔ] "up"
[da] "dog"
[s:] "aerosol spray"
[sʲu:] "shoe"
[haɪ] "hi"

| | | | |
|---|---|---|---|
| [iʔo]/[siʔo] | "Cheerios" | [sr] | "shirt," "sweater" |
| [sa] | "sock" | [sæ:]/[əsæ:] | "what's that?"/"hey, look!" |
| [aɪ]/[ʌɪ] | "light" | [ma] | "mommy" |
| [baʊ]/[daʊ] | "down" | [dæ] | "daddy" |

What is important is not that these words differ from the adult's, but that they represent a fixed sound-meaning pairing.

Most children go through a stage in which they utters only single words. It is interesting to note that even though a child may only be producing one word at a time, he can understand utterances of greater complexity. Controlled experiments show that children in the one-word stage understand simple sentences such as "Ernie washed Bert", distinguishing this from "Bert washed Ernie".

Similarly, a child's one-word utterance may convey more meaning than just the single word. When J. P. says "down" he may be making a request to be put down, or he may be commenting on a toy that has fallen down from the shelf. When he says "cheerios" he may simply be naming the box of cereal in front of him, or he may be asking for some Cheerios. For this reason, the one-word stage is sometimes referred to as the **holophrastic** (whole phrase) stage because these one-word utterances seem to convey the meaning of an entire sentence. This suggests that children have a more complex mental representation of their language than they are able to express and that their productive abilities do not fully reflect their underlying grammatical competence.

## The Acquisition of Phonology

"Baby Blues", Baby Blues Partnership. Reprinted with permission of King Features Syndicate

In terms of his phonology, J. P. is like most children at the one-word stage. The first words are generally monosyllabic with a CV (consonant-vowel) form and the child's phonemic inventory is much smaller than is found in the adult language. It appears that children first acquire the small set of sounds common to all languages regardless of the ambient language(s), and in later stages acquire the less common sounds of their own language. J. P.'s sound system followed this pattern. His phonological inventory at an early stage included the consonants [b], [m], [d], and [k], which are frequently occurring sounds in the world's languages.

The distribution and frequency of sounds in a language can also influence the acquisition of certain segments. Sounds that are expected to be acquired late may appear earlier in children's language when they are frequently occurring. The fricative [v] is a very late acquisition in English but it is an early phoneme in Estonian, Bulgarian, and Swedish, languages that have several [v]-initial words that are common in the vocabularies of young children.

If the first year is devoted to figuring out the sounds of the target language, the second year involves learning how these sounds are used in the phonology of the language, especially which contrasts are phonemic. When children first begin to contrast one pair of a set (e.g., when they learn that /p/ and /b/ are distinct phonemes due to a voicing difference), they also begin to distinguish between other similar pairs (e.g., /t/ and /d/, /s/, and /z/, and all the other voiceless/voiced phonemic pairs). As we would expect, the generalizations refer to natural classes of speech sounds.

Children may produce certain sounds in a way that makes them indiscernible to adult observers. A child's pronunciation of *wing* and *ring* may seem the same to the adult ear, but acoustic analyses of his utterances can show that they are physically different sounds. And in a picture identification experiment the child will correctly identity both a ring and a wing.

Anecdotal reports also show the disparity between the child's production and his phonological representation. An example is the exchange between a linguist and his two-year-old son (linguists love to experiment on their own children). At this age the child's pronunciation of "mouth" is [maʊs].

| | |
|---|---|
| FATHER: | What does [maʊs] mean? |
| CHILD: | Like a cat. |
| FATHER: | Yes, what else? |
| CHILD: | Nothing else. |
| FATHER: | It's part of your head. |
| CHILD: | (*fascinated*) |
| FATHER: | *(touching child's mouth)* What's this? |
| CHILD: | [maʊs] |

It took the child a few seconds to realize that he was pronouncing "mouse" and "mouth" the same. This is probably because his lexical representations of the two words were closer to the adult forms than were his actual pronunciations. Children seem to accurately perceive the adult form, and represent it as such (approximately) in their lexicon, but they are unable in these early years to produce it correctly. Therefore, even at this early stage, it is not possible to determine the extent of the grammar of the child—in this case, the phonology—simply by observing speech production. It is often necessary to use various experimental and instrumental techniques to reveal the child's underlying competence.

A child's first words show many substitutions of one feature for another or one phoneme for another. In the preceding examples, *mouth* [maʊθ] is pronounced *mouse* [maʊs], with the alveolar fricative [s] replacing the less common interdental fricative [θ]; and *ring* is pronounced *wing*, with the glide [w] replacing the liquid [r]. In general glides are acquired earlier than liquids, and hence substitute for them. Similarly, alveolars are acquired earlier than interdentals and replace them in production. These substitutions are simplifications of the adult pronunciation. They make articulation easier until the child achieves greater articulatory control.

Children's early (mis-)pronunciations are not haphazard. The phonological substitutions are rule-governed. The following is an abridged lexicon for another child, Michael, between the ages of eighteen and twenty-one months:

| | | | |
|---|---|---|---|
| [pun] | "spoon" | [maɪtl] | "Michael" |
| [peɪn] | "plane" | [daɪtər] | "diaper" |
| [tɪs] | "kiss" | [pati] | "Papi" |
| [taʊ] | "cow" | [mani] | "Mommy" |
| [tin] | "clean" | [bərt] | "Bert" |
| [polər] | "stroller" | [bərt] | "(Big) Bird" |

Michael systematically substituted the alveolar stop [t] for the velar stop [k] as in his words for "cow," "clean," "kiss," and his own name. He also replaced labial [p] with [t] when it occurred in the middle of a word, as in his words for "Papi" and "diaper." He reduced consonant clusters in "spoon," "plane," and "stroller," and he devoiced final stops as in "Big Bird." In devoicing the final [d] in "bird," he created an ambiguous form [bərt] referring both to Bert and Big Bird. Little wonder that only parents understand their children's first words!

Michael's substitutions are typical of the phonological rules that operate in the very early stages of acquisition. Other common rules are reduplication—"bottle" becomes [baba], "water" becomes [wawa]; and the dropping of final consonants—"bed" becomes [be], "cake" becomes [ke]. These two rules show that the children prefer simple CV syllables. Of the many phonological rules that children create, no child will necessarily use all rules.

Early phonological rules generally reflect natural phonological processes that also occur in adult languages. For example, various adult languages have a rule of syllable-final consonant devoicing (for example, in German hʊnd/ 'dog' is pronounced [hʊnt]. Children do not create bizarre or whimsical rules. Their rules conform to the possibilities made available by Universal Grammar.

## The Acquisition of Word Meaning

How do children figure out the meaning of a word? Most people do not see this aspect of acquisition as posing a great problem. The intuitive view is that children look at an object, the mother says a word, and the child connects the sounds with the object. However, this is not as easy as it seems. As the linguist Lila Gleitman points out:

> A child who observes a cat sitting on a mat also observes . . . a mat supporting a cat, a mat under a cat, a floor supporting a mat and a cat, and so on. If the adult now says "The cat is on the mat" even while pointing to the cat on the mat, how is the child to choose among these interpretations of the situation?[1]

[1]Gleitman, L.R., and E. Wanner. 1982. *Language acquisition: The state of the art.* Cambridge, UK: Cambridge University

Even if the child succeeds in associating the word *cat* with the animal on the mat he may mistakenly interpret "cat" as "Cat," the name of that particular animal, instead of a type of animal. Upon hearing the word *dog* in the presence of a dog, say, a poodle, how does the child know that "dog" can also refer to huge mastiffs, tiny terriers, bulldogs, and greyhounds, all of which look rather different from one another? What about cows, lambs, and other four-legged mammals? Why are they not "dogs"? The child has to figure out that certain words refer to classes of objects and not just to the object in a particular situation. To do this, he must determine what relevant features (four legs, fur, tail, bark, etc.) define that class of objects, and he must do this largely on his own. Nobody provides the child with explicit information on how to extend the use of a word to other entities that the word refers to. In learning the meanings of words, as in other aspects of language acquisition, children are confronted with impoverished data.

The child's early vocabulary provides insight into how children use words and how they construct word meaning. J. P. originally used his word for *sock* not only for socks but for other undergarments that are put on over the feet such as undershorts. Similarly, a child may use the word *doggie* to refer to any four-legged animal or *daddy* to refer to any adult male. This is referred to as **overextension**: The child's word seems to encompass a broader class than the adult's. This might be because he has a different meaning for the word, or, that he lacks familiarity with the more specific terms and actually knows the adult meaning.

Controlled experiments reveal that overextensions are usually based on physical attributes such as size, shape, and texture. *Ball* may refer to all round things, *bunny* to all furry things, and so on. But children will not make overextensions based on color. In experiments, they will group objects by shape and give them a name, but they will not assign a name to a group of red objects. Children are predisposed to attach and extend labels to objects in particular ways. In this instance, they show a *form over color* learning principle.

Similarly, if an experimenter points to an unfamiliar object and uses a nonsense word like *zav*, saying "that's a zav," the child will interpret the word to refer to the whole object, not to one of its parts or attributes, the *whole object* principle. On the other hand, if the experimenter utters "that's a zav" in the presence of an object whose name is already known to the child such as a boat, the child will take *zav* to refer to a part of the boat like the sail. Children initially assume that if an object has one name it cannot have another: a *boat* can't also be a *zav*. This "one name one thing" principle ensures that children are able to learn words that refer to things other than whole objects such as parts and attributes of objects.

Given the poverty of stimulus, principles like "form over color," "whole object" and "one name one thing" facilitate word learning. Without such principles, it is doubtful that children could learn words as quickly as they do. Children learn approximately fourteen words a day for the first six years of their lives. That averages to about 5,000 words per year. How many students know 10,000 words of a foreign language after two years of study?

There is also experimental evidence that children can learn the meaning of one class of words—verbs—based on the syntactic environment in which they occur. If you were to hear a sentence such as *John blipped Mary the gloon*, you would not know exactly what John did, but you would likely understand that the sentence is describing a transfer of something from John to Mary. Similarly, if you heard *John gonked that Mary . . .* , you would conclude that the verb *gonk* was a verb of communication like *say* or a mental verb like *think*. The complement types that a verb selects can provide clues to its meaning and thereby help the child. This learning of word meaning based on syntax is referred to as **syntactic bootstrapping**.

## The Acquisition of Morphology

"Baby Blues", Baby Blues Partnership. Reprinted with permission of King Features Syndicate

Children's acquisition of morphology provides some of the clearest evidence of rule learning. Their errors in inflectional morphology reveal that children acquire the regular rules of the grammar and then overapply them. This **overgeneralization** occurs when children treat irregular verbs and nouns as if they were regular. We have probably all heard children say *bringed, goed, drawed,* and *runned,* or *foots, mouses,* and *sheeps*.

These mistakes tell us much about how children learn language because such forms could not arise through imitation. They tell us that children are acquiring rules and that they apply these rules broadly before learning that there are exceptions such as *mice, ran,* and so on. Some studies of the acquisition of morphology are based on children's spontaneous use of language. Other studies rely on experiments that elicit particular forms from children. A classic experimental study of English-speaking children was based on the "wug test" (Berko, 1958). Children were shown a drawing of a nonsense animal like the funny creature shown in the following picture. Each "animal" was given a nonsense name. The experimenter would then say to the child, pointing to the picture, "This is a wug."

Then, the experimenter would show the child a picture of two of the animals and say, "Now here is another one. There are two of them. There are two ________."

The child's task was to give the plural form, "wugs" [wʌgz]. Another little make-believe animal was called a "bik," and when the child was shown two biks, he or she again was to say the plural form [bɪks]. The children applied regular plural formation to words they had never heard, showing that they had acquired the plural rule. Their ability to add [z] when the animal's name ended with a voiced sound, and [s] when there was a final voiceless consonant, showed that the children were also using allomorphy rules based on an understanding of natural classes of phonological segments, and not simply imitating words they had previously heard. Similar elicitations were done for past tense *-ed* and present tense *-s*, among other forms.

Studies of children acquiring languages with richer inflectional morphology than English reveal that they learn agreement rules at a very early age. For example, Italian verbs must be inflected for number and person to agree with the subject. This is similar to the English agreement rule "add *s* to the verb" for third-person, singular subjects—*He giggles a lot* but *We giggle a lot*—except that in Italian more verb forms must be acquired. Italian-speaking children between the ages of 1;10 (one year, ten months) and 2;4 correctly inflect the verb, as the following utterances of Italian children show:

| | |
|---|---|
| Tu legg**i** il libro. | "You (second person singular) read the book." |
| Io vad**o** fuori. | "I go (first person singular) outside." |
| Dorm**e** miao dorme. | "Sleeps (third person singular) cat sleeps." |
| Legg**iamo** il libro. | "(We) read (first person plural) the book." |

Similar results have been shown for children acquiring other richly inflected languages such as Spanish, German, Catalan, and Swahili. It is rare for them to make agreement errors, just as it is rare for an English-speaking child to say "I goes."

Many languages, including the ones just noted, also have gender and number agreement between the head noun and the article and adjectives inside the noun phrase. Children as young as two years old respect these agreement requirements when producing NPs, as shown by the following Italian examples:

| | |
|---|---|
| E mi**a** gonn**a.** | "(It) is my (feminine singular) skirt." |
| Quest**o** mi**o** bimb**o.** | "This my (masculine singular) baby." |
| Guarda **la** mel**a** piccolin**a.** | "Look at the little (feminine singular) apple." |
| Guarda **il** top**o** piccolin**o.** | "Look at the little (masculine singular) mouse." |

Experimental studies with two-year-old French-speaking children show that they use gender information on determiners to help identify the subsequent noun: *le ballon* (the-masc. balloon) versus *la banane* (the-fem. banana).

Children also show knowledge of the derivational rules of their language and use these rules to create novel words, as illustrated in English where we can derive verbs from nouns. From the noun *Google* we now have a verb *to google*; from the noun *friend* Facebook users derived the verb *to friend*. Children acquire the noun to verb rule early and use it often because there are lots of gaps in their verb vocabulary.

| **Child Utterance** | **Adult Translation** |
|---|---|
| You have to scale it first. | "You have to weigh it first." |
| Don't broom my mess! | "Don't sweep up my mess!." |
| Mommy nippled Anna. | "Mommy breastfed Anna." |
| Will you chocolate my milk? | "Will you put chocolate in my milk?" |

Children also overgeneralize some derivational morphemes such as the *-er* suffix used to mark agents and instruments:

| | |
|---|---|
| cooker | cook |
| brakers | car brakes |
| storier | story teller |
| mistaker | mistake maker |

And they create their own compounds:

| | |
|---|---|
| crow-bird | crow |
| firetruck-man | firefighter |
| mower-blower | gardener |
| sky-car | airplane |

These novel forms provide further evidence that language acquisition is a creative process and that children's utterances reflect their internal grammars, which include both derivational and inflectional rules.

## The Acquisition of Syntax

"Doonesbury" 1984 G.B. Trudeau. Reprinted with permission of Universal Press Syndicate

When a child is still in the holophrastic stage, adults listening to the one-word utterances often feel that the child is trying to convey a more complex message. Experimental techniques show that at that stage (and even earlier), children have knowledge of some syntactic rules. In these experiments, the infant sits on his mother's lap and hears a sentence over a speaker while seeing two video displays depicting different actions, one of which corresponds to the sentence.

Infants tend to look longer at the video that matches the sentence they hear. This methodology allows researchers to tap the linguistic knowledge of children who are using only single words or who are not talking at all. Results show that children as young as seventeen months can understand the difference between sentences such as "Ernie is tickling Bert" and "Bert is tickling Ernie." Because these sentences have all the same words, the child cannot be relying on the words alone to understand the meanings. He must also understand the word-order rules and how they determine the grammatical relations of subject and object. This same preferential looking technique has shown that eighteen-month-olds can distinguish between subject and object in *wh* questions such as *What did the apple hit?* and *What hit the apple?* These results and many others strongly suggest that children's syntactic competence is ahead of their productive abilities, as we have also seen in children's lexical acquisition and the development of other components of grammar.

Around the time of their second birthday children begin to put words together into utterances such as the following:[2]

| | |
|---|---|
| Cat stand up table. | Mommy sock. |
| What that? | Ride truck. |
| He play little tune. | Milk in there. |
| Want that. | Doggie big. |
| Cathy build house. | Bib off. |
| No sit there. | Ride truck. |
| Show Mommy that. | Bye bye boat. |

These early utterances express a variety of semantic and syntactic relations. For example, noun + noun sentences such as *Mommy sock* can be a subject + object relation when the mother is putting the sock on the child, or a possessive relation when the child is pointing to Mommy's sock. When children first produce multiword utterances, they are inconsistent in their use of function words (grammatical morphemes) such as *a* and *the*, subject pronouns like *I* and *we,* auxiliary verbs such as *can* and *is,* and in some languages, verbal inflection. Many (though not all) of their utterances consist only of open-class or content words. During this stage, children often sound as if they are sending a text message or reading an old-fashioned telegram (which contains only the required words for basic understanding). For this reason, such utterances are sometimes called "telegraphic speech," and we call this period of development, the **telegraphic stage**.

Unlike the adult sending a text, however, the child does not deliberately leave out function words. Telegraphic sentences reflect her linguistic capacity at that particular stage of language development. It can take many months before a child uses all the grammatical morphemes consistently.

There is a great deal of debate among linguists about how to explain telegraphic speech: Do children omit function morphemes because of limitations in their ability to plan and produce longer, more complex sentences? Or do

[2]Many of the examples of child language in this chapter are taken from CHILDES (Child Language Data Exchange System), a computerized database of the spontaneous speech of children acquiring English and many other languages. MacWhinney, B., and C. Snow. 1985. The child language data exchange system. *Journal of Child Language* 12: 271–96.

they omit these morphemes because their grammar permits such elements to be unexpressed? On the first account telegraphic speech is due to performance limitations. Since there is an upper limit on the length of utterances a child can produce, and function morphemes are less important to comprehension, they are omitted. On the second view telegraphic speech is an early grammatical stage similar to adult languages like Italian or Spanish that allow subject pronouns to be dropped, as in *Hablo ingles* "(I) speak English."

Some features of telegraphic speech are universal. All children have a tendency to drop the subject of the sentence, as in *Want that* meaning "***I*** want that," whether their language permits it or not (English does not, Spanish does). On the other hand, certain features of a child's telegraphic speech occur in some languages and not others, such as the omission of verb inflection in *Cathy build house*. Children acquiring inflectional languages like Italian or Russian do not drop verb endings.

Although children's sentences during the telegraphic stage may lack certain function morphemes, they nevertheless obey syntactic rules similar to those in the adult grammar. Children almost never violate the word-order rules of their language. In languages with relatively fixed word order, such as English and Japanese, children use the required order (SVO in English, SOV in Japanese) from the earliest stage. In languages with freer word order, such as Turkish and Russian, where grammatical relations are indicated by case markers, children quickly learn this morphology, marking subjects with nominative case and objects with accusative case with few errors.

The correct use of word order, case marking, and agreement rules shows that even though children may often omit function morphemes, they are aware of constituent structure, which, as in adult grammar, may be represented with these (simplified, non X-bar) phrase structure trees:

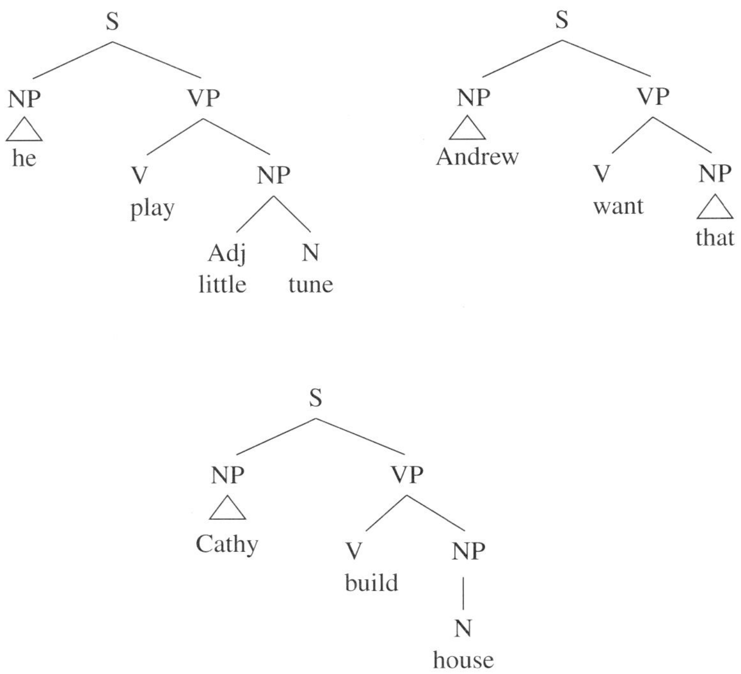

In order to apply the morphological and syntactic rules, she must know what syntactic categories the words in his language belong to. But how exactly does the child come to know that *want* and *dance* are verbs and *song* and *house* are nouns? One suggestion is that children first rely on the meaning of a word to figure out its category. This is called **semantic bootstrapping**. The child may have rules such as "if a word refers to a physical object, it's a noun" or "if a word refers to an action, it's a verb," and so on. However, the rules that link certain meanings to specific categories are not foolproof. The word *action* denotes an action, but it is not a verb; *know* is not an action, but is a verb; and *justice* is a noun though it is not a physical object. But the rules that drive semantic bootstrapping might be helpful for the kind of words children learn early on, which tend to refer to objects and actions.

**Word frames** may also help the child determine when words belong to the same category. Studies of the language that adults use to children show that there are certain frames that occur frequently enough to be reliable for categorization, for example, "you ____ it" and "the ____ one." Most typically, verbs such as *see, do, did, win, fix, turned,* and *get* occur in the first frame while adjectives like *red, big, wrong,* and *light* occur in the second. If a child knows that *see* is a verb, then he could also deduce that all the other words appearing in the same frame are also verbs. This *distributional evidence* is not foolproof, however. "It____ the" can frame a verb, as in *It* ***hit*** *the car*, but it can also frame a preposition, as in *I hit it* ***across*** *the street.* Nevertheless, like semantic bootstrapping, this evidence may be reliable enough to give the child a head start into the complex task of learning the syntactic categories of words.

The most frequent frames typically consist of function words, determiners such as *the* and *a*, and pronouns like *it* and *one*. This suggests that children recognize and learn from function morphemes in the input even though they omit these elements in their own speech. Indeed, comprehension studies show two-year-olds respond more appropriately to grammatical commands such as *Find the bird* than to commands with an ungrammatically positioned function word as in *Find was bird.* This means that children pay attention to the particular function morphemes and not just to the prosody of the sentence, which is the same in the two commands. Other studies show that function morphemes such as determiners and verb inflections help children in word segmentation and categorization.

Sometime between the ages of 2;6 and 3;6, a virtual language explosion occurs. At this point it is difficult to identify distinct stages because the child is undergoing so much development so rapidly. By the age of 3;0, most children are consistent in their use of function morphemes. Moreover, they have begun to produce and understand a variety of complex structures. Following is a sample of Michael's utterances between the ages of 2;1 and 3;2 which illustrate the speed with which children's language development progresses during this period.

**2;1** Monsters eating turkey.
Cow tired.
Derz (there's) Mommy Rabbit sleeping.
Use potty.
Bringing toys.
Take it out.

**2;5** I bang it down like this.
What's that one over there?
I'm gonna dump [jump] in the swimming pool.
I went in the potty last night.
I trying to reach a carrot.
I gotta get those cookies over der [there].
He have a belly ache.
We not strong enough.

**2;7** Her baby is like this.
I didn't like those friends
Why they would be hard?
No, 'cause there's a monster and the monster can [s]care you.
I thought it was a ladder
I see a man who plays football.
He putting the fire in the dragon's mouth.

**2;11** Do you give me a big piece, mom?
We didn't save it 'cause somebody throwed it in the grass.
Mommy, is it ok to take a walk?
I bumped into people I went past and I bumped into those things.
Why does he have colors on his arm?
Now you need to hold the basket.
I like it when it's Christmas.
I can't find a block that's big.
I just want to do it by myself.

**3;2** Watch what I'm doing.
I want her to be the doctor.
Ok, but first I need to stand on here.
I said when I start all these machines you can do it.
Now give it back to me and we put it where all the other things are
I forgot to press the buddons [buttons].
I have it in someplace nobody can see it.
I need to show you what I can sing.
You know what we can hang up here
Mom, can you put sand on this?

In less than a year, Michael has gone from telegraphic utterances to fully formed, grammatical adultlike sentences. His use of coordinated sentences, relative clauses and other kinds of embedded clauses illustrate his knowledge of recursive rules and his potential to produce an infinite range of sentences. By the age of four, Michael, like all children everywhere, will have acquired much of the complexity of the adult grammar.

## The Acquisition of Pragmatics

"Baby Blues", Baby Blues Partnership. Reprinted with permission of King Features Syndicate

In addition to acquiring the rules of grammar, children must learn the appropriate use of language in context, or pragmatics. The cartoon is funny because of the inappropriateness of the interaction, showing that Zoe hasn't completely acquired the pragmatic "maxims of conversation" discussed in Chapter 4.

Context is needed to determine the reference of pronouns. A sentence such as "Surely he loves her anyway" is uninterpretable unless both speaker and hearer understand who the pronouns *he* and *her* refer to. If the sentence were preceded by "I saw John and Mary arguing in the park," then the referents of the pronouns would be clear. Children are not always sensitive to the needs of other speakers and they may fail to establish the referents for pronouns. It is not unusual for a three- or four-year-old (or even older children) to use pronouns out of the blue, like the child who cries to her mother "He hit me" when mom has no idea who did the deed.

The speaker and listener form part of the context of an utterance. The meaning of *I* and *you* depends on who is talking and who is listening, which changes from situation to situation. Younger children (around age two) have difficulty with the "shifting reference" of these pronouns. A typical error that children make at this age is to refer to themselves as "you," saying "You want to take a walk" when they mean "I want to take a walk."

Children also show a lack of pragmatic awareness in the way they sometimes use articles. Like pronouns, the interpretation of articles depends on context. The definite article *the*, as in "the boy," can be used felicitously only when it is clear to speaker and hearer what boy is being discussed. In a discourse, the indefinite article *a/an* must be used for the first mention of a new referent, but the definite article (or pronoun) may be used in subsequent mentions, as illustrated following:

A boy walked into the class.
He was in the wrong room.
The teacher directed the boy to the right classroom.

Children do not always respect the pragmatic rules for articles. In experimental studies, three-year-olds may use the definite article for introducing a new referent. In other words, the child tends to assume that his listener knows who he is talking about without having established this in a linguistically appropriate way.

Implicatures are another part of pragmatics that young children have difficulty with. (Implicatures are discussed in Chapter 4.) An adult hearing the sentence *Some of the children are playing ball* would infer that not all the children are playing ball. This is because adults follow Grice's conversational maxims, among which is the principle that speakers are maximally informative. If all the children were playing ball, a cooperative speaker would say so even though if *all* the children are playing ball then it is logically true that *some* of the children are playing ball. Interestingly, children under the age of seven or often fail to get such implicatures. Various experimental studies have shown that when presented with a description of a scenario in which a stronger, more informative term such as *all* would be appropriate, children readily accept a weaker, less informative *some*. For example, in one experiment the child is shown an animated video in which a mouse, who likes vegetables, picks up all the carrots in the display. A puppet who is watching the animation with the child then says "The mouse picked up some of the carrots." When the child is then asked by the experimenter if the puppet said the right thing, he responds "yes," while adults in this situation would say" No, he picked up *all* of the carrots." In one sense, the child is not wrong in his response—the mouse did pick up some of the carrots—in fact he picked them all up. But, adults use pragmatic principles in such cases while children seem to rely more heavily on the literal or logical meaning.

It may take a child months or years to master those aspects of pragmatics that involve the felicitous use of determiners and pronouns, or the conversational maxims which when flouted result in implicatures. Other aspects of pragmatics are acquired very early. Even in the holophrastic stage children use their one-word utterances with different illocutionary force (see Chapter 4). The utterance "up" spoken by J. P. at sixteen months might be a simple statement such as "The teddy is up on the shelf," or a request: "Pick me up." By age three, Michael was producing grammatically well-formed, and pragmatically appropriate, declaratives, interrogatives and imperatives. And as we will discuss below, bilingual children—even very young ones—understand which of their languages to use in different conversational contexts.

## The Role of the Linguistic Environment: Adult Input

Children deprived of linguistic input show a clear drive to acquire language and may even create a rudimentary linguistic system. But there is little doubt that children require a language environment to develop a mature linguistic system. But what exactly is the function of the linguistic input that children receive? Parameter-setting models of acquisition suggest that children use the linguistic data to extract the underlying rules and parameter settings of their language.

Other approaches to understanding language acquisition afford a much more pronounced and formative role to the input provided by adults. Early behaviorist views as well as some more recent theories that stress the role of general learning mechanisms, hold that the adult input and feedback to the child is paramount. However, most linguists and psychologists now recognize that language is a complex cognitive system that cannot be fully acquired by behaviorist or general learning principles. In the next section, we discuss some of the mechanisms once proposed by behaviorists to account for language acquisition.

## The Role of Imitation, Reinforcement, and Analogy

A common misconception about language acquisition is that children simply listen to what is said around them and imitate the speech they hear. Imitation is involved to some extent, of course. An American child hears *milk* and a Mexican child *leche* and each child attempts to reproduce what he hears. But children's early words and sentences show that they are not simply imitating adult speech. Children use inflectional and derivational processes to produce novel words, and their early sentences diverge from the language of their environment in systematic and interesting ways.

Moreover, even when children are trying to imitate what they hear, they are unable to produce sentences outside of the rules of their developing grammar. The following are a child's attempts to imitate something the adult has said:

| Adult | Child |
|---|---|
| He's going out. | He go out. |
| That's an old-time train. | Old-time train. |
| Adam, say what I say: Where can I put them? | Where I can put them? |

Imitation also fails to account for the fact that children who are unable to speak for neurological or physiological reasons are able to learn the language spoken to them and understand it. When they overcome their speech impairment, they immediately use the language for speaking.

Another proposal in the behaviorist tradition is that children learn to produce correct (grammatical) sentences because adults positively reinforce them when they say something grammatical and negatively reinforce them by correction when they say something ungrammatical. But studies show that parents seldom correct their children, and when they do it is usually for mispronunciations or incorrect reporting of facts and not for "bad grammar." When uttered, the ungrammatical sentence "Her curl my hair" was not corrected because it was true: the child's mother was in fact curling her hair. However, when the child uttered the grammatical sentence "Walt Disney comes on Tuesday," she was corrected because the television program was shown on Wednesday. One researcher concluded somewhat wryly that it is "truth value rather than syntactic well-formedness that chiefly governs explicit verbal reinforcement by parents—which renders mildly paradoxical the fact that the usual product of such a training schedule is an adult whose speech is highly grammatical but not notably truthful."

Adults will sometimes **recast** children's utterances into an adultlike form, as in the following examples:

| **Child** | **Mother** |
|---|---|
| It fall. | It fell? |
| Where is them? | They're at home. |
| It doing dancing. | It's dancing, yes. |

In these examples, the mother provides the correct model without actually correcting the child. Although recasts are potentially helpful to the child, they are not used in a consistent way. One study of forty mothers of children two to four years old showed that only about 25 percent of children's ungrammatical sentences are recast and that overall, parents recast grammatical sentences as often as bad ones. Because parents focus more on the content than on the form of their children's utterances, and allow many ungrammatical utterances to "slip by" while correcting grammatical ones, a child that relies on recasts to learn grammar would be mightily confused.

Even if adults did correct children's syntax it would still not explain how or what children learn from such adult responses, or how children discover and construct the correct rules. Children do not know what they are doing wrong and are unable to make corrections even when "errors" are pointed out, as shown by the following exchange:

CHILD: Nobody don't like me.
MOTHER: No, say "Nobody likes me."
CHILD: Nobody don't like me.
(dialogue repeated eight times)
MOTHER: Now, listen carefully; say "Nobody likes me."
CHILD: Oh, nobody don't likes me.

It has also been suggested that children put words together to form phrases and sentences by **analogy**, by hearing a sentence and using it as a model to form other sentences. In some sense, this must be true. Children must generalize from particular instances to form a general rule. The problem with analogy is that the child must also know when the general rule does not work, as one developmental psycholinguist explains:

> [S]uppose the child has heard the sentence "I painted a red barn." So now, by analogy, the child can say "I painted a blue barn." That's exactly the kind of theory that we want. You hear a sample and you extend it to all of the new cases by similarity. . . . In addition to "I painted a red barn" you might also hear the sentence "I painted a barn red." So it looks as if you take those last two words and switch their order. . . . So now you want to extend this to the case of seeing, because you want to look at barns instead of paint them. So you have heard, "I saw a red barn." Now you try (by analogy) a . . . new sentence—"I saw a barn red." Something's gone wrong. This is an analogy, but the analogy didn't work. It's not a sentence of English.[3]

[3]Gleitman, L., in Searchinger, G. 1994. *The Human Language Series, program 2. Acquiring the Human Language*. Video New York: Equinox Film/Ways of Knowing Inc.

Similarly, based on the sentence "John eats tomatoes" we can say "John eats" with the meaning "John eats *something*." But we cannot analogously say, based on the sentence "John grows tomatoes" that "John grows" to mean "John grows *something*."

Children do not make syntactic errors of this sort. They may overgeneralize a morphological rule or omit function morphemes. But they seem to know enough about syntactic structure not to assign a uniform analysis to sentences with *eat* and *grow* or *paint and see,* each of which has different syntactic properties. Analogy—to the extent it is used by children—must be constrained by the child's knowledge of the general structural principles provided by UG.

## Summary

When children acquire a language, they acquire the grammar of that language—the phonological, morphological, syntactic, and semantic rules. They also acquire the pragmatic rules of the language as well as a lexicon. Children are not taught language. Rather, they extract the rules (and much of the lexicon) from the language(s) spoken around them.

The ease and rapidity of children's language acquisition and the uniformity development for all children and all languages, despite the **poverty of the stimulus** they receive, suggest that the language faculty is innate and that the infant comes to the complex task already endowed with a Universal Grammar. UG is not a grammar like the grammar of English or Arabic, but represents the principles and parameters to which all human languages conform. Children create grammars based on the linguistic input and are guided in this process by UG. Language acquisition is a creative process.

Language development proceeds in stages. During the first year of life children develop the sounds of their language. This begins in the **babbling stage**. They first produce and perceive many sounds that do not exist in their linguistic environment. Gradually their productions and perceptions are fine-tuned to their surroundings. Children's late babbling has all the phonological characteristics of the input language. Deaf children who are exposed at birth to sign languages also produce manual babbling, showing that babbling is a universal, biologically-triggered first stage in language acquisition that is shaped by the linguistic input received.

At the end of the first year, children utter their first words. During the second year, they learn many more words and they develop much of the phonological system of the language. Children's first utterances are one-word "sentences" (the **holophrastic** stage).

Many experimental studies show that children are sensitive to various linguistic properties such as stress and phonotactic constraints, and to statistical regularities of the input that enable them to segment the fluent speech that they hear into words. One method of segmenting speech **is prosodic bootstrapping**. Other bootstrapping methods can help the child to learn verb meaning based on syntactic context **(syntactic bootstrapping),** or syntactic categories based on word meaning **(semantic bootstrapping).** Distributional evidence such as **word frames** contributes both to syntactic and semantic knowledge.

After a few months, the child puts two or more words together. These early sentences are not random combinations of words—the words have definite patterns and express both syntactic and semantic relationships. During the **telegraphic stage,** the child produces longer sentences that often lack function or grammatical morphemes. The child's early grammar still lacks many of the rules of the adult grammar, but is not qualitatively different from it. Children at this stage have correct word order and rules for agreement and case, which show their knowledge of structure.

Children make specific kinds of errors while acquiring their language. For example, they will **overgeneralize** morphology by saying *bringed* or *mans*. This shows that they are acquiring rules of their particular language. Children do not seem to make errors that violate principles of Universal Grammar.

In acquiring the lexicon of the language, children may **overextend** word meaning by using *dog* to mean any four-legged creature. Despite these categorization "errors," children's word learning, like their grammatical development, is guided by general principles.

Several learning mechanisms have been suggested to explain the acquisition process. **Imitation** of adult speech, **reinforcement**, and **analogy** have all been proposed. None of these learning mechanisms account for the fact that children create novel (and non-adultlike) sentences according to the rules of their language, that they make certain kinds of errors but not others, and that they display knowledge of structures for which there is no evidence in the input. Empirical studies of the **motherese** hypothesis show that grammar development does not depend on the grammaticality of the linguistic input.

## References for Further Reading

Bloom, P. 1993. *Language Acquisition: Core Readings*. Cambridge: MIT Press.

Gass, S. and L. Selinker. 2008. *Second language acquisition: An introductory course, 3rd ed.* NJ: Lawrence Erlbaum.

Guasti, M. T. 2016. *Language acquisition: The growth of grammar.* 2nd edition. Cambridge, MA: MIT Press.

Hakuta, K. 1986. *Mirror of language: The debate on bilingualism*. New York: Basic Books.

Ingram, D. 1989. *First language acquisition: method, description and explanation*. New York: Cambridge University Press.

Jakobson, R. 1971. *Studies on child language and aphasia*. The Hague: Mouton.

Lust, B. and Foley, 2004. *First Language Acquisition: The Essential Readings*. Oxford UK: Blackwell Publishing.

O'Grady, W. 2005. *How children learn language*. Cambridge, UK: Cambridge University Press.

Ortega, L. 2009. *Understanding second language acquisition*. London: Hodder Education.

White, L. 2003. *Second language acquisition and Universal Grammar.* Cambridge, UK: Cambridge University Press.

## Exercises

1. *Baby talk* is a term used to label the word forms that many adults use when speaking to children. Examples in English are *choo-choo* for "train" and *bow-wow* for "dog." Baby talk seems to exist in every language and culture. At least two things seem to be universal about baby talk: The words that have baby-talk forms fall into certain semantic categories (e.g., food and animals), and the words are phonetically simpler than the adult forms (e.g., *tummy* /tʌmi/ for "stomach" /stʌmik/). List all the baby-talk words you can think of in your native language; then (1) separate them into semantic categories, and (2) try to state general rules for the kinds of phonological reductions or simplifications that occur.

2. In this chapter, we discussed the way children acquire rules of question formation. The following examples of children's early questions are from a stage that is later than those discussed in the chapter. Formulate a generalization to describe this stage.

| | |
|---|---|
| Can I go? | Can I can't go? |
| Why do you have one tooth? | Why you don't have a tongue? |
| What do frogs eat? | What do you don't like? |
| Do you like chips? | Do you don't like bananas? |

3. Find a child between two and four years old. Note the age in years; months, and play with the child for about thirty minutes. Keep a list of all words and/or "sentences" that are not adult-like. Describe what you think the child means by these words and sentences. Describe the syntactic or morphological errors (including omissions). If the child is producing multiword sentences, write a grammar that could account for the data you have collected.

4. Roger Brown and his coworkers at Harvard University studied the language development of three children, referred to in the literature as Adam, Eve, and Sarah. The following is a sample of their two-word utterances.

| | | |
|---|---|---|
| a coat | my stool | poor man |
| a celery | that knee | little top |
| a Becky | more coffee | dirty knee |
| a hands | more nut | that Adam |
| my mummy | two tinker-toy | big boot |

   One observation made by Brown was that many of the sentences and phrases produced by the children were ungrammatical from the point of view of the adult grammar. Mark with an asterisk any of the above NPs that are ungrammatical in the adult grammar of English and state the "violation" for each starred item. For example, if one of the utterances were *Lotsa book*, you might say: "The modifier *lotsa* must be followed by a plural noun."

**5.** In the holophrastic (one-word) stage of child language acquisition, the child's phonological system differs in systematic ways from that in the adult grammar. The inventory of sounds and the phonemic contrasts are smaller, and there are greater constraints on phonotactic rules. (See Chapter 6 for a discussion of these aspects of phonology.)

**a.** For each of the following words produced by a child, state what the substitution is, and any other differences that result.

*Example*:

spook [pʰuk] Substitution: initial cluster [sp] reduced to single consonant; /p/ becomes aspirated, showing that child has acquired the aspiration rule.

| | | |
|---|---|---|
| **(1)** | don't | [dot] |
| **(2)** | skip | [kʰip] |
| **(3)** | shoe | [su] |
| **(4)** | that | [dæt] |
| **(5)** | play | [pʰe] |
| **(6)** | thump | [dʌp] |
| **(7)** | bath | [bæt] |
| **(8)** | chop | [tʰap] |
| **(9)** | kitty | [kɪdi] |
| **(10)** | light | [waɪt] |
| **(11)** | dolly | [daʊi] |
| **(12)** | grow | [go] |

**b.** State general rules that account for the children's deviations from the adult pronunciations.

**6.** Children learn demonstrative words such as *this, that, these,* and *those*; temporal terms such as *now, then,* and *tomorrow*; and spatial terms such as *here, there, right,* and *behind* relatively late. What do all these words have in common? (Hint: See the pragmatics section of Chapter 4.) Why might that factor delay their acquisition?

**7.** We saw in this chapter how children overgeneralize rules such as the plural rule, producing forms such as *mans* and *mouses*. What might a child learning English use instead of the adult words given?

**a.** children
**b.** went
**c.** better
**d.** best
**e.** brought
**f.** sang
**g.** geese
**h.** worst
**i.** knives
**j.** worse

8. The following words are from the lexicons of two children ages one year six months (1;6) and two (2;0) years old. Compare the pronunciation of the words to adult pronunciation.

| **Child 1 (1;6)** | | | | **Child 2 (2;0)** | | | |
|---|---|---|---|---|---|---|---|
| soap | [doʊp] | bib | [bɛ] | light | [waɪt] | bead | [biː] |
| feet | [bit] | slide | [daɪ] | sock | [sʌk] | pig | [pɛk] |
| sock | [kak] | dog | [da] | geese | [gis] | cheese | [tis] |
| goos | [gos] | cheese | [ʧis] | fish | [fɪs] | bees | [bis] |
| dish | [dɪʧ] | shoes | [dus] | sheep | [ʃip] | bib | [bɪp] |

a. What happens to final consonants in the language of these two children? Formulate the rule(s) in words. Do all final consonants behave the same way? If not, which consonants undergo the rule(s)? Is this a natural class?

b. On the basis of these data, do any pairs of words allow you to identify any of the phonemes in the grammars of these children? What are they? Explain how you were able to determine your answer.

9. Make up a "wug test" to test a child's knowledge of the following morphemes:

| | | |
|---|---|---|
| comparative | -er | (as in *bigger*) |
| superlative | -est | (as in *biggest*) |
| progressive | -ing | (as in *I am dancing*) |
| agentive | -er | (as in *writer*) |

10. Children frequently produce sentences such as the following:

Don't giggle me.
I danced the clown.
Yawny Baby—you can push her mouth open to drink her.
Who deaded my kitty cat?
Are you gonna nice yourself?

a. How would you characterize the difference between the grammar or lexicon of children who produce such sentences and that of adult English?

b. Can you think of similar, but well-formed, examples in adult English?

11. Following is a list of utterances recorded from Sammy at age two-and-a-half:

a. Mikey not see him.
b. Where ball go?
c. Look Mommy, doggie.
d. Big doggie.
e. He no bite ya.
f. He eats mud.
g. Kitty hiding.
h. Grampie wear glasses.
i. He funny.
j. He loves hamburgers.
k. Daddy ride bike.

l. That's mines.
m. That my toy.
n. Him sleeping.
o. Want more milk.
p. Read moon book.
q. Me want that.
r. Teddy up.
s. Daddy 'puter.
t. 'Puter broke.
u. Cookies and milk!!!
v. Me Superman.
w. Mommy's angry.
x. Allgone kitty.
y. Here my batball.

What stage of language development is Sammy in? Explain your answer.

12. Following is a list of overextensions that various children have made. In each case say what the basis is for the overextension. For example, the basis for the overextension of *ball* in example (a) is shape. All the objects in column B are round.

| | A | B |
|---|---|---|
| a. | *ball* | balls, balloon, marble, grapefruits, oranges, pompoms |
| b. | *cookie* | cookies, Cheerios, cucumbers |
| c. | *birdie* | birds, airplanes, flies, bees, kites |
| d. | *bowwow* | dogs, cows, guinea pigs, cats, hamsters |
| e. | *truck* | firetruck, garbage truck, bus, van |
| f. | *dada* | father, policeman, mailman, doctor, men's tie, baseball cap |
| g. | *moon* | moon, half-moon shaped lemon slice, circular chrome dial on dishwasher, half a Cheerio, hangnail |

13. Review Michael's utterances on page 287. Provide two examples of each the following sentence types and the age at which Michael first produced each type of sentence:

a. coordinations (sentences conjoined by *and*)
b. embedded clauses
c. relative clauses